Guidance
and
Counseling
in
the Elementary
School

Readings in Theory and Practice

Edited by

DON C. DINKMEYER

DePaul University

Guidance and Counseling in the Elementary School

Readings in Theory and Practice

HOLT, RINEHART AND WINSTON, INC.

New York • Chicago • San Francisco • Atlanta

Dallas • Montreal • Toronto • London

To my sons, Don and Jim

Copyright © 1968 by Holt, Rinehart and Winston, Inc.
Library of Congress Catalog Card Number: 67–27943

2663201

Printed in the United States of America
1 2 3 4 5 6 7 8 9

Preface

Interest in elementary school guidance and counseling is presently growing at a rapid rate, as evidenced by the numerous articles that have appeared in professional journals and the increased participation in guidance counselor organizations. In 1967 a new journal appeared, called *Elementary School Guidance and Counseling*, thus opening a new channel of communication in this area.

At a time when professional interest is increasing, the federal government has made funds available for elementary school guidance at state and local levels for the training of elementary school counselors. Counselor education programs which differentiate requirements and instructional patterns for elementary school counselors are on the increase throughout the nation. In 1965, through the National Defense Education Act, the government sponsored institutes for this purpose, and by 1967–1968 there were fifteen of these institutes in existence.

One of the reasons for this new interest is the recognition of the importance of early school years in the development of the child. This was indicated especially in the research of Kagan and Moss* and Bloom,‡ among others. Educators note that behavior which was once peculiar to adolescents (rebellion, underachievement, apathy, delinquency, and lack of cooperation) is now frequently observed in preadolescents. This makes it apparent that new approaches are needed to pupil personnel problems at the elementary school level.

This book is intended as a basic text for courses in the theory and techniques of elementary school guidance or as a supplementary text in an introductory guidance course. Because the field is still comparatively new, the book will be useful in acquainting administrators, curriculum directors, teachers, and secondary school counselors with the scope of elementary school guidance. Its main interest, of course, will be for those counselor-educators, counselor education students, and guidance supervisors who need research material appropriate to the elementary school level.

In the author's experiences with organizing graduate courses and in-service workshops in elementary school guidance, it became apparent that sufficient

---

* Jerome Kagan and Howard Moss, *Birth to Maturity* (New York: Wiley, 1962).

‡ Benjamin Bloom, *Stability and Change in Human Characteristics* (New York: Wiley, 1964).

instructional material was lacking and that both instructors and students frequently were unaware of how much relevant material already existed. Ideally, perhaps, students should seek primary sources from the periodical literature. However, many institutions have been unable to keep their libraries supplied in proportion to their increased enrollments. A book of readings such as this will help remedy the situation.

The material included does not provide simple answers. Instead, by acquainting the reader with various philosophies, approaches, and techniques, it makes him aware of the need to develop his own convictions about guidance. The author hopes that students will consult these articles as programs and services are developed and re-evaluated.

The author holds several convictions that influence his classroom teaching, as well as his supervision and counseling of students. Since he applied these convictions in selecting and organizing the material for this book, the reader should be made aware of them:

1. Guidance must start with a consideration of its philosophy, basic concepts, and objectives.

2. Guidance is an integral part of the educational process and must be consistent in purpose with the philosophy and objectives of the elementary school in which it operates.

3. Guidance is for all children, not merely the deviate.

4. Anyone familiar with the development of human personality understands the need for guidance in elementary schools, since many traits related to academic and social progress develop prior to high school where formal guidance is available.

5. Besides being remedial and preventive, guidance must also be developmental. It is an organized effort of the school to help the child develop his maximum potential, both academically and socially.

6. It is essential to the program that the elementary school teacher himself perform certain guidance functions. For this he needs to develop skills in guidance.

7. Although guidance is incidental, it functions best as a planned program providing continuous assistance to the child in his school experiences, helping him to accomplish tasks which lead to his cognitive and affective development. The school curriculum provides the experiences, but it is the guidance functions of the counselor and the teacher which assist the child to succeed in these experiences.

8. A guidance program is most effective when there is cooperation between teacher, counselor, parents, administration, and community.

9. The counselor provides services to the child directly—through counseling, pupil appraisal, and group guidance—and indirectly—through consultation with teachers and parents.

Selecting articles for a book of readings is always a complicated task. Primarily, the choices made had to represent the major issues—actual and philosophical—that concern those involved in elementary school guidance and counseling. And, although a small field exists, articles that express differences of opinion were included also. In cases where no useful material exists, original selections were prepared specifically for this text.

Since role and function of the counselor are such important considerations, various definitions of these are presented. Chapters have been devoted to child study, individual and group counseling, group guidance, and parent consultation. Attention has been given to developing theory and practice for counseling. The book closes with a discussion of the problems of program appraisal.

In his introduction to each chapter, the author has attempted to set the background for the readings, present the theme of the chapter, give his position on the issues discussed, and indicate the contributions of the selections to the issues raised.

The author hopes that these articles will acquaint the reader with materials that are presently available, motivate him to consider the issues, and stimulate the development of creative approaches in his community. Elementary school guidance is essential to the educational process. The author hopes that this set of readings will contribute in small part to improved services to children.

The author wishes to acknowledge his indebtedness to George E. Hill and Merle M. Ohlsen for their careful reading of the manuscript at various preparatory stages. The author also wishes to give special acknowledgment to his wife and family for their assistance and encouragement during the period of the book's preparation.

D.C.D.

CHICAGO, ILLINOIS
NOVEMBER 1967

Contents

Guidance
and
Counseling
in
the Elementary
School

Readings in Theory and Practice

Chapter 1

PHILOSOPHY, BASIC CONCEPTS,

AND ISSUES IN ELEMENTARY

SCHOOL GUIDANCE

This chapter presents a philosophy and principles for developmental guidance, a rationale of human behavior, and the implications of these approaches. An introduction to some of the fundamental issues in elementary school guidance is included.

Pupil personnel services vary in different elementary schools. Some schools emphasize diagnostic evaluation. Other schools are more concerned with remedial counseling for a few children and their parents, and school social work comprises their complete pupil personnel program. Psychological and social work approaches emphasize diagnostic and remedial functions for the exceptional child. This results in a small percentage of the elementary school population claiming most of the specialist's time.

In contrast to these services, developmental guidance offers help to all pupils. This type of guidance has been described by Smith and Eckerson (1963). They say that guidance in elementary schools is usually interpreted as a service to all children in making maximum use of their abilities, for their own good and for that of society. The emphases of this service are on early identification of the pupil's intellectual, emotional, social, and physical characteristics; development of his talent; diagnosis of his learning difficulties, if any; and early use of available resources to meet his needs.

Developmental guidance strives to improve the learning environment of both the school and the home so that learning can take on personal meaning (Munson, 1966). It attempts to reconcile the uniqueness of the individual with

1

the demands of his society and culture. It is not crisis-oriented and does not place a premium on remediation, correction, or therapy.

The intent of developmental guidance is the development of competence in the learner. Grams (1966), in his definition of competence, refers to knowledge, skills, and attitudes which contribute to the process of learning. He considers learning both cognitively and affectively. This theory of learning is concerned with the development of ego strength, not just its repair (Dinkmeyer and Dreikurs, 1963; Tiedeman, 1961).

PHILOSOPHY OF DEVELOPMENTAL GUIDANCE

The elementary school child is at a crucial stage in the formulation of his self-concept. He must learn to develop social relationships and meet educational challenges. The early grades are crucial for developing attitudes toward school, achievement, peers, and society in general. Bloom (1964), in a summary of longitudinal studies of educational achievement, indicates that approximately fifty percent of general achievement at grade twelve was actually reached by the end of grade three. Summarizing a thirty-year longitudinal study, Kagan and Moss (1962) reach similar conclusions:

> The most dramatic and consistent finding of this study was that many of the behaviors exhibited by the children during the period 6 to 10 years of age, a few during the age period 3 to 6, were moderately good predictors of theoretically related behaviors during early adulthood. (p. 266)

This would mean, for example, that children who display intensive striving for mastery during their early years are likely to maintain this attitude toward school work.

The child who has an adequate self-concept functions better socially and academically (Walsh, 1956). This is corroborated by Coopersmith (1959), who discovered a correlation of .36 between a positive self-concept and school achievement.

PRINCIPLES OF DEVELOPMENTAL GUIDANCE

Elementary school guidance is founded on the principles of child development. It is important for the counselor to understand these principles if he is to utilize them (Dinkmeyer, 1967).

1. Developmental guidance is an integral part of the educational process and must be consistent in purpose with the philosophy and objectives of the elementary school in which it operates.

2. Developmental guidance is for all children, not merely the deviate.

3. It is an organized effort of the school to help the child develop his maximum potential, both academically and socially.

4. The elementary school teacher himself must be expected to perform certain guidance functions.

5. Although guidance may be incidental, it functions best as a planned program providing continuous assistance to the child during his school experiences, helping him to accomplish tasks which lead to his cognitive and affective development. The school curriculum provides the experiences, but the guidance functions of counselor and teacher assist the child in succeeding in these experiences.

6. A guidance program is most effective when there is cooperation between teacher, counselor, parents, administration, and community. The counselor provides services to the child directly through counseling, pupil appraisal, and group guidance—and indirectly—through consultation with teachers and parents.

7. It helps the child make full use of his potential talents and capacities (Maslow, 1954).

8. It stresses the perceptual understanding of human behavior in order to maximize the educational process (ASCD Yearbook, 1962; Combs and Snygg, 1959).

9. It emphasizes purposeful and meaningful learning experiences.

10. It discovers and encourages the child's assets, shows faith in him, and recognizes his strengths and efforts (Dinkmeyer and Dreikurs, 1963).

Developmental guidance services are aware of the following pupil needs: developing social relationships, belonging, and identifying; developing independence, making choices, and accepting responsibility for them; growing to understand the nature of work and how it operates in his environment; learning to realistically appraise his attitudes and interests; and learning to plan for his life.

A RATIONALE OF HUMAN BEHAVIOR

Guidance in the schools is based on the assumption that every human being is of value and has a right to optimum development. The guidance program is organized to assist in developing an understanding of the unique goals, percepts, assets, and liabilities of the individual. An understanding of the implications of individuality enables the teacher to facilitate the learning process for each learner. To be effective, guidance services must proceed from an understanding of human behavior. The following assumptions could be used in formulating a theory of developmental guidance:

1. To an individual, his behavior seems caused and purposeful and is decided by the way in which he perceives the field. We must, therefore, learn to comprehend his phenomenological field.

2. Behavior is not only a matter of multiple causation but of movement toward a goal. By recognizing an individual's goal we can understand the direction in which he is moving.

3. Man is a unified organism, a dynamic whole, moving in a definite pattern of behavior. We must learn to understand him holistically rather than by fragmentary analysis.

4. Much motivation in behavior is the striving for significance or self-esteem. It is important to find out how the child seeks to be known and what self-image he attempts to maintain.

5. Man is primarily a social being and cannot be understood apart from his environment.

6. Every person has freedom of choice and therefore is in part self-determined. Each individual has the creative power to make individual interpretations. Man is not only reactive but creative.

7. An individual's uniqueness ultimately proceeds from his creative power. Faust (1966) has noted:

> In the modification of behavior, it is not so much whether a particular stimulus does, in fact, assure the organism of survival that counts, as it is a matter of how the organism perceives the stimulus, or the meaning which the stimulus possesses for the organism's survival. (p. 12)

Combs and Snygg (1959) have noted:

> All behavior, without exception, is completely determined by, and pertinent to, the perceptual field (the entire universe, including himself, as it is experienced by the individual at the instant of action) of the behaving organism. (p. 20)

IMPLICATIONS FOR DEVELOPMENTAL GUIDANCE

The preceding philosophy and rationale imply certain directions for the field of elementary school guidance:

1. Greater emphasis on the role of the teacher in guidance than is necessary at other levels of education.

2. Greater attention paid to the classroom atmosphere, which is an important influence on learning.

3. More individual appraisal and interpretation to pupils and their parents.

4. Procedures should be provided which enable the school to work more effectively with parents. The counselor must be trained as a human relations expert so that he can consult effectively with teachers, parents, and administrators.

5. The elementary school counselor should be recognized as a significant agent of change.

6. Experiences should be provided for the child to develop self-understanding.

7. Education should encourage uniqueness and individuality, which, in the past, it has attempted to minimize.

8. Guidance should be recognized not as a special service but as part of the total educational plan to be integrated into the curriculum.

ISSUES IN ELEMENTARY
SCHOOL GUIDANCE

As one begins a study of elementary school guidance, a number of un-answered questions must be considered:

1. Is the teacher, consultant, or counselor the focal point of elementary school guidance?

2. How does elementary school guidance differ from guidance at other school levels?

3. Is the professional elementary school guidance worker to serve primarily as a counselor providing direct services or as a consultant providing indirect services?

4. What is the relationship of guidance to other pupil personnel services in the elementary school?

5. Which theory of counseling offers the most promise to the elementary school counselor?

6. What are some effective guidelines for consulting with teachers and parents?

7. What is the role of the counselor in diagnostic appraisal and testing?

8. What features should be given most attention in the training of elementary school counselors?

9. What is the role of the guidance program in vocational development?

The author's purpose at this point is not to take a position but to present issues for the reader's consideration. The ensuing articles will acquaint the reader with varied points of view so that he can develop his own position on these issues. The author believes that these questions can best be answered in re-lation to a specific counselor, school, and community.

In the first reading Cottingham reviews the reasons for current interest in elementary school guidance, stressing its developmental and continuous nature and tracing its history through seven different points of view.

Hill believes that the foundation of guidance is an understanding of chil-dren's needs. He reviews almost all pertinent literature on the historical develop-ment of elementary school guidance, discusses the role of the counselor, and ex-amines some objectives for a program.

Faust discusses how elementary school guidance has been hampered because of lack of clear objectives and systematic rationales of human behavior. Guid-ance should be concerned with intellect, curriculum, and noncrisis situations, should facilitate cognition, and should not be remedial or treatment-oriented. Counselors should not be trained to assist students to plan, choose, or make better personal and social adjustments. Instead, they should focus on teachers and the effects of their relationships, subject matter, and instructional methods on the child's learning ability.

Hoyt claims that we still need to define the nature of elementary school guidance. He describes the type of specialist needed to perform such services, and establishes criteria for their evaluation. He believes that the program should be consistent with the purposes of the elementary school, and he emphasizes involvement of teachers and parents. He offers a strategy for encouraging the employment of more elementary school counselors throughout the nation.

REFERENCES

Association for Supervision and Curriculum Development. 1962. *Perceiving, behaving, becoming.* Yearbook of the National Education Association.

Bloom, B. 1964. *Stability and change in human characteristics.* New York: Wiley.

Combs, A., and D. Snygg. 1959. *Individual behavior.* New York: Harper & Row.

Coopersmith, S. 1959. A method for determining types of self esteem. *J. educ. Psychol.*

Dinkmeyer, D. 1967. Child development research and the elementary school teacher. *Elem. Sch. J., 67* (No. 6), 310–316.

———, and R. Dreikurs. 1963. *Encouraging children to learn: the encouragement process.* Englewood Cliffs, N.J.: Prentice-Hall.

Faust, V. 1966. *Role of the elementary school counselor: freeing children to learn.* Address to the Office of Education, U.S. Department of Health, Education and Welfare, Washington, D.C.

Grams, A. 1966. *Facilitating learning and individual development: toward a theory for elementary guidance.* Department of Education, University of Minnesota.

Kagan, J., and H. Moss. 1962. *Birth to maturity.* New York: Wiley.

Maslow, A. H. 1954. *Motivation and personality.* New York: Harper & Row.

Munson, H. 1966. *A rationale for elementary school guidance.* College of Education, University of Rochester.

Smith, H. H., and Louise O. Eckerson. 1963. *Guidance for children in elementary school.* Washington, D.C.: Office of Education, U.S. Department of Health, Education and Welfare.

Tiedeman, D. March 1961. The status of professional theory. Paper prepared for a symposium, *The outlook for guidance today.* Denver, Colo.: American Personnel and Guidance Association.

Walsh, A. 1956. *Self concepts of bright boys with learning difficulty.* New York: Bureau of Publications, Teachers College, Columbia University.

Guidance in Elementary School —
A Status Review*

Harold F. Cottingham

What has happened to point the finger at elementary guidance in the past ten or twelve years? It has been within that period we have seen the most remarkable concern for the movement. Certainly the success of guidance at the secondary level has suggested, "Why wouldn't it work at the elementary?" This was, apparently, a reasonable question. Another factor in its growth is that in psychological theory, we begin to realize that we must look back at the origin, or the cause, of these problems, perhaps earlier than secondary school, in order to prevent them. For this reason it is only logical that guidance in the elementary school has come to the fore also. Certainly, early recognition of problem areas is necessary for early correction.

Along about this same time we also begin to realize in psychological theory that there were many things that affected academic or intellectual performance, not the least of which is emotional or attitudinal development. Seemingly, children have other kinds of problems that may interfere with intellectual performance. Consequently, some sort of service, relationship, or activity, ought to be available to work on this problem. Further, I think we began to realize, although many of us would not verbalize this, and I'm not certain it could be documented in many places, that there were certain areas in which, perhaps, we have not been too successful. Such problems as juvenile delinquency, school drop-outs, failures, and similar difficulties were also attributed to the school, although other social institutions were also responsible.

Along about this time, too, the question of the location or identification as well as the development of talent was cited as a function of the elementary school. There was also some question that we aren't developing boys and girls to their highest ability, that more could be done to develop many of them scholastically. So these are factors again that reflect, I believe, on the guidance emphasis in elementary schools.

We also have had a change in philosophy over a period of twenty years, in which we're now educating not only the intellectual child, or the academic individual, but the total individual. Certainly we are as much concerned about his goals, his plans and needs, as we are about his academic performance, although I grant there may be a philosophic difference of opinion among us on this issue.

* Speech delivered before the American Personnel and Guidance Association Convention, April 1963. By permission.

A little clipping reminds us of this problem with which we're faced. This is from Oconomowoc, Wisconsin. Fourth graders at Greenland School were asked to tell what they would do if they ran the school. "If I ran the school," one youngster wrote, "we would not have Sho Sho Studies, Language, or Seinens. We would not have tests on spelling either." This represents a kind of problem youngster who is trying to communicate but who is doing it phonetically. Not too unsuccessfully, certainly, but not in the terms of good academic spelling standards.

Another reason for the emergence of guidance in the elementary school has been the awareness that teachers themselves perhaps wanted other resources. You and I have worked in schools where the teachers have said, "I would not admit I need help. I am master of this situation; I can do all that needs to be done." I believe we now realize that no one of us has enough skill to handle all needs of all the boys and girls with whom we come in contact. We all have limits. This need for resources has also pointed up the need for additional staff, facilities, material, and people to help children. And lastly, guidance itself has gone through a period of change which we now accept; guidance is not picking up the pieces, not corrective, not remedial, but developmental, preventive, and continuous. This idea, if supported, suggests that elementary guidance is part of the total school, kindergarten through college.

Let's talk briefly about how people have looked at guidance in the elementary school over a period of years. It would be in order to point out the divergence of thinking, as well as agreement in the current situation with regard to viewpoints with which we are faced.

One of the earlier approaches might be called the Services Approach, in which it was felt that we could merely transplant the so-called guidance services, applicable to the secondary school, down to the elementary school level, with some modification, of course. Some publications do not go into great detail as to what modifications might be in order. Illustrative of this point is an earlier book by Ray Hatch, titled, *Guidance Services in the Elementary School*. Incidentally, this book was recently revised under the same title. Another book which also supported his concept was one by Bernard, Zeran, and James called, *Guidance Services in the Elementary School*.

Another position endorses the "guidance in good teaching" concept. This was an early position, and is held by some authorities today. Illustrative of this point of view is the book by Willey, *Guidance in Elementary Education*, which was revised and modified before being reissued about 1959. John Barr of Oregon completed a book in 1958 which took a somewhat similar position. Barr's book is titled, *The Elementary School Teacher and Guidance*.

A third approach might be called the mental health approach, or the problem-centered approach, in which certain authors felt that elementary guidance should be focused on problems of elementary children. Illustrative of this point of view is the book by Detjen and Detjen, called, *Elementary School Guidance*. This is a very helpful book, but does not actually give an explanation of a basic position as to the nature of elementary guidance. A similar book by another man and wife team, Kowitz and Kowitz, also offers a similar approach. This book is entitled, *Guidance in the Elementary Classroom*. In both of these cases, the assumption seems to be that guidance is a mental health problem, or a phase of mental hygiene dealing with problems of children, rather than a designed program within the total school working for the needs of all children.

A fourth approach can be called the school psychologist or specialist approach, in which a highly trained clinician or specialist is seen to be the primary resource person. Gertrude Driscoll's book, *Child Guidance in the Classroom*, illustrates this position. Another publication is the Thayer report edited by Norma Cutts, and called *School Psychologists at Mid-Century*. Both of these publications take the position that only psychologists should perform certain kinds of functions, therapy, for example.

A fifth approach is called the human development or child study approach, in which it is apparently assumed that knowledge of children from a background of developmental psychology is sufficient. This assumes application of this knowledge by teachers, specialists, administrators, and others. Many of the approaches unfortunately do not explain how a whole school can or should implement the appropriate concepts; this limits their value as a philosophic or functional base from which to develop elementary guidance services.

The book by Ira Gordon, *The Teacher as a Guidance Worker*, supports this position. Prescott's book, *Helping Teachers Understand Children*, describing a child study program, also illustrates this approach. A more recent book, *Guidance for Today's Children*, issued by the Los Angeles County Schools, seems to be another statement endorsing the human development approach. This book is a revision of one that was done by the Los Angeles Schools back in 1948.

A sixth approach might be called a coordinated approach, wherein as many activities are brought together, a total program is coordinated for the needs of all pupils. Martinson and Smallenberg's book, *Guidance in Elementary Schools*, also takes this position. This appears to be a more functional, more practical, approach. Ruth Strang of Teachers College has spoken in this vein. Johnson, Peterson, and Evraiff's book, *The Role of the Teacher in Elementary Guidance*, expresses a similar attitude.

The last approach is one that has been called an integrative or individualistic approach. This has been promoted by Esther Lloyd-Jones of Teachers College in a little publication called *Guidance in Elementary Education*, issued in 1958. It contains several interesting case studies of guidance in elementary education and points out various aspects of each problem case. It should be mentioned that the ASCD yearbook, *Guidance and the Curriculum*, also stresses this plan. This publication is not limited to elementary schools, but takes a rather broad look at various levels of guidance, stressing the fact that the guidance function should be integrated with the curriculum—both within and beyond the curriculum. An expression that best exemplifies this philosophy is the quotation, "Instruction is inseparable from guidance, but guidance is separable from instruction."

The next phase of this discussion will look at some of the ways in which these various authors, or writers, appear to agree on the nature of elementary guidance. We begin to approach what might be an answer to some of the basic questions as to objectives or functional aspects of guidance at this important level.

One of the basic principles in which most of the writers seem to agree is the fact that the functions involved must consist of a definite plan to help all pupils, teachers, and parents. This is important in that we are aiming our activities at not only boys and girls but at teachers and administrators and the community. Thus, we have multi-consumer groups as beneficiaries of guidance work.

Another basic position held by many is that the teacher as well as the specialist is involved. Stated differently, guidance exists within and beyond the classroom; within and beyond the curriculum. The classroom teacher, undoubtedly, is a key person in the picture, although on occasion she may be supplemented by other resources in order to meet all the needs of all the boys and girls. Again this points up a problem which some teachers are trying to face with varying degrees of success. Much has been said about creativity and imagination, and occasionally some of us want youngsters to conform to our concept of imagination. A new music teacher was drilling the class in songs that were being acted out as the children sang. After a number of songs in which the children hopped about and waved their arms to represent various subjects, she noticed that one small boy was doing very little acting. "You're not using your imagination, John," she said quite sharply. "The next song will be about flowers; I want you to act like one." John started out willingly enough, but half way through the song, obviously tired, he stopped suddenly and sat down. "John," the teacher called sternly, "get up at once; you're supposed to be a flower. You must have some imagination; now use it." "But I am," the youngster protested. "Then why are you sitting on the floor?" the teacher demanded. Looking up, John quietly explained, "My stem broke!"

A third concept, with which many writers agree, is that the problem areas around which elementary guidance seems to center are three: (1) the acceptance by a child of his own self-picture, or understanding and acceptance of self; (2) satisfactory social relationships or interaction with other individuals. In a recent SRA pamphlet called "Elementary Guidance, A Decade Ahead," Dr. Anna Meeks of Baltimore emphasizes the human relations aspect of guidance. This seems to be a focal point of concern; helping youngsters relate to their peers and others. (3) The need for successful experiences in the academic school setting. How a child gets along in school with respect to intellectual attainment is very important.

A fourth area of agreement is that for both teachers and specialists there seem to be two fundamental steps involved in elementary guidance with regard to the child himself. (1) Understanding children through child study, or analysis of pupil facts, and (2) using this data to help children. The second step is the helping process, often called at various levels assistance, therapy, treatment, or remedy. These function together because it is difficult to help children without some previous data as to their needs and characteristics. We understand or assess, after which we help, just as we hope the doctor gets facts about us before he makes a diagnosis as a basis for treatment. These two steps are inherent in the writing of many of the authors in the field of elementary guidance.

A fifth point, in which some agreement is found, is that the needs of children in general, supported by local studies, determine what should be done for boys and girls in that area. One cannot buy tailor-made programs, since it is unwise to assume that services appropriate for one community automatically fit another. The diversity of pupil needs certainly necessitates a varied approach, both with the individual and with the group situation. Our next point suggests that many authors agree that the teacher herself has a dual role, both as an instructor or teacher and as a guidance person. But, certainly, the methods and materials of instruction which deal with the skills and facts called for by society are somewhat different than the helping procedures built around the psychological needs of boys and girls which relate to their plans, their decisions, their value judgments, and their goals. These are two kinds of roles, both having interaction along with some overlap. The fact that each teacher does have a dual role is significant. This is more important, and probably more realized, at elementary school level than upper level. It is difficult to get some college teachers to talk much about the personnel problems of classroom students. They explain that this is not their responsibility. In effect they say, "You see your counselor, or you go to the dean. I don't discuss these problems." I think elementary teachers see much beyond this point since they see the whole youngster. Sometimes we may not see our differentiated roles in relation to different kinds of pupil experiences; different types of teacher functions ought to be based on different kinds of needs as revealed by children. This should not be an artificial plan to categorize or classify, nor an attempt to arbitrarily dichotomize functions.

Further, we find many authors stating that effective guidance requires trained people, a thorough special knowledge or special approaches by teachers, administrators, or specialists, regardless of title. The basic personal quality sought here is a value structure inherent in our beliefs that will make the youngster want to emulate us, based on the assumption that youngsters do as we do, not as we say. It is doubtful if adults role play accepting a child or being permissive, since children probably see through this, maybe more so than some adults. This personal value structure is needed for a completely professional approach. We need to look at ourselves so that we can help others. Learning is a feeling experience as well as an intellectual one.

In addition to a number of common concepts on which many authorities seemingly agree, there is some evidence that a basic theory undergirding elementary school guidance is also emerging from the literature. Although this theory is far from complete, two or three features characterizing any basic statement can be drawn from a number of sources. Many writers agree that elementary guidance has as its purpose the modification of both pupil and teacher attitudes. Further, a number of writers have indicated that this objective is obtained by the provision of services to children directly, as well as to services to children indirectly, through teachers, specialists, and through the administration. As with basic guidance theory, elementary guidance seems to have as its purpose with children the modification of their behavior through a variety of individual and group experiences. Finally, it seems to be agreed that the elementary guidance workers, whether they be called consultant or counselor or merely a helping teacher, should not be expected to carry out such functions as teaching, discipline, administrative detail, and other routine tasks such as hall and yard duty, except under emergency conditions.

In this next portion of this review, it might be well to examine some of the research and reported evidence on prevailing practices in elementary school guidance. This brief review of current practices will be presented under two headings, namely, organization and philosophy, and functions of elementary guidance personnel. As a source of data for this particular portion of these remarks, two studies in particular were drawn upon in some detail. One of these is in published form and is called "Guidance in the Elementary School" by Louise Eckerson and Hyrum M. Smith, a series of articles which appeared in the summer of 1962 in *School Life*, the official journal of the United States Office of Education. The second study serving as a source of data for these statements is a research report being developed by Rebecca McKellar, a graduate student at Florida State University, who has made a thorough study of the functions and philosophy of a sample of the half-time elementary school counselors in this country. Miss McKellar's study is as yet incomplete, but will be available later this year.

In looking at practices which characterize the organizational patterns and philosophic bases for elementary school guidance programs, several prevailing trends are reported by Eckerson and Smith. They indicate in many instances, based on some twenty-four elementary school guidance programs, that elementary guidance services are frequently a part of a broader pupil personnel program. This pupil personnel program is designed to serve all the children in that particular community. The leadership for guidance organization appears to center on a consultant or guidance person who coordinates a variety of activities involving the school staff, as well as resource personnel within the school and community. Furthermore, it is assumed that the teacher is a vital part of this total plan of action in that she applies guidance principles within her classroom.

McKellar, in her study, sought information about the organization of guidance activities within schools served by elementary counselors. It might be pointed out here that Miss McKellar's study involved 183 half-time (or more) counselors in twenty states. The counselors in Miss McKellar's study serve in a single school, or in about half of the cases, two schools or more. Only fourteen of the sample were actually coordinators or supervisors, but instead were designated as counselors under a guidance person or a school administrator.

One feature of Miss McKellar's study centered around an attempt to determine from the literature certain basic principles of guidance in elementary schools which might serve as a basis for actual practice in the field. In comparing the organizational practices found in sample schools, Miss McKellar reported several practices which seemed to be quite compatible with the guidance literature at the elementary school level. Specifically, the schools that seemed to hold a philosophy most comparable to principles found within the guidance literature as expounded by leaders in the field, used the following organizational policies: the use of a guidance council or committee to develop procedures leading to plans and objectives, the development of guidance functions around periodic research on pupil needs, the development of guidance objectives through cooperative activity involving faculty, administration and guidance people, and finally, the presence of an educational climate which indicated an acceptance by a majority of the school staff of the guidance viewpoint and a willingness to utilize guidance services. As a specific question as to the focal point for organization of elementary school guidance, Miss McKellar asked a direct question on this issue. She discovered that only some twenty-six percent of the elementary counselors saw the teacher as a primary agent for implementing elementary guidance, while almost seventy percent of the elementary counselors saw guidance as a coordinated process involving a variety of school and community personnel.

Moving into the area of functions carried out by elementary guidance personnel, one again finds a lack of solid research on which to base evidences of ongoing practice. Granted that many surveys of opinion and conceived roles of the elementary guidance person have been conducted, there is still a dearth of carefully designed studies which can serve as a foundation for any clearcut trends on the actual duties carried out by a large number of elementary school counselors working half-time or more.

Before citing actual functions carried out by elementary school guidance workers, it might be well to emphasize that Smith and Eckerson suggest that a variety of factors determine these functions. This may account for the lack of terminology, as well as the difficulty in clarifying these functions as typically carried out. Very possibly the existence of these factors will make it difficult for some time to develop any sort of commonly accepted job description of the elementary school counselor. Such a condition may be well and good actually. Some of these factors which have a direct bearing on the kind of responsibility being carried out by elementary guidance counselors are: the attitude and philosophy of the administrative staff, the extent to which other functions and resource units are available in the community, the type of neighborhood and home environment in which the school is located, and the policies followed by the school system with respect to counselor-pupil ratios. In addition, such elements as the education, work experience, and personal qualifications of elementary school guidance persons cannot be overlooked.

Referring again to the study carried out by Miss McKellar, we find that she grouped the functions carried out by elementary school guidance workers into four categories, namely: those related to children, those related to teachers, functions related to parents, and general administrative responsibilities.

Discussing these in order, I would like to report a few of Miss McKellar's

findings which are descriptive of functions performed by her elementary counselor sample. An attempt was made to determine the actual functions carried out
by counselors in each category. Specifically, with regard to helping children,
four functions seem to be most commonly performed: counseling with individual
pupils for better self-understanding, administering tests to individual pupils,
working with pupils who need special help in remedial or emotional situations,
and, fourthly, the orientation of new pupils entering the school during the year.

In the area of teacher assistance, elementary school counselors in this study
indicated that they were most frequently occupied with holding individual
teacher conferences to improve teacher understanding of pupil needs and characteristics, in helping teachers identify pupils who need special help, helping all
teachers to accept and understand children, interpreting pupil data and test results with individual and groups of teachers, and working with individual
teachers on questions relating to student management and behavior change. In
the area of parent services, most frequently listed functions were as follows:
making direct contact with parents at invitation of the classroom teacher or
principal, acting as the liaison person between the home and the school, arranging referrals to out-of-school agencies for physical or psychological diagnosis of
the child with difficult problems, and helping parents in matters of student understanding and management. Needless to say, one very common function was that
of interpreting pupil data to parents. With respect to general and administrative
functions, counselors were involved in a coordination of all guidance functions
in the school, responsibility for organizing and keeping significant pupil data,
maintaining an adequate supply of guidance literature and materials for teachers
and parents, planning and administering the school testing program, and assistance in the placement of pupils in the proper classes.

Referring again to the Eckerson and Smith study of twenty-four guidance
programs, we find a similarity in functions performed although the functions
listed are not categorized as in the McKellar study. Eckerson and Smith, for example, indicate that elementary school guidance consultants are quite often occupied with testing and observing children who were having educational or
emotional difficulties, direct counseling with children whose problems suggest that
school counseling would be beneficial, and consulting with teachers, principals,
and parents to help them better understand normal children and children with
problems. Further, elementary guidance workers in this study spend considerable
time in referring children needing intensive diagnosis to specialists or community agencies available, providing inservice training for teachers in the area of
child development and learning, along with assistance in administering, scoring
and interpreting test results. Some elementary guidance consultants were also
occupied with programs in group guidance involving areas such as personal problems, occupational orientation and study habits; others were responsible for
helping children with physical needs such as clothes, food, and hearing aids;
others reported time spent in interpreting the guidance program to parents and
community organizations and in the conduct of research and evaluative studies
dealing with the effectiveness of the program.

The final portion of this paper is devoted to the discussion of several issues which appear to be confronting the field of guidance in the elementary school at this particular moment. These issues, rather than being derived from research or other opinion studies, have come to the attention of the writer through his experience, examination of the literature, and a consideration of current developments in elementary school guidance through commissions, special studies, and miscellaneous sources.

One of the issues with which we are faced at the moment appears to be the structural pattern which should serve as a model for the development of elementary guidance services within a school or a school system. The heart of this issue seems to be whether or not the focal point is the teacher, a roving consultant serving several schools, or a counselor within each school or a particular assigned group of schools. Naturally, some would argue that we should not look for any sort of structural design which might fit the elementary school, but rather think in terms of functions, letting each school develop its own patterns of structured activities.

Another rather basic area of disagreement centers on the nature and characteristics of elementary school guidance as differentiated from guidance at other school levels. Granted that guidance at any school level has yet to produce its own solid foundation stones, nevertheless, some authorities feel that we have not yet agreed in the guidance profession on characteristics and dimensions of guidance in the elementary school, whether it be a part of the total guidance scheme or not. To date, no one has come up with a position statement, a basic theory, or a series of purposeful directions for elementary school guidance that are acceptable to many of those in the field. Perhaps we will get some answers to this question when the Anna Meeks' study sponsored by the American Guidance Foundation, activated in 1961, comes up with its final report in some three years.

Related to this question of a proper foundation for elementary school guidance is the relationship of guidance at this level to other special services which come under the total personnel tent. The specific services with which elementary guidance is most often confused and perhaps compared are those of school psychology and school social work. In many schools considerable doubt exists as to the distinct roles of so-called specialists in each of these three disciplines. Other professional problems also arise when we raise the question of whether or not the elementary guidance consultant is primarily a therapist or merely a diagnostician. Another similar question hinges on the administrative leadership role of the elementary guidance consultant, whether he be an administrator, that is, a line officer, or merely a staff individual having a consulting or advising role. We have yet to see, I believe, the proper merging of leaders in elementary education and leaders in the guidance movement who must ultimately get together to resolve some of these questions surrounding elementary school guidance. The final professional difficulty focuses on organizational affiliation of elementary guidance people. For example, in the McKellar study referred to above, only one-fourth of the elementary school counselors were members of the American School Counselors Association. Very likely, elementary school counselors hold their primary membership in such organizations as Association of Childhood Education or, perhaps, the American Psychological Association, in a few instances.

One issue which is of vital concern to many individuals is that of clarifying the proper functions which should accrue to the elementary guidance worker. Although we are conducting several research studies in an attempt to determine the most appropriate function in the light of pupil and community needs, there still is no agreement whereby the ideal role and the practices in the field appear to be compatibly related. Eckerson and Smith raise the question whether or not we should seek too much commonality of function when there needs to be considerable variability in the light of local school factors. We are not yet sure, either, with any basis for generalization, of the type of services needed by the teacher and administrator as well as the parent in the community. Eckerson and Smith referred to the chief function being identification and prevention, yet other authorities would go further and speak of remediation, treatment, or even therapy. A final aspect of this role and function question is whether or not our training programs should wait on a job analysis of the actual duties required of elementary school guidance personnel. We are training people at the moment, even though we have no basic guidelines for developing these programs other than the best judgment of counselor educators, elementary educators, and child development specialists.

This question naturally leads us to one of training, which represents another area of difference in elementary school guidance. In a study by George Hill of Ohio State University, a year or two ago, he discovered that a majority of programs in this country did not clearly differentiate elementary guidance training programs in counselor education from those designed to prepare secondary school counselors. Another question in the training field would seem to be to what extent a common core of academic courses or individual experiences underlies the preparation of the child development specialist, the school psychologist, and the elementary guidance consultant. Furthermore, I do not believe that we are in complete agreement yet as to whether or not the elementary guidance person is a generalist or a specialist. Some recent proposals have suggested that we should eventually seek a vertical hierarchy in which there are two types of guidance workers, the general practitioner or the generalist, as opposed to the highly trained specialist who is more akin to what is referred to in the Wrenn report as "the counselor." On the other hand, a variation of this approach might be to develop horizontal variations so that the question of status or hierarchy might not become a threatening one.

The last question we must raise moves into the area of personnel who are to do the elementary guidance work. We have touched upon this issue already, namely, whether the teacher is the focal point or whether a specialist in the area of school psychology, school social work, or guidance is the key figure. An aspect of this question, of course, is the title of the individual, as well as his type of qualifications for this role. Studies by Hart and by Martinson have suggested that we are pretty well agreed on the ideal role of the counselor, yet to date I do not believe that we have enough studies of practice to see whether or not our ideal is within reach or is perhaps too idealistic. Further, there is the ever-present question of terminology wherein we are confronted with a proposal by Patouillet who proposes the term, "child development consultant," which embraces the guidance counselor, the school psychologist, as well as the school social worker. This, however, is not acceptable to some who feel it would be impossible to reach agreement among these disciplines on this terminology. Finally, a basic aspect of the question raised is whether or not the teacher can be equally effective both as a guidance person and in her fundamental, traditional role of instruction. How realistic is it to assume that a teacher should carry this dual role?

As a final conclusion, the writer would like to propose that some thought be given to the implementing mechanics by which a position paper at the national level could address itself to some of these issues in the field of elementary guidance. Such a well-developed position paper sponsored by national organizations and carried out by representatives from elementary education, guidance, and related disciplines could certainly examine some of the fundamental concerns with which we are faced. Hopefully, such a group could offer a theoretical basis within the broad context of a guidance philosophy, could describe dimensions and some of the essential characteristics that should identify elementary school guidance, and, thirdly, point up some of the unresolved issues with which we are yet faced, and, finally, could perhaps propose some next steps by which a unified theory of elementary guidance could be developed.

Guidance in Elementary Schools*

George E. Hill

The idea of guidance in our schools is as old as the concern of a sensitive teacher for one of his pupils. The practice of guidance in our schools is as old as the efforts of this sensitive teacher to help one of his students grow and develop to his fullest potential. Guidance services in our secondary schools and student personnel services in our colleges came into being to meet the needs of the individual— both the individual student and the individual teacher. Guidance services in our elementary schools are developing and expanding rapidly for exactly the same reason.

* A position paper for the American Personnel and Guidance Association Committee on Dimensions in Elementary School Guidance, 1964. By permission.

GUIDANCE AND THE
NEEDS OF CHILDREN

As our understandings of children have developed and as we have come to see more clearly the implications of this understanding for educational practice, four basic needs have come to be widely accepted as the basis for organized guidance in schools:

1. Boys and girls need to mature in their understanding, their acceptance, and their sense of responsibility regarding themselves. Without these three conditions, no person can be his best nor can he live his best with his fellows. Much of this understanding, acceptance, and responsibility comes from his relations with other children and with adults.

2. Boys and girls live in a complex world in which the fullest possible education is imperative if they are to find their most productive place in the world of work. Thus they need to grow in their understanding of education and of work through a more and more mature interaction with their environment, both immediate and vicarious.

3. Boys and girls face the constant necessity of choice making and problem solving. Thus they need to mature gradually in learning how to make choices, to plan their lives sensibly, and to solve their problems rationally and with a high sense of moral values.

4. Boys and girls live in a complex of social settings—the home, the neighborhood, the school, the community, the world. Beginning with the simpler adjustments of home life they day-by-day expand the scope of their adjustments. Thus, day-by-day they face the need for developing those values, those behaviors, those insights which enable them to live with a minimum of fruitless friction and a maximum of maturity in social attitudes and skills.

The guidance services of our schools and colleges have developed to help bring the total impact of the school to bear more effectively upon helping all young people develop along the lines suggested by these four statements.

DO WE NEED GUIDANCE
IN ELEMENTARY SCHOOLS?

The ideal of the dignity, the worth, and the integrity of each person is basic to all aspects of our free school system. Its fostering is not just something that it is nice for us to do—it is an imperative condition for the maintenance of our freedoms and our way of life. Thus, helping children achieve their best, be their best, is a foundation of all good elementary school programs.

The sudden burst of guidance services, and the appointment of staff counselors in elementary schools, during the past decade reflect simply the impact of a few developments which by now are familiar to all of us:

1. The universal acceptance of the educational implications of what we have

learned about child development. For example, if we want a seventh grader to want to make the best of his abilities, we must start helping him learn to want this when he enters the earliest phases of his educational experience. If we want a third grader to be developing wholesome attitudes toward others, we start the processes of socialization in the cradle. Education is a slow, incessant push—not a matter of fits and starts, or leaps and bounds. Thus all educational efforts have to be viewed in terms of the full sweep of the educational effort; including our aids to the fulfillment of the four needs with which we opened this statement.

2. The education of the whole child has become a reality in terms of the common effort of all teachers in all schools. Once regarded as a "progressive" slogan, this is now an accepted axiom. But, not only must the teacher educate the whole child, she must also help him meet and master an explosion of knowledge such as the world has never seen before. Thus the truly professional teacher sees that the full task of full child development in her classroom calls for assistances the teacher once would not recognize. The "self-contained" classroom is not any longer seen by the teacher as being equated with the "self-sufficient" teacher. It is our best prepared, most competent teachers who call upon the special service personnel for consultation and aid in meeting the needs of particular individual children and in planning for a richer learning experience for all of their children.

3. The increasing complexity of choices—and thus of decision making—and the growing awareness that basic attitudes and choices begin early in the child's life have sensitized many teachers and administrators to the need for a critical evaluation of early childhood education and of middle-childhood education as to their impact upon the child's growth in life planning and choice making. The jokes about deciding to go to college in kindergarten are overdone, but there is an undertone of reality in them.

4. Evidence has piled up from many sources that the forerunners of the high school drop-out problems of the problem of underachievement, of the waste of the talents of our girls, of the waste of talent of many children—and especially those from minority groups—lie in the child's experiences from babyhood to adolescence and can not be adequately dealt with if we wait until junior high school. Low aspirations, anti-social attitudes, low self-estimations are attitudes which begin their formation early in life. If the school is to do its best to meet these problems its chief efforts must begin early and must be persistently developmental.

5. We have become increasingly aware of the impact of home life, parental attitudes, and community influences in the determination of the child's sense of self, his sense of his worth—or lack of worth—his aspirations, his values, his achievements. Thus the school, never an island of isolation, has moved even more completely into the sweep of the child's extra-school life. At the same time, the school has come, as its parents have themselves become better educated and more responsible, to develop more fully its program for the fuller involvement of parents in their education of the child.

These five developments have formed the basis for the introduction of organized, staff-directed guidance services in the elementary schools.

DEVELOPING GUIDANCE
IN ELEMENTARY SCHOOLS

While it is not the purpose of this paper to review the literature of elementary school guidance, it is appropriate to point to certain emphases in this literature which have impressed this reviewer:

1. While there is difference of opinion as to roles and functions in elementary school guidance, there is considerable agreement that such needs as delineated in the opening section of this paper will be met only when there is a more concerted staff effort to meet them than now characterizes many schools. Several lengthy books have been written regarding this matter; but two recent brief statements well summarize this conviction (Mathewson, 1962; Meeks, 1963).

2. Certain child needs seem to concern the writers on elementary school guidance more than others. For example, a by-product of the massive concern for the bright, talented, or gifted has been much greater attention to the needs of the "underachiever" and his guidance (National Education Association and the American Personnel and Guidance Association, 1961; U.S. Department of Health, Education and Welfare, Office of Education, 1961). It is clear that attention to the learning needs of children and to the impact of learning problems upon personal development is a primary concern of the elementary school.

The need for earlier and more systematic experiences in life planning, especially as regards future education and vocation, is commanding more and more attention in the elementary schools. The literature on vocational development shows clearly that attitudes toward occupations form early in life, that self-concepts which are basic to educational and vocational planning begin to form early in life, that the impact of parental hopes and biases regarding their child's future begins early in life and is especially influential when the child is young (Davis, 1959; Nelson, 1962 *a* and 1962 *b*).

3. Which children need the help of special service workers—counselors (Wrenn, 1962), guidance consultants (Eckerson and Smith, 1962), or whatever they may be called—and whether the teacher is in a position to provide all the needed help, depends in part upon whether "guidance" is seen as a preventive-developmental effort, or as a remedial-corrective effort. That the preventive-developmental approach is the more widely accepted seems quite clear (Hill, 1963; Smith and Eckerson, 1963). The needs and concerns of all the children are to be met in the modern elementary school. To many of us this means that the staffs of such schools must include specialists in child study, counseling, and developmental planning.

4. The literature on elementary school guidance reveals a serious lack of

research on the special problems of guidance for younger children. Most of the effort to date, and it is productive effort, has been devoted to status studies. Investigators have been trying to discover what is being done in elementary schools in the name of guidance, what educators think ought to be done. This type of study started over a decade ago (Martinson, 1949; National Association of Guidance Supervisors and Counselor Trainers, 1953). The need for more research in the following aspects of guidance for younger children is great:

a. Assessment of the need for, the methods of, and the outcome of individual and small-group counseling with children from pre-school through the upper grades.

b. Investigation of the effectiveness of efforts to involve parents more closely in the complicated processes of helping children mature in self-understanding, and in helping parents understand and accept their children.

c. Further investigation of the educational and vocational concepts of children, how these relate to self-concepts, and the effectiveness of educational efforts to inform children and to encourage them in earlier experiences in life planning.

d. Studies of the significance of models in child development, with implications regarding the possibility of educational provision of models as an important aspect of "environmental manipulation" (Michael and Meyerson, 1962) in schools and communities.

e. Long-term, developmental studies of the outcomes of guidance programs in elementary schools.

f. Studies in depth of differential roles of various pupil personnel workers, with implications for selection and preparation of these workers.

g. Detailed studies of programs for the preparation of elementary school guidance counselors, longitudinally planned to include follow-up evaluation on the job.

5. Another phase of the literature on elementary school guidance that is rewarding as one looks to the experience of those who have been working in the field is the growing number of booklets, guides, and program manuals which come from school systems, both local and state. State departments of education have shown considerable interest and have amassed considerable leadership experience in the elementary school guidance field (Hill, 1963). Some of the manuals that have come from various school districts which impress this writer are:

Guidance in Elementary Schools, a handbook for counselors, principals, and teachers, Los Angeles City Schools, School Publication No. 439, 1948.
Guidance Services Handbook for Elementary Schools in Missouri, Publication No. 94, 1953. (Mowrer and others)
Guidance in the Elementary Schools, Grove City, Ohio: Southwestern City Schools, 1962 (Frost, Quilling, and Van Hoose)
A Guidance Handbook for Adjustment Services in Elementary Schools, Chicago, Illinois: Board of Education, 1954. (DeKoker and others)

Guidance in Elementary Schools, Indianapolis, Indiana: State Department of Public Instruction, Bul. No. 247, 1961. (Shertzer and Pruett)
Elementary School Guidance in Hawaii, Honolulu, Hawaii: Department of Public Instruction, 1960.

PROCEDURES, PROBLEMS, AND ISSUES

As it is now developing in our elementary schools, guidance is emphasizing the following goals and trying to cope with the problems which arise from these attempts:

1. To enhance and make more functional our understanding of all children and to enhance and make more functional all children's understanding of themselves. This means in many schools that teachers have the services of special service workers in testing, counseling, test interpretation, the use of non-testing devices for studying children, and for work with parents in the exchange of information about the children. In other schools it is still assumed that this is the responsibility of the teacher and that she does not need the help of anyone else except in the more extreme cases she may refer to the school psychologist. But it is clear to many that such understandings as these, to be functional, must be tested through self-study, discussion, observation, and study of the world of choices in a personalized setting. In short, the child comes to self-understanding not just by looking at himself but as a consequence of individual and group experiences which help him to see himself in his environment with its demands and to see himself as others see him.

2. To help children with their goal seeking, choice making, and life planning, all good teachers work day by day with their class groups. Many teachers, however, are finding the counselor an aid in several aspects of these matters:

a. Counseling the individual child who needs more help with choice problems, as he sees the need. The counselor can become both an aid to the child and to the teacher by his listening, reflecting, encouraging, and helping with planning and decision making.
b. Working with the teacher to plan—and sometimes actually conducting—discussions of such matters as "Why do we go to school?" "What do the standard tests tell us?" "Why do our daddies have the jobs they do?" and the like.
c. Helping the teachers to find resource materials for units on the world of work and our ultimate place in it.
d. Working with parents, individually and in groups, to coordinate the school's efforts with those of the home. Counseling with parents when their aspirations and the developing goals of the child seem out of harmony.
e. Counseling with small groups of children who have a common concern.

3. To help children develop socially, to mature in their relations with others, requires all the skill, patience, and ingenuity that any teacher can com-

mand. To integrate this development effectively with a productive program for learning the usual academic subjects demands that the teacher effect a proper integration of many phases of the child's experiences. At times children (whose personal and social adjustment has become entangled or frustrated) will need special attention. It is then the teachers especially value the aid of a ready referral source, preferably someone on the staff of their building. This person has time assigned to study the child, talk with him, talk with his parents, and do the many things that help with the processes of individual adjustment require. A counselor on the building staff can be an invaluable help with such problems.

This phase of childhood education is, however, best conceived of as an ongoing developmental program which provides much well-planned opportunity for learning, and not just as remedial effort. Here the classroom teacher may also value the assistance of a skilled counselor. Well prepared in small group processes this counselor helps the teacher plan, and in some instances may conduct, group discussion regarding inter-personal relations and social development. Both as a counselor and as a consultant the elementary school counselor can thus aid with the teacher's job of social education.

4. To help children begin early to grow in their understanding of the role of education in their lives and to help them mature in their own life planning, the teacher must give systematic attention from the primary grades onward to the place of education and employment in the life of the child. Research now shows clearly that any effort at vocational guidance which begins in the secondary schools must be built—if it is to be effective—upon a sound foundation of the following:

a. Systematic orientation to the world of work through instruction, individual study, observation, and exploratory experiences. The elementary school counselor is trained to help teachers develop units on education and vocations and to find materials and resources which will enable the teachers in a school to build a unified approach to the study of these phases of life planning.

b. Enrichment of experiences regarding education and employment through field trips, interviews with workers, viewing of films and other audio-visual materials and the like. The counselor and teacher can work together in planning such experiences.

c. A program of parental involvement in the processes of life planning enables the child to explore and to begin his own planning in an atmosphere of support and understanding. The counselor can be of material aid in parent conferences—group and individual—in presentations to P.T.A.s and other groups regarding the child's problems of life planning, through individual counseling with children, and by many other means to bring about a proper integration of the adult forces playing upon a child as he matures in his own planning.

d. The instructional program of the elementary school needs much attention to experiences which help children develop accepting and respecting attitudes toward the work of all people. Such attitudes are essential to good employment relations in adulthood and are a significant part of our personal values in life. Teacher and counselor will plan such activities as suggested in a-c above with proper regard for values and attitudes.

THE COUNSELOR IN ELEMENTARY SCHOOLS

A good deal has been said in this paper about a guidance worker in the elementary school, the elementary school counselor. Let us summarize briefly what we see as the function of this person on the school staff:

1. The elementary school counselor is a member of the building staff. Thus she is a team member, readily available for close, intimate work with the teachers, the principal, the other special service workers, and the supervisors.

2. The elementary school counselor is an educator, prepared and experienced in teaching in the grades. She knows the work of the teacher, although she will not claim to be an expert in all aspects of all levels of elementary education (Hill and Nitzschke, 1961)!

3. The elementary school counselor will serve a pupil population of four to six hundred. Of course, such figures are strictly rule-of-thumb. It is probably much better to consider total staff for a total pupil population than to single out staff members. For example, we may accept the idea of fifty professional staff members for each 1000 children. This might be forty teachers and ten others; principal, assistant principal, supervisor, special teachers, counselor, nurses, school psychologists, and the like. The point is that we recognize the need for well-rounded and adequate staff resources.

4. This counselor is appointed to a school only after thorough study by the staff of its needs and at least a tentative definition of functions, by the staff. Acceptance by the staff is imperative. Organizational patterns differ too much to lay down a set pattern for this process. But where the work of the school counselor in the elementary school is most effective today is in the schools where the whole staff is involved in the process of planning the program and in selecting the counselor.

5. This counselor will be committed to the following basic principles of elementary school guidance:

a. Our chief concern is the fullest possible development of all children. Each child is a person to be respected, accepted, and encouraged.

b. The guidance effort of the elementary school is an integral phase of the total instructional program. All things done in the name of "guidance" must be viewed in terms of their total educational impact.

c. The teacher is the staff member primarily responsible for a given child or a given group of children. The planning and conduct of her program of

372.14 D6169
C.2

instruction is our chief concern. Guidance supplements and enriches good teaching.

d. The counselor is a building team member, a consultant to children and parents, to teachers and other staff members, a resource person for aid and referral. Her primary role is that of consultant, but a significant secondary role is that of counselor to individuals.

e. A good educational program, at any age level, is built upon each child coming to a better understanding of himself, learning how to understand the world about him and his place in it, learning how to choose wisely and solve his own problems, and learning how to become a more and more mature person in his relations with other people and with himself.

Thus, good guidance is based upon the recognition of the individuality of each child, the acceptance of each child, and the maximum effort to assist each child to become his best.

REFERENCES

Davis, J. 1959. *The acquiring of attitudes toward occupations in the elementary school.* Athens, Ohio: Ohio University. Unpublished honors paper.

Eckerson, Louise O., and H. M. Smith. May–July 1962. Guidance in the elementary school. *Sch. Life.*

Hill, G. E. 1963. Elementary school guidance: criteria for approval by state departments of education. *Couns. Educ. Supervis.*, 2, 137–143.

———. October 1963. The start of a continuous program is guidance in elementary schools. *Clearing House, 38*, 111–116.

———. and D. F. Nitzschke. October 1961. Preparation programs in elementary school guidance. *Personnel guid. J., 40*, 155–159.

Martinson, Ruth A. 1949. *The elementary school counselor in California.* Los Angeles: University of California at Los Angeles. Unpublished doctoral dissertation.

Mathewson, R. H. 1962. *Guidance policy and practice.* Third ed.; New York: Harper & Row.

Meeks, Anna R. 1963. Guidance in the elementary school. In A. J. Jones (ed.). *Principles of guidance.* Fifth ed.; New York: McGraw-Hill.

Michael, J., and L. Meyerson. 1962. A behavioral approach to counseling and guidance. *Harvard educ. Rev., 32*, 382–402.

National Association of Guidance Supervisors and Counselor Trainers. 1953. *National study of existing and recommended practices for assisting youth adjustment in selected elementary schools.* Ann Arbor, Mich.: Ann Arbor Publications.

National Education Association and the American Personnel and Guidance Association. 1961. *Guidance for the academically talented student.* Washington, D.C.: The Association.

Nelson, R. C. 1962 *a.* Early versus developmental vocational choice. *Voc. guid. Quart., 11,* 23–27.

————. 1962 *b. Knowledge and interests concerning sixteen occupations among elementary and secondary school students.* Athens, Ohio: Ohio University. Unpublished doctoral dissertation.

Smith, H. M., and Louise O. Eckerson. 1963. *Guidance for children in elementary schools.* Washington, D.C.: Office of Education, U.S. Department of Health, Education and Welfare.

U.S. Department of Health, Education and Welfare, Office of Education. 1961. *Guidance for the underachiever of superior ability.* Washington, D.C.: The Department.

Wrenn, C. G. 1962. *The counselor in a changing world.* Washington, D.C.: American Personnel and Guidance Association.

Elementary School Counseling*

Verne Faust

For more than a decade the American Personnel and Guidance Association's counselor seismograph has been detecting at least faint underground rumblings of a "new" professional school counselor about to emerge. During the past five years, the tracing on the seismograph chart has indicated clearly that the quake has been gaining momentum. The elementary school counselor is about to be shaken into a full-fledged place on the public school terrain.

During the 1964 APGA national convention, the strength of these rumblings moved the elementary school counselor meetings for the first time, out of dark, hastily scheduled hotel broom closets, into spacious, chandeliered convention rooms, where large audiences of counselor educators met, hoping to prepare themselves for the imminent tidal wave of demand for elementary school counselors about to sweep across the United States.

While sporadic efforts have been made, here and there, to prepare for the tide with descriptions of what the role and function of the elementary school counselor should be, no certain leadership has emerged to point the way. Only one certainty of agreement appears to have been reached: the elementary school counselor should not be simply an image of the secondary school counselor.

* *Developments in Counseling,* 1965, Bulletin No. 18, Bureau of Educational Research and Services, Arizona State University. By permission.

Beyond this, publications (Eckerson and Smith, 1962; Reed and Stefflre, 1963) have referred to the elementary counselor variously as one who works more with parents and teachers, with continuing emphasis on the "different" child, or the child in some sort of difficulty. Occasionally, reference to play therapy can be found. While these references constitute a gross under-description of current thinking, practice, and status of elementary school counseling, it remains to be said that no certain direction of professional image has emerged.

The United States Congress, in 1964, signed into effect a virtual "*title* wave" of its own. Additional authority was added to the National Defense Education Act, granting that preparation of elementary school counselors could be initiated under the auspices of the U.S. Office of Education. It can well be expected that this congressional action will stimulate elementary school counseling perhaps even beyond the remarkable surge which has occurred in secondary school counseling as a result of the original National Defense Education Act congressional legislation.

ELEMENTARY SCHOOL COUNSELING AT ARIZONA STATE UNIVERSITY

The Counseling and Educational Psychology Department at Arizona State University has been preparing, for two and one-half years, to meet the predicted public elementary school demand for counselors. The counselor education program model has been on the drawing boards since this time, and, with the impetus of current national legislation, has been translated recently into a full sixty-hour, or two-year graduate curriculum.

The program first will be undertaken experimentally through a National Defense Education Act Counseling and Guidance Institute, sponsored by the U. S. Office of Education. The interest and support of the U.S. Office of Education, with particular leadership shown in this area by Harold McCully and Ralph Bedell, of the Counseling and Guidance Branch, undoubtedly will contribute considerably toward the present Arizona State University model influencing the character of elementary school counselor education throughout the nation.

RATIONALE OF ARIZONA STATE UNIVERSITY PROGRAM

Perhaps the chief failure for any explicit national leadership in elementary school counseling to emerge to date may be attributed to a critical absence of clearly defined objectives and a rationale of human behavior out of which role and function could grow. This is to say that no leadership has begun with an organized, systematic conceptualization of human behavior, with the counseling program being determined by such a framework. Instead, approaches generally have been atomistic, devoid of continuity, and seldom relating to a common systematic base. We have, for example, heard much about "working with parents," "focusing on the teacher," or other areas. Elementary school counselor curriculum designers have tended to begin with a discussion of areas, focuses, and courses. No substantial effort has been undertaken to permit areas, focuses, and courses to develop out of objectives and a systematic rationale of human behavior.

While the limitation of space in the present report prohibits an exposition of the human behavior rationale out of which grew the elementary school counselor education model at Arizona State University, a brief examination of the objectives can be made.

The premise on which these objectives are based maintains that public school personnel, whether they are teachers, counselors, or administrators, are employees of the tax-supporting society. It is the public—and not school personnel or higher education—which decides what the goals of public education are to be. The public employs personnel to undertake the achievement of these goals. Where the public does not clearly and explicitly define its public school objectives, school personnel must demand clarification or, where this is either inadvisable or not feasible, infer what appears to be the public mandate (Faust, 1964).

The major objective of the elementary school preparation model to be initiated at Arizona State University has been derived through inferential processes, rather than having been gained from explicit public directives.

While we frequently have heard it said that it is the "whole child" we are concerned with in education, more often it is cognition alone which in reality receives the attention of teachers, counselors, and the public.

This is to say, that *"knowing"—knowing how to read, knowing how to manipulate numbers meaningfully, or other content—is most frequently the educational focus; indeed, the current primary goal of tax-supported education.*

Every segment of the elementary school counselor education program has been designed to prepare the counselor to contribute toward the child's functioning maximally at the cognitive level. This is the primary, if not the only, objective of the curriculum.

Whether we, as one kind of educationist, may not agree with current objectives issued to us by the tax-supporting public is another issue. To change these goals—if indeed they require changing at all—would behoove us either to work cautiously in new directions at our present educational posts, or, perhaps, resign our positions, and as a part of the public citizenry, free of certain public school alignments which may leave oneself suspect, attempt to effect change in the public goals of education.

It should be pointed out that the emphasis on "intellectual functioning," the "curriculum," and "non-crisis situations" in the elementary school counseling model initiated at Arizona State University is, in its position, neither new nor unique. At the same time, it is both innovative and unique in its breadth, depth, and translation into a complete counselor education curriculum.

BACKGROUND AND LITERATURE

As long ago as 1918 the Commission on the Reorganization of Secondary School Education, of the National Education Association recognized that a close relationship exists between guidance and curriculum.

More explicitly stated twenty years later, Jones and Hand (1938) supported the contention that ". . . guidance and instruction would be functioning as inseparable parts of a unitary process. . . ."

Despite this point of view appearing sporadically over the years, it never has been, in an important way, translated into practice. Apparently, this has been due, on the one hand, to an absence of leadership in successfully moving beyond a mere statement of the position that counseling and curriculum are "inseparable parts of a unitary process." No thorough effort has been undertaken to establish this position on a theoretical conceptualization of human behavior, with counselor education course work emerging out of the model.

In addition, a tenacious resistance to change on the part of many personnel identified with the earlier guidance movement has shown a shift to the more central core of the student in the educative process. Miller (1961) has, in a noteworthy way, summed up the historical struggle to relate guidance more centrally to learning and the curriculum. On the other hand, he ended his exposition with support of a traditional posture, containing guidance on the periphery of the child in the educative process.

One of the more recent important supporters furnishing a counseling emphasis on intellectual functioning within a non-crises curriculum setting is Wrenn (1962). In *The Counselor in a Changing World* he has stated, "The critical question is whether or not the elementary school will learn from the experience of the secondary school and build a counseling program which is not crisis-oriented." Further, Wrenn has explicitly formulated the contention that the school curriculums of today are ". . . clearly concerned with intellectual growth." He has gone on to say, "The school's primary function can be stated briefly. *It is to facilitate the intellectual development of students who vary in the relation of the intellectual to the social and emotional dimensions of their personality.*"

The apparent impact which Wrenn's book is having on counselors in this country suggests that the posture which he has assumed in regard to intellectual activity of the student, the importance of direct curriculum involvement, and de-emphasizing a focus on crisis situations, may mean that periphery guidance and counseling may, at last, be replaced perhaps as early as within the coming decade. Certainly this seems to be imminently true in the case of emerging elementary school counseling programs.

CENTRAL OBJECTIVE OF THE MODEL

If it is accepted that cognition receives the greater portion of attention in the academic setting, certain implications for educational practice, including the role of the elementary school counselor, as well as counselor educators, become apparent.

The elementary school counselor and the counselor educator possess the same responsibility as teachers and other school personnel. It is assumed in the model for counselor education at Arizona State University that all educationists are to behave in ways which will assist students to learn cognitively at the highest possible levels of efficiency. The elementary school counselor hopefully will possess knowledge, skills, techniques, all the professional competencies, which will add to the probability that public school students will, within whatever innate potentialities they may possess, function cognitively with maximum efficiency.

While it might be imperative for certain other educators to concern themselves with various broad corollary goals, this does not seem to be true in the case of the elementary school counselor. The counselor educator in the present program model acts on the premise that if counselors in the school setting can behave in ways which will allow the intellects of students to function free of crippling anxiety, fear, guilt, and defensive posturing, secondary gains also will be effected (Faust, 1964). Patriotism, civic responsibility, creativity, character development, and personal adjustment, all of which at one time or another have been considered by some voices to be the goals of education, would be expected to result autonomously. This is to say that the kinds of experiences which contribute to effective intellectual functioning also make it possible for effective behavior in other areas.

The goal, the major, most central objective of counselor education, as understood in the present program proposal, is *not* to train personnel to assist students to make better personal or emotional adjustments; nor, for that matter, to aid students in career and educational choices and planning.

The elementary school counselor education program is designed on the contention that if a new world is constructed for children in the classroom, where students feel relatively safe, the central nervous system of the organism will function at high levels of efficiency. As a by-product, positive, efficient identifications will occur with appropriate societal members, accompanied by a self-searching, curious, creative exploration of the world of work, politics, and economic responsibility, so that decision-making may be undertaken effortlessly, or relatively so. Entire guidance and counseling systems or organizations constructed to assist students in choices or decision-making would be practically unnecessary. Certainly, less public school personnel, with less elaborately expensive training, would be necessary to provide students information and a relationship in order to arrive at appropriate career and social choices. It is contended, to reiterate, that individuals who function efficiently (though not pseudo-efficiently) at intellectual levels also will be maximally effective in other areas of human behavior.

DIFFERENCES BETWEEN ELEMENTARY AND TRADITIONAL COUNSELOR EDUCATION PROGRAMS

The broad, basic objective (to facilitate cognition) on which the elementary school counselor education curriculum is anchored is not identical with the objectives of the department's secondary school counselor program. The very nature of the elementary counselor program is new on the scene of professional school counseling in America. It is innovative and experimental. It almost precludes the objectives being similar to those of the department's current goals in counselor education.

This is not to say that the secondary counselor program at this university rejects the major objective—of contributing toward highest levels of cognitive learning—represented by the elementary counselor programs. On the contrary, although not explicitly stated, in many cases the current secondary curriculum would be in support of the central objective stated here.

The elementary counselor education program is more central to what is traditionally called the curriculum core of the school, where the essence of learning, of cognition, occurs. It is less peripheral, less an adjunct to the central stream of the educative process than that represented by the secondary school counselor's role. It focuses less on advisement, less on career and educational planning, less on tests, measurements, and program planning. Also, less emphasis is placed on record keeping.

Further, it functions with less emphasis on direct student contact and work with individuals. While the individual is considered to be of supreme worth, it is maintained that economically his educational welfare can be effectively realized only primarily through teachers and various types of group experiences, all within a particular kind of curriculum design.

The elementary counselor model presented here is less child-treatment oriented, and almost exclusively preventative in nature. Intervention and treatment procedures, techniques, and roles are but a minor working part of the model.

Work with parents and community agencies, while a part of the program, is, by comparison, of much less significance than the central focus on curriculum and the personnel responsible for developing, managing, and carrying out the curriculum in action.

The elementary program focuses more on teachers and the effects of their relationships, subject-matter content, and instructional methods on the learning apparatus of the child. It economically spends more attention on persons, such as teachers and administrators, who will affect, either directly or indirectly, large numbers of students. When working with students it more often is economical to do so with groups, rather than individuals. In illustration, a counselor who works intensively with eight teachers, two hours each week, is contributing to perhaps 240 children. It is conceivable that the counselor-student ratio needs to be 1 to 750 (based on one teacher for every thirty students) rather than 1 to 250, which is a recommended ratio for secondary school programs. The costs of the elementary school counselor can be 200 percent less than that of high school counselors.

Instead of testing, program planning, and record keeping, the elementary counselor is involved in the most economically crucial places, lending his professional role to building a new world for children, making it safe, and so freeing intellects of children to learn.

The program is not designed so much to heal disordered, perplexed, unproductive children, as it is to assist other school personnel in building a new world for children, in which disorder and disease have little opportunity to originate and flourish.

REFERENCES

Commission on the Reorganization of Secondary School Education. 1918. *A report*. Washington, D.C.: National Education Association.

Eckerson, Louise, and H. Smith. 1962. Elementary school guidance: the consultant. Reprint of three articles in *Sch. Life*. Washington, D.C.: Office of Education, U.S. Office of Health, Education and Welfare.

Faust, V. 1964. *Plan of operation for a counseling and guidance institute to be conducted by Arizona State University, under contract with the U.S. Office of Education*. Tempe, Ariz.: Arizona State University.

Jones, A. J., and H. C. Hand. 1938. Guidance and purposive living. *Yearbook of National Social Studies in Education*, Part I.

Miller, C. 1961. *Foundations of guidance*. New York: Harper & Row.

Reed, H. J., and B. Stefflre. April 1963. Elementary and secondary school programs. *Educ. Res., 33*.

Wrenn, C. G. 1962. *The counselor in a changing world*. Washington, D.C.: American Personnel and Guidance Association.

Some Thoughts on Elementary School Guidance*

Kenneth B. Hoyt

INTRODUCTION

Words come easily to those unencumbered by either knowledge or competence in the subject they are addressing. This is true, in part, because neither

* *Elementary School Guidance and Counseling*, 1967, vol. 1, no. 2.
  By permission.

knowledge nor competence is prerequisite to the development of interest or concern. These words are being written on invitation by one who claims both interest and concern for elementary school guidance, but disclaims knowledge or competence in the field. It is hoped that they may prove to have some stimulating value in encouraging those who are knowledgeable and competent in their continuing efforts to develop this badly needed aspect of personnel and guidance services.

THE NEED FOR ELEMENTARY SCHOOL GUIDANCE

There has been no argument with respect to whether or not elementary school guidance is needed for as long as I can remember. The basis of this need must have been present for at least as long as the goals of guidance have been pictured in developmental terms. For more than a professional generation of guidance workers, the goals of guidance have been pictured as developmental as opposed to either preventative or remedial in nature. Those of us in the school guidance field have devoted our major energies to finding and applying ways of helping each and every student in the school make better those decisions they will make whether or not we are present. We have said that optimal individual development will more likely occur if the kind of systematic help the guidance field provides is added to efforts individuals make toward their individual self-development. No one, so far as I know, has ever said (although many have pretended) that these systematic attempts to aid students in responsible self-development should be postponed until the student enters the secondary school setting. The only way the whole concept of school guidance makes sense is to picture it as beginning when the student first enters the school system. This has been true now for many years.

There are three apparent arguments with respect to need for elementary school guidance which have not yet been completely resolved. The first concerns the question of whether or not the developmental problems of elementary school students are serious enough to justify special attention. A wealth of research literature accumulated in the last twenty years demonstrating both the presence of such problems and their crucial nature seems now to have taken care of that problem for most of us. The second argument concerns the efficacy of guidance services at the elementary school level. This argument, because of the absence of a clear-cut body of research knowledge, is still very much with us. We have advanced in this generation to the point of recognizing that the only way of settling it is to install guidance programs in elementary schools and then test their efficacy through sound research procedures. The argument, however, remains and, with the addition of each new kind of specialist in the elementary education field, flames into controversy again among conscientious elementary school administrators.

The third apparent argument concerns itself with whether or not a specialist called the elementary school counselor is needed to perform the guidance function in this setting. The basis of this argument lies in views various individuals have with respect to the need for guidance, the nature of elementary school guidance, the role of the classroom teacher in guidance, and the role and function of other kinds of specialists in the elementary school setting. Like the second, this argument is yet far from being resolved.

In summary, the question of whether or not elementary school guidance is needed was settled in the affirmative long ago. The current questions we face are those concerned with the nature of elementary school guidance, the need for elementary school guidance specialists, and the evidence we require in order to demonstrate the efficacy of guidance in the elementary school. The remainder of this article is devoted to expressions of a concerned, but admittedly ignorant, person concerning each of these three topics.

THE NATURE OF ELEMENTARY SCHOOL GUIDANCE

What should be the nature of guidance in the elementary school? If we had half as much evidence as we now have opinions regarding answers to this question, the future of elementary school guidance would seem assured. It seems quite pointless to answer the question by bravely contending that it should be different from guidance in the secondary school. Who knows? If a pure transplant of the high school guidance program produced better results than something new and different, then that pure transplant should be what survives. It seems even more pointless to answer the question by saying the program should be "developmental" in nature. We don't need words to bring meaning to this field; rather, we need meaning for the words we already possess and use so loosely and casually at the present time.

There seem to be "pilot" programs of elementary school guidance springing up in many states currently using the now available Title V-A NDEA funds. Yet, to an outsider such as myself, it seems exceedingly odd that so many pilot programs can exist that are not part of any sound research design. Where are the master plans in the state departments of education providing for testing the efficacy of elementary school guidance as developed and operated under various *kinds* of concepts? What compacts have been made among various state departments of education for pooling their data accumulated from operation of pilot programs in some comprehensive research design? This would seem to be an ideal time to establish a variety of kinds of elementary school guidance programs under experimental conditions which, in a period of five to ten years, would yield some research answers to the question of the best nature of elementary school guidance in various settings for various populations of elementary school children. If such broadly conceived and truly widespread experimental approaches are being undertaken, those responsible for their operation appear to be keeping secrets from the rest of us. True, we find in almost every state plans for receiving reports from the pilot programs. But where are the plans for what is to be done with the reports? If these remarks do nothing more than make such reports widely available, they will have served their purpose.

If I were responsible for designing and operating a program of elementary school guidance today, my program would be developed around the following kinds of principles. First, I would make every attempt to see that the program was consistent in purposes and goals with the philosophy of the elementary school in which it was installed. I think the principle of making sure this program is really a part of the elementary school—and not something added to the school—must be observed. This principle would guide determination of both the specific activities involved and the speed with which various activities are introduced.

Second, I would operate under a principle that the classroom teacher must be viewed and must view herself as a guidance worker actively involved in the *program* of guidance services. The need for *teacher involvement* and for a *schoolwide program* of services would be given equal emphasis. The guidance activities, for example, of the fourth grade teacher are of vital importance, but of relatively little value if they are seen as encompassing the total range of guidance services extended to the pupils in her class.

Third, I would operate under a principle that guidance in the elementary school must (not *should*) be seen as part of an organized and functioning program of pupil personnel services which is broader than guidance. It is vital that the developmental, preventative, and remedial goals associated with a total program of pupil personnel services be seen as complementary—not as competitive —in the elementary school. I would embrace the principle that the presence of a developmental program of elementary school guidance is not intended and does not purport to eliminate the need for other programs of a preventative and/or a remedial nature. At the same time, I would support with equal vigor that those parts of the pupil personnel program which are called "guidance" should not encompass activities having preventative or remedial goals as primary objectives.

Fourth, I would operate under a principle that guidance in the elementary school demands involvement of parents on a systematic and planned basis. I would think of parents and try to get parents to think of themselves as guidance workers. Guidance isn't something you must be able to spell in order to do. I would reject a principle which stated that only "professional guidance workers" should be active participants in the program of elementary school guidance. I would support a principle which stated that parents of the youngsters I serve can make or break the guidance program—and conferences treat parents as though they were that important. One concrete activity I know I would have would be a systematic program of parent conferences plus widespread appeals to parents urging them to come to school to discuss their children with members of the school staff.

Fifth, I would operate under a principle that guidance in the elementary school requires the presence of professional counselors as key, pivotal, coordinative agents for the entire elementary school guidance program. I would see the coordinative functions of the elementary school counselor as more important (relatively speaking) and the counseling function as less important (relatively speaking) than those of the secondary school counselor. This is, of course, strictly relative because the coordinative function is very important in the secondary school and the counseling function is vital, it seems to me, in the elementary school. If someone asked me to install an elementary guidance program which I thought would work, one absolute requirement I would establish would be that professional elementary school counselors be employed in a ratio of one such counselor for every nine teachers employed in the school. I would favor a counselor-teacher over a counselor-pupil ratio because of the nature and extent of teacher involvement in the guidance program. I would use the number "nine" instead of some other number because I *think* I could defend it to school administrators and school boards—not because I *know* this is correct!

Sixth, I would change the parts of a secondary school guidance program some in terms of their emphasis, but I would eliminate none of those parts. For example, I would emphasize non-testing student appraisal procedures much more than standardized testing and leave the primary task of standardized testing as more of an instructional than a guidance function. I would emphasize teacher referrals as the primary (but not the exclusive) basis on which students come to me for counseling. I would concentrate much attention on small group work with students, on case conferences with parents. I would try to develop systematic means of communication and referral for dealing with other pupil personnel specialists in the elementary school and referral agencies in the community. I would consider problems of relating with secondary school counselors in terms of students transferring to such schools as one of my major tasks.

Finally, I would insist that some goals and objectives for this program be written down in a form susceptible of measurement and that a plan for evaluation be built into the total program. These statements would, in all probability, be ones I had written and then tried to get others to agree with. I would regard this kind of evaluative research as an integral and important part of the total job to be done.

This, then, is the kind of elementary school guidance program I would propose. What is badly needed now is for a wide variety of people to propose a wide variety of programs, to fund all of those which, on the simple basis of logic and professional common sense, appear to hold some positive potential, and then to evaluate this wide variety of programs together in a solidly designed experimental approach.

THE NEED FOR ELEMENTARY
SCHOOL GUIDANCE SPECIALISTS

It should be apparent from what has been said that I believe persons carrying the title of "elementary school counselor" should exist. While I have tried to defend this belief by commenting on the counselor role, there are two essential questions which have been ignored. One is, can the elementary school counselor be defended as needed more than other kinds of specialists in the elementary school? The second is, why should he be called an elementary school "counselor?" These questions need answers. Perhaps answers given by one who is neither practicing in the elementary guidance field nor currently preparing elementary school counselors may be of some interest—even though of little value —to those who are expert in this field.

In one sense, the question of which kind of pupil personnel specialist is most needed in the elementary school is a nonsensical one. That is, it can be viewed as analogous to a question which asks whether one needs food, water, or rest in order to survive—when, obviously, all three are needed. If pupil personnel work was considered as important by school administrators and school boards as we think it is, this question would not be raised. But it *is* raised by such people, and for those in elementary school guidance to ignore it or to protest that it is not a pertinent question would seem unwise. The operational problem is one of developing and implementing a strategy for encouraging the employment of sufficient numbers of elementary school counselors in schools throughout the nation so that the efficacy of elementary school guidance involving such counselors can be adequately assessed.

The wisest basic strategy would seem to be that used so successfully over the last several years in dramatically increasing the number of professional counselors employed in the secondary schools. That this strategy works is attested to by the fact that, as of today, there are more counselors employed in secondary schools than in all other settings combined. The basic elements in this strategy are simple and straightforward: (1) guidance services are pictured as being for *all* students in the school; (2) the goals and objectives of guidance can be and are stated in terms consistent with the goals and objectives of education; (3) guidance is pictured as helping teachers be more effective in their relationships with pupils; (4) counselors are pictured as experienced teachers with special graduate education designed to qualify them for employment as professional counselors; and (5) relationships between counselors and teachers are viewed as of a dual consultative nature—i.e., the counselor is a consultant to the teacher and the teacher is a consultant to the counselor. It is currently popular among some guidance leaders to deny that this strategy has been basically responsible for the widespread acceptance of counselors in secondary schools. Such denials don't alter my firm belief that each element in this strategy has been and continues to be essential.

The second question involves an appropriate title for the professional guidance specialist in the elementary school. It would seem appropriate to identify such persons by the title "Elementary School Counselor" for the following reasons: (1) Such persons should, in their *basic* background of professional graduate education, acquire skills and knowledge similar to those possessed by professional counselors in other settings. (2) The term "counselor" is becoming increasingly accepted in our society as one committed in his professional goals to developmental objectives. (3) Substantial progress has already been made in our professional literature differentiating those carrying the title "counselor" from other pupil personnel specialists. (4) If and when common-core counselor education programs are established through federal legislation, the eligibility of professional guidance specialists in the elementary school may, at least initially, very well depend on whether or not they carry the title "counselor." This last point, it should be understood, is pure conjecture at this time and must be regarded as only a personal opinion. That is, no new legislation has been introduced at the time this is being written which would impose such a restriction.

CRITERIA FOR EVALUATION
OF ELEMENTARY SCHOOL GUIDANCE

How is the worth of elementary school guidance to be demonstrated? What kinds of evidence would suffice to convince elementary schools throughout the nation that the elementary school guidance program should exist? There are no more crucial questions than these to be faced at this time.

Prior to attempting to specify suitable criteria, two important background considerations must be specified. The first involves clear recognition of the fact that doing "something" is generally and under almost all conditions better than doing "nothing." That is, if a reasonably bright, highly conscientious person possessing a sincere interest in and dedication to helping elementary school students solve their problems better were employed as a "counselor," it is highly probable that some "good" things would happen—no matter what his background of education and experience. With the wide variety of specialists now seeking employment in the elementary school, the "something-versus-nothing" approach to evaluation must be viewed as insufficient for use in demonstrating the worth of elementary school guidance. It would answer none of the really pressing professional issues now facing us with respect to desirable professional education, roles, and functions of the elementary school guidance specialist.

The second background consideration involves acceptance of the fact that assessment of criterion measures built in terms of changes in pupil behavior will not be, in most cases, strictly attributable to a "guidance" or to a "counselor" effect. That is, the use of developmental goals and objectives consistent with those of elementary education carries an inevitable handicap of not being able to demonstrate the worth of guidance independent of all other forces operating in the elementary school. This is the same handicap that secondary school guidance has operated under for years. There is no apparent reason to believe that it would or should impede serious efforts aimed at evaluation of guidance in the elementary school.

There are several immediate criteria which appear to hold positive potential for evaluation of elementary school guidance. Included among these would be such things as: (1) an increase in the number of pupils referred by teachers for counseling; (2) more parent-counselor contacts; (3) an increase in the number of contacts with out-of-school referral agencies; (4) a widening of student appraisal procedures; and (5) more funds for elementary school guidance. Each such example of possible immediate evaluative criteria illustrates measurement of factors logically related to effectiveness without itself being a direct measure of effectiveness.

Ultimate criteria appropriate for use in evaluating elementary school guidance should, it seems, be built around pupil behavior. As such, their use must be recognized as factors influenced by things other than guidance but which, at the same time, represent logical effects to which guidance should make some contribution. Included among such criteria are: (1) increases in pupil achievement in the elementary school; (2) decreases in reported pupil disciplinary problems; (3) increases in teacher-pupil relationships; (4) decreases in incidence of tardiness and school absence; and (5) decreases in percentage of underachievers in the elementary school. These represent but a few of the ultimate criteria related to pupil behavior which some may consider appropriate for evaluating the efficacy of elementary school guidance. No attempt has been made here to do more than provide a few illustrative examples.

SUMMARY

The field of elementary school guidance is at a crucial stage in its growth and development. While the need for elementary school guidance appears to be widely recognized, much confusion remains with respect to what it should include or how it should be carried out. A strong plea has been made here for answering such questions through comprehensive programmatic research. It is hoped that these remarks may stimulate those who specialize in this field to undertake the kinds of research called for. The continuing growth of elementary school guidance demands that the personnel and guidance movement accept this challenge.

PROGRAM DEVELOPMENT

AND MANAGEMENT

The philosophy and basic concepts of guidance only become meaningful as they are applied in the guidance program. The crucial step from philosophy to action involves administration and organization, focusing on objectives, role definitions of various professionals within the program, and the interrelationship of the pupil personnel services. Chapter 2 considers those concepts basic to the initiation and administration of a guidance program. The specific services which proceed from a developmental philosophy of elementary school guidance are briefly described in the readings of Chapter 2.

Research in child development has discovered that the early school years significantly influence the child's development of attitudes, values, aspirations, and his basic concept of self. Also, at this age level the child is involved in decision-making processes without much training in thinking and in controlling pressures that might be adverse to academic achievement and personal worth brought upon him by his home environment. A good guidance program at the elementary school level will more than merely recognize an individual's uniqueness; it will seek to develop it. The curriculum, also, must contribute to development of the individual's understanding of himself and the world about him.

PROGRAM IMPLEMENTS PHILOSOPHY

Programs tend to reflect the specific needs of geographical areas, socioeconomic groups, and philosophies of education. However, effective guidance programs must be organized in relation to certain fundamental concepts of program development.

40

Guidance is not a specialized service, but it is an integral part of the educational program, and as such its goal is to reach all students. Its concern is with developmental problems (Lloyd-Jones, Barry, and Wolf, 1958).

The developmental guidance program is directed at discovering the abilities of all children in a continuous, observational system. The student should become more than just the object of a child study; he should participate in his own study by learning to understand himself in relation to his opportunities.

Classroom guidance should not be incidental but a primary responsibility of the teacher. While the teacher does not engage in diagnosis or therapy, he is involved on a daily basis in identifying guidance needs and assisting his pupils to meet the developmental tasks. The teacher can relate the learning opportunities of the school to the emerging interests, goals, and abilities of the child. Guidance conceived in this manner, then, will not be a special function emanating from the office of the school counselor. The program will clearly reflect a collaborative relationship with teachers, parents, and other pupil personnel specialists.

Elementary school guidance is differentiated from secondary school guidance because of the nature of the curriculum and the role of the teacher. Elementary guidance is able to emphasize development of self-understanding and facilitation of learning. Secondary school guidance, in contrast, is more intensely concerned with educational planning and career choice (Farwell and Peters, 1957).

Elementary school guidance theory must recognize the typical dependency of the elementary school child on parents and teachers. The organization of the school and the curriculum at the elementary school level can provide an atmosphere conducive to developmental guidance theory. The teacher typically has a greater amount of time for daily contact with pupils. The curriculum is usually flexible, thus enabling the teacher to develop more effective relationships and perform some of the guidance functions. Guidance can be an integral part of the total instructional program.

PURPOSES OF ELEMENTARY
SCHOOL GUIDANCE

Elementary school guidance services must be twofold in purpose, consisting of objectives for improvement of teaching and development of each child. For teachers, the objectives of elementary school guidance are:

1. Assistance in the total educational program to meet the needs of all students in intellectual, personal, and social areas; promoting understanding of the individual and encouraging adaptation of the program to specific needs, purposes, interests, and maturities.

2. Promoting the early identification of both individual strengths and talents as well as individual liabilities or deviations.

3. Making the teacher aware and sensitive to the child's personal needs, goals, and purposes; enabling the teacher to utilize the principles from educational psychology, child development, learning theory, and guidance in the classroom.

4. Stimulating the study and the use of guidance techniques by the teacher and the total staff, thereby increasing the utilization of pupil personnel data and encouraging the individualization of the total educational experiences.

For the child, the objectives of elementary school guidance are:

1. Assisting the child in the development of increased self-understanding and increased understanding of the relationships of his abilities, interests, achievements, and opportunities.

2. Promoting increased self-direction, problem-solving, and decision-making by the child.

3. Developing wholesome attitudes, convictions, and concepts about self and others which result in the "fully functioning child."

4. Assisting the child to understand, plan, make choices, and solve present and future problems.

5. Developing a sensitivity to the needs of others, resulting in social interest and the desire to cooperate with others and maturing in human relations.

6. Understanding the causal and purposive nature of behavior and using this knowledge in understanding self and others.

7. Assisting the child in the solving of fundamental tasks of life in the areas of work and social development and enabling him to experience success in his tasks.

These objectives cannot be achieved merely by superimposing a set of special services which provide pupil appraisal, counseling, information, and consultation. To achieve the goals in terms of each child, it is apparent that guidance must have an impact upon the curriculum and the way in which the teacher approaches the learning process. Each of the specific objectives indicate that the child has access to the understandings which the guidance staff and the teacher have regarding him. This enables the child to become more efficaciously involved in the learning process.

Guidance, then, is more than a service by the counselor, a contact with the teacher, or a consultation with the parents. Guidance is a process through which the educational experience takes on personal meaning for the child.

Guidance should take advantage of the child's interests, readiness, and the teachable moment. It is a planned service that must consider all of the significant adults important in the development of the child. The classroom teacher, a key person, should have a classroom guidance program which is as definitively developed as his arithmetic or social studies program. This would include objectives, activities, and methods of evaluating the program.

THE INTEGRATED APPROACH
TO ELEMENTARY SCHOOL GUIDANCE

The guidance services offered at the elementary school level must be based on a team approach, where close cooperation and the interrelationship of all pupil personnel services will be a functioning reality. Every teacher should be a member of the guidance team.

The integrated approach provides an opportunity for elementary school guidance to become truly developmental, creative, and unique. This approach would envision individuals in the school who would all be working toward common goals. Fundamental to this approach is an understanding of others and their motives and the development of a sensitivity to one's own attitudes, purposes, and goals.

The implementation of such a program requires not only a continuous evaluation of the nature of the human relationships in the school setting, but also the practical development of channels of communication. One of the procedures fundamental to the development of communication is the formation of the guidance council. The council is composed of representatives of the teachers who meet regularly with administration and the guidance staff in order to discuss needs, problems, and procedures.

Throughout the text there will be specific sections which deal with the role of various professionals in the pupil personnel services area. The role of the counselor will be discussed in detail in Chapter 3. Briefly, the counselor's primary functions involve counseling, consultation, coordination, and the development of in-service training in guidance for classroom teachers. At this time we shall briefly distinguish the primary functions expected of teachers, administrators, psychologists, and school social workers.

The teacher is the heart of the program, involved in identifying guidance needs and facilitating the attitudes and behavior in children. He is concerned with developing a relationship with children which is characterized by a mutual alignment of goals and purposes. In the classroom, emphasis is placed on assimilating knowledge which has personal meaning. The teacher may or may not use tests to help in his understanding of the individual. He provides occupational, educational, and social information. He is concerned that students understand the guidance implications of regular curricular material. He has effective skills in interviewing pupils and parents. The teacher collaborates with the school counselor to provide service beyond that which his skills and understandings permit.

The administrator provides the program with leadership and personal support. Administrators assist by providing adequate physical facilities and schedules which provide opportunities for regular appointments between the counselor and the teacher. The administrator also encourages staff members to participate in in-service education directed at improving guidance skills.

The psychologist, when available as a member of the pupil personnel team, is primarily responsible for the clinical case study. He brings methods and skills in this task which are distinct from those of the counselor or teacher. He is involved in the work with teachers and parents on the problems of one child. He also contributes to the in-service program through case conferences and other forms of consultation. In some schools, psychologists may provide limited counseling assistance with children and have responsibilities in parent education. However, it is assumed that in most instances the psychologist will be used most extensively in clinical case study (Eckerson and Smith, 1966).

The social worker also brings unique skills to the team in terms of his training in case work, which makes him particularly effective in the counseling of students and parents. He is concerned with coordination between home, school, and community in order to promote more effective working relationships. The social worker also collaborates with other members of the staff in assisting teachers to understand the child (Eckerson and Smith, 1966).

Each of the members of the pupil personnel team supplies a vital contribution in terms of his unique skills. The essential difference exists in the focus of the teacher, administrator, and counselor on all pupils in contrast to the typical focus of the psychologist or social worker on the exceptional child.

THE INITIATION OF GUIDANCE SERVICES

In those elementary schools where guidance facilities do not exist, it is important to involve the whole staff in planning for a program. The staff should study its needs for guidance services and develop some tentative definitions of the functions they request. Since local conditions do vary, it is vital that each school system analyze its own situation and develop its own appropriate program.

Planning for the program can begin by scheduling a staff meeting to discuss the possibility of an elementary guidance program for a specific district or school. This could be followed by development of a planning committee composed of teachers, administrators, consultants in the school district, and perhaps lay citizens and parents. This committee would be concerned with relating the educational philosophy of the school system and the guidance needs of pupils, staff, and parents to the functions of the elementary school counselor.

This committee might visit schools which have already developed elementary guidance programs or are in the process of developing such programs. The committee will engage in a survey of needs as perceived by teachers, pupils, and parents. In some instances it will be helpful to the planning committee to contact elementary school counselors who are working in other districts or counselor-educators who have a special interest in the elementary school guidance program. The committee should eventually develop an organizational chart which indicates the role and function of all available pupil personnel specialists and the procedure by which their efforts will be coordinated.

THE DIVISION OF GUIDANCE SERVICES

Any statement regarding services provided by specialists in elementary guidance is made in light of the preceding philosophy and principles which indicate the importance of providing services for all children through the teacher. The division of services only permits the specialist to recognize the services which require his coordination. The following areas constitute the major guidance services:

1. Pupil Appraisal. Early identification of abilities, assets, talents, and liabilities is the goal of the counselor. Information is collected which enables the

teacher to work more effectively with the pupil and assists the pupil to develop an understanding of himself in relationship to his opportunities. A major goal involves the development of self-understanding, self-acceptance, and a more realistic self-evaluation by students. Pupil appraisal, or pupil inventory, includes both standardized tests and nontesting methods.

2. Consulting. The counselor and the teacher collaborate in facilitating the learning of the child. The counselor familiarizes the teacher with guidance techniques in both the diagnostic and therapeutic areas. The counselor may be concerned about helping the teacher understand an individual or perhaps enabling him to work more effectively with the group. In some instances, the counselor demonstrates or assists in the teacher's first experiences with a guidance technique or procedure. The consultant role is directed at providing more guidance services for all pupils.

In his role as consultant, the counselor helps parents understand the objectives of the school guidance program. Consultation to parents includes meetings which help groups of parents understand parent-child relationships. Other meetings with parents develop an understanding of the information that the school has collected about the abilities, interests, and achievements of their children.

3. Counseling. Counseling in the elementary school is considered in two general areas: remedial, or modification of attitudes and behavior; and developmental, emphasizing exploration and self-understanding (Dinkmeyer, 1966). Counseling, then, is not concerned primarily with educational and vocational decision-making. Counseling provides an opportunity for the counselor and the child to survey the facts, clarify feelings, consider alternatives, and develop problem-solving techniques (Dinkmeyer, 1965).

The counseling service includes group counseling, which helps the child to learn to interact effectively within the group. Through group counseling, individuals learn to work within a peer group and with the counselor to explore problems, feelings, attitudes, and values. The counselor's chief aim is to modify perceptions to enable participants to better deal with developmental problems.

4. Classroom Guidance Program. In keeping with the philosophy of developmental guidance, each classroom provides a set of planned guidance experiences. Classroom guidance must consist of a sequential curriculum in the elementary school just as arithmetic, science, and other instructional areas. This program is obviously dependent upon the teacher's capacity to develop a relationship which facilitates learning. The program objective is identification of guidance needs and establishment of plans that enable the child to acquire the guidance learnings (Hill, 1965). The teacher uses specific techniques such as the interest inventory, autobiography, problem inventory and incomplete sentence with every pupil. These techniques help the teacher to engage in teacher-pupil planning, self-selection, and the individualization of instruction. The classroom guidance program also utilizes group discussion on a regularly planned basis.

5. Group Guidance and Information Services. This area includes the kinds

of services which can be done as effectively with the group as with an individual. It would include providing information of an educational, occupational, personal, and social nature. In some instances the counselor would be responsible for conducting group guidance. In most situations he provides the teacher with materials and demonstrates the process of group guidance (Goldman, 1962).

6. Administration, Research, and Evaluation. So that the services provided meet the needs of pupils, teachers, and parents, some time must be scheduled for administration and coordination of the program. This area also includes provision for continuous evaluation and research.

In the first selection, Frances Wilson states the objectives of elementary guidance in terms of services. The contributions of the administrator, guidance specialist, and classroom teacher are set forth. Wilson is one of the early pioneers in elementary school guidance. While reading the ensuing articles in this section, the reader might consider how applicable Wilson's constructs are for current guidance programs in the elementary school.

Patouillet presents a developmental philosophy of elementary school guidance by bringing together the proponents of services and the proponents of guidance as enlightened teaching. He indicates guidance must be concerned about a curriculum that is adapted to the needs and level of maturity of children if it is to assume a developmental approach. The guidance worker is perceived as a consultant in human relations. The reader might compare the major guidance responsibilities of teachers, administrators, and guidance workers as viewed by both Patouillet and Frances Wilson. A strong argument for organization of guidance services around a consultant role is presented.

Smallenburg suggests that a majority of the problems of concern to teachers are directly related to guidance. He develops the characteristics of a good guidance program, with great emphasis on providing for the exceptional child. This article also considers the role of the teacher, counselor, school psychologist, and social worker. One of the major problems in the area of pupil personnel services for the elementary school involves the necessity of clarifying the uniqueness and the interrelationships between the teacher and the specialist in counseling, school psychology, and school social work. Procedures which implement the team approach between these specialists are presented.

The final selection by Johnston provides a practical description of a method of initiating elementary school guidance. This article provides direction for school districts contemplating initiation of a new guidance service. The committee plan enables a school district to develop a program which is tailored to the specific needs of pupils, parents, teachers, and administrators in a given school district.

REFERENCES

Dinkmeyer, D. 1966. Developmental counseling in the elementary school. *Personnel guid. J.*, 45 (No. 3).

————. 1965. *Toward a theory of child counseling at the elementary school level*. Moravia, N.Y.: Chronicle Guidance Publications.

Eckerson, Louise, and H. Smith. 1966. *Scope of pupil personnel services*. Washington, D.C.: Government Printing Office, U.S. Department of Health, Education and Welfare.

Farwell, Gail, and H. Peters. May 1957. Guidance: a longitudinal and a differential view. *Elem. Sch. J., 57*.

Goldman, Lee. 1962. Group guidance: content and process. *Personnel guid. J., 39* (No. 6).

Hill, G. June 1965. Institute on guidance and testing in the elementary school. Chicago: Science Research Associates.

Lloyd-Jones, Esther, Ruth Barry, and Beverly Wolf. 1958. *Guidance in elementary education: a case book*. New York: Bureau of Publications, Teachers College, Columbia University.

Guidance in Elementary Schools*

Frances M. Wilson

One of the important recent national trends in guidance has been the development of organized programs at the elementary school level. These programs have as their major objective development of normal, contented children, at ease psychologically with themselves and with others.

Analysis of programs in several large cities indicates that they are rooted in principles of mental hygiene, and are well rounded in their efforts to help children meet their personal, social, educational, and vocational needs.

Helping children adjust satisfactorily in each of these areas requires the participation of administrators, teachers, guidance specialists, clinicians, community leaders, and parents in a carefully coordinated program. Together they will seek to to accomplish the following:

1. To sensitize teachers to the needs of children for affection, security, a feeling of self-worth, and the opportunity to succeed; and to help teachers to know and use techniques in the classroom which will enable them to recognize and meet each child's needs.

2. To provide a counseling service for all children from the kindergarten through the eighth year, recognizing that guidance is not a privilege accorded the maladjusted, but is a necessity for every normal child.

* *Occupations, The Vocational Guidance Journal*, December 1950, vol. 29, no. 3. By permission.

3. To prepare resource materials to be used by all participating in the guidance program—including printed materials and audio-visual aids.

4. To conduct an in-service training program which will provide continued training in all phases of an effective developmental guidance program.

5. To articulate guidance services with receiving schools.

6. To develop community resources so that they may be utilized efficiently and fully in serving children.

7. To make available clinical services to children whose behavior indicates the need for specialized help.

8. To provide a testing program, utilizing individual and group tests which have well-established reliability and validity.

9. To develop a program of group guidance which will insure each child's receiving help in areas in which group work may rightfully be expected to provide information, develop attitudes, and give opportunity for self-understanding.

10. To explore the curriculum and identify areas of it in which guidance is naturally an integral and dynamic part.

11. To transmit principles of mental hygiene to the home environment of each child through a sound and broadly functioning program of parent education.

12. To supervise guidance services insuring that they flow from an adequate knowledge of the dynamics of behavior.

13. To incorporate research as an essential part of the program.

14. To evaluate the guidance program at regular intervals.

CONTRIBUTION OF THE ADMINISTRATOR

In addition to his basic responsibility for establishing the fundamental mental hygiene philosophy underlying the program, the administrator's second important contribution is the development of the in-service training program.

One important aspect of the in-service training program is faculty conferences which provide an avenue for developing guidance attitudes and training in guidance techniques. Some conferences have been organized effectively around visual aids. The film strip, *All Children Need Guidance*, offers an excellent basis for discussing the emotional needs of children; *Know Your Children* directs thinking toward the use of sociometric measures for identifying the needs of children as reflected through their place in the group.

Recordings of parent interviews, interviews and group discussions with children are also good focal points for faculty discussions.

The administrator can encourage each teacher to study one child in her class carefully and report upon him; a conference devoted to consideration of several case studies will result in teachers appreciating more the needs of all children. When the help of clinicians is available, a case conference presented by them may be provocative.

At other conferences literature in the field may be reviewed, or demonstrations conducted involving observation, the use of rating scales, the writing of anecdotal records, or informal ways of studying children. The dramatization of a case study will be helpful in illustrating how all of these techniques are coordinated in the study of a child's behavior.

The preparation by the faculty of a guidance exhibit is another method of developing its knowledge of the field of guidance as are panel discussions with parents or community leaders. Nor should the value of an ocasional field trip be overlooked. There is nothing fundamentally that requires that a faculty conference be held in the school. A visit to a social agency will help to orient the teachers to the work of agencies, and will encourage them to cooperate more effectively in carrying out agency recommendations. A field trip in industry will add to the teacher's body of information about the world of work, and will enable her to discuss vocational information more realistically.

A third responsibility of the administrator is to insure the supervision of the guidance program. One of the most serious weaknesses of guidance programs in junior and senior high schools has been the widespread absence of adequate supervision. When supervision cannot be supplied by personnel from central headquarters, it is the principal's responsibility to see that the guidance services are adequate. In accomplishing this, the administrator will confer with experts in guidance if he feels his own grasp of the specialized field is inadequate, for measuring the effectiveness of an interview, the value of a group guidance period, or the handling of a case.

Other responsibilities of the administrator will include assuming leadership in the development of a research program, acquainting the community with the nature of the guidance services, and soliciting the help of community leaders in developing the program.

CONTRIBUTION OF THE GUIDANCE SPECIALIST

Since inevitably the cost of guidance services necessitates that a classroom teacher assume broad responsibilities for meeting the guidance needs of children, the specialist should apportion a generous part of her working day to helping teachers develop sound guidance practices within their classrooms. The rest of her time will be devoted to counseling and conducting group guidance programs, especially those of the seventh and eighth years. She will serve also as the referral agent for children needing clinical services, and will assist in the program of parent education by conducting workshops for parents.

The guidance specialist's work with teachers should include various avenues of approach. She may visit the classes of teachers upon their invitation to observe the behavior of individual children so that she may discuss with teachers the needs of particular children, the significance of their behavior, and what the teacher may do in class to help the children. If the teacher grows in fuller understanding of why Sam finds it necessary to approach every new situation with a violent, "I don't want to do that!" she comes to know better the why of negative behavior in all children. When she recognizes that one child is helped to greater freedom through the release of such activities as beating the drum in the rhythm band, or pounding clay, she translates such knowledge to all children.

Grade conferences have also been found singularly effective in developing understanding attitudes, and in practically applying mental hygiene principles. Teachers find it therapeutically good to know that other teachers are faced with similar difficulties in trying to individualize procedures in the classroom. Many times the interchange of practical suggestions is helpful, and the support of the group makes the teacher appreciate that the help she is giving an individual child is more effective than she realized in face of what very often seems negative results. Periods of regression in a child, who is struggling to adjust to the domination of her grandmother who has become only recently a part of the family group, can be faced with greater equanimity by the teacher who recognizes cause and effect relationships. Through grade conferences teachers also have an opportunity to discuss pamphlets and books that they have read, the records of individual children, the significance of the results of sociograms they have made, and interviews that have been held with parents. The grade conferences thus serve as an effective clearing house for ideas and the consideration of practical problems that arise when teachers seek to apply mental hygiene principles in the classroom.

A third important way in which the specialist may acquaint the teacher with specific techniques is through demonstrations. Obviously these demonstrations will be given only at the request of the teacher. Fuller discussion of the techniques in which the guidance specialist will help the teacher develop skill is reserved for the section which follows on the work of the classroom teacher.

The guidance specialist will round out the in-service training of the teachers through offering workshops and courses.

When readiness exists among faculty members, the guidance specialist should assume responsibility for organization of a guidance committee within the school which will include among its members a representative from Kgn-2nd, 3rd-5th, and 6th-8th years; the school nurse and doctor or other clinician where such are available, and a principal or assistant principal. Members of the guidance committee will see many children individually, thus helping to insure that each child will have some individual attention. They will help develop, review, and coordinate guidance materials; and in various other ways provide breadth of service within the school. The committee members thus serve in a sense as extensions of the guidance specialist.

Through special work with groups the specialist will also offer various kinds of help to young people. She will encourage the development of good recreational interests through the organization of clubs, an area of experience which has been lacking for many children in elementary schools. Especially in the middle years and after are they at a place in their social development where the group experience found in clubs has an important contribution to make to their development. The resources of individuals in the community should not be overlooked in this phase of the program for there are many persons with special abilities and talents who have much to give children. Often adults will volunteer to take children whose home environments provide a paucity of happy social experiences on excursions in small groups. These excursions may be as simple as playing ball in the park or fishing in a brook.

If her training is adequate, the guidance specialist will meet in play sessions with children who are faced by particular pressures in their home situation, or who are showing difficulty in adjusting to the school situation. While therapy must be reserved for clinicians, for many children there are important therapeutic values to be found in play sessions provided by one acquainted with the important contributions offered by play for adjustment. In these play sessions, also, the specialist will have an opportunity to observe more intimately the behavior of children with special needs so that she may be in a position to make referral of those children for whom deeper therapy is indicated. Water, doll families, puppets, art materials, and blocks are materials which offer avenues for understanding the children better and giving them an opportunity to grow in the ability to handle the inadequacies, the insecurities, the fears, the pressures in themselves, and the frustrations and repressions in their environment.

Besides her work with play groups, the guidance specialist will offer group guidance to classes, usually in the sixth, seventh, and eighth grades. Free from didacticism, these group guidance periods should utilize all effective methods of group work: dramatizations, forums, moving pictures and film strips, radio programs, recordings and discussions to develop with the student's information and attitudes about getting along with others, vocational opportunities, ethical values, social relations, study habits, leisure activities, selection of high school and course, and the like.

Finally, the guidance specialist will work individually with a number of students whose adjustment problems are not so great as to require clinical care, but are more serious than the teacher or members of the guidance committee are able to handle. The counseling provided should be based upon genuine appreciation of the meaning of behavior, and should recognize that the adjustment process is often of slow growth and cannot be accomplished by an interview, hurried, unplanned, sentimental, or exhortative in tone. Obviously the guidance specialist will be completely free of disciplinary relationships. Since the child's adjustment requires the help of the parents, the specialist will work closely with the parents, appreciating that many of them are faced with difficult problems of adjustment of their own, and that very frequently they need praise, reassurance, and encouragement about the way they are bringing up their children. Good record keeping and the utilization of test results will also be an essential part of the counseling process since only through careful review of her case studies will it be possible for the specialist to evaluate the quality of her counseling, and the trends in the total guidance program. Follow-up is also essential to a good guidance program.

CONTRIBUTION OF THE CLASSROOM TEACHER

The teacher in the first six years of the elementary school spends a far greater period of time with her children than do teachers in the junior or senior high schools. As a result, she has a much richer opportunity to know her children intimately and provide for them through the curriculum and the emotional climate of the classroom, psychological support and release. For too long teachers have failed to recognize the important contribution they make to the adjustment of children. Instead they have tended to minimize their own work because they believe that major contributions to the adjustive process are made only by clinicians.

The teacher is faced by two major needs as she tries to help her children. First, she must be able to know and understand each of them well. Second, where the child is faced by specific adjustment problems, she must be able to provide the help he needs if his problems are not of a kind to require the help of specialists.

To accomplish the first there is no substitute for careful, objective, and continued observation of the child in his many varied daily activities, as he attacks a new learning situation, as he plays with others, as he works by himself, or as he draws. Recording the behavior briefly, objectively, and consistently in anecdotal records will sharpen the perception of the teacher. She will gain also a basis for recognizing trends in the development of individual children, clues to their particular needs, and means for better understanding each child. These anecdotal records, after they have been summarized, will become a part of the cumulative record of the child which the teacher will review at intervals in order not to lose sight of the significant information contained in it.

There are a number of informal ways of learning more about children which the teacher can use. She should not attempt to apply them, however, without recognizing the importance of receiving training in their use. A sociogram of the class will tell the teacher a good deal about the interpersonal relationships functioning in the group. When the language ability of the child permits, she may use interest inventories, or encourage the child to write about his out-of-school experiences. An autobiography written by a child for a teacher whom he knows is sympathetically interested in him will usually tell a great deal. Or the teacher may use the unfinished story to encourage the children to express their reactions to particular situations. With even very young children, the opportunity to draw their wishes will tell the observant teacher a great deal. It does not require a clinician's judgment to realize that a child who wishes for a bureau drawer of his own so that he may have a place for his things is experiencing considerable frustration and deprivation in his home environment. Inviting a child to tell the funniest, the saddest, the happiest experience he has ever had will result in the teacher's knowing more about the experiences of the child and the value he places upon them.

Various feelings of the children will be brought to light through spontaneous puppet plays. The play may involve as simple a situation as "Mother goes marketing." Role playing can be used equally effectively with older children. The dramatic play of children also tells much about them, as do their reactions to carefully selected pictures. Discussions based upon film strips such as *David and His Family*, or stories such as *The Smallest Boy in the Class*, will be productive of significant information. The guidance specialist will help the teacher develop skill in the use of all of these various techniques.

The teacher must do more, however, than merely know the needs of each child; she must also try to meet them. Certain basic help can be given to all children. The teacher can show that she is fond of them; she can praise them generously. She can make them feel easy in her classroom, and can insure some measure of success for each child. Then, too, she can help the children to get along with one another, for each child craves a friendly relationship in his own group. Finally, she can provide for each child the opportunity to express his inner feelings.

SPECIFIC HELP

In addition to supplying this supportive environment for all children, however, the teacher will provide more specific help for some children. For example, careful planning of committee work will make possible the inclusion of a shy child in a group that will encourage him to participate. Assignment of responsibility for a particularly sought-after activity, such as arranging the bulletin board, will often give a child who greatly needs them, prestige and status in the eyes of his classmates. Remedial help for the boy or girl who is insecure because of learning difficulties offers an opportunity for the teacher to help the child grow in self-confidence. Sometimes the development of a particular skill in the field of plastic arts, music, or dancing will give naturally the attention a child craves and provide a focus for praise. Often these same media offer a genuine release of tension and anxiety.

These are a few of the many ways in which the classroom teacher can contribute to the growth and development of the children in her class. Her sympathy, her understanding of children and their needs, and her skill in utilizing opportunities in the group situation will enable her to find countless other ways of providing the guidance services children need. Through the curriculum, for example, she will provide information and experiences which will contribute to the educational, vocational, and social guidance of the children.

CONTRIBUTION OF THE CLINICIAN

The clinical team makes many important contributions to the preventive program—through talks, workshops, demonstration, and case conferences. It conducts the individual testing program; however, its major responsibility is to provide therapy for those children in need of special help. Both teachers and guidance specialists can contribute to the effectiveness of the therapy; first, by referring children for help *early* before personality disorders are too deeply established, interpreting also to the parents the need for such help. Second, they can provide careful descriptions of the behavior of the children. Third, they can help to carry out in the school situation the recommendations of the therapists.

When the guidance program is cooperatively planned and carried out by the administrators, the guidance specialists, the classroom teachers, the clinicians, and leaders in the community, there should result a carefully conceived, practically administered, and dynamically functioning program which will be characterized by a mental hygiene point of view, broad design, and adequate coverage of the needs of every child.

Organizing for Guidance
in the Elementary School*

Raymond Patouillet

The printed word possesses a subtle authority for no other reason than it *is* printed. Also, it is quoted equally to support prejudice and bias and to uphold honest inquiry. And when this printed word is in the third person it takes on the added authority of impartiality. The end result is rather frightening, especially in the field of guidance, where "common sense" so easily leads us to accept uninvestigated hypotheses. So that what I have to say will be clearly understood to be personal, subjective reactions to the subject at hand, I shall use the first person through parts of my presentation.

The problem of defining guidance as this term is used in the school setting has plagued all of us in the field for a long time. Some like to think of guidance as a program of services which may be clearly "defined, recognized, administered, and evaluated. It then is possible to define a guidance program as a program of services which is specifically implemented to improve the adjustment of the individuals for whom it was organized (Hatch, 1951, p. 14). I must confess that this term "adjustment" concerns me a bit and leads me to ask rather bluntly, "Adjustment to what?" Other writers define guidance similarly, as "services to assist the teacher in knowing the pupil and to meet his needs better,

* *Teachers College Record*, May 1957, vol. 58, no. 8. By permission.

as well as to aid the pupil in understanding himself . . ." (Bernard, James, and Zeran, 1954, p. 5).

Others of us shudder at the word services and prefer to think of guidance as enlightened teaching (Kelley, 1955; Lloyd-Jones, and Smith, 1954). A recent book defines guidance as a viewpoint which brings about services which in turn result in an experiential process with pupils (Cottingham, 1956). This statement, in a sense, is an attempt to bring together two schools of thought.

As the reader probably suspects, I neither agree nor disagree with everything that has been said above. In my opinion the proponents of services and the proponents of enlightened teaching are not really as far apart as they would like others to believe. They have simply chosen to stress different dimensions of the same thing. I do believe, however, that the point of stress may well determine the nature of the guidance program. Let's examine these emphases more closely. Both camps agree, for example, that a guidance program involves services. They agree also that the teacher plays a major role in the guidance program. The basic issue is one of relationships and organization. How do people and services in the school setting relate to each other for the good of children? I should like to present some of my thoughts on guidance and on people who are involved in this area, and to suggest a plan of organization as I discuss this question.

GUIDANCE

Guidance is a term that is often coupled with another multi-meaning word, adjustment. This is a potentially dangerous association. We must first define what we mean by adjustment. Adjustment to the status quo, for example, is not necessarily desirable. In a rapidly changing society like ours, marked by a high mobility of the population, it is inadequate preparation for the future. In a democracy it can be fatal, for a democracy is strong to the extent that each individual contributes his greatest potential, his uniqueness developed to the fullest. The democratic answer to manpower shortages is human development rather than identification of talents for assignment to currently critical areas. Guidance can therefore be defined as the maximum development of an individual's potential for his own personal happiness and the welfare of society.

Old and New Guidance

The idea of guidance is as old as the first teacher. A sound curriculum, adapted to the needs of youth and appropriate to their level of maturity, is sound guidance. A program of activities aimed at the development of social competence is likewise sound guidance. In these phases of the school program teachers have always played, and will continue to play, major roles.

More recently, guidance has developed specific techniques which are used by administrators and teachers as well as by school personnel specifically designated as guidance workers. Some of the better known instruments are cumulative records, psychological tests, counseling and group work techniques, and skills in human relations.

Originally, guidance was largely a remedial function, concerned with those in difficulty. The subtle assumption then was that pupils not measuring up to externally imposed standards (of achievement, behavior, and so forth) needed extra help or guidance. Schools soon realized the futility and waste involved in waiting for the casualties, and guidance began to assume a preventive function. The task then shifted to one of identifying potential casualties before they actually got to the disability lists. But even this has proved inadequate. In the face of the titanic struggle between communism and democracy, the optimum development of the individual has become more than the goal of a minority of progressive educators; it has become a necessity for national survival. Guidance is now being forced to assume a developmental approach. This means that it can no longer be solely or primarily concerned with the relatively few severely retarded or disturbed; guidance must be concerned with all pupils and must contribute to the maximum development of each.

Thus, while guidance will continue to serve remedial and preventive functions, its primary focus will be increasingly developmental. For example, rather than emphasizing testing to identify or predict strengths and weaknesses, it will emphasize enriching experiences to stimulate development so that tests will have more to measure. And there's something else here which I should like to make clear. The teacher's role is very definitely not that of junior psychologist, but of one who can translate subject matter into exciting experiences for children. That is the teacher's greatest contribution to education and to guidance.

. . . Everybody's Business

When guidance assumes a developmental approach, it inevitably involves all individuals and agencies which contribute to an individual's development. It is likewise concerned with the many facets of development—emotional, social, and intellectual, for example. The school can no longer arrogate the right to be *the* guidance institution of society. Often, it unknowingly assumes this responsibility, but wise parents have never permitted this. The school does, however, play a critical role. Because it deals with all the children of all the people, it is ideally suited to play the role of coordinator of guidance efforts.

Specifically, the school does not provide therapy, but it does provide a therapeutic climate. It also refers parents and children who need therapy to community agencies organized to offer such aid. Where no appropriate agencies exist, the school assumes a leadership role in establishing them. Similarly, the school does not assume the role of clergyman, den mother, or parent, but it does coordinate their efforts for the good of the child in the school setting.

The Core of Guidance

If guidance is everybody's business, then someone is needed to coordinate and integrate this emphasis in the educational program. The logical person is the guidance worker, and his task involves primarily skill in human relations. This is not to say, of course, that the guidance person need not have unique knowledges and skills in such areas as child development and diagnostic techniques, but rather, that these unique contributions may never be utilized if the guidance person is unable to relate positively to teachers, parents, administrators, community agencies, and groups of children as well as to the individual child within the counseling cubicle.

The guidance worker, therefore, is essentially a consultant in human relations who involves in a cooperative enterprise all those who affect the development of the child.

Mental Hygiene
and Human Relations

Good human relations within a school contribute to a mentally hygienic atmosphere, and a mentally hygienic atmosphere allows people to be their own best selves, thereby encouraging sound human relations. The two are inseparable, and guidance cannot survive where they are not present. In order to insert a wedge into this circular relationship for purposes of study, I shall attempt to define a mentally hygienic atmosphere. I think it might be defined as an atmosphere which promotes physical health, a feeling of personal worth, and communication among members of the school community.

If pupils and teachers are enjoying good physical health, they are released from an area of worry that can in and of itself be disabling and inhibiting to good teaching and learning. Healthy pupils enjoy physical activity and seek to develop physical skills. Children in poor health are apt to look upon physical activity as a threat to their very being and to avoid it. They may react, as all human beings do to frustrating situations, by aggression or by withdrawal, both of which are roads to emotional disturbances.

A feeling of personal worth is a second factor in a mentally hygienic atmosphere. This factor is enhanced when one feels accepted as a person—not despite his differences or even because of them, but, more basically, because he is a human being and by that fact alone clothed in dignity. I do not believe that man gives dignity to man. If that were true, then man could take away dignity from man, a morally untenable position. For example, to fail a child because he is unable by nature to learn a certain task is just as immoral as ruling that no child shorter than four feet six inches shall be promoted to the fifth grade. It should be added that not all experience with failure is of a negative nature. A school program in which one experienced only success would be poor preparation for life. But failure that leads to a feeling of hopelessness, in turn leads to the possibility of serious emotional upset.

A third characteristic of a mentally hygienic situation is communication. This means multi-directional communication, rather than one-way-to-one-person communication. Figures 1 and 2 may prove helpful at this point.

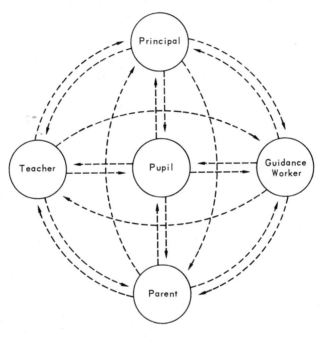

FIGURE 1

Represented in Figure 1 is an open society in which lines of communication are open. The lines in this figure should not be interpreted to be lines of responsibility or authority, however, and the distinction should be kept clearly in mind. Unfortunately, most organizational charts usually clearly indicate lines of authority and little else. These tend to become lines of communication as well (as shown in Figure 2) and suggest a one-way communication process from "top" to "bottom," even though this may not be the intention.

In a situation where there is limited intercommunication, there is obviously limited opportunity to develop interpersonal relations, and potential resources for child development are isolated. Also, where there is a hierarchy of communication, creative energies of those beneath the top tend to be submerged in a feeling of hopelessness.

Thus, physical health, a feeling of personal worth, and multi-directional

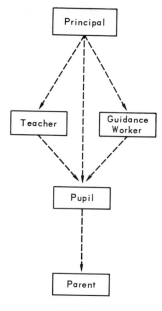

FIGURE 2

lines of communication are basic to sound mental hygiene. In turn, a mentally hygienic atmosphere is basic to human relations and to the guidance program of the school.

GUIDANCE PERSONNEL

In this discussion I shall direct my comments to those people in the school setting who have major guidance responsibilities. If I don't discuss the custodian, it isn't because I think he is not important in the guidance program of the school. If I don't mention the children, it is not because I am unaware of the guidance implications of a first grader's cruel comment to a classmate, "You're not pretty. You can't play with us." I have to establish limits and I am concerned with organizational problems.

The Teacher

In the school setting, the teacher continues to be the key guidance person. Two procedures are especially rich in guidance possibilities: pupil-teacher planning and parent-teacher conferences.

Through pupil-teacher planning, which involves beginning where children are (taking into account their level of maturity, their varying abilities, interests, and other personal characteristics), pupils develop a sense of personal worth and learn the necessity of multi-directional communication. Children learn better when they are dealing with meaningful material and are actively involved in the setting up of course goals, procedures, and evaluation, with the teacher serving as guide and resource person.

Through parent-teacher conferences the guidance responsibility of home and school is clarified and a cooperative, consistent approach is maintained.

The Principal

It is the principal who takes the lead in setting the guidance tone of the school. He involves his staff in policy making, thereby letting them know that they count as individuals. His position as democratic leader demands that he release the creative energies of his staff, rather than project his own needs upon them. He is skilled in human relations, in guiding his professional team through activities aimed at professional development. It has been said that "we do unto others as we have been done unto." This is especially appropriate in the field of teacher-administrator relationships. Teachers find it difficult to accept children as individuals if they themselves are not so accepted.

The Guidance Worker

The school guidance worker (counselor, psychologist, visiting teacher) works primarily with and through teachers as well as with parents and the principal, serving as consultant and resource person to them. The guidance person works with children through the class setting, although individual conferences with parents and children are held if referral to an outside agency is indicated or if individual testing or interviewing is agreed upon by the teacher and guidance person.

I have grouped counselors, psychologists, and visiting teachers together under the general heading of guidance worker because I see an increasing number of similarities and a decreasing number of differences among their respective roles.

The term guidance counselor was probably first used in secondary schools with strong vocational emphases. The guidance counselor now finds himself involved in matters pertaining to educational planning and to personal and social development. He also finds that he is working with teachers, parents, community agencies, and groups of children, as well as with individual children. The term counselor therefore no longer adequately describes his function if we think of counseling as a one-to-one relationship. Thus, the guidance counselor has broadened his area of concern and is beginning to move into the elementary schools.

The role of the school psychologist too is assuming broader proportions. Initially, the psychologist was concerned primarily with the individual exceptional child (Cutts, 1955). He continues to be concerned with testing but has extended his concern to include the mental hygiene of the school. He works with teachers, parents, community agencies, and groups of children as well as with individual children. His area of operations is no longer restricted to the elementary school. The school social worker or visiting teacher is moving in new directions too. Interest in prevention rather than remediation, wider use of referral rather than direct handling of cases, a realization of the need for visiting teachers in other than low-income areas, the growing use of visiting teachers in a consultative capacity, broadening the scope from trying to prevent truancy and delinquency to "helping all children with personal and adjustment problems" (Pearman and Burrows, 1955, p. 9), the extension of social work upward through high school— all of these trends seem to be drawing the visiting teacher closer to the guidance counselor and school psychologist.

It is clear that the teacher is the one who works with the guidance personnel and if she is to be helpful, guidance workers must understand her needs. The following list of functions prepared by a teacher attending the Thayer Conference of school psychologists is pertinent for all guidance workers.

What do I want of a school psychologist?

I want a person to help me with classroom problems on which I need help.

I want one to help me with a solution to my problem rather than give me a *diagnosis* of my problem.

I want one to *help me* solve my problems *within* my classroom setting (as much as possible) rather than to take my problem *from* my classroom.

I want one who may give me ideas on new techniques of teaching but not one who would do them for me.

I want one to give me advice on my relations with my fellow staff members if I need it.

I want one who would be a member of my staff, rather than an *assistant* in the administrative office.

I want one who would be a member of the *team*.

I want one whose personality traits are outstanding.

In teaching, we start with the child and get back to the child. *We are all in this together* (Cutts, 1955).

From a study conducted by the National Association of Guidance Supervisors and Counselor Trainers (1953) I was interested to learn that school systems were recommending the hiring of more guidance counselors, more psychologists, and more visiting teachers for our elementary schools. Frankly, I asked myself whether the schools responding to the questionnaire had comparable perceptions of these different guidance workers. In view of the discussion above, I think we can conclude that the teachers who responded were clearly indicating a need for assistance.

GUIDANCE ORGANIZATION

Let us assume for a moment that we are in an elementary school of 900 pupils; that we have a guidance counselor, a school psychologist, and a school social worker. Figure 3 represents these people. Theoretically, the triangle is taking care of the guidance counseling needs of 900 pupils, the square is respon-

FIGURE 3

sible for the school psychology needs of 900, and the diamond is prepared to meet the visiting teaching needs of 900. In view of the preceding discussion we know that much overlapping of work will prevail and the teacher will not feel that she is getting any concerted assistance.

An alternative plan of organization would be to have three "helping teachers" or "child development consultants," each responsible for the developmental needs of 300 children. Both children and teachers would then stand a better chance of being served.

Of course the question that immediately arises is, What sort of training will these child development consultants need? My answer at this point would be a two-year program of graduate study including courses in guidance, developmental psychology, school psychology, social work, administration, and curriculum (including reading, an area in which teachers say they need help). Such a program is currently offered on an experimental basis at Teachers College, Columbia. The fully qualified school psychologist (a graduate of a four-year program) would still be needed of course, and would serve as consultant in our imaginary school to our three child development consultants. The proposed plan perhaps fills the need for more immediate assistance to teachers within reasonable financial limits.

An intermediate step which is probably necessary for the present is charted in Figure 4. While called child development consultants and performing similar

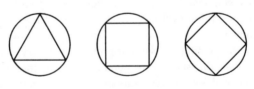

FIGURE 4

tasks, each individual represented might have a different background and contribute unique strengths. The circle surrounding the triangle is the person who has had two years of graduate work in guidance; the one around the square is the two-year psychologist; and the one with the diamond in the center is the graduate of a two-year master's program from a school of social work. These three would work as a team, each serving as consultant to the other two.

SUMMARY

The great need in the elementary school guidance field is to ask ourselves some critical questions. How can we organize more effectively to meet the challenges of our dynamic society? Perhaps an analogy would be helpful. If we use a rowboat to transport four men across a pond, do we use twenty-five rowboats to transport 100 men across an ocean or do we even build one huge rowboat? Perhaps we need to develop new means of transportation.

Whatever is done will have to be done with a thorough understanding of our children and our available resources. And it will challenge the efforts of *all* of us, working cooperatively, to establish the optimal relationship between the two.

REFERENCES

Bernard, H. W., C. E. James, and F. R. Zeran. 1954. *Guidance services in elementary schools.* New York: Chartwell House.

Cottingham, H. F. 1956. *Guidance in elementary schools.* Bloomington, Ill.: McKnight.

Cutts, Norma E. (ed.). 1955. *School psychologists in mid-century.* Washington, D.C.: American Psychological Association, pp. 16–25; 71.

Hatch, R. N. 1951. *Guidance services in the elementary school.* Dubuque, Iowa: William C. Brown Company.

Kelley, Janet A. 1955. *Guidance and curriculum.* Englewood Cliffs, N.J.: Prentice-Hall.

Lloyd-Jones, Esther, and Margaret R. Smith (ed.). 1954. *Student personnel work as deeper teaching.* New York: Harper & Row.

National Association of Guidance Supervisors and Counselor Trainers. 1953. *A national study of existing and recommended practices for assisting youth adjustment in selected elementary schools in the United States.* Ann Arbor, Mich.: Ann Arbor Publishers.

Pearman, Jean, and A. H. Burrows. 1955. *Social services in the school.* Washington, D.C.: Public Affairs Press.

Studying the Elementary Guidance Program*

Harry Smallenburg

Many of the problems that concern teachers are related to guidance. If you were to ask the faculty of an elementary school to indicate some of the major areas with which they need help, you would receive a number of comments such as these:

"We should know more about the children we teach."

"I think we need to use our test results better."

"If someone would help me with just two or three of the youngsters in my class, I could do a better job of teaching the others."

"I need to know more about how to talk with Johnny's parents about his work in school."

"How can I obtain the findings of research studies in psychology, growth, and development?"

"We've been doing a better job of teaching the various subject areas. Now we need to do a better job of teaching our pupils."

Such comments as these add up to a need for a better school guidance program. They reflect a concern for understanding children better and for developing techniques of providing more effectively for their varying needs. A carefully developed and implemented guidance program can do much to help teachers work more successfully with children and to aid pupils in their emotional, physical, social, and intellectual development.

A faculty that wants to strengthen the school guidance program should consider carefully the purposes, characteristics, and techniques of effective guidance services in the elementary school. They should ask: "Why is guidance important in a modern educational program? What are some of the major characteristics of a good elementary school guidance program? What is the guidance role of the classroom teacher? What is the role of the elementary school counselor? Of the school psychologist? Of the school social worker? How can we develop a team approach to guidance?"

This article discusses each of these major questions in a modified outline

* *The National Elementary Principal,* April 1964, vol. 53, no. 5.
By permission.

form. The format may be particularly useful for principals and teachers who undertake a similar study.

WHY IS GUIDANCE IMPORTANT?

The importance of guidance in a modern educational program is evident from the study of current literature.

1. "No society can afford to ignore the fact that one out of every seven men was judged to be mentally and emotionally incapable of serving effectively in its armed forces in time of war," admonished the President's Commission on the Conservation of Human Resources. In its analysis and study of factors most predictive of ineffective performance, the Commission found positive correlation between armed service rejections and separations of men with moderate or acute emotional distress and their poor educational backgrounds (Ginzberg *et al.*, 1959).

2. In a report summarizing twenty-eight different studies of California school dropouts and graduates, a basic recommendation was that "identification of potential dropouts should begin in the elementary grades. Ways of doing this in time to apply procedures are needed" (McCreary and Kitch, 1953).

3. Between 5 and 10 percent of the children enrolled in the public schools have emotional handicaps of sufficient severity that they are unable to learn in school in the way children not thus handicapped can and are unable to employ the type of behavior required in the classroom (California State Department of Education, 1961).

4. Emotionally handicapped pupils who are not identified early and given the help they need to eliminate their handicaps leave school just as soon as they find any opportunity to do so (p. 9).

5. A team of social scientists who surveyed a section of midtown Manhattan, New York City, reported that 23.4 percent of 1660 persons interviewed had "marked, severe, and incapacitating symptoms." Another 58.1 percent were found to have "mild to moderate symptoms." This second figure is not so alarming as it sounds. A survey of physical fitness would probably show few people without some physical ailment or impairment, such as rheumatism or defective vision (Srole *et al.*, 1962).

6. The elementary school is in a favorable position to provide valuable guidance services to children. Parents can approach contacts with school personnel optimistically and constructively. Teachers who work with the children on a total-day basis can know their needs better and make adjustments to provide for optimum growth. The children themselves can change patterns more easily because of their youth and the lessened effect of "typing by their peer group" (Martinson and Smallenburg, 1958, pp. 5–6).

WHAT ARE THE CHARACTERISTICS
OF A GOOD GUIDANCE PROGRAM?

An effective guidance program in the modern elementary school should:

1. Relate to and support the broad objectives of the total educational program.

2. Focus upon the characteristics of pupils—their differences and similarities—physical, emotional, intellectual, and social.

3. Provide systematic ways of gathering information about pupils: for example, cumulative records; standardized tests; interviews, case studies; observation and anecdotal records; conferences with parents; sociograms; and autobiographies.

4. Provide systematic ways of using information with groups; grouping within the class; placement in grades and in classes; and group guidance.

5. Provide systematic ways of using information with individuals through counseling—educational, vocational, social, and emotional.

6. Provide for all pupils but make special provision for the exceptional child.

7. Provide specialized assistance to classroom teachers, such as a counselor, a school psychologist, or a school social worker.

8. Assist teachers and administrators in working with parents through: parent-teacher conferences; PTA meetings; and grade level meetings.

9. Assist teachers and administrators in working with community agencies.

10. Provide for on-the-job growth of the teaching staff in guidance skills.

11. Provide opportunities for research to determine the effectiveness of the guidance program.

WHAT IS THE TEACHER'S
GUIDANCE ROLE?

The elementary classroom teacher is an extremely important guidance worker. This point is stressed in all of the literature on elementary school guidance. As a member of the school guidance team, the classroom teacher, according to *Guiding Today's Children* (California Test Bureau, 1959, p. 236):

1. Observes children's behavior in daily situations.

2. Uses a variety of methods to study children individually and in groups.

3. Takes part in a systematic program of standardized testing.

4. Contributes to and uses cumulative records for each child.

5. Refers children for special study and guidance conference when help is needed.

6. Recognizes children with exceptional needs and knows the special services provided for them.

7. Meets with parents individually and in groups to understand children better and to involve parents in the education of their children.

8. Evaluates the growth and learning of children and the effectiveness of the curriculum.

9. Works with community personnel and agencies in providing for children's educational and social needs.

10. Engages in professional growth activities to deepen his understanding of children.

WHAT IS THE COUNSELOR'S ROLE?

The responsibilities of the elementary school counselor are helpfully defined in an article by Robert N. Hart (1961). In his study, teachers ranked the importance of selected duties for the elementary counselor as follows:

1. Counseling pupils with learning, physical, social, and emotional problems.

2. Interpreting pupil data to parents.

3. Holding conferences with parents regarding any pupil problems.

4. Interpreting pupil data to faculty members.

5. Assisting in placement of pupils in proper classes or in special classes when needed.

6. Acting as a liaison person between school and community agencies on pupil problems.

7. Coordinating the efforts of all specialists working on a case.

8. Acting as a guidance consultant on pupil problems to all staff members.

9. Interpreting pupil data to authorized community agencies.

10. Reporting to the principal annually on what has been accomplished in guidance.

WHAT IS THE SCHOOL PSYCHOLOGIST'S ROLE?

The duties of a school psychologist vary in particular systems and will be influenced by the availability of other specialists, by his professional acceptance by teachers and community, and by the expectations of the administrator and school board. One list of duties representative of many systems states that the school psychologist:

1. Informs school personnel and parents regarding the special services he is prepared to render.

2. Accepts for study individuals referred to him by school personnel.

3. Studies the problems and potentialities of individuals referred to him, formulates procedures to be followed in the case of individual studies, and provides or helps to secure the treatment needed.

4. Confers with school personnel who are working with an individual studied regarding the results of the study, interprets his findings, recommends the treatment needed to correct the individual's difficulty, and suggests ways in which all can cooperate in giving the treatment.

5. Keeps informed regarding the various services available in the community that can be used in helping individuals to solve their problems and is prepared to secure the particular services for the individual who needs them.

6. Helps school personnel to understand the problems and needs that children commonly have at different age levels.

7. Helps school personnel to understand the causes underlying various kinds of behavior and methods of helping each child to develop desirable behavior patterns.

8. Helps members of the community to understand the causes underlying various kinds of behavior and to understand the intellectualness of children, youth, and adults.

9. Promotes and engages in the research that is needed to help each child and youth to work successfully at a rate and at a level commensurate with his potentialities (Bower, 1955, pp. 2–3).

WHAT IS THE SCHOOL SOCIAL WORKER'S ROLE?

Like the school counselor and the school psychologist, the school social worker is an important member of the guidance team. His work has been described as follows (Spence, 1954) :

. . . School social work functions as a profession within the profession of education. It attempts to use unique social work skills on certain problems of children in school. This contribution reflects current philosophy of the elementary school that includes not only the transmitting of knowledge and skills but social adjustment as well.

Such a goal is recognized when school personnel ask:

1. How can we understand and modify attitudes of children, parents, and teachers that hinder a child's progress in school?

2. How can we know more about the child when he comes to school?

3. How can we help children who are unable to learn because of some emotional disturbance?

4. How can we have a closer parent-school relationship?

5. How can we help teachers help individual children in their classrooms?

The school social worker can help in answering some of these questions because social case work functions as a helping process. Social case work promotes effective use of a meaningful relationship wherein mutual acceptance and growth take place. This process stimulates change toward a more satisfying level of experience (p. 111).

HOW CAN A TEAM APPROACH BE DEVELOPED?

The guidance committee approach to staff cooperation is worth considering (California Test Bureau, 1959). Such a committee is an informal advisory group, interested in the study of problems, yet without administrative responsibility. As a "helping" group to teachers, it contributes to the study of children and encourages continuing professional growth. Guidance committees are most helpful if:

1. The committee represents the varied competencies of the school staff.
2. Staff members volunteer because of interest.
3. Communication between the committee, the administration, and the entire staff is fostered.
4. The committee's responsibilities and progress toward its goals are periodically evaluated.
5. The committee is scheduled as an on-going professional activity within the school.

Through the guidance committee, teachers, psychologist, nurse, principal, and supervisor serve as a team to consider mutual problems. They enjoy working together and, of course, grow individually. The committee fosters a guidance point of view which recognizes the complexity of human behavior and avoids ready-made formulas. The interrelations of all members of the staff come into sharper focus, and individualized help is extended to more boys and girls.

On the basis of an analysis such as this, a school faculty can plan specific steps to improve the guidance program. A guidance committee might be set up to survey the guidance services being provided in the school, using as criteria the characteristics outlined earlier in this article. The committee might then identify the two or three greatest needs and report the findings to the faculty. Once the total staff has agreed on priorities, consultant help can be sought.

If special guidance personnel are not available, the principal might discuss with the superintendent the possibility of obtaining such help. In doing so, he might submit data regarding the costs of such services and the values derived from it. If it should prove impossible for the district to employ the specialist help needed, it might be possible for someone already employed in the school district to be reassigned, provided he has the confidence of the teachers and the needed credentials.

Whether or not guidance specialists are available, the faculty who recognize the importance of guidance services in the modern educational program can accomplish a substantial amount if they will carefully study the elements of a good guidance program and plan specific, year-by-year steps for improvement.

REFERENCES

Barr, J. A. 1958. *The elementary teacher and guidance.* New York: Holt, Rinehart and Winston.

Bower, E. M. November 1955. The school psychologist. *Bull. Calif. State Dept. Educ.*, 24, 2–3.

California State Department of Education. March 1961. *The education of emotionally handicapped children.* Sacramento, Calif.: The Department.

California Test Bureau. 1959. *Guiding today's children.* Los Angeles: Office of the County Superintendent.

Cottingham, H. F. 1956. *Guidance in elementary schools: principles and practices.* Bloomington, Ill.: McKnight.

Detjen, E. W., and Mary F. Detjen. 1963. *Elementary school guidance.* Second ed.; New York: McGraw-Hill.

Froehlich, C. P. 1958. *Guidance services in schools.* Second ed.; New York: McGraw-Hill.

Ginzberg, E. *et al.* 1959. *The ineffective soldier: lessons for management and the nation.* New York: Columbia University Press.

Hart, R. N. December 1961. Are elementary counselors doing the job? *Sch. Couns., 9* (No. 2), 70–72.

Knapp, R. H. 1959. *Guidance in the elementary school.* Boston: Allyn and Bacon.

Kowitz, G. T., and Norma G. Kowitz. 1959. *Guidance in the elementary classroom.* New York: McGraw-Hill.

Los Angeles City Schools. 1957. *Guidance in elementary schools.* Los Angeles: Los Angeles City Board of Education.

Los Angeles County Schools. 1948. *Guidance handbook for elementary children.* Los Angeles: Los Angeles County Board of Education.

Martinson, Ruth, and H. Smallenburg. 1958. *Guidance in elementary schools.* Englewood Cliffs, N.J.: Prentice-Hall.

McCreary, W. H., and D. Kitch. 1953. *Now hear youth.* A report on the California Cooperative Study of school dropouts and graduates. Sacramento, Calif.: State Department of Education.

National Education Association, Association for Supervision and Curriculum Development. 1954. *Guidance in the curriculum.* 1955 Yearbook. Washington, D.C.: The Association.

Ohlsen, M. M. 1955. *Guidance: an introduction.* New York: Harcourt.

Spence, Louise C. 1954. Guidance activities of the school social worker. *Guidance for today's children.* 33rd Yearbook of the National Education Association. Washington, D.C.: Department of Elementary School Principals.

Srole, L. *et al.* 1962. *A new report on mental health in the metropolis: the midtown Manhattan study.* New York: McGraw-Hill.

Willey, R. D. 1952. *Guidance in elementary education.* New York: Harper & Row.

Waterford Studies Elementary School Guidance*

Edgar G. Johnston

The guidance movement, originally concerned with vocational choice but expanding its role to include problems of adjustment and personal development, has, until recently, directed its attention primarily to high school and college age young people. A development of the last few years has been the growing interest in guidance opportunities in the elementary school. This interest has been revealed in an increasing number of published articles and books dealing with elementary school guidance, attention in national meetings, and initiation of college sequences for the preparation of elementary school guidance workers.

Despite the rapid expansion of interest, there has not been general agreement on the philosophy underlying the new development or the characteristics of a desirable elementary school guidance program.

Concepts of elementary school guidance have ranged all the way from an emphasis on "the child development point of view" to a watered down version of the high school guidance program. Illustrative of the first approach is the attitude of the elementary school principal who saw no need for guidance consultant service in her school since "such a person couldn't provide help that a good principal wasn't already giving." Asked what she would do if her superintendent insisted on taking advantage of the new provision in the National Defense Education Act to make an elementary guidance consultant available, she replied: "Oh, I guess I could use him to file test results."

At the other end of the spectrum are those who advocate provision of elementary school "counselors" with only negligible changes in function, responsibilities, and preparation from those commonly expected at the secondary school level.

Local conditions vary widely. It would seem appropriate at this stage of development for each school system to analyze its own situation, diagnose guidance needs of its elementary school pupils, and develop an appropriate program on an experimental basis. This is the approach followed by the Waterford Township School District, a suburban school district in Eastern Michigan, with a total school population of more than 16,000 and including 26 elementary schools varying in size and neighborhood background.

In the fall of 1964 a representative Committee on Guidance in the Elemen-

* *Elementary School Guidance and Counseling,* Spring 1966, vol. 1, no. 3. By permission.

tary School was set up under the chairmanship of the Assistant Superintendent for Instruction and Personnel. Included in the membership were the Elementary Coordinator, the Supervisor of Visiting Teacher Service, the Coordinator of Children's Services, the Coordinator of Research, and two elementary school principals. A panel of elementary school teachers met with the committee to present the teacher viewpoint of guidance needs and to react to the Committee's tentative proposals. The final recommendations of the Committee were reviewed by the total group of elementary school principals at one of their semi-monthly meetings.

The Committee on Guidance in the Elementary School was actually an outgrowth of the work of two earlier committees—one concerned with the effects of Promotion and Retention in the Elementary School, and the other a systemwide Committee on School Holding Power. Both of these committees recognized the desirability of earlier attention to the problems which occasion failure and dropout, and both recommended exploration of guidance possibilities at the elementary school level.

The first activity of the Committee on Guidance in the Elementary School was exploration of published materials dealing with guidance at the elementary school level. In addition to volumes devoted to elementary school guidance and articles in professional journals, the Committee found particularly helpful a bulletin from the U.S. Office of Education: *Guidance for Children in Elementary Schools* by Smith and Eckerson (Bulletin 1963, No. 36) and the April 1964 issue of *The Elementary Principal* which is devoted in its entirety to guidance. Sharing of findings from reading helped to guide the Committee's thinking.

A second activity was the visiting by committee members of schools which had initiated guidance programs in the elementary school or were contemplating introduction of such programs. The Chief of the Guidance Division in the Department of Public Instruction was helpful by providing a tentative list of elementary school guidance programs in Michigan and keeping the Committee informed of new provisions in Title V of the National Defense Education Act. In their visits to other schools, committee members were able to profit from the experience of those schools, both in identifying practices to emulate and in appraising approaches which did not seem applicable to Waterford. Consultants with experience in the elementary guidance field also met with the Committee on occasion.

A third—and the most important—phase of the Committee's deliberation was analysis of guidance needs of elementary school pupils in Waterford and consideration of an appropriate design of service to meet these needs more adequately. Here the reactions of the elementary school teachers invited to meet with the Committee and the recommendations of the two committees previously referred to had special pertinence. Also, a community survey conducted in the fall of 1964 presented significant data about social and economic conditions in various sub-communities of the district.

The Committee met monthly from October until April and summarized its deliberations in a series of recommendations which were reviewed by the elementary principals' group and presented to the Superintendent for approval. The major recommendations of the Committee are presented below:

A. Characteristics of a desirable elementary school guidance program:

1. The guidance program should be set up to serve all pupils, not just the gifted, the "slow learners," or the "problem pupils."
2. The approach should be developmental, not crisis-oriented. The concern should be to help all pupils achieve optimum development.
3. The "center of gravity" should be in the classroom teacher.
4. The function of the consultant is to help teachers understand children better and adapt instruction to their needs.
5. The consultant will work primarily with teachers individually or in groups. He may, at the request of a teacher, spend time with a pupil in individual "counseling," but will do so only as assistance to the teacher with whom the continuing responsibility for pupil progress rests.
6. A part of the consultant's responsibility may be to meet with parents individually or in groups, to help them understand their children better. Again, responsibility for continuing relationships rests with teachers and the school administrator.
7. The consultant's role is clearly distinguishable from that of the visiting teacher and the school psychologist or diagnostician. An excellent discussion is to be found in the pamphlet by Smith and Eckerson, *Guidance for Children in Elementary Schools*, pp. 12 and 13.
8. One function of the consultant may be to assist with the administration and interpretation of tests. It should be recognized, however, that "testing" and "guidance" are not synonymous terms.
9. The consultant will assist teachers and administrators to decide on the desirability of referral to other specialists or agencies where appropriate. The consultant is not a therapist.
10. The consultant may initiate meetings and informal conferences with teachers relating to an understanding of *normal* child development and behavior.
11. The consultant may be called on to interpret the school's guidance program to parents and community organizations.
12. A function of the consultant is to carry on continuing evaluation of the guidance program and to conduct, with the help of others, appropriate research.

B. Qualification of elementary school guidance personnel: The role of the elementary school guidance worker is still in an experimental and developing stage. It would be unfortunate to crystallize qualifications and preparation into a definite pattern at this time. At the same time certain characteristics of the program emerge and qualifications of personnel may be tentatively identified as desirable. Those presented below seem to reflect the Committee's thinking at the last meeting.

1. The function of the elementary school guidance worker is distinct from that of the high school counselor as usually defined. Qualifications should be determined with this difference in mind.
2. Successful elementary school experience is generally recognized as essential.
3. Effectiveness in personal relationships is a *sine qua non*. Allen's "Screens for Counselors," a copy of which was distributed to the Committee, may prove a helpful guide in appraising qualifications for the consultant role.
4. Demonstrated ability in group leadership is an important characteristic.
5. Successful relationships with parents, demonstrated in previous teaching experiences, provide an important background.
6. Inclusion in the consultant's preparation of courses in child growth and development, sociology, social work, and elementary school curriculum development are desirable, as well as special course work, seminars, and practicums related specifically to guidance in the elementary school. It does not seem practical or desirable to set up a specific pattern of professional courses at present. It would seem wise for the Waterford School System to work cooperatively with those institutions of higher education from which we recruit teachers, in identifying and developing graduate programs for the preparation of elementary school guidance personnel.

At its final meeting in April the Committee proposed that a pilot program be inaugurated in two schools, hopefully in the fall of 1965, and that announcement of the positions, together with the statement of qualifications, be circulated throughout the school system and to the placement bureaus of the institutions of higher education serving Waterford. It also recommended continuous evaluation of the program and its extension to other schools in the light of experience with the pilot project. At the time of this writing, these steps had been initiated, schools for the pilot project had been selected and applications were being received. Because of the shortness of time before the close of the 1964–1965 school term, it was not possible to complete arrangements for the project to start in September, 1965. It has been under way since 1966.

Chapter 3

THE ROLE OF THE
ELEMENTARY SCHOOL
COUNSELOR

While there is little argument about the need for elementary school guidance services, counselor role and function is still debated. The readings in this chapter will consider the counselor as viewed by teachers, administrators, and elementary school counselors themselves. The rationale for the elementary school counselor is developed.

A committee of the American School Counselors Association (ASCA), under the leadership of Anna Meeks, issued a tentative report in 1959 which dealt with the scope of guidance in the elementary school. The report listed a variety of services which the elementary school counselor might provide and recognized the importance of the classroom teacher in the guidance program. The committee suggested a minimum of thirty hours' graduate work for the training of elementary school counselors. However, their suggestions for graduate study were not particularly innovative. Their only original suggestion was for the training of elementary school counselors in the fields of child development and play therapy. The ASCA committee believed that teaching experience in the elementary school should be a prerequisite for an elementary school counselor.

The 1960 White House Conference on Children and Youth advocated the development of counseling services for the preadolescent and recommended the ratio of one counselor to every 600 elementary school pupils.

The work of the original ASCA committee was continued in 1961 as part of an American Personnel and Guidance Association (APGA) project entitled "Guidance in the Elementary School." In October 1964, Chairman Anna Meeks released a tentative draft of a report, "Dimensions of Elementary School Guidance," which developed the interrelationship between guidance services and the school curriculum. Services were no longer discussed in global terms but focused on efforts to provide educational experiences which fit each child's needs and level of development. Emphasis was placed on providing each child with the maximum opportunity to learn. The report advocated developmental guidance and stressed the importance of the counselor's being a member of the school staff, not a separate specialist. The functions rated as most important were: pupil counseling and consultation; identification of individual differences; needs and problems; working relationships with teachers; and interpretation to staff and community of the guidance program.

The Association for Counselor Education and Supervision (ACES) and the American School Counselors Association (ASCA) formed a joint committee to study the elementary school counselor and report to the conventions of the American Personnel and Guidance Association in 1965 and 1966. Its position paper was more than a description of current status: it described contributions that a guidance specialist could make in an elementary school program. The committee advocated that the guidance specialist be a member of the school staff. The first report, in 1965, named counseling, consultation, and coordination as the three major responsibilities of the counselor. The 1966 report, which is included in this chapter, stressed the importance of the counselor's role as an agent of change by his influence on both the school organization and the curriculum.

THE COUNSELOR'S ROLE

Despite many good descriptions of the role of the counselor, school boards and administrators often have limited understanding of the potential impact of this professional upon the development of the child. Thus, they limit counselors' activities by making them primarily crisis-oriented. In many instances the counselor only has time for the child who is exceptional or who causes the school administration special concern.

The counselor can not function as remedial teacher or records clerk or psychometrician or administrative assistant to the principal. If he did, then we would not expect him to implement the guidance philosophy helpful to individual growth and development. School boards and administrators are facing decisions that will affect the course of elementary education. The role of counselor must be perceived as contributing to the accomplishment of the broad objectives of elementary school guidance.

It is foolish for the counselor to attempt to define his role without first establishing some communication with those other professionals who have an important influence upon his professional function. He needs to communicate with school administrators, psychologists, social workers, and supervisory personnel.

In a study of elementary school principals, ninety-four percent of those responding believed that teaching experience for elementary school guidance counselors was either necessary or highly desirable (McDougall and Reitan, 1963). Sixty-six percent believed that elementary school guidance should be concerned with special services to individual students rather than with the general curriculum for all students. However, it is not clear how these principals interpreted "special services to individual students" and "general curriculum for all students." But, since the principals indicated a belief in the importance of understanding developmental tasks of childhood, we can conclude that they were in favor of the developmental concept of guidance.

A more comprehensive study of elementary school principals was made by Smith and Eckerson (1966). The sample included 5504 principals and was chosen by similar size of school enrollment in various geographical regions. The purpose of this study was to investigate current and preferred elementary school guidance practices in order to make the best use of those individuals responsible for a comprehensive guidance program. Child development consultants (as defined for this questionnaire) included school counselors, school psychologists, and school social workers who spent at least an average of one day a week in an individual school. Three-fourths of the principals in schools without child development consultants expressed need for their services. The majority of elementary school principals reported that their child development consultants worked more with children than with teachers or parents. Eight out of ten principals felt that consultation with parents and teachers and counseling of children were among the consultant's six most important functions. The median number of pupils per consultant was 789. The median number cited by principals as necessary for adequate service was 609 pupils per consultant. Administrators, counselor educators, and school counselors all perceived the counselor's role differently.

The importance of communicating the role of the counselor to other professional groups is dramatized in a brief article in the National Education Association Journal (Ferris and Leiter, 1965). Ferris, president of the Department of Classroom Teachers of the Colorado Education Association, views counselors essentially as specialists for children with special problems. He believes that they might have a negative effect on the close teacher-pupil relationship if they were introduced into it. Leiter, responding in the same article, makes it clear that Ferris has a limited concept of the role of the counselor, and that it is important to develop dialogue with teachers regarding the counselor's role.

As indicated in Chapter 2, it is important that teacher committees are developed at the initiation of and during the program to function as regular advisory councils for the guidance counselor. The guidance role requires joint teacher-counselor planning. Teachers must recognize the ways in which counselors can complement their own services.

Wrenn (1962) secured the reactions of a representative number of counselors in several areas where elementary school counselors could readily be identified and reached. In this survey, two-thirds of the elementary school counselors were female, the majority had master's degrees, and three-fourths of them worked exclusively in grades one through six. While the median student-counselor ratio was one to 690, one-third of the counselors had responsibility for more than 1000 students. This study also showed that elementary school counselors spend considerably more time daily consulting with teachers and parents than do secondary school counselors. They perceive their role as one of service to children directly and indirectly—through contact with their teachers and parents.

Wrenn describes the new outlook in elementary school pupil personnel work as follows:

> This is an emphasis upon the positive rather than upon the negative, upon the identification of pupil characteristics and talents, upon the developmental needs of all pupils rather than deviate and problem students only. (p. 148)

Wrenn urges us to learn from the experience of the secondary school and to develop a counseling program which is not crisis-oriented. In a slight revision of his thinking, Wrenn (1964) provides this description of the role of the counselor:

> I would now describe the function of the counselor in three divisions: 1) serving in a helping relationship to students and teachers; 2) coordinating and developing certain guidance services; and 3) serving as a cooperative member of an education team with team responsibilities. (p. 208)

Ohlsen (1966) surveyed 100 elementary school counselors who were identified as outstanding by their colleagues. These counselors did not use high school counselors as models for their roles, but instead chose to work primarily in the area of developmental counseling and individual consultation.

THE RATIONALE FOR THE ELEMENTARY SCHOOL COUNSELOR

Any rationale for elementary school counseling must proceed from the purposes of education. The main purpose of education is development of the ability to think (Educational Policies Commission, 1961). A counselor who functions in terms of this concept is concerned with facilitating the learning process and the feeling of adequacy and belonging in the learner. This can only occur when classroom teachers become more adequate in their classroom guidance functions. Democratic pupil personnel programs provide services for all children. The normal child is not deprived of services because he is normal. Guidance service is developmental to the extent that it deals with normal developmental tasks and facilitates the learning and development of all pupils. Guidance is never a therapeutic service set apart from the general goals of the educational process.

While guidance can be informal and incidental, it functions best when it is based upon a planned, continuous sequence of experiences which assists the child to cope with both intellectual and emotional development. As Faust (1966) has stated:

The counselor simply translates his depth and breadth of understanding of human behavior, as well as his own personality, into the shaping of a learning climate which will free children to learn efficiently. However, at the same time it should be noted that the role of affect, how the learner feels, is not to be disregarded. For it is through affect that the efficiency level of the intellective processes are principally determined. (p. 8)

ESTABLISHING THE CLIMATE
FOR ELEMENTARY SCHOOL GUIDANCE

Elementary school guidance is dependent upon the development of a co-operative atmosphere between professionals themselves as well as in their relationships with children. The school administrator is a critical factor in the establishment of this climate. He must provide the program with democratic leadership and his personal support. He allots time, facilities, and opportunity for regular contact between the guidance specialist and teachers. He must encourage teachers to work with the guidance specialist and participate in the guidance programs. The school administrator must also provide a coordinating committee of teachers and other specialists in the school system. The counselor can enhance the development of this climate by showing a willingness to listen to and understand the points of view of adults and children. In the development of recommendations with teachers, the counselor should be careful to stress the collaborative nature of their relationship.

The elementary school counselor provides many indirect services for a child through contacts with the school's professional staff and parents. He strives to create a school atmosphere that facilitates self-understanding, learning, and a feeling of adequacy. The counselor who comprehends the significance of his function could serve as an agent of change and make the educational experience in his school more meaningful.

The article by Meeks provides an introduction to the rationale for elementary school counseling. Meeks emphasizes the enhancing of the learning climate for all children. She discusses the significance of the teacher's role and the need for specialized assistance to the teacher through consultation. She recommends both individual and group counseling, and also favors a course in play therapy for elementary school counselors, a position not presented by the other authors in this chapter.

Kaczkowski believes that it is the ability of the counselor to deal with feelings and emotions that makes him unique. He focuses on the importance of assisting the child to build an adequate self-concept. His list of the characteristics of effective counselors, derived from a study by Combs and Soper, indicates the importance of those attitudes which the counselor must bring to a relationship. The counselor's personality and perceptual skill are discussed, as well as practical problems and procedures in the consultant role.

Ohlsen defines the responsibilities of teachers and counselors in the elementary school guidance program and describes the unique characteristics of counseling relationships with children. He establishes guidelines for counseling and consulting with parents and teachers.

The ACES-ASCA committee report on the elementary school counselor describes counselor functions in three major areas: counseling, consulting, and coordinating. The report defines specific professional responsibilities in creating an environment conducive to learning and growth. The report includes some details regarding consultation with parents and teachers and outlines the counselor's responsibilities for participating in curriculum development. The report also includes recommendations for the professional preparation of elementary school counselors. While recognizing the value of teaching experience for the counselor, the report concluded that knowledge of the school program can also be gained through planned experiences in the elementary school at the postgraduate level of teacher training.

REFERENCES

ACES-ASCA Committee on the Elementary School Counselor. April 1965. Preliminary statement of the American Personnel and Guidance Association Convention, Minneapolis.

Educational Policies Commission. 1961. *The central purpose of American education*. Washington, D.C.: National Education Association.

Faust, V. 1966. *Role of the elementary school counselor: freeing children to learn*. An address to the Office of Education, U.S. Department of Health, Education and Welfare, Washington, D.C. 1965.

Ferris, R. R., and Sarah L. Leiter. 1965. Guidance in the elementary school: a teacher can do it best; a specialist is invaluable. *Nat. Educ. Ass. J.*

McDougall, W., and H. Reitan. 1963. The elementary counselor as perceived by elementary principals. *Personnel guid. J.*, 42 (No. 4).

Meeks, Anna. 1964. *Dimensions of elementary school guidance* (tentative draft). Elementary School Guidance and Counseling Committee.

Ohlsen, M. November 1966. *Report to the North Central ACES*. A report by the Sub-committee for Counselor Education Standards in the Preparation of Elementary School Counselors.

Smith, H., and Louise Eckerson. 1966. *Guidance services in elementary schools: a national survey*. Washington, D.C.: Superintendent of Documents, U.S. Government Printing Office.

Wreen, C. G. 1964. The counselor in a changing world revisited. *Teach. Coll. J*. Terre Haute, Ind.: Indiana State College.

———. 1962. *The counselor in a changing world*. Washington, D.C.: American Personnel and Guidance Association.

Elementary School Counseling*

Anna R. Meeks

Significant developments in the decade from 1950 to 1960 brought a recognition that organized guidance programs are as important on the elementary level as on the secondary level.

An increasing awareness that people are the most basic resource for a nation's continued progress and development focused attention upon the academically able student and, more especially, upon the underachieving able youth. Concern mounted for the conservation of human resources as it relates to the secondary youth in matters of "school dropouts," juvenile delinquency and general underachievement of able youth.

Belatedly there came a conviction that we must find means of preventing, rather than trying to remedy, such situations after they occur. This conviction has brought an awareness that any attempt to solve these problems must begin with a strengthened program of counseling and guidance services in the elementary school, for in the early years of the school experience children develop self-concepts and values that determine the motivation for learning and personal development in the secondary school as well as in the adult years of an individual's life.

Research studies in the area of learning have strengthened the school's conviction that any adequate program for the conservation of human resources must be concerned with the development of good emotional, social, and educational adjustment. Efforts to enhance the learning opportunities for every child have emphasized the need to individualize instruction through more effective ways of recognizing and meeting children's needs. An increasing awareness that individual differences not only are great, but that they involve much more than intellectual differences, continues to emphasize the need for elementary guidance programs.

A concept of what this program should be has been slowly emerging in recent years.

Too often elementary guidance has been identified as a process inseparable from teaching. Efforts to meet the needs of children have relied on grouping procedures and curriculum revision with little or no use of special services to the individual. Such a point of view fails to see that the guidance process is concerned with the unique needs of the individual while curriculum is concerned with the common needs of a group of children.

A somewhat later point of view accepts guidance as a specialized service for

* *The School Counselor*, 1962, vol. 10. By permission.

children with severe problems, but not essential for every child unless it might be through the standardized test program.

More recently guidance is accepted as a process through which we can identify the needs of children and help them and their parents in developing realistic goals in order that they may have an opportunity for optimal development. Research studies are showing that a low self-image at school entrance can create barriers to intellectual accomplishment. It follows, then, that the earlier the school identifies the needs of a child and provides for a realistic atmosphere of success and acceptance, the greater will be the chance that the child's self-concept can grow as a basis for progress.

ORGANIZED PROGRAMS

The recognition of a need to provide earlier guidance services has resulted in a developing wave of organized programs of elementary school guidance. The number of schools offering such programs has steadily increased since 1950. In general these programs have been limited to individual school districts or large city and county units. The year 1962 saw the beginnings of statewide programs in at least two states, with the development of certification requirements and of programs for professional preparation especially designed to meet the needs of the elementary school counselor.

There is general acceptance of the importance of the guidance function in the elementary school, but there is not equal agreement on how this function may best be performed nor on who should be responsible for this function. There is a need to better define and clarify the guidance role and function as a basis for determining which personnel must be assigned responsibility for the development of adequate guidance services.

No one seriously believes that elementary guidance is solely a point of view but we have not completely emerged from a "crisis" concept of guidance that serves only those children whose problems become too great to allow them to function in a classroom. A more positive approach is centered in efforts to enhance the learning climate for *all* children. Interest in the development of learning situations that produce creativity and develop leadership is creating a demand for systematic and in-service education for teachers in today's most complex educational program.

QUESTIONS

A number of questions have emerged, and these must be resolved if maximum benefits are to be derived from organized guidance services.

1. What personnel are needed to meet the needs of the child as a learner?
2. When there is a specialist, how shall the guidance functions be delineated?

3. What is the relationship of the guidance specialist to the administrator, teacher, and other members of the school staff?

4. What professional preparation does an elementary school counselor need?

5. How can school counseling be made an integral part of the total educational program?

Guidance in elementary schools is emerging as a process primarily concerned with assisting the child as a learner. Essentially it is the process of helping the child to understand and accept himself in relation to his own needs and to those of his environment. Early identification of each child's needs and interests, interpretation of these to parents and teachers, and counseling for every child would seem to be the chief goals for developing adequate guidance services.

Counseling is a significant aspect of the elementary program. Early counseling helps the child to make adjustments to new and difficult situations and thus strengthens the child's ability to apply his self-understanding to the solution of problems in later years.

Guidance, then, is an integral part of the total educational program, and to be most effective the guidance process in the elementary school must be a part of a continuous guidance process from the child's first contact with school until he has been placed in a "job" or in post-secondary education.

Emphases will change to meet the needs of a developing youth, but essentially guidance will be a process of helping him develop and accept a realistic self-concept as a basis for optimal development.

Techniques and procedures must fit the child's level of development, and it is here that the uniqueness of elementary guidance can be found. The use of toys, of open-end stories and of role playing so characteristic of elementary school counseling offers a different approach.

But the purpose of counseling—a more realistic self-concept and changed behavior—is just as pertinent in elementary guidance as in secondary guidance. Many children will receive individual counseling, but many will work in some form of group activity in order that the dynamics of an interacting group may help the child in his self-evaluation and self-acceptance.

TEACHER'S ROLE

The emphasis upon specialized assistance in no way indicates a lesser guidance role for the teacher. In fact, schools providing effective guidance services consistently report an enhanced role for teachers that recognizes guidance as that part of the teacher's responsibility directly related to the provision of conditions necessary for effective learning.

Every attempt to improve the learning climate in a classroom has made new and heavier demands upon the teacher's time and ingenuity. Gradually we are accepting the idea that the teacher has a *right* to expect specialized assistance in meeting the varying needs of children in her class. Administrators and teachers accept this concept and urge a clarification of the role and function of guidance in the elementary school, so that the development of organized programs can proceed at a faster rate.

While there is some evidence that universities are developing programs for the professional preparation of elementary counselors, there is a need for many more programs that give attention to the unique needs of various developmental levels of elementary children. Practicums in counseling must allow for experience with elementary school children. Play therapy and courses in human development and in the psychology of learning are musts for potential elementary counselors.

PROSPECTS

The decade from 1950 to 1960 has seen remarkable growth in interest, understanding, and know-how in elementary guidance and has provided a readiness for professional leadership for the future development of organized programs.

The American School Counselor Association has had a committee working to clarify some of the issues mentioned above. A tentative report in 1959 at the APGA Convention in Cleveland aroused considerable interest. The response to meetings on elementary guidance in subsequent conventions gave evidence of the genuine interest and concern for the development of effective programs of elementary school guidance.

The work of the ASCA Committee is continuing as a part of the APGA project for the study of elementary school guidance. An initial survey of existing guidance programs is providing the basis for further study of the direction and trends evident in the expansion and development of these services. ASCA will be responsible for the preparation of a statement designed to suggest a desirable approach to the development of effective elementary school guidance. Such a statement will be developed after a larger committee has had an opportunity to study existing programs.

This statement will be followed with a period of research to determine the effectiveness of suggested organizations and techniques. Then APGA will release a statement of basic principles which can guide the development of the emerging and rapidly expanding program of elementary school guidance.

The decade of the sixties challenges us to bring vision, creativity, and unceasing effort to the development of effective elementary school guidance in order that all children may find an opportunity for optimal development in a climate that minimizes barriers to learning through genuine individualization of instruction.

The Role and Function of

the Elementary School Counselor*

Henry R. Kaczkowski

In the past year or two, elementary school guidance has received a considerable amount of attention. This attention will reach meteoric proportions in the next few years, partly because of the values inherent in the type of guidance program being stressed and partly because additional state and federal money is now available for the execution of the program. However, a moment's reflection on the situation will point to the fact that ideas about what constitutes an elementary school guidance program are not necessarily new. For example, the New York City school system had developed a rather comprehensive program in 1955. What is new is that most school systems are trying to develop a rationale for the ongoing guidance programs. Schools have become aware of the fact "that one professional person cannot be all things to all people" (Stripling, 1964, pp. 11–14).

One of the basic problems in the development of a rationale for an elementary guidance program is that of relating guidance to pupil personnel services and instructional programs. Pupil personnel services not only embrace guidance services but also such activities as attendance, health services, special psychological services, visiting teachers and so on. The problem posed by the pupil personnel services concept is that of coordinating the efforts of the various specialists such as counselors, nurses, school psychologists, school social workers, and psychometrists. Since each "expert" is interested in some "part" of the student, it is essential that a team approach be evolved so that the total child can be considered. The inherent weakness in the service concept is that of compartmentalization of the individual to the point of complete vitiation of the counseling process.

Generally speaking, three strategies can be employed to reach the typical goals of guidance: remedial, preventative, and promotional (Stewart and Warnath, 1965). Stewart and Warnath define these terms in the following manner:

1. *Remedial guidance* is concerned with the correcting of some aspect of the maturation process that has gone awry.

2. *Preventive guidance* discovers and removes blocks in the environment that could potentially handicap the development of the individual.

3. *Promotional guidance* is concerned with promoting these skills, attitudes, and habits that lead to becoming a fully functioning person.

The inherent weakness in these strategies as they are commonly executed is

* Paper prepared especially for this book of readings.

that they lead to a considerable amount of social engineering. The activities are so structured that the individual loses considerable flexibility. He is incapable of achieving what Patterson (1959) calls "responsible independence." The attitude of "I know what is best for you" must be avoided by the counselor. It is easy to adopt this attitude especially when dealing with elementary school children. The counselor (and the teacher) by virtue of maturity, training, and experience at this level of instruction tend to overlook the uniqueness of the child while assisting him to become a socialized being within society.

To many staff members the relationship between guidance activities and instructional aspects appear to be worlds apart. For the most part, the instructional phase is viewed as inculcating basic skills and knowledge. The gap between the two widens as one proceeds up the instructional ladder. However, some of the early definitions of guidance stated that it was concerned with the individualization of instruction (Willey and Andrew, 1955). If one examines the situation carefully, a high degree of relationship between instruction and guidance should exist. This is not to imply that every teacher is a counselor, but that the entire school staff can make vital contributions to the guidance program because everyone in the school system works with the same material: Pupils. The individual student in his quest to answer "Who am I?" needs the services of both the school staff and counselors. Each can enhance his self-concept by providing a sense of identity and a ground for reality testing (Stewart and Warnath, 1965). A coordinated effort is required because activity in the classroom focuses almost exclusively on the cognitive aspects while guidance programs, particularly counseling, deal primarily with emotion and feeling.

Lafferty (1962) believes that "there is overwhelming evidence that [one's] self-concept is related to successful function in learning and in later adjustment in life." He quotes Symonds (1951) on this point:

> Parents should be extremely sensitive to the attitudes they express toward children. . . . It is important that children be referred to with warmth, appreciation, encouragement, confidence rather than with criticism, disparagement, and disappointment. . . .
> The fact that concepts of self are a reflection of the attitudes expressed toward a person by others indicates the power that parents and teachers have in determining the kind of selves that children will develop.

There is a belief among some schoolmen that the bulk of reading problems are due to improper self-functioning rather than to lack of skill and know-how in reading. Gordon Allport (1961) points out that teachers are very skillful in teaching matters of fact. However, matters of importance (his term for values) are rarely discussed in class. Yet the child needs values to evaluate things in order to develop his self-concept, which in turn affects his life style. Lecky (1945) in developing his concept of "self-consistency" points out that self-identity and reality may have little congruency. "The very fact that we strive to be true to ourselves involves resistance to the acceptance of that which is inconsistent. Thus, resistance may be recognized as normal and necessary. Indeed, a unified organization (person) could not be maintained without it." In other words, a person who considers himself a poor speller (and has this idea continually reinforced by the teacher) cannot be helped by remedial procedures unless his attitude toward spelling and, in turn about himself, is altered. In citing some of his experimental work in the area of spelling, Lecky points to individuals who have "unconsciously" set a goal of so many misspelled words per page. Words spelled correctly on one page are misspelled on another in order to maintain the "proper quota." In an elementary school setting a counselor can play a vital role in helping the teacher to recognize the existence of this type of problem. In addition, he can, with the help of the teacher and other staff members, reduce the debilitating effects of this condition.

A casual examination of the literature in the field of elementary guidance reveals that the task of the counselor is almost always defined in general rather than specific terms (Crow and Crow, 1965). The duties typically mentioned are: counseling, group work, screening, test administration, parent conferences, consulting with teachers, working with underachievers, in-service training, and remedial work. On occasion, explicit tasks are spelled out. Many of the neophyte counselors looking for specific techniques will find a few of them after arduous labor, but they are not found in typical educational sources. Since the cupboard is bare, there is a tendency to adopt without careful examination the same techniques and procedures used with adolescents and adults. Using a strictly cognitive approach to resolve problems in guidance can only result in chaos.

One of the biggest stumbling blocks is the matter of vocabulary. The adult meaning of a word and a second grader's interpretation of the word can literally be worlds apart. The writer was exploring with a second grader the types of things he liked to do. The pupil said that one of his favorite pastimes was to watch the "late show" on TV. At times it was easy to form a hypothesis that the lack of sufficient sleep could contribute to the boy's poor performance in school. Tempered by the counseling approach, the discussion centered on the importance of the "late show" in the boy's life. It soon became apparent to the writer that the boy's examination of the situation was a bit incongruous. So from the point of clarification, he asked the boy what he meant by the "late show." "Well, I call the 'early show' the 'late show' because I am fifteen minutes late in seeing the start of the movie."

Of the myriad tasks allotted the elementary school counselor, two will concern him the most: counseling and consulting with teachers. The latter activity is one of the most frequent tasks mentioned while at the same time being the least explicitly defined. Usually vague generalities are offered as the kinds of things about which the counselor is "consulted." After pondering a typical list, a counselor feels that he has to play the role of a supervisor, principal, and confessor. To add to the anxiety of the counselor, the lists of the kinds of things he counsels about are as vague as the list on consultation or they are simply transpositions of what goes on in interviews with adults. It is hoped that a supervised practicum can alleviate most of the fears of the neophyte elementary school counselor. In the next few paragraphs these two concerns will be explored more thoroughly.

Most textbooks define counseling as a "relationship," and by maintaining this "relationship" a change in behavior will occur. Lafferty (1962) contrasts two types of approaches in counseling:

These (therapies) are essentially based upon the idea that some children grow up in a situation where they have never had or experienced a close relationship with a mature adult, and therefore by replacing this lack with a relationship in a psychotherapeutic situation the youngster is able to change his behavior. While this is a simply stated idea it is, perhaps, one of the most important cornerstones of the schools' current attempts to alter behavior in children. . . . Still another system may be referred to as supportive therapy, a system under which a significant or mature adult takes interest in a youngster and lets him know that this adult will stand with the youngster. The person essentially sympathizes and lets the youngster know that he can understand the nature of his concerns, and worries. It is a sustaining form of therapy and few of its advocates maintain that it produces much in the way of drastic change in behavior. . . . This writer does not wish to infer that these are essentially ineffective schools of thought, but rather raises the question of whether or not we should look for other, more immediate ways of altering behavior. The proposition stated above may be restated simply: There are no known totally effective ways in which behavior might be altered.

Essentially Lafferty is drawing attention to the idea that a strictly cognitive approach tends not to be effective in changing the behavior of pupils. What is needed is another ingredient: emotion. By combining cognition with emotion we have Ellis's (1962) notion of rational therapy. The essential idea underlying this therapy is that in reality emotions are biased, prejudiced, and opinionated forms of thinking. Inherent in the concept is Lecky's (1945) notion of "self-consistency." "Neurosis, in other words, consists of stupid behavior by a non-stupid person."

As mentioned earlier, counselors tend to feel that they are hindered rather than helped by counseling theory. The above explication is a good example of some of the problems encountered by a counselor when he tries to translate theory into action. "Is there any way I can become a 'good counselor' without being weighted down with a myriad of counseling approaches?" Fortunately, an article by Combs and Soper (1963) can provide a partial answer to the dilemma. In reviewing the literature Combs and Soper state, ". . . effective relationships seem dependent upon the nature of the helper's attitudes and ways of perceiving himself, his tasks, his client, and his purpose" (pp. 222–226). They also observe that Rogers concluded "that almost any kind of behavior may be helpful to an individual if the intent of the helper is to help." Combs and Soper seem to concur with Rogers, stating that "apparently, what makes an effective professional worker is a question not of what methods he uses, but of how well he has learned to use his unique self as an instrument for working with other people."

In their own particular study Combs and Soper list the following characteristics of the effective counselor: (1) he perceives from an internal rather than an external frame of reference; (2) he sees in terms of people rather than things; (3) he sees people as able rather than unable; (4) he sees people as dependable rather than undependable; (5) he sees people as friendly rather than as unfriendly; (6) he sees people as worthy rather than unworthy; (7) he sees himself as identified with people rather than apart from people; (8) he is able to cope with his own problems; (9) he is not afraid to reveal his true self; (10) he tries to free people rather than control them; (11) he is altruistic rather than narcissistic; (12) he is concerned with larger rather than smaller meanings.

One can generalize from the above study that it is more important to have internalized a particular philosophy of life rather than a set of techniques. It is the attitudes that a counselor brings into the "relationship" that maintain it rather than a bag of tricks. That "change" is brought about by the counselor acting as an agent of the client rather than as an agent for society. Consequently, counselors should be more concerned about their perceptual organization rather than their ability to master counseling theory. Performing a personal synthesis in regarding one's self-concept is more important than striving to achieve an "A" in a guidance course.

In addition to counseling, the other major concern of elementary school counselors is that of "consulting with teachers." Very often this is reduced to generalization on mental health aspects of classroom management procedures. It is true that classroom teachers are vitally concerned with adverse results of some of their actions. The eternal question asked is "Did I do right in this ease?" This question can be interpreted in many ways, all of which focus on the sense of worth of the asker. "Do I dare to admit the fact that at times I feel imperfect in my relationship with others?" "What will my students think of me now?"

The essential procedure used with the teacher is the same as used with the pupil: exploration of the self-concept. The typical problem faced by the teacher is that of conflict: I would like to help Johnny but I am not willing (as yet) to do it at the "expense" of 25 other pupils. There is no tailor-made solution to this type of problem. By establishing a "relationship" the problem can be alleviated for most teachers. Another type of problem is that of the failing student. Most teachers feel that this type of person should receive some type of help. However, the counselor does not offer assistance in the form of outlining remedial procedures but looks for the emotional blocks to learning. This means observing the student in a variety of situations and employing sociometric procedures. It means using tests, not necessarily for assessment or diagnostic purposes, but for appraising performance in stress situations. Very often the report on a "failing" student will place the teacher in a conflict situation. "From this report I gather that it is my attitude toward the youngster that may be responsible for his poor reading. It cannot be so. After all, all I have been telling him is that he is a poor reader."

This type of consultation brings into focus an organizational problem on the elementary level. When and where are you going to do it? First of all, you need a private setting to carry this type of interaction. The typical teachers' lounge affords very little privacy. It calls for an office removed from the heavy traffic of the school. The classroom can be used for this consultation. However, the classroom is usually filled with children. It is surprising what big ears children have. If the conversation is held in the hallway, the teacher is continually worried about what is going on in the classroom. After all, in most schools the amount of noise reflects the degree of discipline the teacher can enforce. The end result is a squirming teacher who is interested in a quick solution rather than an exploration of the problem. In addition, the consultations must be crowded in during a limited time period: before school, after school, recess, and lunch hour. For the most part, this proves unsatisfactory because the teacher may have more requests for consultation than time to carry them out. To keep everyone happy the counselor may resort to prescribing a favorite remedy: try to understand the youngster.

The solution to the above problems may be in reorganizing the elementary school. A departmentalized approach that frees the teacher for professional tasks other than teaching would yield many benefits. For example, when the music, art, or physical education teacher conducts the class, the teacher could schedule a time block to consult with the counselor, parent, or nurse about a given youngster in an unhurried fashion. The biggest single drawback of this plan is that it costs money to hire extra teachers. A variation of the plan is to hire a single "floating" substitute to take over the class when consultation is deemed appropriate.

There is one other problem that arises when the counselor acts as a consultant to the staff. What kind of interaction should the counselor have outside the "professional" contact he has made with the teachers? Can he be one of "the boys" and engage in idle banter or partake in drinking coffee with some teachers during recess? Most counselors see nothing wrong with participating in these types of activities. After all, Snygg and Soper (1963) feel that effective counselors identify themselves with people rather than remain apart from them. The writer's observations on this issue have led him to conclude that his effectiveness as a consultant is reduced the more time he spends being "one of the boys." Why? First of all, it takes time away from his performing his task as a consultant. Second, it reduces his availability to the staff. Third, it tends to reduce consultation periods to gossip time. Fourth, it affects the degree of trust that the staff has in the counselor. Is he going to talk about me to somebody else? This does not mean that the counselor should not participate in social activities with the rest of the school staff. It does mean that he must be continually aware of the great professional responsibility he has when he deals with other staff members. His aloofness is a sign that he cares to give his best to all concerned.

There are many other types of interactions that should be discussed. Among them are parent conferences and the counselor's relationships with the administration and other members of the pupil personnel team, such as nurses, school psychologists, and social workers. Because they have just been enumerated rather than discussed does not mean that they are unimportant. All of the points considered concern the pupil in some way and are therefore important to the over-all success of the guidance program but more importantly, to the self-enhancement of each pupil within the school. Unfortunately, time permits only a cursory mention of these considerations and their contribution to the guidance program.

I have tried to point out some of the problems that confront the elementary school counselor. The problems highlighted here are those that have frequently come up during my brief work as an elementary school counselor. Probably in another setting other problems would have arisen. Many may be confused rather than helped by this exposition but I will nevertheless offer the following in conclusion: By virtue of your training as elementary school counselors you have one asset that most staff members lack. Because of this one talent you are in a position to enter into a unique relationship with pupils, teachers, parents, and administrators. The help given through the counseling relationship is immeasurable. What is this gift that you have? You, better than anyone else in the school, are able to deal with affect. It is not your sophistication in dealing with test data or your ability to draw a sociogram that make you invaluable. It is your ability to deal with feelings and emotion that makes you unique. Techniques become unimportant when you want to help an individual to become a person. Your training can very often help make this a reality.

REFERENCES

Allport, G. 1961. Values and our youth. *Teach. Coll. Rec.*, *63*, 211–219. New York: Columbia University.

Board of Education of the City of New York. 1955. *Guidance of children in elementary schools*. New York: The Board.

Combs, A. W., and W. Soper. 1963. Perceptual organization of effective counselors. *J. counsel. Psychol.*, *10* (No. 3), 222–226.

Ellis, A. 1962. *Reason and emotion in psychotherapy*. New York: Lyle Stuart.

Crow, L., and A. Crow. 1965. *Organization and conduct of guidance services*. New York: McKay.

Lafferty, J. C. 1962. *Values that defeat learning*. A paper prepared for The Eighth Inter-Institutional Seminar in Child Development. Mimeographed.

Lecky, P. 1945. *Self-consistency: a theory of personality*. New York: Island Press.

Patterson, C. H. 1959. *Counseling and psychotherapy: theory and practice*. New York: Harper & Row.

Stewart, L. H., and C. F. Warnath. 1965. *The counselor and society*. Boston: Houghton Mifflin.

Stripling, R. O. April 1964. Trends in elementary school guidance. *Nat. elem. Princ.*, *63*, 11–14.

Symonds, P. M. 1951. *The ego and the self*. New York: Appleton.

Willey, R. D., and D. C. Andrew. 1955. *Modern methods and techniques in guidance*. New York: Harper & Row.

A Rationale

for the Elementary School Counselor*

Merle M. Ohlsen

Recently we have heard a lot about elementary school counselors. Some teachers and principals are enthusiastic about the idea. Others have doubts; they often ask such questions as: What will be his qualifications? With whom will he work? How will his work affect what I do? Wouldn't it be better to reduce class size and relieve teachers from some of their non-teaching duties so that they could give pupils more individual attention rather than to employ counselors? Ferris (1965) asks some of these questions; he also expresses the fear that having a counselor work directly with the pupils would damage the close relationship that usually develops between an elementary teacher and his pupils. Those who have seen what elementary school counselors can do for pupils, parents, and teachers take the opposite view (Brison, 1964; Kaczkowski, 1965; Lambert, 1954; Leiter, 1965; Mahan, 1965; Meeks, 1963; Ohlsen, 1964; Wilson, 1956, and Zeller and Garber, 1964); they believe that the counselor enhances the development of a close working relationship between a teacher and his pupils. They also believe that he helps pupils by counseling them, by consulting with their teachers, and by counseling their parents concerning the children's problems. In other words, they believe that he fulfills functions that we cannot expect teachers to fulfill.

PRINCIPALS' PERCEPTIONS

Though he recognizes the need for an elementary school counselor's services, Waetjen (1965) contends that most elementary school principals would oppose the idea of employing counselors. In part, he thinks that the resistance to specialists arises out of the specialists' failure to adapt to the elementary school setting. He also believes that it may stem from the idea that teachers can handle all the problems that arise within their classrooms. As he sees it: "The challenge to elementary school principals is twofold: first, to examine their resistance to having counselors in the elementary schools; and second, to differentiate the organization and functioning of the elementary school so that the counselor may emerge" (pp. 59–62). It is his hope that the research and demonstration centers selected by the Research Commission on Pupil Personnel Services will help solve these and other similar problems.

McDougall and Reitan (1963) deplored the idea that no one had sys-

* *Guidance Journal*, Fall 1966, vol. 5, no. 2. By permission.

tematically surveyed the opinions of elementary school administrators and used their opinions in developing elementary school guidance programs. From their survey of elementary school principals' opinions (from Idaho, Oregon, and Washington) they found: ". . . that the majority of responding principals favor the viewpoint that elementary guidance be concerned with specialized services to individual pupils rather than general curriculum guidance for all pupils." Preference is also expressed by the majority for personnel engaged in full-time guidance rather than a combination of part-time teaching and guidance duties. Seventy-five percent of the responding principals favored special certification for elementary guidance personnel and a majority also favored additional salary beyond the teaching salary schedule.

> The reaction of the principals was solicited regarding problems in establishing elementary guidance programs. The most frequently mentioned problems were in the areas of program, finance, gaining school and community acceptance for the guidance program, and obtaining adequately trained elementary guidance personnel.

> Principals expressed their judgment concerning the major differences between elementary and secondary school guidance. Areas mentioned most often were the greater emphasis on the preventive aspects of guidance at the elementary level; the lesser need for occupational and vocational guidance in the elementary school; the need for more parental involvement at the elementary level; and the need for understanding developmental problems peculiar to childhood and pre-adolescence (McDougall and Reitan, 1963, pp. 348–354).

In other words, these elementary school principals have a pretty good idea of what should be expected of the elementary school counselor. At least their ideas agree with the authors cited earlier who react favorably to having such a person employed in the elementary schools. If these principals accurately reflect the attitudes of most principals, then the climate for introducing the elementary counselors is more favorable than Waetjen perceives it to be.

THE TEACHER'S CONTRIBUTION

Important as the principal's perception is, attention must also be given to what the effective teacher contributes to normal development of children. He recognizes the importance of teaching subject matter, but he also knows that having children memorize facts and practice basic skills are not sufficient. He tries to get children excited about learning by exhibiting interests in the intellectual activities that excite them, by raising challenging questions, by helping them learn to challenge others and evaluate others' ideas as well as their own, and by helping them locate and use information in making decisions. Besides increasing their desire to learn, he tries to improve their ability to educate themselves. He also tries to understand his pupils; to help them understand and accept themselves, including what they have a right to expect from themselves; to help them understand, accept, and work with important others such as classmates, parents, and teachers; and to help them discover and develop special interests, abilities, and aptitudes. He is interested in his pupils as individuals and he is able to convey to them that he is interested in them. He is aware that what children learn is a function of their needs, community and family backgrounds, previous educational experiences, and the atmosphere within the classroom as well as their learning potential. He recognizes that he must be concerned about both the conative and cognitive aspects of learning.

EXPECTATIONS FROM THE COUNSELOR

Based upon the above definitions of the elementary school teacher's responsibility for guidance, the elementary school counselor should be expected to help the teachers to further normal social, emotional, and intellectual development of his pupils, to better understand his pupils, to discover and try to remove blocks to learning, to make effective use of such school specialists as the school psychologist, school social worker, remedial teacher, and speech therapist, and to refer certain pupils and parents to out-of-school personnel and agencies for treatment. In fulfilling these functions the counselor consults with teachers, counsels children, and counsels parents concerning their children's school adjustment problems. Since he is primarily concerned with normal children and the prevention of serious school adjustment problems, he does short-term counseling, tries to help teachers discover problems early, and tries to help them improve the learning atmosphere within the classroom.

A WORKING RELATIONSHIP
WITH CHILDREN

Like those who counsel adolescents and adults, the elementary school counselor tries to develop an accepting, trusting relationship with his clients. He uses his knowledge of the counseling process, of human behavior, and of each client and his environment to try to understand each client's problems as the client sees them, and in the elementary school, to try to help the child, his parents, and his teacher to understand the forces at work within the client and his environment. At the same time, the counselor recognizes that insight in and of itself is not sufficient, and for many clients it is not necessary (Ginott, 1958); these children can learn to change their behavior without understanding why they had problems.

One of the unique characteristics of this relationship is the counselor's ability to listen—to make a personal investment in each client, and at the same time to maintain separateness. When a counselor is at his best he can feel deeply with a client without experiencing countertransference. Moreover, he is able to convey this commitment to his clients and his expectations from them. He also is able to convey to children what they may expect from him, including his willingness to talk to them whenever they have something bothering them and they want to talk to someone privately, they must realize that they can seek assistance without waiting for a referral from an adult. Contrary to what many authors have said, staff members in the Illinois demonstration centers have found that children will seek help on their own when such action is accepted by teachers and counselors. Apparently elementary school children trust counselors more quickly than either adolescents or adults, but counselors tend to have greater difficulty communicating with them than they do with older clients. Kaczkowski (1965) believes that children's limited vocabulary accounts for a large part of this difficulty. Often a child does not know the best word to express a feeling, or he knows only a single meaning for a word which has many meanings and the counselor assumes another meaning, or he uses a word incorrectly and the counselor assumes a correct meaning for the word. Nevertheless, these counselors have found that even primary school-age children can better convey verbally what bothers them than any noted authors have indicated. True, the counselor must listen very carefully, be patient and try to help the client fumble for words, or even teach the client new words to express his feelings. On some occasions the counselor also must use play materials to communicate, but not as often with normal children as psychotherapists have indicated one must with disturbed children. Further support for this idea comes from Moustakas (1959). He describes play therapy as a form of preventative mental hygiene for normal children.

What do these normal children talk to counselors about when they seek a counselor's assistance? They talk about a wide variety of problems from "I can't learn to read," or "My teacher doesn't like me," to "My little brother messes up my homework," or "My new puppy was killed." When, for example, a child thinks that his teacher does not like him, it helps just to have another adult at school listen to him and try to understand him. All that some very young children need is more experience in relating to adults and help in discovering that all adults who accept them do not have to relate to them as their mothers do. The typical normal child requires only a few sessions in order to help him and his teacher and/or parents identify and remove his blocks to learning. When, however, the counselor concludes that a child cannot be helped with a few individual sessions, perhaps he should ask himself whether the child could be best helped in a group. Children who are shy, or have difficulty making friends, or have difficulty participating in class discussion, or have better ability than their performance indicates often can be helped in small groups.

COUNSELING PARENTS

In counseling parents the same basic relationship is required. The principles for counseling adults apply, but at the same time school counselors will have to try to limit themselves to helping parents deal with their children's school adjustment problems. Other problems will have to be referred to other agencies. This writer believes that eventually such services will be provided by agencies jointly supported by the local school district and mental health agencies. Now much can be done to help parents prevent school adjustment problems through cooperative efforts of school and community mental health personnel, to provide group counseling for parents and seminars on child rearing for parents. Often the latter can be provided through the local school district's adult education program.

CONSULTING TEACHERS

Functioning as a consultant for teachers is a very important aspect of every counselor's work, but it takes on more than the usual significance at the elementary school level. Most elementary school teachers work within a self-contained classroom in which they are the primary source of influence outside of the home for an entire school year. Fortunately, the typical elementary school teacher cares about his pupils, and he tries to understand them. Hence, he is quick to recognize the need for help from a counselor who can appreciate what he is trying to do for his pupils and who will also try to empathize with him. To benefit fully from what this counselor has to offer him, the teacher must trust the counselor—must believe that he can talk freely without fear of being criticized or evaluated. However, he will appreciate the counselor's help in criticizing and evaluating himself. Thus, the counselor must not be a line officer in the administrative staff. Though he uses his counseling skills to establish a relationship which is very similar to that which a counselor establishes with his clients, it is different. Rather than helping a teacher deal with his personal problems, the counselor tries to help the teacher discover why the pupil for whom the teacher sought assistance feels and behaves as he does; to help the teacher discover how he feels toward the child; to help the teacher discover and remove the blocks to learning, and often this requires visits to the teacher's classroom as well as private conferences with the teacher and case conferences with several teachers (Ohlsen, 1964) ; and where appropriate, to help the teacher make a referral to a school specialist or to an out-of-school specialist.

The counselor also consults teachers when he needs assistance in understanding his clients. In fact, asking teachers to help him is often the best way for a counselor to develop a relationship which encourages teachers to seek his assistance, but it must not be done for that purpose. If it is done merely for the purpose of manipulating teachers into seeking his help, teachers will see it for what it is and resent it. Counselors do need teachers' help in understanding their clients, and they had better seek teachers' aid only when they genuinely feel the need for it. There is no substitute for sincerity.

PROFESSIONAL BACKGROUND
AND PREPARATION

Of the questions noted at the beginning of this paper that teachers and principals often ask, only two remain to be answered: (1) Wouldn't it be better to make the classes smaller or to relieve teachers of some of their non-teaching duties so they could give more attention to their pupils rather than to use the funds to employ counselors? and (2) What will be the counselor's qualifications? Granted, reducing class size and providing other assistance to reduce time in non-teaching functions would enable most teachers to work more effectively with their pupils. However, such change would not alleviate the need for counselors. The duties defined in this paper for counselors require specialized professional preparation which most teachers do not have.

With reference to the qualifications of the elementary school counselor, McDougall and Reitan (1963) found that the elementary principals whom they polled also recognized the need for elementary school counselors to have special preparation not ordinarily required of teachers. If one looks at the responsibilities that principals would like most for them to assume (counseling children, consulting parents, helping teachers learn to use appraisal techniques to understand children and to identify children with special talents, and interpreting the guidance program in the community), one can readily understand why they prefer persons with elementary school teaching experience and want them to have special preparation in such courses as principles of guidance, individual testing, tests and measurements, and counseling theory.

Hill and Nitzschke (1961) reported that most master's degree level persons in elementary school guidance (and that is about the level of training of qualified persons at present) come chiefly from the elementary school teaching ranks. Even as late as 1961 they found that few graduate institutions had well-defined programs for the preparation of elementary school counselors. Major emphasis in the preparation programs existed in the areas of psychological foundations, guidance principles, counseling theory, and analysis of the individual. Moderate emphasis was placed upon the practicum, organization and administration, and research. Minor emphasis was placed upon information service, group work, social foundations, and remedial work. Nitzschke's findings on required courses suggest that graduate programs are similar today. However, he did note an increase in concern for preparation of elementary school guidance workers.

CONCLUSIONS

Finally, there is an important job to be done by the elementary school counselor and it is one which teachers cannot be expected to do. Moreover, special professional preparation is needed to prepare him for his work with pupils, parents, and teachers. At present more attention must be given to developing graduate programs to help elementary school counselors meet their professional responsibilities. More attention should be given to mental hygiene, personality development, the study of group process, group counseling methods for both children and parents, and the practicum, including in addition to supervised counseling, specific assistance in learning to function as a consultant to teachers and to apply their knowledge of group dynamics in helping teachers understand the forces at work within their classrooms.

Laymen are beginning to recognize the need for this service, and they are doing something about it. In the current session of Congress, Congressman Gibbons introduced a bill (House Bill 11322) to provide these services for at least primary school children. Though Congressman Gibbons defined the job to be done much as this writer defined the role of the elementary school counselor, he gave his specialist the title of child development specialist. The point is that funds for these services may soon be provided. Hence, the counseling and guidance profession must be prepared to act quickly and wisely in the interest of children. Professional leaders must cooperate in defining the job to be done, in planning graduate programs for the many persons who will be needed to fill the jobs, in recruiting and selecting persons for the training programs, and in using these specialists wisely once they are placed in the schools. Beginning with demonstration centers like those sponsored by the Guidance Department in the Office of State Superintendent of Public Instruction in Illinois shows great promise as a method for introducing these programs.

REFERENCES

Brison, D. W. April 1964. The role of the elementary school counselor. *Nat. elem., Princ., 43,* 41–44.

Ferris, R. R. September 1965. Guidance in the elementary school: a teacher can do best. *Nat. educ. Ass. J., 54,* 48.

Ginott, H. G. 1958. Play group therapy: a theoretical framework. *Int. J. Group Psychother., 8,* 410–418.

Hill, G. E., and D. F. Nitzschke. October 1961. Preparation programs in elementary school programs. *Personnel guid. J., 40,* 155–159.

Kaczkowski, H. R. 1965. *Role and function of the elementary school counselor.* A paper read before the Mount Zion Conference for Illinois Demonstration Center Personnel and Consultants.

Lambert, H. S. 1954. Program of guidance in eight elementary schools. *Guidance for today's children: fifty-third national elementary principal's yearbook,* 225–236.

Leiter, Sarah L. September 1965. Guidance in the elementary school: a specialist is invaluable. *Nat. educ. Ass. J., 54,* 49.

Mahan, T. W. February 1965. The elementary school counselor: disturber of the peace. *Nat. elem. Princ. 44,* 72–74.

McDougall, W. P., and H. M. Reitan. December 1963. The elementary school counselor: as perceived by elementary principals. *Personnel guid. J., 42,* 348–354.

Meeks, Anna R. March 1963. Elementary school counseling. *Sch. Couns., 10,* 108–111.

Moustakas, C. E. 1959. *Psychotherapy with children.* New York: Harper & Row.

Nitzschke, D. F. April 1965. Preparation programs in elementary school guidance: a status study. *Personnel guid. J., 43,* 751–756.

Ohlsen, M. M. 1964. *Guidance services in the modern school.* New York: Harcourt.

Waetjen, W. B. February 1965. Counseling services for the elementary school. *Nat. elem. Princ., 44,* 59–62.

Wilson, Frances M. 1956. Realities in the guidance programs in elementary schools. *Sch. Couns., 3,* 41–44.

Zeller, R., and R. Garber. 1964. *Demonstration centers for elementary guidance.* Mimeographed guides for Demonstration Center counselors and consultants.

Report of the ACES-ASCA Joint Committee

on the Elementary School Counselor,

April 2, 1966 (Working Paper)*

Miss Sarah L. Leiter, Chairman / Mrs. Verna Barke
Dr. Louise Eckerson / Mrs. Joan Helpern / Dr. Walter Lifton
Dr. Raymond A. Patouillet / Dr. Hyrum M. Smith

PREFACE

The purpose of this statement is to identify and provide guidelines for the development of the role of the guidance specialist in the elementary school as perceived by the membership of the Association for Counselor Education and Supervision and the American School Counselor Association. Guidance for all children is accepted as an integral component of the total educational experience in the elementary school. Guidance is defined as a continuing process concerned with determining and providing for the developmental needs of all pupils. This process is carried out through a systematically planned program of guidance functions which are a vital part of the elementary school's organized effort to provide meaningful educational experiences appropriate to each child's need and level of development.

The teacher's many responsibilities in the guidance process are recognized and respected, but the significant complementary role of personnel in addition to the teacher is also acknowledged. Other specialized professional personnel add new dimensions to an already ably functioning administrative and teaching staff,

* By permission.

providing additional knowledge and professional skill to strengthen existing programs and offering new services where there is evident need. Such additional personnel are essential if the elementary school is to provide the maximum opportunity for learning, enabling each child to learn effectively in terms of his own particular abilities and his own developmental process.

The elementary school guidance specialist, as one of these additional professional persons, has a significant contribution to make in the cooperative process of identifying and providing for the developmental needs of children. The elementary school has an opportunity to reach all the children of our society if we staff it so this is possible. Adding a guidance specialist will certainly not be a panacea. It will, however, be one effective way of providing additional professional resources to a school staff as it seeks to make educational experiences more meaningful to all pupils. The purpose of this ACES-ASCA Policy Statement is to describe, not what presently exists, but the contributions which a guidance specialist could make to an elementary school program.

PROFESSIONAL IDENTITY

The identity of the secondary school guidance specialist has been reasonably well established through the years and has been clearly stated in the ASCA Statement of Policy for Secondary School Counselors, published in 1964. The identity of the elementary school guidance specialist is in the process of developing.

The guidance specialist in the elementary school is a member of the professional staff of an individual elementary school who provides additional knowledge, understanding, and skill in the area of child growth and development and the behavioral sciences so that 1) individual pupil needs may be recognized and met more effectively, 2) experiences in the school may be made meaningful to all pupils, and 3) change in the school experiences may be more readily initiated when needed in terms of the developmental needs of pupils.

The guidance specialist makes his contribution to other staff members, parents, and pupils through the processes of consultation, coordination, counseling, interaction, and participation in efforts to develop meaningful school experiences and to initiate change when appropriate for the welfare of the child. He is a specialist in child growth and development with a broadly based multidisciplinary background in the behavioral sciences and a high degree of competence in human relations. He has thorough knowledge of the elementary school program including curriculum, the learning process, and school organization.

PROFESSIONAL RESPONSIBILITIES

The counselor as a member of the professional staff of an individual elementary school will share the responsibility for contributing to the positive growth and development of all children. He will contribute his knowledge and skill to that of parents and other staff members in the following ways:

A. Participating in creating an environment conducive to learning and growth for all children by:

1. Helping members of the school staff to understand the effect of their behavior on children, the interaction between the child and adults, and the importance of this interaction in the development of the child's self-concept and relationship with his peers.

2. Being a member of the group considering innovations in the school program, pointing out the psychological effects of such changes on the child.

3. Planning with the teacher ways to foster acceptance and valuing of individual differences in addition to academic achievement.

4. Maintaining a constant interest in the needs of the individual and the welfare of the pupil population while interacting with other staff members, equally concerned about the individual pupil but with additional responsibilities and different preparation and background.

5. Providing and interpreting significant research data about the developmental needs of all children and the relation of these needs to the learning process.

6. Maintaining a constant emphasis on the need for continuing evaluation of the school's effort to meet individual pupil needs.

B. Helping parents to understand the developmental needs of all pupils and working with parents to meet the individual needs of their own children in the school situation by:

1. Providing and interpreting information about the developmental needs of all children; helping parents to continue growth in understanding of behavior which is to be expected at different ages, of problems which are part of normal growth, of crises which may be expected in the process of growing up in home and school, and of ways of helping the child meet these concerns.

2. Providing and interpreting information about the uniqueness of each child; helping parents to develop further understanding of behavior which is unique and acceptable for one child and of the parent's natural concern for his own child.

3. Interpreting for parents the meaning of the school program, helping them to understand what the school is trying to do for their child, and determining the extent to which follow-up of the school's efforts is being made at home.

4. Counseling with individual parents and groups of parents in meeting specific needs.

5. Serving as a consultant and providing counseling when the need is indicated for individual parents and groups of parents
    a. in exploring new ways of helping a child
    b. in developing an understanding of the factors affecting children in the parent-child relationship
    c. in providing increased understanding of a child's potential, motivation, and unmet needs
    d. in providing an opportunity for parents to express their own feelings about the child and the school
6. Providing information about the school and community resources available to the parents and child and helping the parent to use these resources as needed.

C. Helping the individual child to grow in self-understanding and in positive maximum use of his potential by:

1. Consulting with the teacher and other staff members about individual pupil needs, with priority given to pre-school and primary grade children.
2. Mobilizing and coordinating the resources of the school for the development of the individual.
3. Observing and studying pupil behavior in the classroom and other school situations.
4. Counseling with individual pupils and groups of pupils when this process is selected as the most effective way of helping the child at a particular time.
5. Maintaining a continuing relationship with children in the regular school program beginning with the pre-school conference so crises intervention is possible when needed.
6. Consulting with the teachers and other staff members in exploring new ways of helping a child.
7. Participating in changing the environment for the child when this is the best solution for the welfare of the child, initiating this change if necessary.
8. Interpreting findings of research in relation to the child's awareness and acceptance of himself.
9. Identifying and facilitating referral of children with serious problems to other school or community services; serving as case manager, coordinating information from many sources, preparing case material for use by appropriate persons or agencies, providing liaison with these persons or agencies as the case develops.
10. Initiating efforts to provide needed referral services when these services are not available; participating with the teacher in dealing with the problem until the service can be provided.
11. Consulting with the teacher to determine the effect of the services of other persons on the child's learning and behavior in the classroom.

D. Participating in curriculum development and change by:

1. Interpreting the emotional effect of curricular experiences and materials on the child's concept of himself and on his relationships with others.
2. Sharing in the development of materials which are sensitive to the needs of children of varying interests and which help children develop realistic concepts of themselves and their environment.
3. Planning with teachers ways by which young children may approach an understanding of the world of work and may become aware of and develop their own strengths in dealing with people, ideas, and things.
4. Initiating change in the curriculum when appropriate for the welfare of the child.

The Counselor will contribute his knowledge and skill through the following processes:

A. *Counseling:* It is the premise of this statement that counseling both individually and in small group situations can provide assistance to children in the normal process of growing up as they seek to understand themselves, meet the developmental tasks of childhood, learn effectively, and develop realistic self-concepts. Emphasis is on the child as a learner in the school situation.

1. *Individual counseling* is the process of establishing with the child a relationship which enables him to communicate his needs, to explore his feelings, to learn about himself, to set goals and develop self direction in moving toward these goals. Often the child is trying to communicate his need for help and this provides an opportunity for the counselor to develop a greater understanding of the child and to become more sensitive to the child's needs. Such counseling is not necessarily a communication of words on the part of the child. The content of the counseling process will reflect the developmental level of the child and may be through play media rather than verbal communication. The counselor represents to the child a non-evaluative adult in a helping relationship.
2. *Group counseling* is the process of establishing relationships with a small group of children enabling them to communicate with the counselor and each other certain identified needs. Such counseling is particularly helpful in personal and social growth as children have an opportunity to react and interact and to work out some of their behavioral changes. Group counseling provides a major learning experience in human relations.

B. *Consultation* is the process of sharing with another person or group of persons information and ideas, of combining knowledge into new patterns, and of making mutually agreed upon decisions about the next steps needed. The Counselor as a professional person with a background in child growth and development and the behavioral sciences helps parents to grow in understanding of their children in the school situation. He may provide insight for the parent about the child's potential, his motivation, and his unmet needs. In turn the Counselor learns from parents about their children and offers them a chance to express their feelings about the child and the school.

C. *Coordination* is the process of relating all efforts for helping the child into a meaningful pattern. The Counselor member of the school staff coordinates the organized effort of the school and community for the individual child as a learner in the school situation. Coordination is the method used to bring into focus the school's total effort in the child's behalf, eliminating duplication of effort and insuring follow-through on decisions made and policies established. This involves close working relationships between the counselor, teacher, parent, and other school and community personnel whose contacts with the child in the school situation are significant.

PROFESSIONAL COMPETENCIES AND PREPARATION

The functions to be performed by the Counselor in the elementary school determine the personal qualifications and the professional preparation required for this position. To carry out the functions described above the Counselor will need:

1. Depth of knowledge in:
   child growth and development
   theories of counseling
   group dynamics
   interpersonal relations
   psychology of learning
   personality dynamics
   curriculum of the elementary school
2. Background and understanding in:
   community and culture
   elementary school program
   curriculum trends and developments
   basic goals of guidance
   organization of pupil personnel services
   research procedures
   reading program
   world of work
3. Specialized skill in:
   observation and interpretation of behavior, particularly the interpretation
       of feeling from non-verbal behavior
   consultation with parents
   counseling—individually and with groups
   interpretation of the methods by which children communicate their needs

use of toys, art, and other media for communicating with the child
case conferences and case records
statistics
educational measurements
psychological testing
organization and administration of guidance services
4. Personal qualifications which include:
courage to bring about change
valuing of the individual
initiative
high degree of sensitivity to the feelings of children and adults
scholastic aptitude
emotional stability
competence in human relations
depth and variety of interests

The following statements are pertinent to counselor preparation of the counselor as a Counselor:

1. The preparation should be broadly based, multi-disciplinary in nature. Such a program would include study in several disciplines—anthropology, economics, education, philosophy, psychology, and sociology. It is hoped that appropriate programs designed specifically for elementary school counselors will be cooperatively planned by the university and college departments concerned.

2. An individually planned program of graduate study should be based on the undergraduate program and professional experience of the person concerned.

3. The individual's previous work experience is especially significant. The value of teaching experience in the elementary school is recognized but it is felt that knowledge of the school program and processes can be gained through a planned program of experiences in the elementary school as a part of the graduate program. Such experiences would include supervised field experience and/or an internship program providing firsthand knowledge of the curriculum and of the reality of working with children in groups. The value of different types of work experience is also recognized, especially in the development of skill in human relations and understanding of the community. The prospective counselor should be encouraged to gain work experiences in addition to those directly related to education.

4. The Counselor will work as a member of the team providing pupil personnel services. This perspective should be established in the program of preparation.

5. The Counselor must also see himself and the school as an integral part of a total community effort. Understanding of community structure and resources is essential in the program. There will be a need for clearly perceived relationships and definition of functions in working with community personnel.

Chapter 4

THE GUIDANCE COUNSELOR
AS CONSULTANT

Consulting is one of the primary functions of the counselor. Some educators believe that consulting is the only feasible approach in the elementary school because of the large number of pupils to be served by each counselor. They see no other way of implementing the developmental approach than through consultation with teachers, parents, and administrators. Others, including the author, do not believe one must choose between consulting or counseling, but maintain that the two functions supplement each other. Counseling serves to help the counselor understand the child, and enables him to consult more effectively. The consultant relationship provides the counselor with a better understanding of the environment in which the child lives.

This chapter differentiates consulting from counseling, develops some of the premises that support the consultant function, and presents the rationale for consulting. The nature of the consulting relationship with teachers is discussed, and consulting procedures are presented. Attention is given to the implications of the consultant role for counselor education.

THE DIFFERENCE BETWEEN CONSULTING
AND COUNSELING

Consulting is a process by which teachers, parents, principals, and other significant adults in the life of the child communicate about him. The consultation is held at the request of those significant adults who are in need of assistance or information that will increase the effectiveness of their work with a child

106

or a group of children. The child is usually not present at the discussion. Consultation involves coordinating and exchanging information. Joint planning and collaboration is emphasized in contrast to the superior-inferior relationships of some consultation situations. The purpose of the consultation is to consider all of the available data and formulate decisions about future procedures. Recommendations that ensue usually consider the uniqueness of the teacher as well as the individuality of the child.

In contrast, counseling occurs in a one-to-one or small-group situation where there is a child or children in need of a personal relationship with the counselor. The counseling process facilitates changes in perceptions, convictions, attitudes, and behavior through the communication that occurs during the counseling. The author's purpose here is not to discuss the relative merits of the two functions but to define the difference in roles.

ADVOCATES OF CONSULTATION

A number of leaders in the field of guidance and counseling have favored the consultant role. One of the first was Patouillet (1957), who took the position that the school guidance counselor should serve as a consultant, or resource person, working primarily with teachers, parents, and the school principal. His article is included in Chapter 2 of this book.

Wrenn (1962), writing for The Commission on Guidance in American Schools, underlined the importance of consultation. His primary recommendation was that the counselor work with both students and staff on the most unique function of the school: development of the intellect. Wrenn advocated a counseling program based on the developmental needs of the total range of students rather than on the remedial needs and crisis points in the lives of a few students. This focus can only be achieved through an adequate emphasis on consultation in the guidance service.

Wrenn had an opportunity to review his thinking by discussing his report in a majority of the states and receiving written reactions to it. In a talk entitled "The Counselor in a Changing World Revisited" (1964), his slight revision in thinking indicated he would now give even more importance to the consultant role.

Hyrum Smith and Louise Eckerson of the U.S. Office of Education have always been advocates of consultation as the major focus for the guidance service. Their study (1966) asked elementary school principals to list the six most important functions for child development consultants (that is, guidance counselors). Over three-fourths of these principals included consultation with parents, consultation with teachers, and counseling with children among the most important guidance functions.

Principals clearly consider consultation to be a primary function of the elementary school counselor. Oldridge (1964) did a study contrasting the psychotherapeutic role with the consultant role in an elementary school district. In the schools which utilized therapy, the primary function of the guidance worker was counseling children who suffered from emotional maladjustment. In the schools which utilized consultation, guidance workers accepted any type of referral, although only emotionally maladjusted children were considered in this study. At the beginning of the study, the guidance personnel involved showed no significant preference for either of the two roles. At the end of the study, they showed significant preference for the consultant role. During the study, nine of the ten schools shifted their preference significantly in favor of the consultant role. The consultant role was preferred both by guidance workers and school staffs. There was little evidence that psychotherapy was more effective than consultant procedures.

The Joint Committee of the Association for Counselor Education and Supervision and the American School Counselor Association have identified consultation as one of the three major responsibilities of the counselor (ACES-ASCA Report, 1966). This report can be studied in detail in Chapter 3.

THE RATIONALE FOR
GUIDANCE CONSULTATION

The rationale for guidance consultation proceeds from the belief that only consultation—indirect service involving teachers, parents, and administrators—can fulfill the objectives of elementary school guidance: developmental help for all children. Because of the counselor-pupil ratio, an emphasis on counseling is inevitably an emphasis on remedial guidance, with the result that relatively few children are reached. Consultation, on the other hand, meets the problems of increased demands for services.

The rapid knowledge explosion has forced the teacher to become concerned with new developments in the curriculum, often resulting in less time being available for child study. Consultation remedies this situation, permitting the teacher to examine the impact of the instructional process on children.

Consultation should result in increased guidance competencies by the teacher, in contrast to providing a service that is used primarily to refer children to a specialist. Consulting helps the teacher develop an understanding of human behavior which he can apply in all of his contacts with children. In this way, consultation may reduce the number of children needing individual attention at a later date.

One of the critical needs at the elementary school level is to integrate the guidance function into the educative process and curriculum. Consultation provides an opportunity for the counselor to serve as an agent of change. He can help the school staff analyze its philosophy, policy, and procedures as they affect the total development of the children.

The teacher also must play a key guidance role in the elementary school. The consultant can help him by demonstrating guidance procedures and supplying material for the classroom guidance program. The consultant helps the teacher understand the affective aspects of the instructional process: the effect of his behavior on his pupils.

One of the beliefs upon which the counselor as consultant operates is that guidance services can be improved most extensively through increasing the effectiveness of the teacher. If the counselor is to be viewed as a vital member of the educational team, he must make a primary commitment to the consultant role.

THE RELATIONSHIP
WITH ADMINISTRATION

Research studies of elementary school principals have indicated that the majority of principals believe the guidance counselor should serve as a consultant. However, in some schools there is confusion between the roles of the principal, counselor, and other specialists.

The consultant role, as we have described it, can only operate effectively in a school system where there is an atmosphere of trust and acceptance. For this, the cooperation of the principal is essential. It is the principal who provides not only the physical facilities but also the atmosphere which fosters professional growth. The counselor himself has no supervisory or administrative responsibilities over teachers but serves as a specialist who helps them achieve their primary objectives with their pupils.

THE CONSULTING RELATIONSHIP
WITH TEACHERS

The guidance counselor is a specialist in human relationships. As a consultant, he is particularly valuable because he is actively engaged in the teachers' problems and provides a helping relationship for them.

Consulting is a collaboration: The specialist does not provide ready answers. The teacher and the consultant work together to understand and resolve problems. They formulate hypotheses and tentative recommendations that are mutually acceptable, and they should schedule a follow-up meeting to enable them to evaluate the effectiveness of their recommendations.

The consultant's relationship with the teacher is based upon mutual trust and respect, and requires that consultant and teacher share the same goals. In many ways it is similar to the counseling relationship in that it provides an atmosphere for cooperative problem solving. It avoids mere advice giving or vague generalizations. The consultant listens, empathizes, and concentrates on the teacher's perception of the situation.

In observing counselors at work, one mistaken attitude quickly becomes apparent. Counselors tend to listen to students and promote their self-understanding and decision-making ability; but counselors' work with parents and teachers is usually devoid of involvement and is often nothing more than mere advising. Counselors must not forget that the techniques involved in establishing a relationship apply when dealing with teachers and parents, as well as when dealing with children. Consulting with parents will be developed more extensively in Chapter 10.

CONSULTING PROCEDURES

The counselor is trained to provide sensitive insights into the dynamics of human behavior. He assists the teacher in understanding and dealing with the uniqueness of the child. In many instances, he is a mediator between the child and the significant others in his environment.

It is up to the consultant and the teacher to decide upon the type of information needed to understand the child. The teacher can provide anecdotes and samples of work. The consultant can provide unique observations of the classroom situation. Classroom observation by the consultant focuses on understanding the interaction between the child, his peers, and his teacher. The consultant attempts to answer the following questions: What is the social meaning of this behavior? What are the consequences of the interaction? How does the child seek to be known? What is the self-image he is maintaining? If the consultant is not acquainted with the child, he may conduct a brief diagnostic interview enabling him to check the impressions he obtained through observation.

The consultant and the teacher then meet to discuss the information they have collected in order to develop some hypotheses and tentative recommendations. Recommendations are developed on the basis of the teacher's personality and his capacity to carry them out. The consultant contributes his understanding of the dynamics of human behavior. He helps clarify specific factors about the child which are significant for the educational process. It is vital to remember that the first recommendations are tentative, and that they must be re-evaluated before they are permanently established.

Although the consultant has his most dramatic effect upon teachers in helping them in their dealings with an individual or a group, he also will be responsible for in-service programs. Such programs should help the teacher develop a general understanding of human behavior, learn the relationship of the curriculum to the child, and be able to examine the effect of instructional methods on the learning process.

IMPLICATIONS FOR
COUNSELOR EDUCATION

Because of the emerging role of the counselor as consultant, particular care must be given to the selection of the elementary school counselor. He must be capable of relating effectively with adults as well as with children. He must be able to communicate effectively with a variety of people in the child's life.

Counselor education must include course work which will provide skills in human relationships and communication. It must also provide experiences in consultant relationships with teachers as well as children. The practicum must include experiences within school settings working with the concerns of teachers and administrators. This will enable the counselor to become aware of the problems involved in establishing the atmosphere for consultation.

Eckerson and Smith believe that the elementary school child's needs call for a particular guidance approach distinct from that used with adolescents. They suggest that the functions of the guidance consultant require the development of a new discipline. They present the roles of the guidance consultant, school social worker, and school psychologist, and they suggest a number of innovations for the selection and preparation of consultants. In their estimation, the teacher continues to be the person who works most closely with each child, but his opportunity to teach is enhanced by the presence of the guidance consultant.

Lee proposes that guidance consultants should assist teachers in working with children and parents. He sees the consultant as one who increases the effectiveness of the teacher. He specifies collection, interpretation, and utilization of information as functions which facilitate the planning of programs for individual children. While he lists work with parents, individual children, or groups of children, he emphasizes assistance to the teacher to make him more effective in the educational process with the child.

The article by Dinkmeyer describes a consultant program also directed at increasing teacher competency with pupil personnel problems. He discusses specific procedures in establishing the consultant relationship and in diagnosing and modifying behavior.

Kaczkowski believes that consultation primarily helps the staff to evaluate the affective aspects of the instructional process. Recognizing that consultant suggestions tend to be met with resistance, he explains the importance of helping the teacher and the class accept procedures that enhance individuality. The basis for an effective working relationship with the school principal is discussed. In contrast to Faust, Kaczkowski believes that consulting should adhere to many principles of the counseling relationship. He feels that parents should be helped to develop an understanding of their child's behavior.

Faust states that consultation differs from counseling in its focus on external variables rather than on the teacher's feelings. This definition of the consultant role implies that each school should employ two counselors: one as a consultant and the other for counseling of children and teachers. This dichotomy would be new to the counseling profession. Consultation would occur most often through in-service course work and staffing of cases. The article makes a valuable contribution by clearly differentiating the roles of consultant and curriculum specialist.

REFERENCES

ACES-ASCA Joint Committee on the Elementary School Counselor report. April 1966.

Oldridge, B. December 1964. Two roles for elementary school guidance personnel. *Personnel guid. J.*, *43* (No. 4).

Patouillet, R. May 1957. Organizing for guidance in the elementary school. *Teach. Coll. Rec.*, *58*, 8.

Smith, H., and Louise Eckerson. 1966. *Guidance services in elementary schools: a national survey.* Washington, D.C.: Superintendent of Documents, U.S. Government Printing Office.

Wrenn, C. G. 1964. The counselor in a changing world revisited. *Teach. Coll. J.*, Terre Haute, Ind.: Indiana State College.

———. 1962. *The counselor in a changing world.* Washington, D.C.: American Personnel and Guidance Association.

Elementary School Guidance:
The Consultant*

Louise O. Eckerson / Hyrum M. Smith

Fifty years ago, the school boy's world was small, and man remained in it. Cities were communities in which people had roots and knew each other, and the streets were safe at night. Jobs were plentiful, the schools were uncrowded, the dullard dropped by the wayside, and teachers could teach those who wished to learn.

Now, fifty years later, the child in elementary school begins to feel adult pressures, and youth problems relating to college admission as well as underachievement, dropouts, and delinquency. The times demand that children be prepared to meet the challenge of a forward-looking society, that they be equipped in education, physical health, and emotional stability to work at jobs which do not yet exist. Guidance, starting in the early school years and continuing at least throughout school, is a partial solution to the gigantic problem of preparing youth for the unknown future.

The elementary school guidance movement, focused on facilitating a sound educational foundation in the child's early years, is spreading throughout the

* *School Life*, July 1962, Washington, D.C.: U.S. Department of Health, Education and Welfare, Office of Education. By permission.

country. It has gained momentum—even without financial encouragement from the National Defense Education Act, which has accelerated guidance in secondary schools. Its existence is just beginning to be recognized by representation at the State level, although State certification rarely makes any distinction between the qualifications required for guidance personnel in elementary and secondary schools. Only a few colleges and universities have initiated graduate programs specifically tailored to prepare the guidance consultant who works with young children.

The guidance movement for children in the lower grades has received its impetus from local educators and parents who believe that professional assistance given to the child at an early age will prevent his developing serious problems later. Across the country, the aim of early guidance is summed up in two words, "identification and prevention."

A review of some outstanding programs in elementary schools suggests the following definition: Guidance in the elementary schools assists *all* children directly, and indirectly through their teachers and parents, in making maximum use of their abilities for their own development and for the good of society. The emphasis is on the early recognition of intellectual, emotional, social, and physical strengths and weaknesses, on the developing of talents, on the prevention of conditions which interfere with learning, and on the early use of available resources to meet the needs of children.

Community planning for "identification and prevention" has centered attention on designating the services most needed within a school, and then looking for the person with education and experience to perform those services. Many communities have chosen an elementary school teacher who seemed to possess the necessary insight and encouraged him to supplement his education with courses relating to guidance and, subsequently, to assume the role of guidance consultant. Usually, the only graduate program available to him was designed as preparation for guidance work and counseling with adolescent students whose problems were conceived to be largely educational and vocational.

The elementary school child's needs do not call for emphasis on educational and vocational counseling; few of these youngsters are mature enough to make valid decisions for themselves by means of the counseling interview, nor are they concerned with choices of courses or vocations. The problems of grade-school pupils are caused by conditions which interfere with learning in school, and these may be attributed to tensions in the home, physical defects or poor health, poor social relations, emotional blocks, and intellectual limitations, as well as unsatisfactory methods of instruction and pupil-teacher relations. What, then, should be the qualifications of a guidance consultant who would be able to identify early signs of trouble in a child and get remedial help for him?

There is no simple answer, for children have many kinds of problems. For example, if a child's reading problem is caused by faulty reading techniques, perhaps a former teacher in the primary grades with courses in guidance and remedial reading might be highly qualified to handle it. If, however, his reading difficulty is caused by emotional stress in his home or lack of social adjustment, or by a visual defect or his physical condition, a specialist in another field might possess the requisite knowledge and understanding to identify the source of trouble and take steps toward helping him.

In addition to poor readers, elementary school classrooms hold children who are retarded, aggressive, withdrawn, unloved, undernourished, overweight, defective in speech and hearing, and who have a host of other limitations. Classrooms also hold gifted and talented children whose abilities are not recognized or challenged, and whose mediocre performance is accepted at home and at school. What qualifications should the consultant have to work with these children?

The function of the guidance consultant, dictated by the varied needs of children, raises the question: Are guidance services in elementary schools developing as a new discipline? If guidance functions at this level are not teacher functions, nor the functions of the high school counselor, then it is possible that the guidance of young school children may be moving in the direction of a new discipline requiring a new focus on professional preparation. And if so, what should be emphasized?

Some educators believe that early guidance is an extension of the elementary school teacher's job and that consequently only a person with teaching experience can effectively work with teachers in the child's behalf. And some believe that no essential difference exists in the functions of guidance personnel at the elementary and secondary school levels. Others maintain that guidance of elementary school children require the knowledge, insight, and techniques possessed by the school psychologist, school social worker, clinical psychologist, psychiatric social worker, or school nurse.

The profusion of specialists nominated for the post of being responsible for the guidance of grade-school children attests to a diversity of opinion, both on problems and on remedies. Each specialist sees the problems which children bring into the classroom, or develop there, as they pertain to his branch of knowledge. Also, each specialist who attempts to diagnose a difficulty may be limited to some extent in his grasp of those causal factors which lie outside of his particular field. Each has depth in the knowledge and techniques of his own discipline; each has breadth without depth in some aspects of allied disciplines. Which professional emphasis with what techniques will be most effective in helping children with their problems is a debatable question. Since the answer awaits clarifying evidence, it seems practical to encourage experimentation and evaluation of pilot programs before standardizing guidance services and the qualifications for guidance personnel in elementary schools.

In some states specialists who have different professional titles but whose services overlap are working in elementary school guidance programs. In California and Connecticut, for instance, schools recognize the contributions of graduate preparation in guidance, psychology, and social work by using persons with professional training in these fields in their guidance programs. A pamphlet published by the Connecticut State Department of Education (1955) delineates the similarities and dissimilarities in the preparation and roles of the guidance consultant (and counselor at the secondary level), the school social worker, and the school psychologist. It has this to say of the common aspects of their functions:

> a. Each tries to help pupils to utilize their abilities more fully, to overcome problems, to understand themselves more clearly, and to make better progress in school. . . . As a part of this help, each studies pupils' backgrounds, abilities, and psychological forces. Each works with the pupil individually or may seek special help for him from others.
> b. Each renders service in cooperation with the school staff. The teacher has the major educational responsibility for each pupil; the social worker, psychologist, and counselor are concerned with facilitating the work of the teacher. . . .
> c. Each develops and maintains information and records about pupils. . . .
> d. Each has a real interest in research. . . .
> e. Each of the three professions shares with other school personnel a responsibility for working with parents and community groups to facilitate the progress of individual children and also to interpret the work of the school. . . . (pp. 36–38)

The pamphlet answers the question, What are the distinctive emphases of the work of each of the three professions? "The *social worker* has emphasized work with pupils who have, or appear likely to have, serious problems of school adjustment which also involve aspects of social or emotional adjustment. These problems often can be more successfully solved if home or other community forces are utilized to help and the social worker has a major role in work with both parents and community social agencies. . . . The *psychologist* has emphasized work with pupils who have serious learning or behavior difficulties due to mental, physical, or emotional handicaps and for whom an intensive clinical psychological diagnosis is sought by the school. . . . The *counselor* has emphasized work with all pupils in the school on educational . . . and personal problems which are common among the age groups with which he is working" (pp. 36–38).

Writing about elementary school guidance services, Raymond Patouillet (1957) says: "The school guidance worker (*counselor, psychologist, visiting teacher* [now generally called social worker]) works primarily with and through teachers as well as with parents and the principal, serving as consultant and resource person to them. The guidance person works with children through the class setting, although individual conferences with parents and children are held if referral to an outside agency is indicated or if individual testing or interviewing is agreed upon by the teacher and guidance person. I have grouped counselors, psychologists, and visiting teachers together under the general heading of guidance worker because I see an increasing number of similarities and a decreasing number of differences among their respective roles." (p. 435)

In discussing the role of the elementary school guidance consultant, Patouillet adds: "The term counselor therefore no longer adequately describes his function if we think of counseling as a one-to-one relationship. . . . The guidance worker . . . is essentially a consultant . . . in human relations who involves in a cooperative enterprise all those who affect the development of the child."

Patouillet's proposal for meeting the personnel needs of elementary school guidance programs is twofold: (1) Utilization of persons who have already completed programs in guidance, psychology, or social work; and (2) a two-year graduate program which cuts across the areas of guidance, psychology, and social work. His proposals are not intended to eliminate the need for and use of itinerant school psychologists and school social workers who work intensively with children on a referral basis.

Both the Connecticut pamphlet and Patouillet recognize common functions belonging to three disciplines which are important to the guidance of young children. This idea presents a challenge to determine through experimentation and research the best procedures for selecting and preparing persons to fill children's needs for guidance.

The consideration of guidance personnel recruited from fields other than teaching was recommended by the 1960 White House Conference on Children and Youth:

> That all States require the certification of guidance counselors and other specialized personnel. That the qualifications for certification be continually reviewed and strengthened in accordance with the latest research findings in the field; and *that they recognize and give credit to appropriate training and work experience in lieu of classroom teaching* (italics are ours).

A program designed to serve in lieu of classroom teaching might resemble an internship required by the University of Michigan in preparing school psychologists. Such an internship could be planned to familiarize both social workers and psychologists with the practices and problems of teachers and children at the elementary school level. William Clark Trow (1961) describes the internship:

> All students preparing to become school psychologists will enroll for a practicum requiring three hours a day for a minimum of one semester in the University School. During this time under the guidance of a special supervisor they will attend a number of different grades and classes ranging from the kindergarten through grade 12, participate in instructional as well as measurement and guidance activities, and study and follow through on individual instructional and adjustment problem cases. We believe that this range of experience will be even more valuable than that of teaching a particular grade or subject for a year or two. (pp. 84–85)

Such an internship could give social workers and psychologists a firsthand knowledge of elementary schools. Just as a teacher gains his understanding of children and schools by his course in practice teaching, the psychologist and social worker could supplement their formal preparation with experiences provided by an elementary school internship. This supervised internship might well give them a broader understanding of children of all ages than they would gain from three years of teaching experience in the sixth or the first grade.

Universities are beginning to organize graduate programs to prepare guidance consultants for elementary schools. Among them is Teachers College, Columbia University, which offers one-year, two-year, and three-year programs. It recommends the two-year sequence for those who will work on a local elementary school staff. It is inevitable that more and more graduate schools will specify courses to prepare elementary school teachers, and perhaps persons with undergraduate majors in behavioral sciences, for guidance in elementary schools.

Hill and Nitzschke (1961) report information given by 154 directors of master's degree programs recommended for elementary school guidance personnel. They conclude:

> Preparation programs for guidance workers in elementary schools are as yet not well-defined. Some of these programs make little, if any, differentiation between preparation for the elementary school and preparation for the secondary school. Very few universities have clearly planned programs for the preparation of guidance workers in elementary schools . . . It would seem that the time is at hand for leaders in elementary education and in guidance to combine their judgments to formulate a clearer definition of "elementary school guidance." (pp. 155–159)

Who should be selected and how he should be prepared to achieve the goals of elementary school guidance may vary from school to school because the problems of large number of children differ from community to community —from slums to suburbs, from industrial to agricultural areas, from native to foreign culture groups. Moreover, a school's need for guidance services varies in proportion to the available services of social workers and psychologists. Each school, before employing a specialist, should therefore analyze the problems of its student body and select the person whose education and experience prepares him to offer the required services, regardless of his title.

When school social workers and school psychologists are selected as guidance consultants, they may wish to retain their identity in name. However, many people have the mistaken belief that social workers help only the poor, and that psychologists work only with the unbalanced. For this reason, it might serve the purposes of public acceptance as well as uniformity if such noninstructional specialists, engaged in helping children learn in school, were known by a single title such as counselor, child consultant, or guidance consultant. (The term *guidance consultant* is used here to differentiate between guidance personnel in the elementary school and counselors in the secondary school, and to indicate the major function of the former—which is usually designated as consulting with teachers and parents.)

It seems most expedient at this time to suggest tentative procedures without commitment to any one. Standardizing the qualifications now for guidance personnel in elementary schools without clear evidence from research that persons with those qualifications make the best guidance consultants for all schools may jeopardize the program by limiting its scope and quality. Therefore, the following hypotheses are offered to encourage experimentation in the selection and graduate preparation of guidance consultants:

1. That the candidate's background be rich in liberal arts with the undergraduate major in elementary education, or perhaps in psychology, sociology, or related areas.

2. That the candidate be required to have had several years' employment in a related field in a school, clinic, or comparable agency. In such work, through experiences in living, he gains background and maturity, both necessary qualifications of a guidance consultant. Some work experience with adults is also desirable.

3. That flexibility characterize the planning of a graduate student's program. It should not be assumed that every candidate for a degree in elementary school guidance has had the same background and needs the same courses. An appraisal of the candidate's academic history and experience may reveal that he is familiar with some information, concepts, and techniques important in work of the guidance consultant. An individualized graduate program also makes it possible for a prospective guidance consultant to take courses to meet special needs of a particular school in which he expects to be employed.

4. That the preparation for guidance consultants be specifically tailored to the functions of elementary school guidance, which may be telescoped and expressed for convenience, as "identification and prevention." The professional knowledge and techniques required in these functions are found in such fields as elementary school education, guidance, psychology, social work, and health. Therefore, professional preparation may well include these fields.

5. That a comprehensive and extensive internship in elementary school guidance be accepted in lieu of teaching experience.

6. That appropriate professional experience in working with children be accepted in lieu of teaching experience.

7. That the candidate qualify in personality characteristics. It is difficult to evaluate objectively the quality of personality that can reach and assist children and consult with adults who work with children. With an awareness of traits to be sought, however, an approach might be made to a subjective evaluation of personality.

A promising candidate may be described in these terms: He is a person who enjoys helping others and who, by responding sensitively, is able to produce an atmosphere of mutual liking and respect with both children and adults. His natural endowment and education give him significant insight into the feeling and thinking of people, especially children, and an appreciation of their values, which may differ from his own. He is able to help parents and teachers understand the child who needs to belong or who needs to be alone; to encourage, rather than stifle, those tendencies that lead to creative thinking and to respect both areas of conformity and areas of individuality.

Education anticipates strides in communicating a vast increase of knowledge to students through the use of programmed instruction (teaching machines), airborne television, language laboratory equipment, and other new teaching equipment and teaching techniques. It is logical to expect the schools to meet the bombardment of knowledge with new techniques and personnel. The most efficient teacher cannot do the job that the times demand and also serve as guidance consultant as well as psychologist and social worker. These persons are needed by the significant number of children who have major problems and by the much larger number of children who occasionally need specialized assistance. In addition, all children profit indirectly from the continuous presence of a guidance consultant who helps understand the perplexing phases of a normal child's development and the danger signals of trouble.

The teacher will continue to be the person who works most closely with each child. He will have the opportunity to teach children who are ready to learn when deterrents to learning have been reduced through the services of guidance consultants and other pupil personnel.

Guidance consultants are at the center of guidance programs in elementary schools. Patterns of selection and preparation of these persons now are varied. As the movement grows, experimentation and evaluation should determine the preparation which can contribute most effectively to the needs of children. In the meantime, we urge schools to use an eclectic approach in organizing elementary school guidance programs within pupil personnel services to the end that each child shall benefit from a cooperative effort of all professional personnel.

REFERENCES

Connecticut State Department of Education. 1955. *The team approach in pupil personnel services.* Hartford, Conn.: The Department.

Hill, G. E., and D. F. Nitzschke. October 1961. Preparation programs in elementary school guidance. *Personnel guid. J., 60* (No. 2), 155–159.

Patouillet, R. May 1957. Organizing for guidance in the elementary school. *Teach. Coll. Rec., 58,* 8, 431–438. New York: Columbia University.

Trow, W. C. February 1961. Diagnostician, Ed.S., and Ph.D. programs for school psychologists in Michigan. *Amer. Psychologist, 16,* 84–85.

White House Conference on Children and Youth. 1960. *Recommendations, composite report of forum findings.* Washington, D.C.: U.S. Government Printing Office.

Is a Guidance Consultant

Needed in the Elementary

Schools?*

J. Murray Lee

The answer to the question proposed by the topic is yes. It is obvious, however, at least in a great many school systems in Illinois, that school personnel don't feel that is the answer for there are few guidance consultants in the elementary schools. Some states have made excellent beginnings in this area including our sister state of Missouri, which recently provided some state support for elementary counselors. All of us are well aware of the tremendous problem of dropouts. During the 1960's, the Department of Labor estimates some 7.5 million youngsters will drop out of school before graduating. About 2.5 million will not go beyond the eighth grade. We are well aware that studies of dropouts show that these pupils are poor readers, have poor self-concepts and poor peer acceptance. It is only too apparent that these three factors have their roots in the elementary school.

The White House Conference on Children and Youth (1960) reported that "No reliable data exist on the prevalence of childhood psychiatric disorders. But in 1955, 1,200 outpatient psychiatric clinics in the country reported that about 212,000 children under the age of twenty-one have been under diagnosis or care during the war" (p. 39).

Here again emotional disorders have their roots in early childhood as well as in situations in the present. We have been operating elementary schools for a long time without guidance consultants. The simple answer seems to me that teachers need a great deal more help and assistance in working with children and parents than is now available in most schools.

The last five years have seen some other startling developments take place in elementary education. A few of these include Paul Torrence's significant studies on *Creativity in Children,* Ken Wann's study on *Intellectual Development of Young Children,* new approaches to the culturally deprived, pressures to start reading at a much earlier age, newer mathematics, individualized reading, newer approaches to science, newer approaches to develop thinking in children such as Suchman's *Scientific Inquiry,* introduction of foreign languages, increasing interest in improving the social studies, educational television, pro-

* *Illinois Guidance and Personnel Association Newsletter,* Fall 1963. By permission.

grammed instruction, team teaching, various methods of organizing pupils for instructions, including ability grouping in some schools. Is it any wonder that teachers and principals feel harassed by these proposals?

If the pace of developments have been rapid in the last five years, we can expect marked increase in the next ten years. The modern computer makes possible educational research on a scale that was previously only dreamed of. For instance, a couple of our doctoral students are working on dissertations which involve measures of thirty-one variables from grades four to six. The inter-correlation tables of these thirty-one variables was just a minor phase of their study. One phase covers 700 T tests. The analysis of such data several years ago would have been utterly impossible.

It is obvious from a great many studies that problems of children in school have their roots in the elementary school. Some of my friends who have had experiences with elementary counselors have informed me that due to the efforts of the elementary counselors they have fewer problems in the secondary school. I have just one study to quote, but this study, I am sure, could be multiplied many times. This study was done by William E. Paulo on improving reading in the Junior High School. It was a study made in California in which able readers with IQ's from 90–110 were compared with a comparable group two or more years retarded in reading. The conclusions of the study as reported in the September, 1963 issue of *Childhood Education* are:

a. The failure pattern unique to the disabled reader group had been a long-term one, originating for *each child* in the first grade where he was placed in the lowest group.

b. This pattern of failure with its accompanying self-perception had had a markedly negative effect upon the attitudes of the disabled readers toward school and reading.

c. By the time he had reached junior high school age, the disabled reader's negative attitude toward reading was firmly fixed as an integral part of his total personality.

The usual testing program in most elementary schools is limited to intelligence tests and achievement tests. It is clear from the recent research that these provide very inadequate means of identification, that these two measures are inadequate in a modern elementary school. We also need measures for creativity, anxiety, and the self-concept. Teachers will certainly need assistance in gathering and interpreting this kind of information. They will also need help in working with teaching methods involving discovery, inquiry, and creative approaches. These two areas help define the kind of abilities that the guidance consultant should have.

Dr. Eli M. Bower in an article in *Educational Leadership* for October, 1963, described a three-act play about a group of men who were fishing on the bank of a swiftly flowing stream. In Act I there were a host of drowning children in mid-river. The fishermen jump in and manage to save one or two of them.

In Act II the fishermen move upstream where the current is less swift so they can pull out and save a greater number of children. As Act III opens, one fisherman is seen departing upstream. When asked by his companions where he is going, he replies, "I'm going upstream to find out who's throwing those kids in." The role of the elementary guidance consultant would be to stand upstream and keep so many children from being thrown in.

Dr. Cottingham's speech at the APGA Convention in Boston was reproduced in the Fall 1963 issue of the NEWSLETTER of the Illinois Guidance and Personnel Association. He defines some seven approaches to elementary counseling. You can decide whether the following proposal constitutes an eighth or not. The consultant should serve as an extra pair of eyes for the teacher to help him see children in situations differently than he would otherwise, an extra pair of hands to help gather more data concerning children, an extra brain to look at this data somewhat differently than the teacher might look at it, and as an extra mouth to occasionally help teachers interpret children to parents; certainly a pair of ears would be extremely helpful to listen to the teacher's side of the story. Thus, out of this concept grows a list of functions of the guidance consultants. The functions of the guidance consultant should be as follows:

1. To make possible an increase in the amount of significant information which can be gathered concerning children.

2. To help teachers better interpret such information and plan programs for individual children. This would mean working with individual teachers and with groups to help them better understand children.

3. To help teachers work with parents.

4. To work closely with the principal in determining the unique needs and problems of the school.

5. To help teachers to experiment with new ideas and evaluate results in terms of changes in children.

6. Occasionally to work with individual children or groups of children. The direct work with children, however, would be a minimum part of the total working load.

The term guidance consultant rather than guidance counselor has been used throughout. This is a term used in the new Bulletin (1963, no. 36) of the Office of Education U.S. Department of Health, Education and Welfare in *Guidance for Children in the Elementary School*. Their concept of the guidance consultant is more closely related to the concept of the school psychologist or school social worker than has been set forth here. The stress here is on helping the teachers do a better job rather than on loading them down with individual case work. In the long run it would seem that this will accomplish more and result in greater changes in the school program.

For a counselor to be effective I believe he should work with no more than twenty teachers and 600 children.

What kind of a training program would be needed to produce this kind of person? First, start with an experienced elementary teacher, one who had had at least two or three years of successful teaching in the elementary classroom. Second, there would need to be adequate training in measurement, including individual testing and personality assessment, if possible. Third, he should have an adequate background in child development. Fourth, he should have an adequate background in instructional theory, especially in some of the techniques of discovery, scientific inquiry, and he should know something about modern proposals for curriculum improvement. Fifth, he should have experience in working with groups of teachers and parents under supervision.

REFERENCE

White House Conference on Children and Youth. 1960. *Children in a changing world*. Washington, D.C.: U.S. Government Printing Office.

The Consultant in Elementary
School Guidance*

Don C. Dinkmeyer

There is a real need for a clear-cut definition of the role of the guidance specialist in the elementary school. At present, we find members of various professions working with varying levels of effectiveness in the elementary school guidance program.

Many schools service their entire guidance program through the school psychologist and his perception of the task. This program frequently is diagnostically strong but lacks the scope of a guidance program. Other schools use a social worker as their source of guidance. Here, greater emphasis is placed on individual counseling and home-school contacts. Some school systems use personnel who would be more closely aligned by their education with the members of the American Personnel and Guidance Association. For these people there has not been a definite philosophy for their program, and as a result, they frequently function in a manner similar to the high school counselor.

We would like to present another view of the role of the guidance specialist in the elementary school. This will be called the Role of the Consultant in Elementary School Guidance. It will attempt to include the psychiatric, psychological, social work, and guidance viewpoints. It will recognize that this service goes

* *Guidance Journal*, Spring 1962, vol. 1, no. 4. By permission.

on in a school, and as a result, must function in relationship to school administration, teachers, and children. This program seeks to keep in mind the need
for services to all children. It is based on the belief that in practice the teacher
must serve in the role of doing the original diagnostic work, and that the teacher
must carry on certain counseling services in the elementary school. This does
not make the teacher either a school psychologist or a psychotherapist, but it
does make her a key person both in detecting difficulties and in assisting in the
successful management of behavior difficulties.

This role of the guidance consultant arose from a need on the part of administration, the teaching staff, and the guidance specialist to build a program
with real payoff. Careful inspection of the literature related to elementary guidance soon convinced us that there was a need for a new look at elementary
school guidance; and that there was a body of knowledge available which could
serve as a solid foundation for this new approach.

The major purpose of this program is to maximize the development of each
child. It was felt that there was a real need for earlier identification and effective
handling of the adjustment problems of pupils. It was felt that the elementary
school program should not be just a repetition of high school guidance; but
that it needed to consider the specific characteristics of the children, and to
recognize the role and the relationships of the elementary teacher to her class.

Counseling, then, should be an added service which results in improved
guidance by teachers, not in less guidance by teachers. This program, then, only
works through establishing an effective relationship with the teachers. This can
be done by in-service education and through close contact with their actual classroom situations. Obviously, it is most effective when it produces a change in a
child or situation.

The program attempts to assist teachers in dealing with guidance problems
at their level of demonstrated competency. It strives continuously to raise the
competency of the teacher. It does not seek to build a large "private case load"
but to help the teacher solve the problems in her classroom. It recognizes that
many problems are directly related to the relationship between the teacher and
the child, and until this relationship is improved, frequently, outside contact
cannot be efficacious. The consultant is concerned with establishing a continuous
flow of information between each classroom and his services.

The teacher serves as a screening device and as the person who carries out
the daily relationship with the child. She selects the type of child she feels
needs special assistance. Once a contact has been established with the consultant, she also carries out recommendations. Recommendations must always
be formulated after observation of the child in the classroom setting, study of
the cumulative record, and some personal contact with the child. Suggestions to
the teacher are always tentative in the sense that she knows her situation and
her capacities, and hence recommendations must be realistic for this child,
teacher, and setting.

The guidance consultant performs a number of functions in relationship to the testing program, the coordination of services, referral, individual pupil counseling, group counseling, preventive mental hygiene, the promotion of research, and parent education. For the purposes of this paper, we shall attempt to stress the function of a consultant on learning and behavior problems.

The guidance specialist begins each school year by explaining the purposes of the program to the total staff. This should be done verbally at a total staff meeting, and in writing to all concerned. The consultant should be available for any questions related to his specific relationship to the classroom teacher. Once the original clarification of role has been presented, observation in all classrooms is a primary task. This observation must be with a purpose. It is to look for: behavior problems, learning difficulties, and difficult group relationships. However, the consultant must do more than merely observe as a motion picture camera; he must also act to establish purpose and causation as related to the behavior he is observing. The child is seen in the classroom setting in order to come up with a realistic diagnosis and plan for treatment. The teacher's handling of the child and the child's response soon makes clear the "psychological movement" that is going on in the social setting. This enables the specialist to develop practical recommendations that fit a specific situation in contrast to the classical generalizations that frequently arise from individual testing. Thus, the child is seen in relationship to the teacher, the group, the learning atmosphere, and the specific learning task.

Teachers are requested to provide a list of children with whom they especially desire help. They are also requested to list suggested times when they might meet to discuss the situation with the specialist.

The list should give the name of the child and a specific description of the learning or behavioral difficulty. At this point the teacher should indicate what she has attempted to do about the problem, how the child has responded, and any background information that is pertinent. Insofar as possible, anecdotal records related to this child's specific problem are requested. Access to the pupil's cumulative record should be available at the time of referral.

Regularly scheduled appointments should be set up with all the teachers to discuss their problems. While it is important that each teacher feel free either to use or not to use the service, it is also important that the consultant have some opportunity to develop a relationship with the teachers so that they are able to choose whether they can benefit from the service or not. This can only be done if the consultant is aware of the time each teacher is available for consultation.

It is apparent that a major part of the consultant's work is to fill in the gaps in the teacher's education. Typical teacher education programs do not provide the teacher in training with skills in handling guidance problems. Textbooks do not address themselves to this problem, frequently, and college instructors often are unable to stimulate interest in problems that college students do not have; or the college instructors are not qualified by their experiences to answer the questions of the rare student who has raised a guidance problem. The elementary guidance specialist must come up with real answers to meet the concerns of the teacher on the job. It is obvious that his batting average on recommendations must be fairly high or the teacher will not continue to come to him with her problem. The consultant can only be successful when recommendations are mutually developed, tested, and revised when the situation warrants such action. This provides an exciting challenge to the specialist in child development and guidance, for here he is able to see certain principles work with a variety of children and teachers. There is continual opportunity for him to check his theories in relationship to the laboratory of the classroom.

Aside from regularly scheduled appointments with the teachers, there should be provision for other in-service contacts. These contacts can be facilitated through pre-school workshops, institute days, staff bulletins, and released time for professional meetings. A variety of topics can be handled in such meetings and through written materials. Obviously, they should be topics of concern to the staff, preferably selected by the staff.

Some topics which are effective include: Individual Differences, Diagnostic Cues, Influencing the Child, Understanding the Child's Life Style, Changing Goals and Behavior, Learning as an Emotional Disability, Discipline, Cumulative Records, Recording and Using Anecdotes. It is also productive to schedule opportunities for groups of teachers to discuss mutual problems related to guidance. If the consultant is able to develop a good working relationship with a high percentage of the teachers, he will also find them contacting him regularly through notes in his mailbox or on an informal basis.

The diagnostic skills of the teacher can be developed in many ways. Careful inspection and analysis of achievement test results can be most productive. Interest inventories, check lists, problem inventories, all help give a view of the life space of the child. The typical paper and pencil personality test can be of value not only as a screen, but when used to see the specific response of the child to certain questions. Creative writing and the development of autobiographies provide other insights. The teacher can be trained to be more effective, in observing, as she comes to recognize certain principles. The consultant assists her to see that each child must be understood in terms of the child's subjective view, that all behavior is purposive, and that there is a unity and pattern in the life style of each child. Each child tells us much about himself if we will only develop and use both the "third eye" and "third ear."

The treatment procedure is more difficult to dicuss in general. It must be based on a thorough understanding of a specific child, a specific situation, and the teacher's capacity for managing the total situation. This necessitates adequate diagnosis and the recognition that many children are best understood when a tentative diagnosis is formulated. This tentative diagnosis is sometimes stated to the child in terms of "Would you like to know why you are acting the way you are?" or "Could it be?" or "Is it possible that?" This tentative testing of the diagnosis of the child helps to formulate the recommendations. The recommendations are tested in the classroom and are always subject to revision when experience with this specific child indicates they are inappropriate. This obviously places a great emphasis on regular communication between the consultant and the teacher.

This guidance approach implies that each child should be following an educational program tailored to his specific developmental rate and his specific needs. This can only be accomplished when adequate developmental information is available, and functional cumulative records are developed. Biweekly staff meetings to discuss the meaning of a child's behavior in the light of his cumulative record are held. These meetings are not only used as a typical case conference, but to illustrate general developmental and guidance principles.

This program places its emphasis on sharpening the guidance skills of all the teachers. Some individual pupil counseling is accomplished but only after thorough screening and an indication that the problem cannot be managed on a consultant basis with the teacher. Most counseling contacts are designed to be short-term, and to produce specific recommendations for the classroom teacher. At present, children who need intensive, long-term counseling are not handled in the school setting. The consultant assists in making arrangements for them with other facilities.

Group counseling is another method used to spread the services. Some group counseling is being done by teachers who have been specially trained and who work under the supervision of the guidance specialist. This work is usually done with groups of fifteen set up on the basis of grade levels. The guidance consultant also does some group counseling with the children who have specific problems which are similar and appear to be helped effectively through a group approach. These children are selected in consultation with all the teachers concerned.

This program, in action, has been a rewarding one, both for the consultant and the teachers. It has provided the opportunity to test a specific role in guidance and to see many teachers develop skills in understanding and guiding individual children more effectively. It appears that a wider scope of diagnostic services is possible when all teachers are concerned, in contrast to the individual psychological examination by the specialist. This implies that all teachers must be made aware of the kinds of behavior which indicate the need for service, and that they must have available certain tools which enable them to locate children with problems.

The Elementary School Counselor as Consultant*

Henry Kaczkowski

The roles that an elementary school counselor can normally assume are those of counseling, coordinating, and consulting. The literature does not adequately describe the consulting function of the counselor. Some of the descriptive phrases that are used to denote this function are: (a) advisory capacity; (b) sounding board; (c) enhancing cooperation and respect; (d) practicing human relationship; (e) achieving teamwork. Although some sociologists like Ronald Lippitt have made detailed analyses of the consulting function in other helping professions, the elementary school counselor lacks a definitive statement which could guide his action in this area of work. It is the purpose of this paper to explore a possible course of action which an elementary school counselor could utilize in a school setting.

The consultive work of the counselor reflects a blending of his psychological orientation with the educational viewpoints of the school. It can be grouped into two main activities: (a) Acting as a mediator between the child and his concerns and significant others. At certain times a child can only modify his behavior if significant persons in his life (i.e. teacher and parents) change their behavior toward him. (b) Helping the principal and the teachers to examine the impact and consequences of instructional procedures on the children. The counselor helps the staff to evaluate the affective aspects of the instructional process. Since the school is a dominant force in the life of a child, the overall purpose of the school structures the consultive work of the counselor. The school and the child are both concerned about success and failure in educational experiences. The counselor by counseling the child and consulting with teachers and parents helps to enhance the academic and social progress of the child.

An additional factor that structures the consultive work of the counselor is the instructional process itself. The teacher's task is to take an aggregate of individuals and integrate them into a group so that select tasks for the group can be acquired. The teacher's mission is not only to provide an atmosphere that is conducive to individual growth and development but to foster a group elan that enhances the socialization of the aggregate. When the class becomes a psychological entity, the teacher can use certain principles of group dynamics to facilitate the development of norms and levels of aspirations for the individual

* *Elementary School Guidance and Counseling*, 1967, vol. 1, no. 2.
By permission.

and the group. The teacher will normally ask the counselor for assistance (a) when her professional skills are not adequate to help a child operate successfully in the classroom, or (b) when the class does not operate successfully.

The teacher's concern with academic achievement does not necessarily mean that she ignores the social and emotional aspects of the child. It does point up the fact that disruptions to the instructional process have priority over the intrapersonal concerns of the child. The teacher's failure to see beyond the immediate classroom situation and view the child's behavior pattern as a result of many factors very often impedes the work of the counselor. When a counselor acting as a mediator for the child asks the teacher to modify certain classroom procedures in order to enhance a behavioral change in the child, his suggestions tend to be met with resistance and hostility. Two factors are responsible for this behavior on the part of the teacher. First, the teacher fails to understand that the proposed modifications in her behavior are as important as the counseling relationships. The success that the child has in coping with and mastering his environment has a therapeutic value. A second factor that inhibits a cooperative attitude is the teacher's fear of losing the group cohesiveness of the class. She feels that if she gives special attention to one member of the class the rest of the class will resent this action. One of the possible manifestations of this resentment is the failure of the class to cooperate in certain educational procedures. (If Bill does not have to do his homework, neither do we.) The counselor has to reassure the teacher that special attention to one child can be interpreted as manifest concern for all of the children in that class. The rest of the class should see the action as meaning that measures needed to enhance the individuality of each child in the room will be taken whenever the situation demands it. The teacher and the counselor must periodically tell the class that variable treatment of individuals is needed in order to preserve the unique attributes of each person. In essence, each pupil should feel that he can receive special attention when circumstances warrant it.

Although teachers are intimately concerned with the instructional process, and the counselor does spend a certain amount of time with them, the counselor should not ignore the principal of the school. The counselor should always keep in mind that the principal is not only responsible for the work of the teacher but very often for the work of the counselor. He is a person whose cooperation is essential for the ultimate success of the program within the school. It is essential that the counselor and principal reach agreement on several matters.

First of all, they must reach at least a tacit agreement as to what the counselor will do in the school. Although there may be a system-wide policy statement concerning the work of the counselor, the perception that each principal has of the role of the counselor is variable. Second, operational matters concerning individual students should be clarified: when can a child be seen, how much time do you spend with him, may sessions be tape recorded, confidentiality of information, etc. Third, operational matters pertaining to teachers should be reviewed: when teachers can be seen, parent-teacher-counselor confer-

ences, confidentiality of information, etc. Fourth, the counselor's staff responsibilities to the school should be examined. For example, should any of the
counselor's time be devoted to the general welfare of the school program (i.e.,
supervise the playground at noon)? If the counselor and principal enjoy wholesome interpersonal relations, the school's instructional program and guidance
services will be enhanced.

The various illustrations in this paper have pointed out that the counselor
acting as a consultant can act in an advisory capacity or as a sounding board
for ideas. The request for help can either be in terms of specific problems or it
can be formulated in somewhat general terms. Does the counselor react differently
to a specific request (e.g., how can I stop Johnny from running around the
room?) than he does for help with general problems (e.g., what are some of
the ways in which we can evaluate the effectiveness of our new math program?)?
To a certain degree the counselor is in a dilemma: Should he bring into operation certain specific skills so that a "right answer" is generated or should he
employ certain interpersonal dynamics and let the person asking the question
answer it himself? Ordinarily the counselor does not want to create a dependency
situation, but on the other hand he does not know if the teacher is capable of
solving her own problem. Lurking in the back of the counselor's mind is the
question "How will the rest of the staff interpret my actions with this teacher?
There is always the possibility that if the staff views me as failing to give help to
teachers then they will also see me as failing to give help to children." For all
practical purposes "guidance is dead" as far as this school is concerned. Although
there are times when the counselor cannot help the teacher either personally
or by means of a referral, he must be seen by the staff as overtly caring for
the concerns of the teacher.

In order to resolve the above dilemma, the counselor should ask himself
the question, "What kind of person asks for help?" Basically a teacher asks
for help when her skills are unable to (a) help the child to operate successfully
in the classroom or (b) when the class does not operate successfully. The principal asks for help when his skills do not enable him to solve problems concerning the school program, staff, or students. However, the teacher and principal
who ask for help have certain traits in common. Their personality structures are
sound enough to enable them to realize that a conflict situation exists which they
cannot resolve through ordinary means. From past experiences they also realize
that unresolved conflicts tend to generate anxiety. To a certain degree they tend to
value their self-esteem and do not attempt to use a new tactic to resolve a problem
for fear of failure. Those teachers and principals who never ask for help from
anyone tend to have a weak personality structure. They find many actions
threatening to their personality structure and continually mask their true feelings
by using a variety of defense mechanisms. These individuals need to enter some
form of counseling or therapeutic relationship before they can use the consulting
services of the counselor. Fortunately, they only make up a small portion of the
school staff.

Essentially, then, a person who asks for help is one who feels that he needs help. Before the actual steps of seeking help take place, several conditions must be present. First, the counselor must be seen as a person capable of giving help. Second, the school district must have both an explicit and implicit policy that it is both right and proper for school personnel to express themselves on a variety of topics without fear of being penalized. Third, the principal must accept each staff member and respect his worth. It is impossible to have a meaningful consultation if the atmosphere is one of fear and distrust.

A review of the above shows that what has been discussed are the essential conditions for a counseling relationship. This is not to say that counseling and consulting are the same thing. For one thing, the goals of consulting are somewhat structured. It is to say, however, that consulting calls for many principles of human relationship that are found in counseling. The nature and the kind of interaction that occurs during the consultation will have a definite impact on whether a change will take place or not.

Since the counselor is skilled in interpersonal relations, the art of consulting should not be too difficult for him. The first step, as in counseling, is to structure the situation. Essentially, this requires the teacher or principal to answer the question, "What do you want?" The second step is for the counselor to answer the question, "What can I give you?" The interaction that follows this introductory phase should be characterized by the counselor following the principles common to all human relationships: acceptance, respect, openness, empathy, and trust.

In one sense it is immaterial whether the consultation is about a specific problem or a general problem. The consultation focuses on the particular concern of the staff member. As mentioned earlier, consultations differ from counseling in that they are not interested in personality reorganization of the teacher or principal. The fundamental purpose of the consultation is to make the staff member more assertive in respect to a problem in a school setting that demands either a specific action or a more generalized approach to the problem. The counselor does not "teach" the staff member anything. The staff member has asked for help because he is fearful to act: He feels his self-esteem will be lowered if he fails. However, he cannot ignore the problem either for he fears the anxiety that will be generated by his inaction. Virtually all staff members who seek consultation ask the same question: "Will you please help me grow professionally?" The task of the counselor is to provide the atmosphere whereby professional growth is possible by following the principles common to all human relations. The counselor listens to ideas of how the problem may be resolved, explores with the staff member some of the methodology that could be used, helps review the possible consequences of action, and may be asked to evaluate whether a procedure was successful or not. Probably the most important contribution the counselor can make is by helping the staff member remove the psychic stalemate. He does this by reinforcing the staff member's sense of worth.

The third type of consultation has been discussed in part. This type of consultation calls for the counselor to interact with school personnel and with parents. The purpose of the consultation is to secure some type of modification of the environment or the behavior of those consulted so that the process of counseling can be enhanced. This may be in terms of a reduction of homework, changing the hour of going to bed, waiving a standardized test, etc. Theoretically, the dynamics of the counseling relationship itself should be strong enough to bring about change in the child. However, it should also be kept in mind that an elementary school child is a growing and developing organism. Therefore, he is subject to certain pressures in the environment which can impede the results of the counseling relationship. Hence, in some instances, the counselor must consult with what is termed "significant others" so that helpful modifications can be made in the environment. Once again the counselor employs the principles of human relations in this type of consultation. Sometimes the needed cooperation from a "significant" person is not obtained. The counselor does not force the issue. He seeks help elsewhere. If the counselor finds that the counseling relationship has been strongly affected by outside forces so that the client finds it impossible to modify his behavior, a referral should be made to the appropriate agency.

The counselor's consultation with parents is somewhat different from that with a teacher. When acting as a mediator between a child and his parents, the counselor may have to assume a teaching function. In essence, the counselor communicates a psychological understanding to the parents so that they may better comprehend the behavior of their child. For example, parental over-protection may be responsible for the child's inability to cope with certain classroom procedures. In order to help the child the parents may have to alter their child-rearing practices so that they are more adaptive and flexible. When the family style is altered the counselor should not condemn or ridicule previous practices but should point to the therapeutic values of the changed behavior of the parents. Some parents may refuse to cooperate with the counselor. In these circumstances, if the child's behavior interferes with the welfare of others, a referral should be made to the appropriate agency. Otherwise the counselor must help the child solely through the counseling relationship or drop the case.

This paper has been primarily concerned with the counselor acting as consultant. It pointed out that since the counselor works in an educational setting his work is affected by the goals of that institution. Since the chief function of the school is to instruct children so that they acquire a common set of learning tasks, the counselor is consulted about many factors that disrupt the instructional process. It was pointed out that the consulting role has three aspects to it: (1) teachers ask for consultation when their skills are unable to (a) help the child operate successfully in the class, or (b) when the class does not operate successfully; (2) the principal may ask for assistance about matters pertaining to students, school programs, or staff members; (3) the counselor may seek consultation with school personnel or parents when he feels that certain modifications in the environment or in the persons consulted will enhance the counseling process. The three types of consultation incorporate the principles of human relations in their mode of operation. Very often it is said that the principal task of the consultation is to remove the emotional blocks to learning. One can expand that idea and say that the principal goal of elementary guidance is to help the child have a meaningful educational experience.

The Counselor as

a Consultant to Teachers*

Verne Faust

The present material offers a role description of the counselor as a consultant, perhaps the role which is generally least understood and most confused with counseling. While consultation is undertaken with children, parents, administrators, and referral agencies, generally the greater share occurs with teachers. Consequently, the present discussion will limit its examination to that of consultation with teachers.

The counselor as a consultant differs in several ways from the counselor as a "counselor." The primary differences are in (a) *focus,* and (b) the *kinds of relationships that he develops within the schools* (Faust, 1967a).

FOCUS

The consultant focuses on some unit (such as a child, instructional method, course content, etc.) that is external to the counselee, or teacher. In such cases, the teacher may simply be in need of information regarding child development, or the kinds of expectations that he may have for a particular child or for his entire class (McGehearty, 1965). The counselor, as a consultant, and the teacher focus on the child, class, or some other unit external to the teacher. It amounts to an exploration of data, information, ideas, all within a relatively safe, accepting environment. This is not to say that the person of the teacher, his feelings, conflict, and need systems are rigidly avoided at all times. Nevertheless the consultant maintains the relationship through focusing on external, rather than internal, variables. And so it is, that while a clear-cut definition of roles of the

* *Elementary School Guidance and Counseling,* 1967, vol. 1, no. 2.
By permission.

guidance specialist is still in process (Dinkmeyer, 1963), these rules are becoming increasingly clear.

WHEN AND HOW A CONSULTANT TO TEACHERS?

Generally, a consultant relationship is established at those times when the teacher indicates a simple need for information or human behavior data exploration. The teacher's request is usually short and to the point. At the conclusion of the consultant contact, both teacher and consultant generally feel satisfied that the task has been relatively well completed. There are few "loose ends hanging" in the relationship. All that remains is for the teacher to use or translate the results of his consultation contact into the curriculum.

Types of Consultation with Teachers

Consultation with teachers is most often, though not exclusively, practiced through (a) an in-service course work type of experience, and (b) the staffing of cases. In-service training generally revolves around the mental apparatus, that is, a study of what makes children, or all people, tick. It should be noted that this type of consultation avoids a pedantic, purely didactic classroom teaching approach. Only data that teachers can easily and quickly identify with are treated. Only when teachers can become *personally* involved with the course work can the consultant hope to see his efforts rewarded by teachers becoming excited about the in-service program, about education as a profession, and most importantly, about the welfare of children in the learning climates that the teachers can ultimately design.

Staffing of cases, as consultation, simply involves teachers who play minor or significant roles with a child, coming together with the consultant, sharing data regarding the child, and developing a course of action to be taken in problem-solving. Again, the focus remains largely on the child, not the teacher.

Too Much Consultation?

Teachers who frequently "run to the consultant for answers" may provide cues for the consultant to inquire what meaning this behavior could possibly have. It may be that he would eventually confront the teacher with a need to explore this behavior. The consultant may discuss with the teacher the advisability of moving into a counseling, rather than a consulting, relationship. If this is inadvisable, the consultant may take other steps. In order to protect himself from being overwhelmed or manipulated, or from feeding an over-dependency relationship or other perhaps unrealistic need-system of the teacher, he may point out to the teacher the limitations of his consulting time, and so reduce these contacts by placing them on some numerical or time appointment basis.

RELATIONSHIPS OF THE CONSULTANT IN THE SCHOOL

Inasmuch as the consultant relationship requires very little risk on the part of the teacher's openly examining himself, in the consultant role the elementary school counselor is freer to move within the various interpersonal strata of the school. The consultant, as a relatively non-threatening figure, may eat lunch with teachers, use the faculty lounge, attend teacher social functions, etc. However, at those times when teachers request counseling in this setting, sensitization training, or other process experiences that might come under the heading of counseling, the consultant will refer the teacher, or teachers, to the counselor who visits the school on only a counseling basis.

In the consultation relationship, the elementary school counselor does not provide a relationship setting for the teacher (or other consultee) to invest extensive or deep-level dimensions of himself. The teacher is not so exposed; he takes fewer personal risks. He need not, therefore, invest as much trust in the consultant's not retaliating against him later, in the everyday, socially competitive setting. This enables the consultant to interact with relative freedom outside the consultation setting, at almost any social level. In this way, then, the consultant relationships within the school differ markedly from those he might establish if he were to function as a counselor for teachers.

Perhaps the major implication of these definitions of the consultant's role for the student personnel program structure is the absolutely requisite condition that each school should employ at least two counselors: one for the role of counseling and consultation with children, and one for consolidation with teachers, parents, administrators, and referral agencies. The second counselor would engage both children and teachers in counseling. This would mean, of course, that two counselors would be employed for every two schools (of approximately twenty-five teachers), or an average of one counselor per school (Faust, 1967*b*).

THE CONSULTANT VERSUS THE CURRICULUM SPECIALIST

In reality, curriculum development comprises the counselor's major consultant focus, inasmuch as it is the total curriculum world of the child that the counselor works to influence. All that happens to the child, whether through textbook content, the teacher, scheduling, etc., is, in fact, an acceptable definition of "curriculum" for the counselor. For purposes of differentiating roles and function, curriculum development is tentatively limited to focusing on content, instructional methods, and program design, but without particular emphasis on teaching personnel.

The consultant is a full-fledged member of any curriculum development committee or undertaking. He is not simply a part-time consultant who is sometimes invited to sit peripherally on the committee.

The Curriculum in the Light
of Human Behavior

The consulting role is designed in a specific, carefully delineated way in the curriculum development process. The consultant does not contribute as a specialist in content, nor as an expert in instructional methods and other curriculum areas. Such experts are found among teachers themselves and, most certainly, among curriculum supervisors. *The consultant's highly specialized contribution resides in his examination of all suggested curriculum practices in light of his depth and breadth of preparation of the dynamics of human behavior.* His depth and breadth of understanding of human behavior exceed that of perhaps all other personnel in the school. (Only the school psychologist's background in human behavior generally is comparable to that of the elementary school counselor. The school psychologist, however, is diagnostically oriented toward crisis situations, while the counselor is developmentally oriented toward all children.)

At many, perhaps most, points, the counselor-consultant may have nothing to contribute to curriculum development meetings and individual teachers. However, when concepts, principles, materials, and teacher behaviors in some way possess a special significance in view of what is known about human behavior, the counselor may contribute pertinent data (Faust, 1967b).

For example, the consultant would not advise teachers on the approach they should use in teaching reading. Such decisions are the teachers' responsibility, within the policy structure of the school. It is the teachers' or administration's decision, or both, regarding, for example, what effect phonetic analysis may have on the learning apparatus of the child. To what extent does this one facet of teaching reading enhance or detract from freeing the intellect for learning? The counselor simply contributes his specialized background in human behavior.

THE KEY QUESTION FOR THE
COUNSELOR AS CONSULTANT

The counselor as a consultant to the teacher may be found at the mutual agreement of teacher and consultant, in the classroom, where the teacher's instructional methods may be observed. The observations are invariably in a frame of reference that inquires, "To what extent do the specific methods under study enhance or impair learning apparatus functioning?" The counselor is not in the classroom in order to assist the teacher in a global development of instructional methods. This is the responsibility of a curriculum supervisor. The counselor in the consulting role within the learning climate simply cannot, as the curriculum supervisor can, keep up on the literature on instructional methods, the latest textbooks, research, etc. The consultant simply examines the methods which are finally worked out by the teacher, for the effect these methods may have on smooth, efficient functioning of the mental apparatus in the learning process.

REFERENCES

Dinkmeyer, D. C. 1963. The consultant in elementary school guidance. In H. Peters, A. Riccio, and J. Quaranta (eds.), *Guidance in the elementary school*. New York: Macmillan.

Faust, V. 1967 *a*. *Child development counseling in the elementary school*. Boston: Houghton Mifflin.

————. 1967 *b*. *Developing guidance programs in the elementary school*. Boston: Houghton Mifflin.

McGehearty, L., and J. Pierce-Jones. 1965. *Child behavior consultation: IRCOPPS research at Texas*. University of Texas Press. Mimeographed.

Chapter 5

TEST UTILIZATION

FOR GUIDANCE PURPOSES

Child study and pupil appraisal have always been closely associated with guidance and counseling. Historically, guidance originated with attempts to appraise abilities related to vocational decisions. For many people, testing and guidance are synonymous; for others, testing is considered the most important guidance process. Diagnostic appraisal of the exceptional child has been the primary service provided by many pupil personnel specialists.

Child study in the elementary school is concerned with the identification of talent and ability, as well as with the diagnosis of liabilities and deficits. This chapter presents articles that discuss the purpose of tests in the school program and the proper utilization of test results, as well as the preferred procedures of presenting results to groups and individuals (teachers, parents, and pupils). This chapter focuses only on the testing aspect of pupil appraisal. Nontesting approaches to pupil appraisal are described in Chapter 6.

Educational testing in the United States has experienced phenomenal growth since World War II, with currently almost one million tests per school day being given (Lyman, 1963). On the national scene the most intensive administration of standardized tests is found in grades three through nine (Bauernfeind, 1963). However, it is apparent that interpretation and test utilization are minimal in the elementary school.

The developmental guidance theory suggests some of the following emphases for the use of tests: deciding what purpose the testing program should accomplish and then formulating each test to that purpose; determining who needs information on test results and specifically what kind of information; encouraging the student to use tests as a method of self-study. In previous approaches the student was considered only as an object of study.

THE PURPOSES OF TESTS

In the past, tests have been used primarily to diagnose or predict. The major purpose of the elementary school guidance testing program, however, should be an understanding of the individual as he is, in order to provide him with appropriate educational experiences and development of self-understanding. A well-organized testing program should provide for the study of all children, not just exceptional ones. A testing program must be aligned with the purposes of elementary school guidance as discussed in Chapter 2. Properly used, tests can be of considerable assistance in achieving the objectives of the elementary school guidance program.

In opposition to current use of tests—providing information to parents and teachers about children—there must be increased emphasis on the direct use of test results with children. Tests are used by school administrators to establish groups, identify children for special programs, serve as a basis for curriculum planning, provide information regarding the selection of materials for a specific group, and enable teachers to plan appropriate learning experiences. These purposes are all basic to the organization and administration of the school program.

The purposes of tests should be closely related to the objectives of elementary school guidance: facilitation of the learning process for the individual; assisting the child in the development of increased self-understanding; assisting in the development of realistic plans; and helping teachers and parents develop an understanding of the child.

PRINCIPLES OF TEST UTILIZATION

Those who plan the testing program of a school must be willing to struggle with the question, "What do students, teachers, counselors, and administrators want to know?" It is vital that all persons in the school system participate in a coordinated effort during the selection and utilization of tests. It must be decided if tests are to be used primarily for institutional decisions, such as selection and placement of pupils, or if they are to be used for individual decisions. Tests can be used more effectively to predict the performance of a group than of an individual. The use of tests in individual cases requires considerable skill in communicating results, and should be selected to serve the purpose of those who need the results. If test results cannot be *applied* by teachers, the test is useless in the learning process. A test should also be selected so that it provides students with information to assist in the decision-making process.

The following principles are involved in test utilization:

1. A test must be valid for the purpose for which it has been selected. Tests must be able to predict other measures.

2. A test must be reliable; that is, repeated rankings of the test must be consistent. The test should also meet practical considerations, such as time available for testing and cost of testing materials.

3. Test scores are not absolute measures of behavior, and should not be used as such. They should always be considered in relation to nonstandardized information and observations by staff members.

4. When interpretations of tests are presented, individuals must be made aware of the amount of variance expected in a person's score when he is examined repeatedly with the same test.

5. In test interpretation it is important to have the person who is receiving the information (pupil, teacher, or parent) report his estimate of the results prior to receiving information. This early estimate helps in identifying errors in the individual's perception and provides a clue to his feelings.

6. Individuals should always be allowed the opportunity to react to what they have learned. They ought to be given a chance to state, in their own words, what they feel they have obtained from the test interpretation and what they believe are the implications of this information.

USING TESTS TO FACILITATE LEARNING

In the past, tests have had little impact upon the learning process in schools. They were used to provide a summary of the progress of a group or an individual, but they had no *direct* effect on the continuous instructional process.

Ideally, tests could be used to identify an individual's or a group's special talents or weaknesses, either of which can help the teacher plan an instructional program that will be certain to consider the needs of the pupils. Teachers and pupils can make realistic plans about the level and amount of work that can be expected of them. Skillful test interpreters can usually provide a general classification report which may provide clues for group planning and the organization of pupils into sections. However, test developers appear to offer little help to the teacher with her primary responsibility, the instructional process (Bauernfeind, 1965).

In this chapter Bauernfeind describes a method by which the teacher is supplied with a record of each student's answers to a test. This enables the teacher to plan for both the group and the individual. This kind of specific pupil information is really the best that the testing program can offer to the teacher.

COMMUNICATING TEST RESULTS

Interpretation of a test can determine the success of the test. Those persons involved in the test—students, teachers, and parents—must be made aware of the significance of the results and should be expected to benefit from a knowledge of the precise and well-formulated interpretation of an individual's (or a group's) performance on a test. Thus, the job of the test interpreter is a difficult one. Many persons rely on his judgment, and many classroom programs are created out of his recommendations. Among his characteristic qualities are the following:

1. Thorough understanding of any specific test and its implications.

2. Preinterpretation awareness of the meaning of possible results in terms of each individual taking the test.

3. Knowledge of statistical concepts, such as the nature of the norm group with which an individual is being compared.

4. The interpreter should obtain a self estimate from the tested person prior to providing him any test information with questions like "How do you think you did?" "On which of the tests do you believe you did best?"

5. Sensitivity to the individual's feelings about the test and his own results.

6. Awareness of the importance of providing time and opportunity for the individual to react to his own performance on the test.

As the article by Lister and Ohlsen and the selection from Leonard indicate, test interpretation with pupils has considerable potential. It is particularly important, when dealing with students, for the interpreter to become involved in the relationship that he establishes, for the students must be made to feel that he is interested in how they feel about themselves. Estimating test performances before receiving actual test information will help the school guidance counselor identify pupils' attitudes that should be discussed (Ohlsen, 1965).

In some instances the test interpreter will be aware that the pupil does not understand or can not accept the information that is provided. When a pupil receives information that does not fit into his self-image, it is important to provide an opportunity for him to discuss these findings. Facts alone are not sufficient. We must discuss the individual's feelings with him before he can accept the facts and use them in making decisions. Pupils should never leave a test interpretation session until they have had a chance to react to results, clarify their feelings, and restate in their own words the meanings and implications of the test.

It is important that the elementary school child realize that his score is taken at a point in time and is never to be considered a final estimate of his ability. A test must be understood as something which adds to the knowledge about the child, not as the sole source of information about him.

The counselor-pupil ratio in the elementary school dictates that teachers be used more extensively in test interpretation. Counselors then become engaged in training teachers through in-service sessions. In-service training provides the teacher with a background regarding tests and measurements in general, but it is always done in terms of specific test results. Teachers should have available summaries of group and individual results when the counselor is conducting test interpretation sessions. The primary purpose of in-service training is to improve the teacher's understanding of his pupils. An effective method for in-service training is provided in Womer's (1966) case study of Mary Nelson.

The group meeting with teachers provides an opportunity to discuss general principles and to clarify misunderstandings. During this meeting, it would be valuable to utilize a role-playing theme in which the counselor interprets specific tests to one of the teachers, who takes the role of the pupil. Role playing should be extended to provide opportunities for all of the teachers to take on the role of test interpreter. Teachers might be divided into groups of three in which one teacher assumes the role of the child; one the role of the teacher; and the third evaluates the interpretation process. The counselor should also provide time for individual conferences with teachers who desire additional assistance.

Teachers then become the providers of test information to pupils, with the counselor available for test interpretation upon the request of teacher or pupil.

Some plans should be developed for providing test results to parents. In this chapter, Ricks provides an excellent rationale and set of procedures for telling parents about test results. The setting and the type of information provided will obviously differ according to the school district and its policies. Practical considerations suggest that an effective way to conduct test interpretations might be to group parents according to the ages of their children—primary, intermediate, and junior high school age. In a group meeting, the counselor would provide information regarding the testing program—its background, limitations, and implications.

The meeting of parents could make use of charts and other visual aids to clarify the meaning of tests and should provide ample time for questions. The meeting consists of group conferences with the teacher in which the application of tests to a specific age level is interpreted. Perhaps a teacher-pupil-parent conference might be scheduled to review individual interpretations where requested. Individual conferences with parents should always be conducted in an atmosphere similar to that which has been suggested for student conferences. Parents should be asked to state what they expected their children would do. Parents should also be asked to explain what they have learned from the test interpretation and what they believe to be the implications of this information.

The first article in this section poses a fundamental question regarding the relevance of tests for the schools: Can tests facilitate the learning process? Bauernfeind proposed a method for more effective use of tests by classroom teachers. Through item analysis, the teacher is provided with information for planning both group instruction and individualization of the educational process.

Lister and Ohlsen investigated the extent to which self-understanding was increased and maintained by fifth, seventh, ninth, and eleventh graders. They propose that appropriate test interpretation can increase self-understanding in elementary school students as well as in high school and college students.

Leonard's study investigated the capacity of elementary school students to develop realistic perceptions of their scholastic aptitude. He determined that students were not accurate in their estimations. Group test interpretation was provided and one month later pupils were asked to rate themselves again. Results indicated that pupils' self-estimates did move closer to reality following a discussion of their ratings on the test. Group test interpretation, accomplished in this fashion, appears to facilitate more realistic pictures of academic potential.

Ricks concurs with the principles that parents have a right to know about their children, and that the school is obligated to communicate understandable information to them. He emphasizes meaningful communication of test information through attention to content, language, and presentation.

REFERENCES

Bauernfeind, R. October 1965. *Can tests facilitate the learning process?* 30th Educational Conference, Educational Records Bureau.

————. 1963. *Building a school testing program.* Boston: Houghton Mifflin.

Lyman, H. 1963. *Test scores and what they mean.* Englewood Cliffs, N.J.: Prentice-Hall.

Ohlsen, M. 1965. Increasing the use of self-understanding. *Educ. Leadership, 22.*

Womer, F. 1966. *Interpreting standardized test results: a case study,* Unit 5. Chicago: Science Research, Testing Extension Service.

Can Tests Facilitate the Learning Process?*

Robert H. Bauernfeind

Can tests facilitate the learning process? The very fact that this question is being asked suggests that there is something amiss in the relationship between test developers and classroom teachers. First, we know that standardized achievement tests are very popular on the American scene. Probably a healthy majority of schools give a battery of achievement tests at least once a year in grades 4–8, and many give such batteries once a year in grades 3–12. Evidence for this statement comes from sales records of major test publishers, and statewide studies such as those of Gipe and Shellhammer (1961) in California and Frank Womer (1963) in Michigan. Moreover, some studies we have been conducting at Northern Illinois University indicate that teachers are considerably more interested in standardized achievement scores than they are in other types of scores—mental ability, multiple aptitudes, interests, or what have you.

So we have a situation where teachers indicate a high level of interest in achievement tests; where schools do in fact provide a regular program of standardized achievement testing; and yet, here we are, asking ourselves whether tests can facilitate the learning process.

* Speech delivered at the Educational Records Bureau Conference, New York, October 1965. By permission.

The problem, I think, is that there is a basic discrepancy between the views of the test developer and those of the classroom teacher. The test developer is essentially concerned with the classification process; he is primarily interested in providing reliable rankings of pupils within some norms group—local norms, state norms, national norms, or others. If the test developer can establish that Johnny scored at the 25th percentile within some norms group on a social studies test—and that Johnny would again score pretty close to the 25th percentile if he took the same test a second time—the developer feels that his job is well done. He has provided reliable evidence of Johnny's classification within a norms group—that is, whether Johnny is above average, average, or below average within that norms group.

The teacher, on the other hand, typically does not especially care about these classifications, however reliable they may be. True, such classifications will help her in ability groupings, in parent conferences, and in recommendations regarding promotion, but they do *not* help her directly in facilitating the learning process.

In effect, the dialogue goes something like this: The test developer says, "Johnny scored at the 25th percentile in social studies, and we know that this score is highly reliable." The teacher asks, "But what should I do next to help Johnny in his social studies program?" And the test developer responds, "We don't know, but we can tell you that his 25th percentile classification is highly reliable."

I firmly believe that this suggested dialogue cuts through to the problem under discussion: The test developers, concerned about reliability, validity, and norms, have been offering a service that does not help the teacher in his primary responsibility—academic instruction.

Fortunately, we are beginning to see movement toward a closer relationship between the test developer and the classroom teacher. A major step, it seems to me, is to expand our efforts in developing the idea of the rights analysis," or the "right response record." In these plans, the teacher is given both a classification report on each pupil's norms standing, and also a systematic record of every right answer and every wrong answer each student got on the test. Thus, on a 75-item test of achievement in social studies, the teacher is told not only that Johnny scored at the 25th percentile within some norms group, but she is also told that Johnny was correct in his answers to items 1, 2, 3, 6, 7, 9, and so on, and that he was wrong in his answers to items 4, 5, 8, 10. A perceptive teacher, looking at the record of wrong answers, can, I am convinced, reach a number of judgments (or hypotheses) regarding past misunderstandings and possible next steps for Johnny's growth in social studies.

How are we doing in developing these types of reports? Not very well, I'm afraid. I have checked with two of the major test publishers, and I found in both cases that fewer than five percent of schools ask for the return of achievement answer sheets from the scoring center. In the remaining 95-plus percent of schools, apparently the teachers are given classification data only. My hunch is that these latter schools raised questions which led to this symposium: "Can tests facilitate the learning process?" If the teacher doesn't know which questions were missed by her pupils, the tests *cannot* facilitate the learning process. Without some sort of rights-and-wrongs analysis, the testing program is going to miss the mark as far as the teachers are concerned.

When one administers a 75-item test, and reports back only norms scores for pupils and school averages, he has been grossly inefficient in his use of the test results. This is quite a bit like the English professor who reads student essays ranging from ten to twenty pages each, and then marks each with a grade —A, C+, D—, etc.—with no other accompanying comments. Happily, we are confident that elementary and high school teachers are typically not this insensitive, and that many of them would be concerned with specific pupil strengths and weaknesses as indicated on the standardized examination.

Along the same line, we should also mention the enormous values of item-by-item analyses for group instruction. Again, if we focus only on classification, we might report to a seventh-grade teacher that her pupils attained a mean score of 48 on the social studies achievement test—and that this mean of 48 is well above the national average for seventh graders. But again the teacher may ask us what she can do to help her pupils further. To shed light on this question, the test publisher can report the percent of correct answers to each question on the test. Let me cite some examples.[1]

One question in a social studies test reads as follows:
Compared to India, the United States

(*)   has fewer people per square mile.
( )   is more rural.
( )   has about the same population.
( )   has proportionately fewer city people.
( )   has a larger population.

In one large school system on the West Coast, twenty-one percent of the sixth graders marked this question correctly; thirty-two percent of the seventh graders marked it correctly; and thirty-five percent of the eighth graders marked it correctly. In an eighth-grade group in a Chicago suburban school, forty-two percent marked the item correctly. We need not argue here whether the intensive overpopulation of India is an important learning for junior high pupils; but, if you believe that it is, these data clearly suggest a major need in planning the curriculum for these schools.

---

[1] The four test items cited are taken from the *STS Educational Development Series*, Advanced Level, Form A (I) prepared by Scholastic Testing Service, Inc., Bensenville, Illinois. See the adaptation of the STS Rights Analysis Form and directions for its use at the end of this reading.

Here is another question from this same social studies test:
The U.S.A. has risen to the position of a leading world power mainly because of its

(*)   industrial strength.
( )   desire to conquer the world.
( )   opposition to communism.
( )   form of government.
( )   geographical position.

In the same four groups cited earlier, the percents correct were 21, 24, 26, and 28. Again, we need not argue whether industrial strength as a requisite to world power is an important learning for junior high pupils; but, if you believe that it is, then clearly a curriculum need in these schools has been shown by these data.

Here is a question from an arithmetic test:
To multiply 1086.736 by 100, you should move the decimal

( )   one place to the left.
( )   two places to the left.
( )   one place to the right.
(*)   two places to the right.
( )   none of these.

In these same four groups, the percents correct on this item were 33, 37, 44, and 36. If one believes that junior high students should be able to relate multiplication by 100 to decimal position, it appears that these schools need to provide their pupils with much more work in this area.

Obviously, if one is using a total achievement battery comprising 300, 400, or 500 test items, there is a tremendous amount of information to be gained from rights analyses of each item in each grade. Here is just one more example. In a test entitled "Solving Everyday Problems" designed to measure student growth in guidance understandings, the following item appears:
If a friend does something that makes you angry, it is usually best to

( )   stop being friends with him.
( )   yell at him.
( )   plan something to make him angry.
(*)   tell him, "That makes me angry."
( )   tell yourself that you're not really angry.

In these same four groups, the percents correct on this item were 14, 14, 22, and 27. Most of the wrong answers occurred on the alternative—"tell yourself that you're not really angry." This foil, of course, is not only a logical absurdity, but it suggests the mechanism of repression which is of great concern to mental hygienists. If the teachers in these schools are concerned with self-understanding and self-expression as an educational objective, these rights analyses data clearly indicate a specific direction for further instruction and class discussion.

We need to bear in mind the fact that these percents correct were obtained only because these schools asked the test publisher for such reports. If the schools had not ordered these services, they would have received only general classification data—that is, percentiles on the total test score—for each pupil and for each class average. They would then have had no evidence on how each pupil, and the class as a whole, performed on each test question.

While these types of rights analyses can now be developed through data processing techniques,[2] there is usually a time lapse of 3–6 weeks in getting such information back to the teachers. Thus, there is one further suggestion that I would like to offer:

During the past two years I have been working on a new program with a junior high school in one of Chicago's northern suburbs. In this program, students are tested with an extensive achievement battery during the first week of school in September. At the end of the last testing session, each student is given four replica answer sheets—one for the English test, one for the social studies test, one for the mathematics test, and one for the science test. Each student copies his answers from the master answer sheet onto these replica answer sheets; the replica answer sheets are then put in each teacher's box that same evening.

The next day, then, each teacher has a complete record of each student's answer to each and every question on the test in that teacher's subject field. And, during the first or second session of each class, the teacher can obtain a record of total class performance on each item. This record of class performance on each item—along with the replica answer sheets showing each student's response to each item—gives the teacher a wealth of information for planning both group instruction and individual help for individual students.

How well does this program work? Estimates provided by the building principal are that about half of the teachers use this response record intensively, and that about half have not gotten involved in the project. For those teachers who *are* using the record, we would say that they are getting the maximum use from the testing program. In fact, there is nothing more that the testing program can give them. With this abundance of information regarding specific student understandings and misunderstandings, it is only a question of teacher competence and creativity to plan new learning experiences around the test results.

Without these records of specific item responses, the teachers would get back, about two weeks later, simply a record of each student's position within

---

[2] The California Test Bureau's "Right Response Record" provides an excellent model of what can be done in a data-processing program.

some norms group. And, after looking at the array of percentile scores and Grade Equivalent scores only, the teachers would very likely ask, "How can tests facilitate the learning process?"

STS RIGHTS ANALYSIS FORM

Teachers should check to be sure they have the correct Rights Analysis sheets for their subject tests as follows:

LASS	Test 7 and 10
Mathematics	Test 8
Science	Test 9
Reading	Test 6

When the students have filled in their Rights Analysis sheets for the particular subject test, ask the students to indicate by a show of hands how many marked answer (a) on question 1, how many marked answer (b) on question 1, and so on. Your master record would then look something like this:

1. a 8
   b 12
   c 1
   d 4
   e 1

2. a 2
   b 1
   c 19
   d 3
   e 1

After you have recorded the information on your master record, collect the forms from the students.

The data collected will give the teacher (1) the number of students recording certain answers and (2) the specific answers recorded in response to the questions on the subject test.

REFERENCES

Educational Development Series—Advanced Level, Form A. 1963. Bensenville, Ill.: Scholastic Testing Service.

Gipe, M. W., and T. A. Shellhammer. 1961. A study of standardized group testing programs in California public schools. *California Schools, 32,* 264–277.

Womer, F. B. 1963. *Testing programs in Michigan schools 1963.* Ann Arbor, Mich.: The University of Michigan.

The Improvement

of Self-Understanding

through Test Interpretation*

James L. Lister / Merle M. Ohlsen

This study appraises outcomes of test interpretation as well as the effect of an orientation to that testing upon student motivation for test interpretation. It investigated the extent to which self-understanding was increased and maintained by fifth, seventh, ninth, and eleventh graders. Since a rationale for stressing improved self-understanding in test interpretation was recently presented by Ohlsen (1963), none will be presented here.

The writers' previous review of the literature (1962) on test interpretation in counseling led them to conclude that exclusive reliance upon information-giving approaches to test interpretation had been generally ineffective in increasing student self-understanding. Few of the studies reviewed devoted attention to students' feelings concerning what they learned about themselves during test interpretation. In addition, most of the studies were based on secondary or collegiate students, and interpretations to students below eleventh or twelfth grade seemed generally ineffective in promoting increased self-understanding.

An analysis of test manuals, and even some of the other literature on the use of tests, suggested that thorough knowledge of the tests to be interpreted and skill on the part of the test interpreter in communicating appropriate information to the student are adequate for successful test interpretation. Though these are necessary, they do not seem sufficient to increase self-understanding. The review of literature suggested that the following three other conditions influence increased self-understanding: (1) student participation in the test interpretation process; (2) ability of the test interpreter to recognize and deal with students' feelings about test results; and (3) orientation to testing. Inasmuch as the writers concluded that the first two were essential, they elected to study the effects of orientation.

Counselors were selected with care to insure skill in enlisting student participation and in coping with students' underlying feelings. Approximately half were masters' level persons with supervised practicum experience in counseling.

* *Personnel and Guidance Journal*, April 1965, vol. 43, no. 8.
This paper is based upon the results of Cooperative Research Project No. 1344 supported by the U.S. Office of Education, University of Illinois. By permission.

Except for three who had completed doctorates, the rest were doctoral candidates. Each was provided with a manual (Lister and Ohlsen, 1962, Chapter 5) which described the test interpretative process in detail. After each had become familiar with the material in this manual, he was checked out in a role playing interview with Lister. Such interviews were tape recorded and discussed in detail with each counselor. Test interpretation sessions with students were also recorded and checked to determine whether counselors were continuing to use prescribed methods.

It was hypothesized that a pre-testing meeting in which students were told about testing and how they could use test results would result in: (a) greater motivation to have tests interpreted, and (b) greater self-understanding following test interpretation.

PROCEDURES

A total of 787 students from four similar school systems served as subjects: 380 students in grades five, seven, nine, and eleven from two schools received the experimental treatment (the orientation presentation), and 407 students in the same grades served as a control group (no orientation presentation) in the other two schools. The unequal number of cases in the two groups resulted from slightly different enrollments in the control and experimental schools.

It was recognized that an unequal distribution of socio-economic class membership could possibly influence both motivation for interpretation and effectiveness of test interpretation. To minimize this possibility, the socio-economic level of each subject was determined by categorizing the father's occupation according to a modification of the *Dictionary of Occupational Titles* classification system (U.S. Employment Service, 1949). On this basis, random numbers were used to obtain equal proportions of experimental and control subjects within each socio-economic category.

A battery of standardized tests was administered to students in both treatment groups. In grades five and seven the battery consisted of the Iowa Tests of Basic Skills, Form 1; the Henmon-Nelson Tests of Mental Ability, Form A; and the What I Like To Do: An Inventory of Children's Interests. In grades nine and eleven, the battery included the Iowa Tests of Educational Development, Form X-38; the Henmon-Nelson Tests of Mental Ability, Form A; and the Kuder Preference Record, Vocational Form CM.

Before the tests were administered, the experimental group received the orientation presentation in self-contained classrooms (grades five and seven) and English classes (grades nine and eleven). Members of the research team read prepared statements which discussed why tests were given, the kinds of tests the students would be given, and what they could expect from such tests. Students were encouraged to ask questions at any time during the presentation, and speakers were instructed to remain alert to any evidence that students had questions or misunderstandings. Time was provided for questions and discussion at the completion of the prepared statement. Usually there was some discussion, but the amount varied from classroom to classroom.

Motivation for obtaining test interpretation was operationally defined in terms of students' responses to a counseling request form. After completing the test battery, students were given the request form and asked to indicate whether (a) they wished to have a test interpretation interview, (b) they did not wish to have such an interview, or (c) they preferred to postpone their decision concerning participating in test interpretation.

After one week the students indicating the third choice were asked to make a final decision as to whether they wanted to have their tests interpreted. Thus, the final response to the request form represented the two levels of motivation considered in this study.

The students stating that they did not wish to receive a test interpretation were contacted by the senior author and encouraged to participate. When they were told that they had invested their time in taking the tests and that the investigator wished to make the service available to them also, only about one percent objected to participating. Consequently, everyone except these few had their test scores interpreted.

A self-rating scale similar to the one described by Berdie (1954) was used to obtain students' self-estimates with reference to each of the scores provided by each of the three tests. Students were required to compare themselves with others their own age on a five-point scale. For example, the following item was used to obtain fifth and seventh graders' perceptions of their reading comprehension:

Compared with others your own age, how well do you understand what you read? For example, how able are you to get meaning out of things you read?
( ) very much more than most pupils my age
( ) somewhat more than most pupils my age
( ) about the same as most pupils my age
( ) somewhat less than most pupils my age
( ) very much less than most pupils my age

These data were obtained from both control and experimental subjects on four occasions: (a) before the tests were administered, (b) after testing, (c) after test interpretation, and (d) sixty days after test interpretation. Prior to using this self-reporting device it was administered twice, four days apart, in another similar school system to appraise its reliability. Median test-retest reliability coefficients of approximately .60 (significant beyond the .01 level) were obtained for the three tests.

The low reliability of self-estimates, high reported intercorrelations among achievement subtests, and intercorrelations among self-estimates led to the decision to consider self-rating accuracy in terms of the three broad areas of achievement, intelligence, and interests rather than specific subtests.

To determine accuracy on each of the four rating occasions, students' ratings were compared with their earned percentile ranks on the corresponding subtests. If, for example, a student checked "somewhat less than most students my age," he was given a rating of 4 (the range was from 1 for "very much more than most students my age" to 5 for "very much less than most students my age"). If his earned percentile rank on the subtest was 43, he would be given a rating of 3 (the range of percentile ranks was divided into five bands: band 1, 90–99; band 2, 75–89; band 3, 25–74; band 4, 10–24; band 5, 0–9). The absolute difference between these ratings on each subtest was subtracted from a constant of 5. These resulting values were then summed to obtain composite accuracy ratings for achievement and interests. Rating accuracy on the single-score intelligence measure was determined by subtracting the difference between the self-estimate and the earned percentile rank from the constant 5.

The approach to test interpretation emphasized three factors: client participation, the presentation of information by the counselor, and counselor response to student affect.

Encouraging Client Participation

During the interview, the counselor provided the student with copies of the tests to aid in recalling the nature of the tests as they were discussed. Each student was asked to estimate his performance on each subtest by checking a five-point scale (see Table 1). He was also encouraged to express in his own terms the meaning of his test results and to contribute non-test information about himself which would add meaning to the results under consideration.

Providing Information. The counselor defined each subtest in terminology appropriate to the maturity of the student. For example, the Vocabulary Test of the Iowa Tests of Basic Skills was described as a test that "measures how well you understand words you read and hear others use." After each subtest had been defined, the student placed a check mark on a five-point scale to estimate his performance. When this procedure had been completed for all parts of the test battery, the counselor placed an "X" on the same scales to correspond with the student's earned percentile ranks. As indicated in Table 1, test performances were discussed with the student in such terms as "did as well as most your age," "did very well," etc., rather than as percentile ranks.

Difficulties were anticipated in determining whether comparatively small differences between self-estimates and earned percentile ranks should be considered significant or within the range of chance variation. To enable counselors to make such judgments reliably, the following steps were taken. Standard errors of measurement, originally expressed in raw or standard score units were converted to percentile rank units. These standard error of measurement equivalents varied according to the scale intervals in which they were used. For example, on the Vocabulary Test of the Iowa Tests of Basic Skills, in grade five one standard error of measurement would correspond to 3, 8, 10, 8, and 3 percentile rank units in the five respective scale intervals. A set of tables containing these equivalents was prepared for use during test interpretation. When counselors noted differences for which they could not readily determine significance, they re-

**TABLE 1/ TEST INTERPRETATION INTERVIEW FORM FOR
GRADES 5 AND 7**

Counselor_____   Student's Name_____

School_____   Date_____

I. Achievement

	Did Very Poorly	Didn't Do As Well As Most	Did As Well As Most	Did Better Than Most	Did Very Well
1. Vocabulary					
2. Reading					
3. Language					
4. Work-Study Skills					
5. Arithmetic					

II. Learning Ability

It's Very Difficult	It's Difficult	Learn As Easily As Most	It's Easy	It's Very Easy

III. Interests

	Like It A Lot Less	Like It Less	Like It As Well As Most	Like It More	Like It A Lot More
1. Art					
2. Music					
3. Social Studies					
4. Active Play					
5. Quiet Play					
6. Manual Arts					
7. Home Arts					
8. Science					

ferred to these tables to obtain the standard error of measurement for the subtest under consideration. One standard error of measurement was extended from the student's check mark toward the counselor's "X" and one standard error measurement from the counselor's "X" toward the check mark. When these lengths overlapped, it was concluded that chance would account for the observed differences.[1]

Responding to Feelings

The counselor faced two general problems in conveying test results to students. First, the counselor had to be sure that the student cognitively understood the test results. For example, he had to remain alert to make sure the student did

---

[1] It is recognized that this use of the standard error of measurement is actually an inappropriate technique for two reasons. First, the standard error of measurement of the subtest was applied to the student's self-estimate. Second, this use of the standard error of measurement is not an appropriate technique for determining profile *differences*. Nevertheless, the method used did provide test interpreters with a reasonably simple, workable technique which seemed to be better than any other available. To compensate for inadequacies of this method, larger observed differences were required for significance.

not infer ability from scores on interest inventories or fail to distinguish between his classmates and students in the national norm group as the standard for his self-estimates.

Second, the counselor had to identify accurately and respond appropriately to the feelings elicited by the test information. The counselor tried to respond in ways that showed acceptance and understanding of the feelings the student was unable or too fearful to express. He tried to help the student formulate and express both positive and negative feelings and reactions.

The student often found it difficult to accept test information that was inconsistent with his self-estimates. This occurred when test performances were underestimated as well as overestimated. No effort was made to defend the tests or convince the student that he should agree with the results; instead, the counselor helped the student explore his feelings about the discrepancies between his test scores and self-estimates.

TABLE 2/ CHI-SQUARE TESTS OF INDEPENDENCE OF TREATMENT AND MOTIVATION CATEGORIES

Grade	Chi-square	p^*
5	3.38	N.S.
7	22.19	$< .001$
9	5.09	$< .05$
11	3.48	N.S.

* Differences favor experimental group.

RESULTS

The first major hypothesis, that orientation would be associated with a higher degree of motivation for test interpretation, was tested by a chi-square test with one degree of freedom. One test was conducted for each of the four grade levels. Table 2 reveals two values of chi-square significant beyond .05, suggesting that the experimental treatment was associated with higher motivation for learning test results in grades seven and nine but not in grades five and eleven.

It is difficult to explain why this experimental treatment resulted in higher motivation in only two grades. Considering the total sample, however, 76.4 percent of fifth graders, 77.2 percent of seventh graders, 92.9 percent of ninth graders, and 87.2 percent of eleventh graders requested test interpretation interviews. The chi-square value of 92.8 with three degrees of freedom computed from these data was significant beyond the .001 level. Thus, the failure of orientation to be associated with higher motivation may not mean the same for grades five and eleven, since the unequal base rates suggest that it would have been more difficult to have effected a significant difference in grade eleven (Meehl and Rosen, 1955).

The second major hypothesis, that orientation would be significantly related to increases in accuracy of self-estimates following test interpretation, was tested by computing point-biserial correlation coefficients between the gains made from post-testing to post-counseling and the group type, i.e., experimental control. Table 3 contains the separate coefficients computed for achievement, intelligence,

TABLE 3/ RELATIONSHIP OF ORIENTATION TO ACCURACY OF SELF-ESTIMATES

Grade	Type of Test	r_{pb}	p
5	Achievement	.025	N.S.
	Intelligence	.041	N.S.
	Interests	−.083	N.S.
7	Achievement	.022	N.S.
	Intelligence	−.108	N.S.
	Interests	−.018	N.S.
9	Achievement	.113	N.S.
	Intelligence	.081	N.S.
	Interests	−.013	N.S.
11	Achievement	.074	N.S.
	Intelligence	.070	N.S.
	Interests	.009	N.S.

and interests at each grade level. Since none of the values of r_{pb} was significant, it was concluded that the orientation treatment, as used in this study, does not result in increased accuracy of self-estimates following interpretation.

In addition to testing the two main hypotheses, the data were also examined (a) to determine the extent to which test interpretation resulted in increased self-undersanding, and (b) to ascertain whether such increases were associated with motivation for learning test results.

Since it had been determined that the experimental treatment was unrelated to increased self-understanding, it was possible to conduct the remaining analysis on the total sample. It was predicted that significant increases in accuracy of self-estimates would occur from post-testing to post-counseling and that such gains would be maintained during the follow-up period. Table 4 (columns one and two) presents the values for the *t*-tests computed to test these two hypotheses.

From these results, it appears that test interpretation produced significant increases in self-understanding for all grades and types of tests (column one). A significant decline, however, was noted in accuracy of self-estimates during the sixty-day follow-up period (column two). Additional *t*-tests were computed to check the possibility that a net increase in accuracy may have occurred over the period from pre-testing to follow-up. The *t*-values in the third column of Table 4 suggest that a net increase in self-understanding did occur during the period covered by this study.

TABLE 4/ CHANGES IN ACCURACY OF SELF-ESTIMATES

Grade	Type of Test	Pre- to Post-Interview		Post-Interview to Follow-up		Pre-Interview to Follow-up	
		t	p*	t	p‡	t	p*
5	Achievement	5.56	<.001	2.42	<.02	3.70	<.001
	Intelligence	7.43	<.001	.73	N.S.	2.87	<.01
	Interests	6.29	<.001	4.23	<.001	1.96	<.05
7	Achievement	13.01	<.001	6.47	<.001	6.70	<.001
	Intelligence	5.36	<.001	3.08	<.01	2.39	<.02
	Interests	7.99	<.001	1.51	N.S.	3.23	<.01
9	Achievement	13.34	<.001	3.16	<.02	4.01	<.001
	Intelligence	8.68	<.001	4.45	<.001	4.50	<.001
	Interests	10.45	<.001	8.32	<.001	.025	N.S.
11	Achievement	5.73	<.001	3.67	<.001	1.84	N.S.
	Intelligence	3.62	<.001	2.28	<.02	1.16	N.S.
	Interests	8.53	<.001	4.39	<.001	4.13	<.001

* Significant increase in accuracy of self-estimates.
‡ Significant decrease in accuracy of self-estimates.

On an a priori basis it was reasoned that students expressing a desire to learn about their test results would, as a result of such motivation, possess greater readiness to accept and integrate the information received during the interviews. It was therefore predicted that students in the higher motivation category would

TABLE 5/ RELATIONSHIP OF MOTIVATION TO CHANGES IN ACCURACY OF SELF-ESTIMATES

Grade	Type of Test	r_{pb}	p
5	Achievement	.067	N.S.
	Intelligence	.038	N.S.
	Interests	.038	N.S.
7	Achievement	.183	<.02
	Intelligence	.088	N.S.
	Interests	.167	<.02
9	Achievement	.242	<.001
	Intelligence	.013	N.S.
	Interests	−.068	N.S.
11	Achievement	.065	N.S.
	Intelligence	.051	N.S.
	Interests	−.060	N.S.

evidence higher gains in self-understanding following an interpretation of their test scores. This hypothesis was tested by computing point-biserial correlation coefficients based on the gains made by the high- and low-motivation groups. The values of r_{pb} presented in Table 5 clearly support acceptance of the null hypothesis for grades five and eleven. However, the significant values of r_{pb} noted for self-estimates of achievement and interests in grade seven and achievement in grade nine tentatively suggest a relationship between motivation and ability to modify self-perceptions through a knowledge of test results.[2]

While one cannot determine from these data the extent to which the emphases upon counselor response to feelings and student participation facilitated the observed growth in self-understanding, they do offer a tenable explanation for the results. It is possible that experiences designed to promote continued self-exploration might also serve to maintain the level of self-understanding observed immediately after test interpretation. Considering the research on immediate loss by forgetting, these findings appear to have significant implications. From the results, the investigators conclude that appropriate test interpretation can increase self-understanding in elementary school students as well as in high school and college students.

REFERENCES

Berdie, R. F. 1954. Changes in self-ratings as a method of evaluating counseling. *J. counsel. Psychol., 1* (No. 1), 49–54.

Levitt, E. 1961. *Clinical research design and analysis in behavioral sciences.* Springfield, Ill.: Charles C Thomas.

Lister, J. L., and M. M. Ohlsen. 1962. *The effects of orientation to testing on motivation for and outcomes of test interpretation.* Cooperative research report number 1344, University of Illinois.

Meehl, P. E., and A. Rosen. 1955. Antecedent probability and the efficiency of psychometric signs, patterns, and cutting-scores. *Psychol. Bull., 52,* 194–216.

Ohlsen, M. M. 1963. Interpretation of test scores. In *The impact and improvement of school testing programs.* 62nd Yearbook of the National Society for the Study of Education. Chicago: The University of Chicago Press.

U.S. Employment Service. 1949. *Dictionary of occupational titles.* Washington, D.C.: Division of Occupational Analysis, Government Printing Office.

---

[2] The probability of finding 3 of the 12 values significant at the .05 level is less than .02 (Levitt, 1961).

Utilizing Test Results

in the Elementary Classroom*

George E. Leonard

It is accepted as a basic goal of education in general and counseling in particular that each individual understand and accept himself. Counseling aims to aid each individual in developing a realistic perception of his strengths and weaknesses. If a student has a poor self-concept or thinks of himself as being a failure in a learning situation, he has little enthusiasm in the classroom. Further, it would seem that, in many cases, secondary school students either have developed an unrealistic perception of their scholastic aptitude or have no idea of their true capabilities. Consequently, these students often either make unrealistic educational and vocational plans or do not make any plans at all. In many cases, the efforts of the school counselor are hampered by the resulting nebulous level of aspiration.

It would appear, then, that it would be of benefit if students could be aided to begin developing greater knowledge concerning their scholastic aptitude before high school. Two questions immediately arise, however:

1. Can elementary school students grasp the concept of individual differences?

2. Can elementary school students apply this concept to themselves?

In the school year 1962–63, an experiment was conducted at the laboratory school of Kent State University to see if the foregoing questions were real or hypothetical problems. A third grade class and a sixth grade class were utilized in the experiment.

PROCEDURES

The Lorge-Thorndike Intelligence Method Test was administered to both classes in November, 1962. Both classes were considerably above-average in intelligence, although the range in each class was from slightly below-average to superior as shown in Table 1.

The first step in the experiment was to discuss with the student groups the concept that all of us can do some things better than some others and some not as well as some others. The discussion was introduced in one class with the question, "Who is the fastest runner in the class?" The teacher then led the class into

---

* *The School Counselor*, October 1964, vol. 12, no. 1. By permission.

TABLE 1/ DISTRIBUTION OF THIRD AND SIXTH GRADE CLASS IQ'S

	Range of IQ's	Median IQ	Mean IQ	N
Grade 3	95–138	116	116	26
Grade 6	88–134	115	113	30

a discussion of the differences among individuals in their ability to perform certain things and the importance of being aware of one's own strengths and weaknesses.) Students were then asked to rate themselves in comparison with "boys and girls all over the United States." This necessitated a look at the map in the third grade.

SELF-RATINGS

Third grade pupils were given a dittoed sheet upon which ten figures were outlined. They were asked to color the number of persons whom they thought they *could* surpass in doing school work. Sixth grade pupils were asked to rate themselves on a vertical bar graph as to the percent of boys and girls whom they thought they *could* surpass in doing school work. It was assumed that asking students to rate themselves in deciles would compensate for the variation of each score indicated by the standard error. Next, the students estimated deciles were compared with the actual decile in which their score placed them. The results are shown in Table 2.

TABLE 2/ MEANS AND STANDARD DEVIATIONS OF ACTUAL AND ESTIMATED DECILES OF THIRD AND SIXTH GRADE GROUPS

	Grade 3		Grade 6	
	Actual	Estimated	Actual	Estimated
Mean Decile	7.84	6.23	8.14	5.65
S.D. of Decile	2.22	2.15	3.72	2.30

These findings indicate that the elementary students in the study tended generally to underestimate their level of scholastic aptitude. An examination of the means and standard deviations of the actual and self-estimated deciles of pupils indicates that the self-estimates tended to be lower and less variable than the actual decile. Further investigation of the results indicates that pupils of higher ability generally tended to underestimate their potential, while pupils of lesser ability tended to overestimate their scholastic aptitude.

Correlations between the actual and self-estimated deciles of pupils reveal a low positive (.20) relationship in the third grade and a negative (—.41) correlation in the sixth grade. Differences between mean actual and estimated deciles are significant at the one percent level in the sixth grade and at the five percent level in the third grade.

The second stage of the experiment consisted of presenting to the pupil groups their decile rating on the Lorge-Thorndike and discussing the results with them. This was done one month after the initial self-rating. In each case, students were given horizontal line graph profiles of their results which differed completely from the self-rating forms. In order to guard against memorization of their ratings, pupils were not allowed to keep the profiles.

One month after the pupil groups were given the profiles of their results, they were asked to rate themselves once more. The results are shown in Table 3.

TABLE 3/ MEANS AND STANDARD DEVIATIONS OF ACTUAL AND ESTIMATED DECILES OF THIRD AND SIXTH GRADE GROUPS

| | Grade 3 | | Grade 6 | |
	Actual	*2nd Estimate*	*Actual*	*2nd Estimate*
Mean Decile	7.84	7.01	8.14	6.77
S.D. of Decile	2.22	2.19	3.72	2.93

The results indicate that pupils' self-estimates did move closer to reality following a discussion of their rating on the Lorge-Thorndike. Further, variability of self-estimates increased (although not significantly), indicating some movement away from the previous tendency toward the mean.

Product-moment correlations and tests of significance between actual and self-estimated deciles are summarized in Table 4.

TABLE 4/ CORRELATIONS AND TESTS OF SIGNIFICANCE BETWEEN ACTUAL AND ESTIMATED DECILES

| | Grade 3 | | Grade 6 | |
	r	t	r	t
Actual Decile and 1st Estimate	.20	2.07*	—.41	5.92‡
Actual Decile and 2nd Estimate	.38	1.1	.35	1.93

* Significant at 5% level.
‡ Significant at 1% level.

DISCUSSION

It would seem that elementary school pupils may not have a clear picture of their abilities. The results of the experiment indicate that elementary pupils probably can apply the concept of individual differences to themselves and that group test interpretation may be a useful technique in aiding these students to develop a more realistic picture of their potential.

The results raise several questions and cannot be taken as being conclusive. Why, for example, did third grade students seem to have a more realistic self-perception than sixth grade pupils? Further, would the same results be obtained with a more nearly normal population? If similar results were obtained, the technique described would seem to have value for the teacher or elementary counselor interested in making more use of test results. A caution must be stated, though, in that the person utilizing test results in this fashion should become thoroughly familiar with the test beforehand.

On Telling Parents about Test Results*

James H. Ricks

Like any other organization dealing with people, a school has many confidences to keep. School administrators, teachers, and especially guidance workers inevitably come to know items of private information. A gossip who carelessly passes such information around abuses his position and his relationship with his students. It is both right and important that some kinds of information be kept in confidence.

What about test results? Do they belong in the category of secrets, to be seen only by professional eyes and mentioned only in whispers? Or is their proper function best served when they become common knowledge in the school and its community? (In some towns, names and scores have been listed in the local newspaper, much like the results of an athletic contest.)

We think neither extreme is a good rule. Sometimes there is reason to make group data—figures such as the average and the range from high to low—generally public. Seldom should individual results be published except for the happy announcement of a prize won, a scholarship awarded, and the like. But short of general publication, school guidance workers face a particularly important question: Should parents be told their children's test results?

Hard questions, often, are hard because they deal with genuinely compli-

* *Test Service Bulletin*, December 1959, no. 54. The Psychological Corporation. By permission.

cated problems. Simple "solutions" to such questions are likely to be a trap rather than an aid if their effect is to divert our attention from the difficulties we truly face. Simple rules or principles, on the other hand, can be of real help as one tackles complex problems and situations. This article will present some rules that we have found useful in facing questions such as:

"What should I say when a mother wants to know her son's IQ?" "Should we send aptitude test profiles home with the children?" "We feel that parents in our school ought to know the results of the achievement tests we give, but then it's hard to explain the discrepancies between these and the teachers' grades."

No single procedure, obviously, can be appropriate for every kind of test. Nor for every kind of parent. To Mr. Jones, a well-adjusted and well-educated father, a report of his daughter's test scores may enhance his understanding of her capacities and of what the school has been giving her. To Mr. Green, a somewhat insecure and less knowledgeable man, the identical information may spark an explosion damaging to both child and school. And the counselor or teacher often has no sure way of knowing which kind of person he will be reporting to.

Two principles and one verbal technique seem to us to provide a sound basis for communicating the information obtained from testing. The two "commandments" are absolutely interdependent—without the second the first is empty, and without the first the second is pointless.

The first: *Parents have the right to know whatever the school knows about the abilities, the performance, and the problems of their children.*

The second: *The school has the obligation to see that it communicates understandable and usable knowledge.* Whether by written report or by individual conference, the school must make sure it is giving *real* information—not just the illusion of information that bare numbers or canned interpretations often afford. And the information must be in terms that parents can absorb and use.

Few educators will dispute the first principle. It is in parents that the final responsibility for the upbringing and education of the children must lie. This responsibility requires access to all available information bearing on educational and vocational decisions to be made for and by the child. The school is the agent to which parents have delegated part of the educational process—but the responsibility has been delegated, not abdicated. Thoughtful parents do not take these responsibilities and rights lightly.

The parents' right to know, then, we regard as indisputable. But, to know what?

Suppose that, as a result of judicious testings, the school knows that Sally has mastered social studies and general science better than many in her ninth grade class, but that few do as poorly as she in math. In English usage she stands about in the middle, but her reading level is barely up to the lower border of the students who successfully complete college preparatory work in her high school. The best prediction that can be made of her probable scores on the College Boards three years hence is that they will fall in the range which makes her eligible for the two-year community college, but not for the university. She grasps mechanical concepts better than most boys, far better than most girls. Looking over the test results and her records, her experienced teacher recognizes that good habits and neatness of work have earned Sally grades somewhat better than would be expected from her test scores.

All of these are things Sally's parents should know. Will they know them if they are given the numbers—Sally's IQ score, percentiles for two reading scores, percentiles on another set of norms for several aptitude tests, and grade-placement figures on an achievement battery?[1]

Telling someone something he does not understand does not increase his knowledge—at least not his correct and usable knowledge. We are reminded of the guide's observation about the tenderfoot. "It ain't so much what he don't know, it's what he knows that ain't so that gits him in trouble." Transmitting genuine knowledge requires attention to content, language, and audience. We have already referred to some of the characteristics of parents as an audience. Let's look at the other two elements.

Content means that to begin with *we* must ourselves know what we are trying to get across.

We need to know just what evidence there is to show that the test results deserve any consideration at all. We need equally to know the margins and probabilities of error in predictions based on tests. If we don't know *both* what the scores mean *and* how much confidence may properly be placed in them, we are in trouble at the start—neither our own use of the information nor our transmission of it to others will be very good.

Content—what we are going to say—and *language*—how we are going to put it—are inseparable when we undertake to tell somebody something. In giving information about test results, we need to think about the general content and language we shall use and also about the specific terms we shall use.

To illustrate the general content-and-language planning: a guidance director may decide that he wants first to get across a sense of both the values and the weaknesses of test scores. One excellent device for his purpose would be an expectancy table or chart. Such a chart can make it clear to persons without training in statistics that test results are useful predictors *and* that the predictions will not always be precise. Local studies in one's own school or community are of greatest interest. But the guidance director who lacks local data may still find illustrative tables from other places helpful in preparing parents and students to use test results in a sensible way. (An example is given in Table 1, with references to others that may be found elsewhere.)

Specific terms used in expressing test results vary considerably in the problems they pose. Consider, for example, the different kinds of numbers in which test results may be reported.

---

[1] The implied "No" answer to this question does not, of course, refer to those few parents trained in psychometrics—perhaps even to a point beyond the training of the school staff. Parents include all kinds of people.

IQ's are regarded as numbers that should rarely if ever be reported as such to students or to their parents. The reason is that an IQ is likely to be seen as a fixed characteristic of the person tested, as somehow something more than the test score it really represents. The effect, too often, is that of a final conclusion about the individual rather than that of a piece of information useful in further thinking and planning. Few things interfere more effectively with real understanding than indiscriminate reporting of IQ scores to parents.

Grade placement scores or standard scores of various kinds are less likely to cause trouble than IQ scores are. Still, they may substitute an illusion of com-

TABLE 1/ THE CHART FOR THE BOYS' CEEB VERBAL RESULTS *

Of Each Ten Boys in the Tenth Grade Whose VR + NA Scores Are in the	*On the CEEB SAT-V When They Are Seniors, How Many Will Score*				*And How Many Will Score 500 or Above*
	399 and lower	*400–499*	*500–599*	*600 and over*	
Top quarter of the class	½	2	4	4	4 out of 5
Second quarter	2	4	5½	½	3 out of 5
Third quarter	6	4½	3	1	2 out of 5
Lowest quarter of the class	4				Very few

* The guidance director found, in the classes of 1953 and 1954, 101 boys and 85 girls who had taken the *Differential Aptitude Tests* (including Verbal Reasoning and Numerical Ability) in their Tenth Grade years and the *Scholastic Aptitude Test* of the College Entrance Examination Board as Seniors. Since the CEEB reports two scores—Verbal and Math—there were four sets of data: Boys—Verbal, Boys—Math, Girls—Verbal and Girls—Math. (For more data from this school, see the *Journal of Counseling Psychology*, 1954, I, 106–115, and 1955, II, 229–230). The other three charts were similar in appearance. For additional illustrations of expectancy charts and tables, see Test Service Bulletins 38 and 53; the *Differential Aptitude Tests* Manual, third edition, pp. 62–64; and the *Modern Language Aptitude Test* Manual, 1959 edition, pp. 15 and 16.

munication for real communication. Standard scores have no more meaning to most parents than raw scores unless there is opportunity for extensive explanations. Grade placements *seem* so simple and straightforward that serious misunderstandings may result from their use. As noted in a very helpful pamphlet,[2] a sixth-grade pupil with grade-placement scores of 10.0 for reading and 8.5 for arithmetic does not necessarily rank higher in reading than he does in arithmetic when compared to the other sixth graders. (Both scores may be at the 95th percentile for his class—arithmetic progress much more than reading progress tends to be dependent on what has been taught, and thus to spread over a narrower range at any one grade.)

Percentiles probably are the safest and most informative numbers to use *provided* their two essential characteristics are made clear: (1) that they refer

---

[2] M. R. Katz, *Selecting an Achievement Test*. E. and A. Series No. 3, 1958, page 26. Available free from Educational Testing Service, Princeton, New Jersey.

not to percent of questions answered correctly but to percent of people whose performance the student has equalled or surpassed, and (2) who, specifically, are the people with whom the student is being compared. The second point—a definite description of the comparison or "norm" group—is especially important in making the meaning of test results clear.

Much more can be said about the kinds of numbers used to convey test score information. Good discussions can be found in a number of textbooks.[3] But a more fundamental question remains: *Are any numbers necessary?*

We intend nothing so foolish as suggesting a ban on the use of numbers in reporting test results. But we have been struck repeatedly by the fact that some of the very best counselors and many of the best written reports present numerical data only incidentally or not at all.

Along with the two "commandments" at the beginning of this article, we mentioned a verbal technique. Generally, we dislike formulas for writing or speaking. This one, however, seems to have advantages that outweigh the risks attending its suggestion. It's just a few words:

"You score like people who. . . ." Or, to a parent, "Your son (or daughter) scores like students who. . . ."

The sentence, of course, requires completion. The completion depends on the test or other instrument, the reason for testing, and the person to whom the report is being given. Some sample completions:

. . . people who are pretty good at office work, fast and accurate enough to hold a job and do it well.

. . . people who don't find selling insurance a very satisfactory choice. Three out of four who score as you do and become insurance salesmen leave the job for something else in less than a year.

. . . students who find getting into liberal arts college and getting a B.A. degree something they can attain only with extra hard work. On the other hand, they find a year or two of technical school interesting and they probably do well in the jobs to which that leads.

. . . students who are disappointed later if they don't begin a language in the ninth grade and plan to take some more math and science. It's easier to head toward business later if you still want to than to go from the commercial course into a good college.

. . . students who don't often—only about one out of four—manage to earn a C average their freshman year at State.

. . . students who have more than average difficulty passing in arithmetic— you [*or, to a parent,* he] may need some extra help on this in the next few years.

Many more samples will come readily to mind. The most important thing to note is that a satisfactory report combines two kinds of information:

1. the test results of the individual person, and

---

[3] See, for example, Chapters 17 and 18 in *Measurement and Evaluation in Psychology and Education,* by Thorndike and Hagen (New York: Wiley, 1955), or pages 556–563 and 584–588 in *Appraising Vocational Fitness,* by Super (New York: Harper, 1949).

2. something known about the test or battery and its relationship to the subsequent performance of others who have taken it.

Also, a satisfactory completion puts the school or the counselor out on a limb, at least a little. Some variant of "That's not so!" or, more politely, "How do you know?" will be the reaction in some cases, probably less frequently voiced than it is felt.

Well, let's face it. The decision to use a test at all is a step out on a limb. Some limbs are broad and solid and the climber need feel little or no anxiety. Some are so frail that they offer only hazard, with the bait of an improbable reward. We climb out on some limbs of medium safety because there is evidence of a real chance that they will help us, and those whom we test, toward a worthwhile goal.

The words of the formula need not actually be used in each case. Sometimes percentiles, grade placement scores, or a profile may be what the parents should receive. But it is well to try first mentally stating the meaning of the results in the language suggested above. If this proves difficult or discomforting, a warning signal is on—reporting the numbers is likely not to be constructive in the case at hand!

The audience of parents to which our test-based information is to be transmitted includes an enormous range and variety of minds and emotions. Some are ready and able to absorb what we have to say. Reaching others may be as hopeless as reaching TV watchers with an AM radio broadcast. Still others may hear what we say, but clothe the message with their own special needs, ideas, and predilections.

The habit of using the formula, and of thinking a bit about what answer to give if the response is a challenging or doubtful one, puts the interpreter of test scores in the strongest position he can occupy. In the case of achievement tests, it requires him to understand why and how the particular test or battery was chosen as appropriate for his school and his purpose. In the case of aptitude (including scholastic aptitude or intelligence) tests, it requires him to examine the evidence offered in the test manual and research studies to back up the test's claim to usefulness. And it reminds him always that it is in the end *his* thinking, *his* weighing of the evidence, *his* soundness and helpfulness as an educator or counselor that is exposed for judgment—not the sometimes wistful ideas of the test author or publisher.

The school—or the counselor—*is* exposed for judgment when telling parents about the abilities and performances of their children. The parents have the right to know. And knowledge in terms they can understand and absorb is what the school must give.

Chapter 6

GUIDANCE AND
THE CLASSROOM TEACHER

Elementary school guidance began in the classroom with teachers who were concerned about individual pupils. At first it was often sporadic, and depended upon the interests of the teacher, with some teachers neglecting guidance entirely and others providing it regularly. Good teachers, however, have always carried on many activities which actually come under the heading of guidance.

Developmental guidance in the elementary school requires an organized program in each classroom and is dependent upon effective procedures by classroom teachers. It is an important and inevitable part of the teacher's responsibility; it is an integral part of the educational program, not an optional activity. The rationale that underlies good teaching is also responsible for the effectiveness of guidance procedures.

This chapter presents the rationale for guidance in the classroom, the teacher's guidance responsibilities, characteristics of the helping relationship in the classroom, procedures for classroom guidance, and the relationship between teacher and counselor.

THE RATIONALE FOR
CLASSROOM GUIDANCE

Guidance is an emphasis within the educational process; it is not a service adjunctive to education (McCabe, 1958). The objectives of elementary school guidance as set forth in Chapter 2 can only be achieved through full use of the classroom teacher's guidance potential.

The child is in the process of developing attitudes toward himself, others, and the world of achievement. A teacher obviously can have considerable effect upon this development. Davidson and Lange (1960) found that children's perceptions of their teacher's feelings toward them correlated positively and significantly with their self-perceptions. Roth (1959) found that self-concepts and feelings of adequacy have considerable influence upon school achievement. In a study of fifth- and sixth-grade children, Coopersmith (1959) found that a correlation existed between a positive self-concept and school achievement.

The organization of the elementary school accentuates the importance of the teacher's role. The teacher in the elementary school has more contact with the pupil than the teacher in the high school. The comparatively flexible curriculum provides more opportunity for the teacher to adapt to individual differences and relate subject matter to personal needs and self-development. The teacher is in a position to observe the child more extensively and to gather information that the counselor does not have access to.

Guidance and instruction are complementary phases of the educational process. In a 1954 article entitled "Student Personnel Work as Deeper Teaching," Lloyd-Jones and Smith described what a guidance relationship should be. The guidance program cannot be effective if teachers do not cooperate with counselors to maximize the child's educational experience.

Perceptual research has shown that no individuals have exactly the same experience or derive the same learning from a new experience (Kelley, 1950). The perceptual approach to understanding behavior is the basis for adaptation of educational programs and underlines the significance of the teacher in elementary school guidance.

Recognition of the teacher's importance in guidance is not a new development in education. Some of the earliest approaches to elementary school guidance —by Barr (1958) and Willey (1960)—described guidance primarily in terms of good teaching. The human development approach advocated by Gordon (1956) stressed the teacher's understanding of child development. The book by Lloyd-Jones, *Guidance in Elementary Education* (1958), is another example of this approach. Other authors who have developed the importance of the role of the classroom teacher in guidance include Caldwell (1960), Garry (1963), and Johnston, Peters, and Evraiff (1959).

GUIDANCE RESPONSIBILITIES OF
THE CLASSROOM TEACHER

The teacher has a function in the guidance process that can not adequately be handled by any other adult in the child's milieu. Classroom guidance is concerned with assisting each child to have personally meaningful learning experiences. The essence of classroom guidance occurs in the teacher-pupil interaction. Although some educators have suggested that all teachers are, in a sense, guidance workers, they have not yet described specific responsibilities, objectives, and techniques. These must be set forth if classroom guidance is to be effective. Guidance responsibilities of the classroom teacher include:

1. Modifying the classroom environment and adapting instruction to meet the unique needs of individuals.

2. Providing information to the counselor from observation, anecdotes, work samples, and other classroom activities.

3. Integrating guidance with the curriculum so that the guidance possibilities in various areas are realized.

4. Providing educational, occupational, personal, and social information to pupils through regularly scheduled group guidance classes.

5. Serving on guidance committees that help establish the purpose of various services and provide the counselor with feed-back on the program.

6. Participating in case conferences on individual children.

7. Participating in in-service education programs designed to improve the effectiveness of the guidance program.

THE CLASSROOM ATMOSPHERE

Elementary school guidance functions best in a school with good relationships between children and adults, in an atmosphere that builds confidence, avoids threat, and creates feelings of security. Such a school is one that provides planned success experiences for individuals.

Physically the classroom should be attractive and provide a stimulating environment for learning. The teacher and the students should share information, ideas, attitudes, and feelings. The teacher-pupil relationship should be one of mutual trust and respect which encourages the child to assume responsibility for himself. Cooperation should be emphasized rather than competition.

A study by Lewis, Lovell, and Jessee (1965) showed that sixth graders who perceived a therapeutic teacher-pupil relationship received significantly higher achievement test scores than did students who perceived a nontherapeutic teacher-pupil relationship. This study demonstrated the importance of the interpersonal relationship in positive student change.

While developmental guidance emphasizes an understanding of the individual, the group unit is also an integral part of the guidance function. Led by the teacher, the group structure should facilitate the development of a democratic climate for group living and build cohesiveness within itself. The teacher must be able to comprehend group dynamics. He should regularly schedule group discussions which will permit the students to express their feelings and develop plans. The group guidance process fosters the development of self-understanding and self-evaluation, provides the opportunity to give and receive love, and offers the atmosphere to test reality. To conduct the classroom discussion effectively, the teacher must help the children become aware of their desires and provide opportunities for developing solutions to problems. Group guidance will serve to create the sense of belonging to a peer group and owing responsibility to it. The group relationship tends to develop the teacher's sensitivity to the child's emotions, attitudes, and values. Teachers with this sensitivity are able to create a genuine individual relationship such as the one which Moustakas (1966) portrayed so explicitly.

THE HELPING RELATIONSHIP IN THE CLASSROOM

The guidance point of view in the classroom involves the process of helping children grow toward goals that they feel are worthwhile and attainable (Caldwell, 1960). The teacher must act as coordinator of goals in what is known as a "helping relationship." Some of the teacher's actions that contribute to a helping relationship are: being concerned and attentive when the child has something to say; helping the child clarify feelings about himself and others; showing an understanding of his feelings; accepting the child as he is, thus enabling him to accept himself; being kind but firm, so that the child learns there are limits to what he may do, encouraging self-evaluation; giving recognition for effort, even if the job is not completed or perfect; focusing on the child's strengths and assets; and helping the child to explore possible solutions to a problem by presenting alternatives for his consideration.

OBJECTIVES OF CLASSROOM GUIDANCE

The teacher directs the learning process by involving children in problems that are personally meaningful to them (Dinkmeyer, 1964).

Both guidance and the curriculum provide help in the development of the individual's capacities. As the teacher studies his pupils, he adjusts the curriculum to meet individual differences (ASCD, 1955). Pacing and self-selection promote harmony between the specific developmental level of the child and the curriculum.

Guidance services as proposed by Hill (1965) provide direction for the program and a standard by which to judge the effectiveness of classroom guidance services. The guidance services help the child to:

1. Understand himself and become aware of his potentialities.

2. Accept responsibility for what he is and how he functions.

3. Develop a wholesome attitude toward educational and vocational responsibilities.

4. Mature in his ability to solve his own problems; to plan, and to make choices and decisions.

5. Mature in understanding human behavior and the nature of social relationships.

6. Adjust to the demands of life, especially in relationship with others.

7. Mature in a sense of values and the achievement of high ideals.

UNDERSTANDING MOTIVES AND PURPOSES

The teacher's main responsibility is to facilitate the learning process and impart information to the child. However, if the teacher is not able to understand the child in terms of his cultural setting, the way he finds his place in the group, his percepts, attitudes, and values, then he will be unable to help the child achieve the educational goals. Teachers need a psychological frame of reference which will provide insight into the reasons for a child's immediate behavior, and suggest effective responses to the child's behavior.

The child's behavior becomes more meaningful when the teacher recognizes that it is purposeful and directed toward a goal. Children primarily desire to belong; it is within the group that they can fulfill themselves. The child who is not discouraged finds his place through useful contribution to the group. A discouraged child, on the other hand, has a "useless side" (Ansbacher and Ansbacher, 1956). This has been described by Dreikurs as participating in either active-destructive or passive-destructive behavior (Dreikurs, 1957). Misbehavior and lack of cooperation are the child's mistaken ways of gaining social status. The four goals of misbehavior as described by Dreikurs (1957) are: attention getting; demonstration of power; getting even; and displaying real or assumed deficiency in order to avoid tasks at which the individual believes he will fail. The motivation of misbehavior is explained in greater detail in the article by Dreikurs, which appears in this chapter.

CLASSROOM GUIDANCE TECHNIQUES

Identifying the guidance needs of pupils is most effectively accomplished through the application of guidance techniques to regular classroom activity. By such application, the teacher can gather information which will help him facilitate the full development of his pupils. Some of the techniques that can be used to identify guidance needs include:
1. Observation.
2. Cumulative records.
3. Interview.
4. Autobiography.
5. Work samples.
6. Creative writing.
7. Interest inventories.
8. Sociometrics.
9. Problem inventories.
10. Scattergram.
11. Sentence or story completion.
12. Health records.

In addition, there are some teaching techniques designed to help the individual meet his needs. These are:

1. Individualizing instruction so the child is able to work in terms of his own interests and at his own pace.

2. Allowing the child to select materials which will reflect his own interests and capacities.

3. Joint planning by teacher and pupil.

4. Teacher-pupil evaluation of progress in recognizing guidance needs, which calls for continual reassessment.

5. Planning group meetings on a regular basis to discuss problems and to make plans.

6. Use of bibliotherapy—dynamic interaction between the reader and literature. The reading of books accompanied by follow-up activity can produce significant changes in individuals (Cianciolo, 1965).

7. Group guidance material such as that developed by Ojemann (article in this chapter) which provides a sequential program for the elementary school.

8. Encouragement: helping the child feel worthy by recognizing his assets. Encouragement provides more opportunity for success than failure (Dinkmeyer and Dreikurs, 1963).

The above lists merely provide a survey of classroom guidance techniques. The articles by Caldwell, Dinkmeyer, and Simmons will describe some of the techniques at greater length. The reader interested in more detailed information on classroom techniques is directed to the following sources:

Caldwell, E. 1960. *Group techniques for the classroom teacher*. Chicago: Science Research Associates.

DeHaan, R., and J. Kough. 1956. *Helping children with special needs*. Chicago: Science Research Associates.

Dinkmeyer, D. 1965. *Child development: the emerging self*. Englewood Cliffs, N.J.: Prentice-Hall.

Garry, R. 1963. *Guidance techniques for elementary teachers*. Columbus, Ohio: Merrill.

Gordon, I. 1966. *Studying the child in school*. New York: J. Wiley.

Kough, J., and R. DeHaan. 1955. *Identifying children with special needs*. Chicago: Science Research Associates.

THE RELATIONSHIP OF THE
TEACHER AND THE COUNSELOR

The teacher and the counselor must be aware of and have respect for each other's guidance functions. They must cooperate and collaborate for the benefit of the child. The counselor complements and facilitates the work of the teacher. He can only achieve the total objectives of guidance through the teacher. The teacher observes the child, identifies guidance needs, and records daily progress.

The counselor contributes his knowledge of human behavior and his capacity to deal with affect. He may visit the classroom to observe, provide the teacher with guidance materials, or serve as a consultant. The consulting relationship, which is discussed in detail in Chapter 4, emphasizes collaboration. The counselor develops a schedule allowing time for incidental and formal contacts with all teachers. This enables the counselor and teacher to make full use of each other's knowledge, perceptions, skills, and experiences. The most desirable relationship occurs when the counselor is viewed as a member of the teaching staff, not as an administrator or supervisor.

DEVELOPING CLASSROOM GUIDANCE COMPETENCIES

One of the ways to develop the teacher's guidance competencies is through in-service training. This could include parent conferences, study of child development, development of meaningful records, and training in specific guidance techniques. The in-service training program may also be used to acquaint the teachers with professional guidance materials available through various commercial concerns.

Consultation is another way of developing classroom guidance skills. The counselor, at the request of the teacher, can come to the classroom to demonstrate a technique. In other instances he may come to observe the teacher's use of a technique and discuss with him its effectiveness. Consultation also includes discussion of individual or group problems which the teacher might be experiencing.

McCabe presents guidance as an emphasis within the educational process itself, not as a separate service. He develops series of hypotheses about personality, the helping process, guidance in the classroom, and guidance organization. These hypotheses form a strategy for achieving the objectives of guidance in the classroom setting.

Dreikurs proposes that teachers can be educated to understand the purpose and goals of behavior. Teachers can become sensitive to the goals of the child by observing interaction between children and the child's reactions to the teacher's corrective efforts.

Gordon describes guidance as a basic part of the teacher's daily work. He focuses on the child's development of himself as well as on improvement in the child's skill and knowledge. He offers practical suggestions for increasing the teacher's effectiveness.

Caldwell emphasizes comprehension of the child's feelings. In the classroom, assessing the self-concept can be accomplished by sentence and story completion and pictorial teaching techniques. Caldwell includes methods of small- and large-group guidance and makes recommendations for increasing the teacher's guidance skills.

Dinkmeyer presents a set of principles which comprise a rationale for classroom guidance, and sets forth the objectives of the elementary school guidance program. He also discusses techniques for identifying the child's guidance problems and effecting changes in his attitudes and behavior.

Simmons illustrates how a sixth-grade guidance program was developed. This program utilized analyses of tests on completion sentences, teacher-pupil and teacher-parent conferences, and self-evaluation by pupils.

The Human Relations Program at the State University of Iowa, developed by Ojemann, recommends that teachers and children be taught to comprehend the causes of human behavior. Methods of utilizing the causal approach to human behavior and examples of curricular experiences are presented. This article includes considerable proof of the validity of causal orientation.

REFERENCES

Ansbacher, H. L., and R. Ansbacher. 1956. *The individual psychology of Alfred Adler.* New York: Basic Books.

Association for Supervision and Curriculum Development. 1955. *Guidance in the curriculum, 1955 yearbook.* Washington, D.C.: The Association.

Barr, J. 1958. *The elementary teacher in guidance.* New York: Holt, Rinehart and Winston.

Caldwell, E. 1960. *Group techniques for the classroom teacher.* Chicago: Science Research Associates.

Cianciolo, Patricia. May 1965. Children's literature can affect coping behavior. *Personnel guid. J.,* 63 (No. 9), 897–903.

Coopersmith, S. 1959. A method for determining types of self esteem. *J. educ. Psychol., 59,* 87–94.

Davidson, H., and G. Lange. December 1960. Children's perceptions of their teachers' feelings toward them related to self perception, school achievement, and behavior. *J. exp. Educ., 29,* 107–118.

Dinkmeyer, D. September 1964. How do you think of yourself as a teacher? *The Instructor, 74,* 11.

————, and R. Dreikurs. 1963. *Encouraging children to learn: the encouragement process.* Englewood Cliffs, N.J.: Prentice-Hall.

Dreikurs, R. 1957. *Psychology in the classroom.* New York: Harper & Row.

Garry, R. 1963. *Guidance techniques for elementary teachers.* Columbus, Ohio: Merrill.

Gordon, I. 1956. *The teacher as a guidance worker.* New York: Harper & Row.

Hill, G. June 1965. *The institute on guidance and testing in elementary school.* Chicago: Science Research Associates.

Johnston, E. G., Mildred Peters, and W. Evraiff. 1959. *The role of the teacher in guidance.* Englewood Cliffs, N.J.: Prentice-Hall.

Kelley, E. 1950. *Education for what is real.* New York: Harper & Row.

Lewis, W., J. Lovell, and B. E. Jessee. 1965. Interpersonal relationship and pupil progress. *Personnel guid. J., 54* (No. 4).

Lloyd-Jones, Esther. 1958. *Guidance in elementary education: a case book.* New York: Bureau of Publications, Teachers College, Columbia University.

————, and Margaret Smith, 1954. *Student personnel work as deeper teaching.* New York: Harper & Row.

McCabe, G. July 1958. Guidance in the classroom—a series of hypotheses. *Educ. Adminis. Supervis., 44,* 213–218.

Moustakas, C. 1966. *The authentic teacher.* Cambridge, Mass.: Howard A. Doyle Publishing Co.

Roth, R. 1959. The role of self concept in achievement. *J. exp. Educ., 27,* 265–281.

Willey, R. 1960. *Guidance in elementary education.* Revised ed.; New York: Harper & Row.

Guidance in the Classroom —

a Series of Hypotheses*

George E. McCabe

Currently there are two major points of view regarding the role of guidance in education: one emphasizes the use of intensively trained specialists to work individually with students needing assistance—specialist-centered guidance. The other point of view advocates the use of intensively trained guidance workers as consultants to teachers—teacher-centered guidance.[1] The former approach advocates the periodic *removal* of the student from the educational mainstream so that he may be worked with under clinic-like circumstances free from the education-administrative context and the attributes of authority and evaluation which go with it. The latter approach advocates the use of guidance workers as consultants to teachers who will work with students within the administrative context of the educational institution. According to this point of view guidance

---

* *Educational Administration and Supervision,* July 1958, vol. 44. By permission.

[1] Esther Lloyd-Jones discusses these as "Centrifugal and Centripetal Guidance Programs for Children" in the *Teachers College Record,* 1949, 51, 7–13.

becomes an emphasis *within the educational process itself*, rather than a service which is adjunctive to it.

One's position with respect to these points of view depends on his assumptions regarding the process by which people are helped to grow. What follows is a tentative series of hypotheses on which the writer bases his present conclusions about professional practice in the field of guidance, and his conclusions regarding a desirable organizational structure for guidance in the public schools.

SOME HYPOTHESES
REGARDING PERSONALITY

1. Given our biological inheritance, personality is what it is as a result of an individual's history of interpersonal relationships.

2. An individual's attitudes, values, feelings, and habitual ways of reacting have been *learned* from his interpersonal experiences.

3. An individual's attitude toward himself (his self concept) is learned from his experiences, and determines the quality of his perceptions of the people and events around him.

4. In order to protect his concept of self the individual tailors reality. He sees things as he *needs* to.

5. An individual's behavior is a function of reality *as he sees it*.

6. In order to defend his concept of self, and to tailor reality to meet his needs, the individual shuts himself off from (denies) conscious awareness of significant portions of his life experience.

7. In varying degrees individuals are deprived of conscious self-determination because their behavior is determined for them by attitudes and feelings they have learned to deny (repress). They are motivated, in part, by feelings of which they are not aware.

8. The most fully functioning personality has greater access to his own experience; finds it necessary to deny less; is able to see people and their behavior with less distortion; is less likely to perceive the great variety of people and events around him in a limited number of stereotyped ways. Such a person is consciously self-determined to a greater degree.

SOME HYPOTHESES REGARDING
THE HELPING PROCESS

1. New attitudes, values, and feelings toward the self and others and, therefore, new ways of perceiving and behaving, can be learned as the result of the proper kinds of new (corrective or developmental) interpersonal experiences.

2. Psychotherapy, for example, is a series of corrective interpersonal experiences between a person seeking help and a therapist. Helpful (developmental) interpersonal experiences are not confined to psychotherapeutic sessions. They can develop in a variety of situations, many being non-professional and unplanned.

3. A "corrective" or "developmental" interpersonal experience is more likely to develop in situations in which a professional person consciously uses himself (his personality) to meet the developmental needs of others.

4. In a classroom situation a teacher can do this. While the teacher is not practicing psychotherapy, and the interpersonal experiences which develop in the classroom are not likely to be as *intensive* as in the therapist's office, he or she has the advantage of more extensive contact, and the opportunity to exploit "life events"[2] therapeutically, or, in an educational sense, developmentally.

5. Usually the therapist must use words (the interview) as a medium for establishing an interpersonal experience, that is, he must use words for the re-creation of the kinds of experiences to which the therapist must react therapeutically. The teacher has living situations to which to react. The manner in which he uses his "self" *as a teacher*, meeting situations as they arise in the classroom, determines whether he is providing a "developmental" interpersonal experience.

6. The teacher, *as a teacher*, is apt to be more effective as a guidance worker than as a guidance counselor who has sporadic contact with youngsters in "non-living" situations, and who does not have the professional training necessary to equip him to develop through the medium of the interview the kind of deep, intensive interpersonal experience which characterizes psychotherapy.

SOME HYPOTHESES REGARDING GUIDANCE IN THE CLASSROOM

1. Some of the characteristics of the "developmental" or "corrective" milieu which the effective teacher establishes are:

a. A high degree of acceptance of pupils.
b. An emphasis on the importance of self-evaluation and a de-emphasis on the importance of evaluation by others.
c. A high degree of awareness of and acceptance of feelings.
d. An atmosphere in which pupils find it increasingly safe to be *themselves* —in which they can find fuller awareness of self.
e. A milieu in which limits are more often a necessary part of the social situation, and less often a projection of the personal needs of the teacher.
f. A situation in which limits are imposed gently, but firmly, with respect for the feelings of pupils who do not like them.

2. The essence of guidance is to be found in the teacher-pupil interaction. "Guidance tools and techniques" such as sociometric charts, anecdotal records, problem check lists, autobiographies, etc., are useless unless they assist the

---

[2] The "clinical exploitation of life events" is the keystone of the milieu therapy described by Fritz Redl and David Wineman in their companion volumes, *Children Who Hate* and *Controls from Within*, Glencoe, Ill.: Free Press, 1961.

teacher to interact with the pupil with greater understanding—with greater empathy.

3. Guidance is an interpersonal *process*. It is unusual to find a diagnostic device which can produce a "fact" or a "series of facts," knowledge of which solves a pupil's problem.

4. Guidance materials injected into a course of study can be helpful *if* they elicit from pupils responses which indicate attitudes and feelings, and *if* the teacher is skillful in facilitating class interaction around these responses in accordance with some of the principles indicated above. Of central importance is the empathetic capacity of the teacher. The curricular material is an aid to be used or *mis*used.

SOME HYPOTHESES REGARDING THE PROCESS BY WHICH TEACHERS ARE HELPED

The preceding hypotheses emphasize teacher-pupil interactions as the central aspect of the guidance process. What follows is a series of hypotheses regarding the process by which teachers can be helped to grow into greater effectiveness in their role.

1. A teacher's classroom behavior represents an implementation of his concept of self, to a great degree.

2. Teachers interact with pupils in the way they *need* to.

3. They need to interact with pupils the way they do because of the way in which they see themselves and others.

4. Everyone (teachers and pupils) resists seeing himself and others differently—resists change.

5. Because teachers are human—and therefore resist change by defending their concept of self—the consultant (supervisor) does not help them to develop by telling them *how* to develop. In varying degrees, everyone is protected against this sort of judgmental attack on his concept of self.

6. The consultant, in working with the teacher (and the teacher, in working with the child) must judge the extent to which the other is sufficiently uninvolved emotionally on a given subject to be able to perceive it without distortion; to be able to deal with it on a straightforward, intellectual, information and advice-giving basis. If it is an area of distortion due to emotional involvement the approach must be *emotionally* rather than *cognitively* based.

7. When a teacher's ability to deal effectively with a classroom situation is hampered by his own emotional involvement, the consultant's role is to provide an understanding and acceptant (empathetic) interpersonal experience in which the teacher is gradually freed (feels safe enough) to explore and recognize his feelings, and, eventually, to change his perceptions because he *feels* differently.

8. In such situations the consultant functions as a counselor dealing with the

teacher's feelings about himself, and others, and with the situation itself, which the consultant keeps as the focal point of the counseling.

SOME HYPOTHESES REGARDING ORGANIZATION FOR GUIDANCE

The foregoing hypotheses regarding the nature of the guidance process, and the process by which teachers can be helped to contribute more fully to the process, serve as premises for the following conclusions regarding a desirable organizational structure for guidance in public schools.

1. The greatest opportunity for guidance is to be found in daily pupil-teacher interactions.

2. The central emphasis of guidance programs should be on the improvement of the quality of teacher-pupil interactions.

3. A major portion of the time of guidance workers should be devoted to individual and group consultation with teachers.

4. The emphasis of guidance programs should be on the improvement of the quality of the educational experience in the classroom, a function which only the schools can perform, and not on the performance of clinical services which are properly the function of other agencies better equipped to offer them.[3]

In conclusion, it should be stated that because of the truly enormous number of teachers who must be educated to carry on this nation's program of universal public education, teacher education institutions cannot be as selective in admitting students nor offer training programs of comparable intensity to those offered by sister professions in the human relations field such as psychiatry, clinical psychology, or social work. The result is that many of our teachers have not worked through the basic attitudinal problems which block their implementation of the principles of child psychology and learning to which they think they are committed at the time they receive their credentials. Teachers, therefore, particularly need an opportunity for the kind of systematic consultation which is characteristic of the clinical professions. This should be the primary function of a guidance department.

---

[3] The relationship between the full use of guidance resources within an institution and the utilization of specialized community resources is discussed by the writer in a chapter entitled "Utilizing Every Resource" in *Student Personnel Work as Deeper Teaching*, Esther Lloyd-Jones and Margaret Smith (eds.), New York: Harper & Row, 1954.

Do Teachers Understand Children?*

Rudolf Dreikurs

We have no statistical evidence for the extent to which teachers are able to understand children. However, it seems that many cannot cope with simple forms of disturbing behavior in the classroom because they are unaware of the child's motivations in behaving as he does. Knowing them, many teachers would respond differently.

Some teachers understand children through empathy. They sense what the child wants and needs, and react constructively. Their knowledge and understanding is usually not acquired during their professional training, since the psychology taught in most institutions does not provide sufficient information that can be applied to the classroom situation and to any individual child that does not behave well or does not learn.

This state of affairs is neither the fault of the teachers nor of the training institutions. It is the result of the present state of psychology and psychiatry which is plagued with divergent and often contradictory ideas and theories. Educators have to rely on the data which the field of psychology provides. An autocratic teacher will seek and find evidence for the assumption of an innate goodness or badness, intelligence or dullness in each child. Consequently, he will attempt to "tame" with punitive restrictions all bad impulses he encounters. The more democratic the educator is, the more he will follow psychological theories which assume that deficiencies are due to detrimental experiences of the child that have to be replaced with better training methods. The more "modern" educator may be affected by the psychoanalytic literature and be inclined to be overpermissive, avoiding repressions which may cause emotional maladjustment. Others may rely on data about learning, growth, and development provided by various, often unrelated, research studies of experimental psychology.

This kind of psychological information does not provide the teacher with insight into the reasons for the child's immediate behavior, nor for the proper psychological responses to it. However, there is one psychological approach which does permit an immediate understanding of any child. It is the teleo-analytic approach, developed by Alfred Adler and his co-workers, which regards behavior as purposive. Whatever the child does, right or wrong, good or bad, is understood by the purpose, the goal, which the child has set for himself.

It may be necessary to explore why the teleo-analytic approach has not been recognized universally heretofore for its extreme significance and value. There is, first, a general scientific resistance, because, historically, teleology was a

* *School and Society*, February 1959, vol. 87. By permission.

theological concept; a divine scheme set the goal for each man. The modern teleologic concept concerns itself with the goals which each individual sets for himself.

Another reason for scientific rejection of the teleological approach is the element of self-determination which it implies. As long as science was strictly mechanistically and deterministically oriented, there was no room for individual self-determination. Man was entirely determined, either by his heredity or by his environment, or by both. Goal-directed behavior assumes free choice, limitations of deterministic influences, whether from within or from without the individual. Such assumptions were totally unacceptable to the scientific world at the time when Adler and his collaborators fomulated a teleological approach in psychology. Recent developments in the basic sciences, in physics, and contemporary changes in epistemology point to creativity, self-determination, and teleological mechanisms as natural phenomena, fortifying Adler's psychological concepts. Other psychological schools move in the same direction, away from a strictly causal determination to the concepts of perceptions and goals influenced by the individual himself.

Teachers who are exposed to a training in the teleo-analytic approach suddenly become aware not only of the child's motivation, but of their own often highly detrimental role in fortifying and supporting mistaken goals. Four characteristic goals are observed behind disturbing or deficient behavior. Every child, as a social being, wants to belong. He can only fulfill himself within the group; within it he is trying to find his place. As long as he is not discouraged, he will seek his place through useful contribution, through conformity or initiative, as the situation may require. He becomes disturbed only if he is discouraged and does not think he can succeed through his own strength and ability and useful means. Then he adopts disturbing approaches, still under the assumption that they will provide him with a place in the group.

Such a misconception may lead a child either to attract attention, to demonstrate his power to the figures of authority, to get even for all the hurts he has received, or to display real or assumed deficiency in order to be left alone and avoid any tasks where he is sure to fail. These are the four goals which we found in disturbing behavior. A teacher who is not aware of them not only fails to counteract them, but often actually intensifies them by her reaction.

Teachers can be taught to become sensitive to the goals of a child. There is, first, *observation*. In the interplay of a small group of children, teachers can learn by mere observation to distinguish the goals of each child, be they attention, power, revenge, or display of deficiency. One has merely to observe what actually happens between the child and other children. By seeing what happens, one can deduce what the child intended to bring about.

Once the teacher has a tentative impression about the child's goals, she can confirm it by the observation of the child's reaction to her *corrective efforts*. A child who talks out of turn may do so either to keep the teacher busy with himself or to demonstrate his power to resist her demands. The distinction will be obvious when the child is admonished to be quiet. If his talking was merely a bid for attention, then he will be satisfied with the attention he got and stop—but not for long; soon he tries again to attract the teacher's attention. He will behave quite differently when he is talking for the purpose of defeating the teacher. Her demand for quiet will move him not to stop talking but, rather, to more violent forms of disturbance. After all, he wants to show the teacher that he can do as *he* pleases, and that she has no power to stop him.

Another reliable diagnostic tool in determining the child's goals requires more skill. It consists of the child's reaction to a *disclosure* of his goals. When asked why he misbehaves, the child cannot tell because he actually does not know the reason; he is not aware of his goals, which may be quite obvious to the trained observer. A correct explanation of the purpose of his behavior usually evokes what may be called a "recognition reflex." The child becomes aware of what he does, although he did not know it before.

The most reliable indication of the child's goals is at the same time one of the most distressing aspects of the teacher-child interaction. If the teacher wants to know for what purpose a child misbehaves, she merely has to watch her own *spontaneous and impulsive reaction*. If she merely feels annoyed and is inclined to reprimand the child, then it is most probable that he merely made a bid for her attention. If she feels deeply provoked, showing him that he cannot do that to her, then he probably just wanted to show her exactly that he *can*, to demonstrate his power. On the other hand, when she feels deeply hurt, wondering how anyone can be so mean, then she really reacts as the child wanted her to react—that is, to be hurt. And when she is inclined to throw up her hands, feeling that there is nothing she can do with this child, then he wanted to be left alone.

One can fully appreciate the disastrous consequences of the teacher's inability to understand the child's goals when one realizes that most are inclined to respond to the child's provocation in exactly the way described above. In this way, then, the teacher who tries to correct the child actually does only what the child wants, and succumbs to his intentions while attempting to counteract them. Without learning to understand the child's goals and *to deal with them effectively*,[1] the teacher simply is no match for any disturbing child.

The crucial question is how long will it take before all teachers receive this kind of training which seems to be so essential for their ability to deal with children in a democratic atmosphere. Most teachers are fully aware that they need help and assistance, training and information. However, school authorities are not prone to embarking on new courses. Too many accepted standards and principles would be upset and many vested interests threatened both in teaching and publishing. Therefore, one might be pessimistic about the prospects of developing new approaches in training teachers were it not for the fast-rising awareness that we may be confronted with a bankruptcy in our educational approaches.

[1] The technique is described in detail in the author's books, *The Challenge of Parenthood* and *Psychology in the Classroom*.

The realization of the dangerous state in which education finds itself is prompted by a variety of events: Sputnik, the recognition of our deficiency in scientific training, and the rising number and violence of juvenile delinquents. But more clearly pointing to the bankruptcy of our educational procedures is the number of children who make poor social and academic progress, and particularly the increasing number of those who are expelled from school because of academic or social maladjustment. At a time when parents are obliged by law to send their children to school, the schools assume the right to send the children back home because they do not know how to cope with them. The situation probably will become so bad before long that not only the community but also the teachers and the administrators will recognize the need for a reconsideration of some of the basic principles that underlie our present educational system. Then the time may come when new systems which have proven their effectiveness may have a chance to be implemented on a large scale.

Elementary Guidance:

Just Good Teaching?*

Ira J. Gordon

In this time of confusion over educational goals and procedures, one point of general agreement is that guidance is "good." Of course, what is meant by guidance, and particularly guidance in the elementary school, is subject to widely different meanings.

The age of rocketry and space exploration has brought with it such terms as "guided missile" and "inertial guidance systems." These are devices the expert decides are needed, and builds into the rocket. Some people see children and rockets as similar: they know what direction children *should* take, and so they conceive of school guidance as something done to children to build this direction into them.

There are many people in education, however, who feel that children have their own directions already inside them, who feel that children want to learn, to grow, to develop their capacities. They see guidance as the provision of experiences so that all children can develop their potentialities, come to know themselves better, and make wise decisions for themselves.

* *The Instructor*, March 1961. By permission.

A third view of guidance sees it as testing to find out who possesses academic talent, and then siphoning this group off from the "great unwashed" to receive rigorous training of their "minds," with no concern for anyone's personality development.

The findings of research regarding how children grow suggest that the second view, that guidance at all levels is concerned with the development of the total personality, is not only the wisest but also, from the teacher's position, the most practical definition.

Such a view of guidance places the classroom teacher on the front line. After all the organizational, curricular, and administrative decisions are made, it is she who actually establishes the classroom climate and provides the day-to-day learning setting in the classroom. She may have the assistance and support of specialists, but the primary, direct guidance responsibility is hers.

What practical steps can she take to increase her efficiency? What are the limits of her responsibility? What does she need to know?

PRACTICAL SUGGESTIONS

First, she can increase her understanding of the children in her class. She needs not only "book learning" about child development, but also specific information about the youngsters in her room. She can begin by (1) making a survey of the home backgrounds through home visits and by having the children describe, in their own words, their perceptions of home, (2) providing many activities offering choices and carefully observing and recording the choices the individual children make, (3) using sociometrics to gain insight into peer relationships, (4) learning, either through in-service experiences or through action research activities, to become sensitive to the feelings, the personal meanings back of children's behavior. She can adopt a "why" point of view, asking herself, in effect, how a child may feel who behaves in certain ways.

Second, she can survey community resources available to serve those children whom she cannot help. In spite of her best intentions, she is prohibited by the limits of her training and the very nature of the classroom situation from being a "therapist." She can find out who is available, and how to refer persons to him.

Third, she can recognize the relationship between instruction and guidance in the elementary school. She can seek ways to be creative in allowing for—nay, encouraging—individual differences. We are still a long way from using our knowledge of the individuality of the child to enhance his learning in the classroom. Research shows that the teacher who instructs with the child's self in mind, who works to make each child feel good about himself, not only reaches the academic goals for her class but also achieves such guidance goals as increasing the child's awareness of his capabilities and his knowledge of various aspects of his personality.

Fourth, she can evaluate her efforts through action research. Too often we try something new and evaluate it simply as good or bad. The classroom teacher can use simple but effective action research tools to really test her efforts.

For example, a fourth-grade teacher might begin by planning a new approach to a boy who has been passed on to her as a difficult youngster, resistant to authority, and unable to read. She will keep a record of both the boy's behavior and her own response. She can set up for herself a list of suggested experiences, in keeping with the idea that even this boy wishes to learn, to understand himself, to be accepted, to grow. She can jot down some ideas on how she plans to show him that she is attempting to understand his feelings.

Her data, a record of what actually occurs as she uses her plan, can then be evaluated at the end of each month or so. She has facts with which to test her ideas of how to work with this child. Her evaluations will suggest new plans, and she can continue. At the end of the year, she not only can see what has been done for this child, but she has accumulated many significant understandings which can be applied to aiding other children.

SUMMARY

Guidance in the elementary school is carried on, then, as a basic part of the daily work of the teacher. It is supplemented by the specialist who can perform his role by working with individual pupils or by consulting with individual teachers, or perhaps more usefully, by working with teacher groups to enable them to better understand child behavior. The focus of elementary guidance is the individual child. The goal is not therapy, but self-development. It is more than just good teaching, because it recognizes and emphasizes the self-development of the child in addition to the increase in skill and knowledge. Its concern is to enable *each* child to feel worthy, to release his capacity for growth, to come to terms with both himself and his environment.

Guidance Competencies in the Classroom*

Edson Caldwell

1,000 HOURS A YEAR!

One-thousand hours a year! Who has one-thousand hours to do anything in today's busy world? I can give a firm answer—the elementary teacher. Not only

* *Elementary School Guidance and Counseling,* 1966, vol. 1, no. 2. By permission.

count the hours, but count the opportunities allotted to the teacher to create a learning environment and then assist in its fulfillment. That many hours to be filled with close, continuous, purposeful contact with young lives that depend upon one helpful adult for instruction and guidance. What kind of a world awaits them? Who knows? Half of today's fifth graders will work at jobs that do not now exist. It is likely that each one who becomes employed will need to learn five different jobs in a lifetime. Yet this does not diminish the power of the teacher's personality and presence—he is still the greatest force in education. No magic or merchandise or mechanism devised by the genius of man can match the impact of the teacher.

In one thousand hours, what can happen? If these hours are well-planned, purposeful, and carried out with a heart full of commitment, then much can be realized in terms of the goals of guidance, provided, of course, that this teacher has acquired some competencies in both individual and group guidance activities. The high school counselor counts himself fortunate if he can maneuver even one or two full hours a year for assisting each of the students counted in his case load. Not so the elementary teacher!

I often ask teachers in my guidance classes, "When do you find time for guidance?" Evasively, most say they want to find the time but never manage to do so. Then I discover upon occasion some who say, "I do guidance all the time." One eager young fellow, now a school psychologist, pondered the query, toyed with it, then smilingly phrased his answer. "When it's warm, I move in!" This shows the necessity of comprehending the child's feeling and developing a significant relationship. Now the main question can be posed: What are some of the more basic guidance activities that can invite and challenge the elementary school classroom teacher?

BEING ATTUNED TO HUMAN FEELINGS

If there is any single competency that is fundamental to guidance it is the capacity to be aware of human feelings. Emotions are the "raw stuff" of guidance. Bankers derive their activities from the use of money. Chemists are concerned with atoms. Musicians invent harmony from vibrations. Accordingly, guidance workers become absorbed with the ebb and flow of human feelings. Individuality, that most precious quality that makes each person unique, is shaped by private feelings about the things the individual experiences around him. Only as we discover the dimensions of these feelings do we get to know and understand the behavior of an individual. Back of behavior are the emotions that generate the actions. Suppose a person feels lonely, then many types of resulting activity can be understood. Knowing the feelings of the child, not just his pattern of performance in the curriculum, is basic to understanding who he is and what he can become.

When I visit a classroom this focus on feelings is the first dimension I try to assess. If a child is not participating, asks for individual help, or shows rebellion, does the teacher discover the feelings first or does he try to "get at the facts?" It is one role to be a District Attorney and an interrogator; it is quite another to get below the surface level and find the flow of feelings that produced a person's behavior.

When a boy gives up on a puzzling problem in arithmetic and wads up his paper, does the teacher deal with the particular mistake made, or does he have the competency in guidance to deal with the deeper problem—how does this boy face difficulty? If he deals with the underlying feeling, then a possible *counseling* relationship is set up, leading later to any instruction needed. This dual approach of the teacher-counselor distinguishes the professional from the amateur, however warm-hearted his intentions may be.

Classrooms have climates. They have moods. Children respond to both the visible and invisible factors that concern their existence in today's increasingly accelerated technological society. I recently asked an enthusiastic young teacher about the source of her zest for facing a class of third graders each day. "How do you like to start your day?" I asked. She took a deep breath, then revealed her whole heart.

"First, I try to find their feelings and set the tone for the day. Maybe I sense it already from informal observations. I know that each day is different, often very different. I wonder what they are concerned about this morning. What is on their minds. Let's get it out of the way or use it if we can. What should we try to do today? How can we work it out? As they respond, I put their ideas on the blackboard and we work out plans together.

"Then the rest of the day I shift gears. I just sit back and help it happen. Instead of being a teacher and leader up front, I move to another desk at the back of the room. There I 'listen' a lot. I'm a counselor and helper. I try to circulate around the room every now and then so that I don't miss anybody. I get to every person before recess. Each person is so wonderfully different and he grows a little bit every day."

It's easy to see why Toni loves teaching. She has found the fascination of following feelings and channeling them into constructive directions. She doesn't have to fight feelings—they are on her side.

It is an art to capture and corral the diversity of emotions that come into a classroom. Yet, it is the quality and depth of human feelings that make immortal music, great drama, lasting art, or a masterpiece in literature. Reading *Moby Dick* is an emotional experience.

Following feelings is like watching the flow of a river from its source in some high hidden mountain canyon all the way to the sea. The gathering flow sometimes plunges swiftly and spectacularly. Sometimes it wanders widely through marshes or meanders aimlessly—but it has a destination and moves toward it. Or, it is like a game of golf. Feelings don't go where we try to direct them and they often get lost for a while. No one knows in advance where the ball —call it "ego" if you wish—will be. Each time the ball must be played according to where it lies at that very moment. Guidance, with its focus on feelings, is likewise an adventure, sometimes quite unpredictable, but always quite profitable.

The discovery of feelings revolves around the teacher's ability to find the self-concept of each child. His behavior, his work, his aspirations are shaped by this basic foundation of his personality pattern. There are, fortunately, many techniques that a teacher may employ in revealing the self and in discovering ways to deal successfully with its development.

THE OPEN-END SENTENCE

One of the easiest and most revealing instruments to employ in the classroom is the open-end sentence. It lends itself to a variety of uses. Any answer is accepted and any sentence may be completed in many different ways. Each teacher can compose his own list, but such items as these will prove significant:

At school I like to _____

After school I usually _____

My parents expect me to _____

Report cards make me feel _____

I get worried when _____

I wish I could _____

Erasures are significant and also omissions—both evidences that the situation is difficult to respond to and involves avoidance. Greater freedom and depth of response will be given if names are not requested, only age and sex. Tallies can be made of the replies to certain questions and the general results used for classroom discussion purposes. This way the teacher can anticipate the spectrum of feelings in advance. It is an intensely satisfying and helpful experience to bring such feelings out into the open where each child can make comparisons and have his own understandings deepened. Consensus is not sought, but group evaluation of the various wholesome and unwholesome aspects of the emotions revealed.

THE UNFINISHED STORY

Language activities, both written and oral, offer many guidance activities. The unfinished story of a "problem" story gives each child a chance to respond to a difficulty in terms of his own feeling. These can be adapted to the proper level of difficulty and designed to meet an immediate or forthcoming situation. For example:

> Roger, age eleven, has been asked by his mother to baby-sit with his two sisters, age five and three, while she goes to the dentist. This comes after school when he had planned to try out for the local Little League Team. What do you think he should do and why?
>
> Carol, age nine, has been getting an allowance of fifty cents per week. She helps set the table twice a day and clears away the dinner dishes, cares for her

own room, and takes care of the family Persian cat. She finds one of her girl friends gets $1.00 a week for doing chores and another $1.50 per week. (Finish the story).

The various answers can be reviewed by the teacher and brought back to the class for evaluative discussion. Often it helps to put some of the more significant solutions or comments on the board, noting both positive and negative aspects. Above all don't "preach" or "moralize"—let them find the solution.

PICTORIAL TECHNIQUES

At the kindergarten-primary level the best technique for expressing feelings is not verbal or written but through pictorial expression. Invite pupils to draw pictures on such topics as "My Home," "My Family," "What I Do After School," "What Makes Me Mad," or "My Responsibilities." No one is forced to do any of these and children are invited to show their drawing to the class and tell about it if they wish. Each drawing offers a fine opportunity for the teacher to discover inner feelings by employing the "Tell Me Technique," which implies that the child is not placed in the position of answering questions, but in that of an open response to "Tell Me About This Picture." Much can be learned from these personal "productions" and the accompanying comments. They offer an excellent basis for teacher-pupil communication. In them the child's world comes alive. Some teachers like to keep these in individual folders for occasional review with the pupil. With the child's permission, several pictures may be selected to show for a coming parent conference.

PUPIL APPRAISAL

The basic approach in elementary school guidance is child study, conducted for the purpose of developing an individual and on-going appraisal of each youngster. In addition to the regular information in the cumulative record as to family background, health, grades, and test results, there is a need for folders to include some of the child's own "productions." These can be drawings like those mentioned above, samples of work in each subject, or any work that the student feels is worthy of keeping for the record. As he gets a better paper in a school subject, call him aside for consultation and clip this improved paper over the old one. Also valuable are timed observations, two-minute checks, efficiency observations (such as time utilized in study vs. time lost), anecdotal records (including both positive and negative incidents), accounts of stories told or materials brought to school for display, etc. These compose an excellent basis for a private "talk it over" session with the pupil. Together teacher and child can go over materials, look for progress, enjoy an occasional laugh, and plan for future additions. Again, close attention to the child's self-concept is basic to understanding his performance. If someone contributed to the class by singing a song, bringing materials, helping on playground, or doing some act of appreciation, the class might be involved in evaluating the activity and deciding if the accomplishment deserves special recognition. A special note is then added to the individual folder.

SMALL-GROUND GUIDANCE ACTIVITIES

The elementary teacher is fundamentally a group worker. Reading groups, socialized art activities, bulletin board committees, class officers, safety patrol squads, and demonstration groups in science are frequent classroom activities, especially in the middle and upper grades. After a lecture and demonstration on sociometrics as a device for grouping, a young teacher sighed hopefully, "I'm glad to know there's an organized way to do this."

Sociometry provides a basis for studying the network of "underground" choices that children make from day to day. Good teachers can usually spot most of the first choices, but the second and third ones are largely invisible—but they are there. Ralph Garry's book, *Guidance Techniques for Elementary Teachers* (Columbus, Ohio: Merrill, 1963), gives a good review of the mechanics of the sociometric technique, especially that of the follow-up of the second sociogram and its analysis. Studies now show that unless remedial steps are taken, the child who is an "isolate" in the second grade is likely to still be one in high school and all through life. Isolation, even partial isolation, and loneliness can seriously cripple the development of a child. Evaluative and preventive steps, through sociometrics, can be undertaken early.

Study groups can be very close, personal associations—for one lets another know his mistakes. Last fall I visited some classrooms where the teachers, amazingly, never had to preside over a class to get it started after recess or intermissions. Each morning, however, preliminary discussions of "being in charge of myself" had been held. Study time, work, recreation, recitation, and free time were carefully planned individually each day. Children worked in voluntary groups or alone, as previously agreed upon. Much guidance had preceded this achievement—in fact six weeks of special effort. The progress made and the atmosphere created paid off in greater accomplishment and individual maturity. During the year there was a better grasp of the most important branch of human knowledge, one recommended by Socrates long ago—self-knowledge.

LARGE-GROUP GUIDANCE ACTIVITIES (CLASSROOM SIZE)

I visited a sixth grade recently and was pleased to observe a lively discussion on "acting grown up." I was still more gratified when I noted that a girl with a very pronounced speech defect spoke up frequently and that the class waited patiently to hear her ideas, displaying not the slightest sense of embarrassment. It takes very sensitive work with a class to create a classroom climate like that. All the road signs read, "FEELINGS FIRST."

Actually the skills used in guiding the non-directive, human relations type of discussion closely approximate the same techniques used in good interviewing. I like to hear teachers in discussion sessions "mirror" feelings with statements like this (feeling level words underlined) :

"Anyone *agree* or *disagree* with Nancy's ideas about counting to ten to hold your temper?"

"Who else can help us find out how we *feel* about tests?"

"Tom has told us about some of the things that make him *angry*. Anyone else want to tell what *upsets* him?"

Note that the teacher does not take a position, but facilitates the expression of true feelings from the class. If he or she takes a stand, then pupils will tend to agree with the teacher instead of revealing their own reactions. By playing up and bringing out *positive* feelings and writing them on the blackboard, the tone of the discussion can usually be constructive. Even if it isn't, the teacher should allow the class to be honest. New information, new situations, or further discussions can be planned for the future where the class will be able to evaluate ideas and actions. Generally, it is best to work toward pupil-led discussions.

Films that present problem situations can be effective tools for discussion purposes. Stopping the film at critical points can be helpful and give students a chance to analyze the action thus far or give identification to the underlying problem.

A powerful force in making a problem come alive for discussion purposes can be found in the use of role playing. The unstructured situation gives room for spontaneous expression of feelings. The role playing must make the problem come alive for the class and be stopped in time to allow discussion of the feelings involved, the possible solutions, and to permit revised enactment of the scene. This allows for "reality testing" in a marvelous way. A mistake in a classroom role playing situation is not crucial, as it might well be at home or in view of outsiders.

GAINING COMPETENCY
IN GUIDANCE ACTIVITIES

Without some concluding statement, I fear this presentation would appear to be like the Mother Hubbard dress referred to by Lincoln when he said, "It covers everything and touches nothing." How are teachers to learn the principles and techniques underlying such activities as those just reviewed? Probably not by reading books on guidance. Probably not by taking a college course on guidance. Probably not by exposure to this article.

It is not expected, certainly, that teachers, even very excellent teachers, can merely read about such activities and then immediately try them out successfully in the classroom. That would be like expecting a person to start playing baseball after reading a quick summary of the rules. It takes observation—carefully supervised observation—in order to discern the principles involved in these guidance activities. The application of actual practices and sequential procedures will be learned by seeing such activities in action and by participating directly in them. But how are teachers to have such opportunities?

The main point underlying this entire article can now be proposed. *A good elementary school guidance program provides a service to teachers as well as pupils.* A vital part of this service involves direct assistance to classroom teachers in learning guidance competencies. Actual demonstrations in the classroom or at meetings with teachers will usually be needed, followed by later observations or consultations to see if further assistance is needed.

The elementary school counselor, it seems evident, needs to be a widely experienced and highly competent individual at many grade levels. He should be able to come into a classroom, on invitation, and assist with a guidance activity in whatever way is agreed upon as most comfortable to the teacher. Often a counselor takes one class while the teacher observes an activity in another room. If a counselor or guidance worker cannot offer this kind of direct classroom assistance, not much will happen to reach the main mass of elementary school students so far as the guidance program is concerned.

Guidance competencies, like creativity, cannot be forced, cannot be imitated, cannot be prefabricated. Like good music, however, they must be experienced to be understood and learned in order to be possessed. In the last analysis, all educational progress revolves around what actually happens to the individual, particularly the one in the back row. There should be no reluctance, therefore, to emphasize the fact that what happens to individual pupils in the day-to-day activities of the classroom is what matters most.

And who is closest to the individual? We are back to those 1,000 hours a year again. Who holds those hours holds the inner key. No magic or merchandise or mechanism can match the impact of the classroom teacher!

Elementary School Guidance
and the Classroom Teacher*

Don C. Dinkmeyer

As schools increasingly seek quality educational experiences for all children, consideration is being given to the nature of the elementary school guidance program. This investigation has included a review of the role of administration,

* *Elementary School Guidance and Counseling*, 1967, vol. 1, no. 1.
   By permission.

consultants, and the teacher in guidance services. While guidance has been established in the secondary schools for a number of years, the guidance program in the elementary school has frequently been poorly conceptualized and haphazard.

Some schools have assumed that all staff members function in the area of guidance regardless of their training or the accessibility of a guidance consultant. In these situations we usually find some teachers performing adequately while many teachers assume few of the responsibilities of a broad classroom guidance program. Other schools have made little pretense of developmental guidance for all children. They have featured programs which focus only on diagnosis and therapy for the exceptional child. Finally, we can observe a growing number of schools that have hired an elementary school counselor or consultant and have developed a planned program of classroom guidance through teachers.

We now see considerable evidence about us that there is a generally accepted awareness of the importance of elementary school guidance. The American School Counselor Association has had a study of elementary school guidance under way since 1957. The 1960 White House Conference on Children and Youth placed an important emphasis on the extension of counseling services to meet the needs of the pre-adolescent. Recent federal legislation has subsidized elementary school guidance. The need for guidance services is related closely to the fundamental principles of democratic education. Schools which provide education for all and which stress choice, self-actualization, and citizenship training will consider elementary school guidance an essential service.

Perhaps the most significant research has been that which has shown that there is a significant relationship between the child's academic achievements and his concept of self as a functioning student (Roth, 1959). All of this suggests a need to investigate the role of the teacher in the elementary school guidance program. It is fundamentally true that a good educational program is one that is developmental. It is generally acknowledged that all education is individual. If a school program is to have meaning and be significant, it must reach the individual. No amount of administrative manipulation or curriculum planning will necessarily be effective until we are able to reach the individual child. This implies that guidance must be more than incidental.

PRINCIPLES UNDERLYING ELEMENTARY SCHOOL GUIDANCE

The type of guidance in the elementary school that we shall be discussing is the foundation of effective instruction. Classroom guidance is based on certain fundamental principles:

1. Guidance is for all children, not merely deviates or exceptional children.
2. Guidance is concerned with the growth of the whole child: intellectually, socially, emotionally.
3. Guidance is developmental in nature, not merely remedial or preventive.

4. Developmental guidance is directed at helping the child know, understand, and accept himself. The child becomes a participant in self study, not the object of child study.

5. Guidance provides the individual with assessment of self, the opportunity to plan and choose, and to be responsible for the consequences of choice.

6. Guidance may be incidental, but it functions best when it is based upon a well organized, developmental, and sequential program that is continuous.

7. Guidance takes into consideration needs and developmental tasks while focusing on individual purposes and goals.

8. The guidance program is provided for all through the teacher in the school setting and is also facilitated by an educationally oriented counselor.

9. Guidance focuses on the strengths and assets of the individual.

10. Guidance that is developmental focuses on the encouragement process. It strives to build self-confidence.

11. The guidance program is most effectively activated when it is a cooperative enterprise between the teacher, guidance counselor, administration, and community resources.

THE PURPOSES AND OBJECTIVES OF ELEMENTARY SCHOOL GUIDANCE

The purpose of elementary school guidance is to facilitate learning in the child and modify pupil, teacher, and parent attitudes. It should make possible the mutual alignment of pupil and teacher purposes. The purposes of elementary school guidance are in direct alignment with the objectives of elementary education. The broad objectives of elementary school guidance include:

1. Assisting teachers in the total educational program to meet the needs of all students in intellectual, personal, and social areas. Promoting understanding of the individual and encouraging adaptation of the program to specific needs, purposes, interests, and maturities.

2. Promoting the early identification of both individual strengths and talents as well as individual liabilities or deviations.

3. Making the teacher aware of and sensitive to the child's personal needs, goals, and purposes. Enabling the teacher to utilize the principles from educational psychology, child development, learning theory, and guidance in the classroom.

4. Stimulating the study and the use of guidance techniques by the teacher and total staff, thereby increasing the utilization of pupil personnel data and encouraging the individualization of the total educational experiences.

Specifically, in terms of the child, the goal of the program is:

1. to assist the child in the development of increased self-understanding, and increased understanding of the relationship between his abilities, interests, achievements, and opportunities;

2. to promote increased self-direction, problem solving, and decision making by the child;

3. to develop wholesome attitudes, convictions, and concepts about self and others which result in the "fully functioning child";

4. to assist the child in understanding, planning, making choices, and solving present and future problems;

5. to develop a sensitivity to the needs of others, a social interest in and a desire to cooperate with others;

6. to understand the causal and purposive nature of behavior and to use this knowledge in understanding self and others;

7. to assist the child in the solving of fundamental tasks of life in the areas of work and social development.

PRINCIPLES OF HUMAN DEVELOPMENT

Developmental principles help the teacher function more effectively with children. There is a pattern to behavior and it is vital that the teacher recognize and focus on the pattern and avoid being confused by details. Behavior often appears contradictory until seen in relationship to the pattern.

The teacher must become acquainted with certain fundamental assumptions related to the understanding of personality. Knowledge of a theory of human development provides a basis for understanding behavior. The following assumptions have been of value in providing direction for classroom guidance:

1. Human personality is best understood in its unity. The teacher focuses on the pattern and the psychological movement the child displays instead of considering isolated situations. Psychological movement should be understood in terms of holism.

2. Behavior is goal directed and purposive. Each psychological movement has a goal and behavior is directed by the dominant motive. These goals must be recognized as being subjective, creative, and frequently unconscious, or dimly perceived by the individual. The goal becomes the final cause or final explanation. As one is aware of the purpose of misbehavior, suggestions for corrective action are often implied. The goals of misbehavior can be understood in terms of: attention getting, the struggle for power, the desire to get even, or the display of inadequacy, or assumed disability, as described by Dreikurs (1957).

3. Motivation is best understood in terms of understanding the way in which the child strives for significance. Always ask, how does this help the child find his place or maintain his reputation?

4. Behavior and misbehavior make sense to the individual. The individual must be understood in terms of his phenomenological field, the entire world including the self as it is experienced by the individual.

5. All behavior has social meaning. Behavior must always be seen within its social context and the interactions it produces. Misbehavior in the classroom often makes sense in terms of the social rewards it can secure.

6. Belonging is a basic need of all humans. The child desires to identify and belong and we can both understand and correct his behavior by utilizing this need.

7. The development of social interest is crucial for adjustment. The child's capacity to give and take, his social interest, is an expression of his mental health.

The style of life is a unifying principle that helps us comprehend the consistent movement the child makes toward certain goals. This style of life is the frame of reference for all his attitudes. It reflects his private logic and basic convictions. The style of life helps us to become familiar with the child's private logic and uniqueness. Some styles of life may be characterized as "those who need to be more than others," "those who are willing to demonstrate their inadequacy," "those who mainly want excitement," "those who set their own rules," and "those who are committed to provoking" (Mosak and Shulman, 1962). As the teacher becomes aware of the specific life style of a child he can function more effectively in working with that child.

GUIDANCE IN THE CLASSROOM

The teacher's guidance role can be described in terms of identifying guidance needs and changing attitudes and behavior. It is crucial to develop an effective relationship with children. This relationship should be characterized by a mutual alignment of goals and purposes. Mutual trust and respect are essential conditions but the responsibility for change resides in the pupil.

TECHNIQUES FOR IDENTIFICATION

One of the skills available to all teachers is that of observation. Observation is most meaningful when one has a comprehensive understanding of personality and is able to see behavior in relationship to a style of life. Systematic anecdotal records are an aid in the identification of guidance needs. Suggestions regarding adequate anecdotal records emphasize the importance of presenting a word picture of an incident in the life of the child (Dinkmeyer, 1965). Teachers must be aware that the behavior of the child provides an excellent opportunity for developing insight into his motives. If behavior is understood in its unity as being purposive, then the actions of the child express his atttudes, goals, and expectations. This emerging pattern points to the motives of the child.

There are a number of techniques that can be mentioned briefly at this point which require further study. These would include sociometrics, pupil questionnaires such as "Guess Who" and "Who Are They?", incomplete stories or sentence completion tests, and the Pupil Interest Inventory. Early recollections, the earliest specific incident the child can recall, are most revealing of the child's self-concept and his attitude toward life. The place of the child among the siblings, family constellation, and particularly his perception of his position, provide clues in understanding behavior.

All of these techniques can be used to assist the teacher in systematically beginning to understand more effectively the values, goals, and motives of children. Teachers can be assisted in this type of study by the use of an organized child study outline. The case study and discussion by the entire staff can be most profitable. After the collection of data the teacher should begin to have available some answers regarding the child's purposes and values. He should be able to assess the developmental tasks which the child is presently concerned with. Most of all, he should be able to formulate specific ideas about more effective corrective actions to utilize in future interactions with the pupil.

TECHNIQUES FOR CHANGE OF ATTITUDE AND BEHAVIOR

The teacher must become involved in much more than merely identifying problems. Pupil personnel services in the elementary school have long been concerned with the identification process, and far too many psychological reports have been filed on children without appropriate action being initiated. Curriculum experiences can be used to help meet the needs of the child intellectually, socially, and psychologically.

GUIDANCE LEARNINGS

It is important that we recognize certain basic guidance learnings which give direction to elementary school guidance. The guidance learnings I shall refer to were originally listed by Hill (1965). These guidance learnings are not the exclusive concern of the counselor but should be the concern of all teachers. The guidance learnings include:

1. the need to understand oneself, to mature in self-understanding, to become aware of one's potentialities.

2. to mature in accepting responsibility for oneself, for what one is and how one functions.

3. to mature in understanding the role of education and the role of work; to develop a wholesome attitude toward these responsibilities in life.

4. to mature in the ability to make choices and decisions; to plan.

5. to mature in the ability to solve one's own problems.

6. to mature in understanding human behavior and the nature of relationships.

7. to mature in one's adjustment to the demands of life, especially in relationship with others.

8. to mature in a sense of values and the achievement of high ideals.

These learnings provide the rationale for the necessity of the classroom teacher functioning in the area of guidance. The guidance learnings can give direction to the elementary school curriculum in its broadest sense.

The teacher can engage in certain corrective or therapeutic techniques himself. After asserting the individual's capacity and purposes, attempts should be made to individualize instruction. This can be done by teacher-pupil planning and teacher-pupil evaluation. The program involves self-selection and pacing. In some instances the use of programmed materials and programmed instruction techniques will assist in the individualization of instruction. Teachers should become increasingly aware of the technique of bibliotherapy—the use of a book as a means of helping the child understand a personal problem. The regular use of group discussion on a planned basis in the classroom as problems occur is helpful in establishing group expectations (Dreikurs, 1957).

There is need for an increased utilization of group guidance material and process (Goldman, 1962). A number of commercial materials are now available from various publishing houses. Some school districts have also developed their own curriculum guides in group guidance. The Ojemann (1961) materials from the University of Iowa provide an excellent sequential program in self-understanding.

One of the most effective techniques at the disposal of the classroom teacher is encouragement (Dinkmeyer and Dreikurs, 1963). Here he helps the child to feel his worth and facilitates the development of his security. He provides more opportunities in the classroom for success than failure, actually arranging experiences so that the child develops a sense of accomplishment. It becomes important in this process that children are valued and accepted as they are. Having this faith in the child's ability enables him to build his own self-respect. This type of teacher recognizes a job well done, and is willing to give recognition for effort, even when work is not complete or perfect. The group is used to enhance the development of the child. It is important that the child be helped to be sure of his place within the group. The teacher utilizes interests to enliven instruction. Emphasis is placed on recognizing and focusing on strengths and assets.

Some children can be most effectively assisted as they are permitted to experience the consequences of the situation. As an individual becomes impressed with the disadvantage of disregarding order, it is not necessary to become personally involved in punishment. The consequence can frequently express the power of social order and goes far beyond that of any individual teacher. The creative teacher will find many opportunities to utilize natural and logical consequences (Grunwald, 1955).

The therapeutic approach implies that the teacher is kind and firm, respecting both himself and the child. He teaches individual children, not subjects. He is alert to non-verbal behavior which reveals the goals of the child's psychological movement. This teacher uses responsibility to enhance the individual's development. The psychological approach is preferred to the logical approach. He does not require the child to first earn responsibility, but he uses responsibility for the therapeutic effect it may produce on the irresponsible child. This teacher sets limits early and if possible has the rules and limits developed by the group. When there are violations he permits the consequences to occur instead of talking about what might happen. At times the teacher, as an effective technique, uses disclosure to produce insight for the child into his own goals. He may confront the child with his current goal and his private logic and enable him to see the possibilities for change to more efficient goals and logic by saying, "Could it be?" or "Is it possible?" and then alluding to the child's goal. This is followed by assisting the child to clarify his purposes and see alternatives.

The teacher then becomes a part of a broad-based guidance program. This guidance program typically consists of:

Pupil Inventory and Pupil Appraisal

Guidance Consulting

Counseling: Individual and Group

Group Guidance and Information Services

Coordination and Research

The program is activated most efficiently in the elementary school through counselor and classroom teacher cooperation. Obviously, the teacher is most effective if he has available an elementary school counselor or consultant who is able to assist in the appraisal and counseling of certain individuals. The consultant helps the teacher to understand test results and in some instances may be of assistance in the articulation of pupils throughout the elementary school. At times the consultant leads or demonstrates certain group guidance activities or consults with teachers about specific pupils. The consultant uses pupil-personnel records with teachers so they become meaningful in helping make educational decisions with children.

Thus, we come to the fundamental question, is the teacher a guidance worker in the elementary school? It would seem apparent that the teacher is concerned with assisting each child to achieve the developmental tasks and to do this he must assist individuals in clarifying understandings about self and others. If this teacher is involved in understanding, accepting, clarifying, encouraging, and building an adequate concept of self, then he takes on specific guidance functions. It seems most apparent that if the goals of guidance are ever to be achieved in terms of the principles and objectives we have laid down for all pupils, then it is only through the teacher, assisted by a competent consultant, that we can hope to reach all children.

REFERENCES

Dinkmeyer, D. 1965. *Child development: the emerging self.* Englewood Cliffs, N.J.: Prentice-Hall.

——, and R. Dreikurs. 1963. *Encouraging children to learn: the encouragement process.* Englewood Cliffs, N.J.: Prentice-Hall.

Dreikurs, R. 1957. *Psychology in the classroom.* New York: Harper & Row.

Goldman, L. February 1962. Group guidance: content and process. *Personnel guid. J., 60* (No. 6), 518–522.

Grunwald, B. 1955. The application of Adlerian principles in a classroom. *Amer. J. indiv. Psychol., 11* (No. 2).

Hill, G. June 1965. *Institute on guidance and testing in the elementary school.* Chicago: Science Research Associates. Not mimeographed.

Mosak, H., and B. Shulman. 1962. Lectures given at the Alfred Adler Institute, Chicago. Not mimeographed.

Ojemann, R. 1961. *A teaching program in human behavior and mental health.* Ames, Iowa: State University of Iowa, Iowa Child Welfare Research Station.

Roth, R. June 1959. The role of self concept in achievement. *J. exp. Educ., 27,* 265–281.

A Guidance Program

for Preadolescents*

Science Research Associates

Although the average elementary teacher has an excellent knowledge of her pupils, there are factors affecting individual attitudes and preventing self-understanding that may remain undiscovered by the teacher for the entire school year.

A new and effective technique for discovering many of these hidden factors has been developed by Ida Harper Simmons, sixth-grade teacher in the Children's School of the National College of Education. It employs sets of completion sentences, followed by an exploration of pupil responses in individual teacher-pupil conferences at intervals throughout the year. The method was studied over a four-year period and information obtained from sixth-grade pupils was carefully evaluated. The findings then became the basis for the development of a sixth-grade guidance program.

While the techniques to be described were carried out in only one grade of a single school, the method may be adapted for use in upper elementary grades in other schools.

At the Children's School of the National College of Education the sets of completion sentences, or attitude inventory, given four or five times during the school year and followed by careful analysis and teacher-pupil conferences, served these purposes:

1. Aided the teacher in understanding the individual child.

2. Helped the teacher to draw conclusions about ten- or eleven-year-olds in general.

* Science Research Associates Special Guidance Report, 1962. By permission.

3. Assisted the child in understanding himself, so that he could appreciate his strengths and face his weaknesses.

4. Helped pupils to perceive the purposes of learning and encouraged them to establish good study habits.

The first set of completion sentences was given early in the year, after rapport between pupils and teacher had been well established. The list was introduced by an explanation of the purposes, namely, to help the teacher become better acquainted with each child and to help her understand sixth-graders in general. The pupils were assured that the information would be confidential. They were directed to decide upon their own answers, and not to discuss them with their friends.

TYPICAL COMPLETION SENTENCES

Sentences can be tailored to fit the needs of a particular class. In general, the first set includes the following:

1. I'm proud of myself because . . .
2. My best work in school is . . .
3. I could improve myself by . . .
4. I wish my classmates would . . .
5. I could help my class improve by . . .
6. I do my lessons because . . .
7. The kind of friend I like best is . . .
8. I wish my teachers would . . .
9. I wish my parents would . . .
10. I wish . . .

Miss Simmons learned much from observing pupils while they wrote. She detected those who were at ease in expressing their ideas. She also tried to distinguish between those who appeared unable to express themselves because of lack of writing ability and those who apparently could not express themselves for emotional reasons, so that these pupils could be given the necessary help.

When pupils asked whether they must answer all questions, they were told that they need not answer those about which they had no definite opinion or feeling. The teacher expected fewer answers on the first set than on each of the sets of completion sentences to be given later.

RESPONSES ARE REVEALING

A careful examination of responses revealed much about each child. Jim left sentence 1 blank. Perhaps he hesitated to enumerate his own good points, or he might have sincerely felt that he had little to feel proud of. Betty wrote, "I try to work very hard in school and do all my work." Here was a girl who tried hard to please. Her reaction might indicate parent pressure or feelings of social inadequacy that would bear careful watching in the future.

Carl wrote, "I think I'm a good student and a good athlete." Joe responded with "I think I'm capable of knowing how to do something for other people." Rita said, "I feel that mostly I'm a good student in school and that most of my friends take my opinion for various things." From such statements the pupils were guided toward objective self-evaluation.

Sentences 2 and 3 were of value in comparing the child's achievement with his estimate of his ability, as well as in establishing some goals in learning. The fourth and fifth sentences revealed the child's peer relationships and social adjustment.

Sentence 4 (I wish my classmates would . . .) revealed much about the individual's adjustment to the group. The contented child found it easy to respond, ". . . be the same as they are right now," or ". . . do nothing; I like them the way they are." On the other hand, the teacher detected warning signs in responses such as ". . . would not pick on me"; ". . . think twice before they laugh at others"; ". . . associate with me more"; and ". . . stop picking on me because I am weaker."

THE PUPIL'S RESPONSIBILITY

The pupil's thinking was directed to his own responsibility in the group by sentence 5 (I could help my class improve by . . .). An average preadolescent will usually respond with an honest evaluation of his own faults. The teacher found that it is sometimes easier for youngsters to write responses dealing with personal faults than to admit virtues.

Sentence 6 (I do my lessons because . . .) often puzzled the pupils at the beginning of the school year. First responses included such statements as these: ". . . I have to and I like some of them"; ". . . I know I'm supposed to"; ". . . then I can get a good job"; ". . . I feel better inside"; ". . . my teacher wants me to."

The preceding replies pointed up a learning factor that is too often overlooked at the middle-grade level. At this level pupils have passed the point where learning to read or acquiring a mathematical skill is an adventure. As a result, many perceive no immediate purpose for further learning.

Responses to sentence 7 (The kind of friend I like best is . . .) typical of a beginning sixth-grader included the following: ". . . someone who is nice to me"; ". . . a girl who likes the same things I do"; ". . . someone who is interested in sports"; ". . . the kind that always likes me." It has been observed that the child who is having difficulty in making friends will be inclined to respond to this sentence in one of two ways. Either he will put down a specific name, or he will state that he likes a friend who is just like himself.

Sentence 8 (I wish my teachers would . . .) is one that a teacher might hesitate to include, and pupils hesitate to complete. The class often indicated surprise at the sentence. However, its presence in the list was well worthwhile for several reasons. By their responses—or by failing to respond—the pupils gave the teacher some indication of her rapport with her class. Pupils did not usually hesitate to give honest answers after the teacher had casually explained that the whole purpose of the questionnaire was to help pupils understand themselves and to help acquaint the teacher with the feelings and problems of each member of the class.

A sampling of responses included the following: ". . . be more understanding"; ". . . let me act like I'm older"; ". . . have just a little more patience"; ". . . let me listen to the World Series"; ". . . explain directions a little more clearly"; ". . . help me more in math."

USING CLASS DISCUSSION

Such statements were examined objectively by the teacher. Sometimes, when a recurring comment justified it, class discussion clarified a situation. In other cases it was observed that some child's need for special help had been overlooked.

A word of caution is offered regarding this area of pupil-teacher relations. There are times when pupils need to understand the cause-and-effect factor in behavior—even the behavior of teachers. The comment "I wish my teacher wouldn't raise her voice," or ". . . wouldn't get angry with me," may indicate that the teacher is short on patience. On the other hand, such responses may signify that pupils need guidance in accepting the responsibility for and the consequences of their own behavior. The teacher should accept some comments on this sentence simply as expressions of the child's temporary hostility. It must be added that positive answers give the teacher the sense of security that she needs.

Sentence 9 (I wish my parents would . . .) was considered from many points of view. The ten- or eleven-year-old child is nearing adolescence and is beginning to test his independence in the home situation. These children are beginning to feel that parents do not understand them. (This may be true, since the beginning of personality changes at adolescence often perplexes parents.)

Typical comments concerning parents were as follows: ". . . spend more time with me"; ". . . give me a chance to explain"; ". . . let me spend money without worrying what I'm going to do with it"; ". . . see my view on things"; ". . . wouldn't nag me."

Other responses to sentence 9 that threw light on the child's behavior in school included these: "I wish that Mommy would marry someone who would be nice to me"; "I wish my mom would have a conference so she'd know what I need help on"; "I wish my parents would help me more at home."

Responses to sentence 10 (I wish . . .) were as varied as the interests of sixth-graders. Certain responses were indicative of pressures felt by the children, both at home and at school. An illustrative example is "I wish I could have good grades."

In responding to sentence 10, a child often expressed a desire that a teacher would not be able to discern in any other way. Jane's hidden fears concerning her mother's health were revealed in the sentence "I wish that my mother's heart trouble wasn't there, and that she was always well and she would live a long happy life." Helen's statement, "I wish I could be more outgoing," indicated the desire of this shy girl to learn to relate to others. Ellen, a passive and unattractive girl, revealed her deep need when she wrote, "I wish I could be teacher's pet."

Individual conferences were held with each child after the first set of completion sentences was given. Children were not required to discuss all of their responses, some being accepted without comment. It was found that the time could be spent more profitably in clarifying obscure items or in establishing a better teacher-pupil understanding. At these conferences, results of full achievement tests were discussed along with the completion sentences.

During these conferences the teacher helped the child compare his opinions of his academic achievement with the results of his tests. She helped the child analyze his difficulties and sometimes planned a program for strengthening his weaknesses. It was noted that giving a pupil assurance that his reading or mathematical achievement, for example, was satisfactory often served as an excellent incentive for further achievement. Moreover, conducting teacher-pupil conferences early in the school year did wonders in establishing a good relationship between pupils and teacher.

The public school teacher with a large class may doubt whether time could be made available for a program of individual pupil conferences. It was found that once the conferences were under way, pupils were usually eager for their turn. At the same time, they co-operated fully in giving the teacher a chance to confer with the other pupils in the class. The teacher set up her office in the corner of the classroom and conferred with individual pupils while the rest of the class worked on an assignment. In as little as ten minutes per pupil, an invaluable relationship was established between pupil and teacher.

GIVING THE SECOND SET

The second set of completion sentences was administered shortly before the close of the first semester. It could be given earlier if deemed advisable. The form varied somewhat from the first set, so that the pupils were not tempted to repeat the same responses.

Typical sentences in the second set were as follows:

1. Since September, I think I have made progress in . . .
2. I still need to improve in . . .
3. I do my lessons because . . .
4. The kind of friend I like best is . . .
5. I think our class has made progress in . . .
6. Our class could improve by . . .
7. I could help my class improve by . . .

8. My teachers could help more by . . .

9. I wish . . .

It appears that devices of this sort are less effective if given too often. However, the first list may have been administered too early. At the National College of Education the teacher sensed when the class was ready for the second set of completion questions, and expected more complete and analytical responses than in the initial set.

In most cases, Miss Simmons observed that pupils were maturing in their ability to evaluate their strengths and weaknesses. Pupils had begun to see their progress and point out their specific weaknesses. For instance, Debby now mentioned her careless mistakes in arithmetic. Another pupil mentioned the need to spend more time on weekly spelling lists. Certain aspects of progress and need for improvement had shifted from academic work to behavior and attitude.

The teacher can use the completion sentences to measure her success in motivating learning if she examines responses to the sentence "I do my lessons because . . ." and compares replies given on the first list with those given on the second. For example, if the teacher compares an early response of "I do my lessons because my teacher wants me to," or ". . . because I know it is for my own good," with a later response of ". . . because they're fun and because I want to pass with flying colors," or ". . . I like them and enjoy doing them with the class," or ". . . usually they're a lot of fun," or ". . . some I find to be interesting," she can readily detect a change in pupil attitude.

The teacher did not expect that her class would be in complete accord as to the fun and interest involved in learning. However, information from the completion sentences was used to identify pupils who still regarded learning as a chore that must be done to achieve some remote goal. These children would receive extra attention and encouragement as motivation to learning.

The child who still finds it difficult to evaluate himself or his peers with the second set of completion sentences may well need the teacher's special attention and guidance. This may also be true of the pupil who has too many complaints about his classmates' attitudes and behavior.

EFFECTIVE METHODS

One of the most effective methods of pupil evaluation used at the National College of Education is a teacher-pupil conference immediately followed by a parent-teacher conference. These conferences are regularly scheduled at the end of each semester. An outline that includes a brief written evaluation of physical, emotional, and adjustment factors; work habits; and subject-matter area is used as a guide for the conferences. Report cards may also serve as a basis for the conferences.

Experience has proved that a greater degree of communication prevails in the procedure just described than in the often advocated teacher-parent-pupil conference. If the conference procedure is carefully explained to the class, acceptance and co-operation can be readily obtained.

It became evident that the success of a conference plan of this kind depends largely on the degree of rapport that has been established between teacher and pupil. The pupil must sense that the teacher is honest and sincere in her evaluation. The teacher must allow the child enough time to analyze and comment. A question such as "Is there anything we should add here?" or "Do you think we should change any of these comments?" has usually met with a good response. Such a response provides an excellent insight into the thinking of a pupil. It also stimulates a teacher toward improvement of pupil motivation in certain areas of academic learning.

FOLLOW-UP ACTIVITIES

Experience indicated that the pupil conference was much more valuable if it had a follow-up. This step involved certain changes in class procedure, some individual help, and sometimes another pupil conference. After the parent-teacher conference, the parents were encouraged to discuss the evaluations with their child.

It became evident that the dual conference (teacher-pupil and teacher-parent) method also provided certain advantages.

1. Teacher-pupil conferences helped to eliminate the pupil attitude conveyed by such statements as "Teacher gave me a C in arithmetic." They revealed that many eleven- and twelve-year-olds have many surprising misconceptions regarding evaluation.

2. Brief individual conferences guided pupils toward intelligent self-evaluation. Competition or comparison with classmates is almost inevitable during a group discussion of evaluation, whereas individual conferences aided in developing an objective self-evaluation that is invaluable as pupils enter adolescence.

3. In the conference situation the pupil often revealed apprehensions, interests, and desires much more freely.

4. As a result of the conference with the child, the teacher had in mind the necessary information, and was able to interpret the child and his progress during the conference with the parents.

5. Pupil morale improved and teacher-pupil rapport was more firmly established. Pupils reacted favorably when their evaluation was clearly discussed with them prior to the teacher-parent conference.

6. Good relationships were built through guiding pupils to understand themselves and their peers.

7. Parents were convinced that the child understood his progress better and felt himself more a part of the parent-teacher-pupil team.

8. Pupils who had learning difficulties, or who previously had felt they were constantly being talked about, were given a greater sense of individual worth.

After the first conference, pupils eagerly asked when another would be scheduled. Rather than indicating a dread or a dislike for conference time, pupils encouraged parents to make appointments with the teacher. From the teacher's standpoint, the time and effort required by pupil conferences was amply rewarded.

PUPIL EVALUATION

It was noted that pupils were able to evaluate themselves more readily during the second semester of the school year. They were given the opportunity to set their own goals and, either individually or as a group, they planned toward the achievement of these goals.

The completion sentences for the last portion of the year were directed toward further evaluation and goal setting. An extra sentence was added to this third set: "Before the end of the term I need to. . . ."

Typical comments regarding improvements to be made before the end of the term were ". . . improve in social studies"; ". . . be more sure of what I'm doing and not be afraid I'm doing it wrong"; ". . . work harder in spelling and science"; ". . . improve in reading and a little in math."

The fourth or final list was similar to the one administered early in the year, thus offering a basis for evaluating the year's growth. Generally, pupils now found it easy to complete the sentence "I'm proud of myself because. . . ." Many indicated pride in some area of academic accomplishment as is illustrated in the following responses: ". . . I have progressed in reading and arithmetic"; ". . . of what I did in crafts, gym, and math"; ". . . my arithmetic has come up so much."

Other pupils had different reasons for feeling proud. It was Dianne who wrote, "I'm proud of myself because I feel I did something this year in the way of understanding things better and knowing other people better." Renee's response reflected her feelings of security: "This year I have made many friends and have gotten good grades. I feel that other people enjoy my friendship and that makes me happy."

ESTIMATING PROGRESS

Responses revealed that what is progress in the eyes of a ten- or eleven-year-old is often seen differently by an adult. A striking example of this was the case of Raymond, a brilliant boy who had had problems in social adjustment. During the school year Raymond had completed many excellent projects in science, including one on solar energy; yet on his final evaluation he wrote, "My greatest accomplishment this year is to climb the tree without being afraid."

The techniques used by Miss Simmons at the National College of Education differ little from those used in the average elementary school. Yet these methods have demonstrated the value of establishing teacher-pupil understanding for the purpose of creating an environment for learning that is so necessary with pre-adolescents.

The study indicates that during the preadolescent period a foundation can be established for self-understanding and self-evaluation, as well as for understanding others, and for developing positive attitudes toward learning. Such a foundation will pave the way for an easier adolescence and a greater degree of success in adult life.

The Human Relations Program
at the State University of Iowa*

Ralph H. Ojemann

Some years ago when we were making observations of parental and teacher behavior toward children, it was observed that parents and teachers tended to deal with child behavior as a surface phenomenon instead of taking account of the factors underlying or causing the behavior. Observation also indicated that such an approach to behavior tended to produce conflicts and emotional strains in both adult and child.

For example, if a child attempted to overcome a feeling of inadequacy by "pushing" to be first so often that it interfered with class activity, the teacher who approached this behavior as a surface phenomenon would try to stop it by such methods as reprimanding the child, making him go to the end of the line, or sending him out of the room. She tended to do this without thinking about or inquiring as to the causes of the behavior. Since the feeling of inadequacy remained in spite of the scolding, going to the end of the line, or leaving the room, the child would still be under a strain and would attempt more vigorous action or a different approach. The teacher would soon observe that her attempts to stop the behavior were not successful. She would tend to intensify her attempts to stop the pupil's interfering behavior and the whole round of strains would rise to a new level.

Observation of the behavior of parents toward children tended to reveal a similar situation. Analyses of parental behavior often revealed a sequence somewhat as follows. In the early years of the child's life, parents would try to control him by telling him what to do, punishing him, coaxing him, and so on. When these procedures failed after years of trial some parents would give up. This left

* *Personnel and Guidance Journal,* November 1958, vol. 37. By permission.

the child to his own devices for meeting problems and he often failed to find satisfying and cooperative solutions. Other parents would doggedly persist, only to meet with increasing resistance and conflict.

WHAT THE EARLY
OBSERVATIONS SUGGESTED

An analysis of such behavior on the part of parents and teachers suggested that if they could extend their insight into and appreciation of the causes of behavior and change from a surface approach to an approach that takes account of the dynamics of behavior, the chances of blocking strong motivations in the child (and also in themselves) would be lessened and the chances for cooperative or mutually satisfying interaction would be increased.

A test of this hypothesis was made in the case of teachers in a study by Wilkinson (1939). Through the use of an experimental and control group it was shown that as the teacher acquired more insight into the backgrounds, ambitions, worries, and concerns of pupils, conflict between teacher and pupil tended to lessen and the pupils' attitudes toward school tended to change in a more favorable direction.

A close examination of the idea that teachers and parents can guide children more effectively and produce less emotional conflict if they approach the child's behavior in dynamic terms suggested that we were dealing with two cases of the larger problem of the relation of one person to another. The reactions of a teacher toward a child or a parent toward a child are essentially reactions of one person toward another. This observation suggested the question, will the hypothesis hold in any human relationship? If we change children to approach behavior dynamically, will that help them in getting along with adults and with their associates?

When we examined the whole problem still more closely we noted another aspect. After a child learns about the factors that underlie behavior, theoretically he could apply this learning not only to the behavior of others but also to his own actions and to the guiding of his own development. For example, if he learned that over-aggressive behavior is often motivated by a feeling of inadequacy, and if he learned something about how feelings of inadequacy develop and how they can be overcome, he would have something to help him interpret his own over-aggressive behavior or his own feelings of inadequacy. The question then became, if we change children so that they appreciate the differences between the surface and dynamic approaches to behavior, will that affect their relationships with others and their relationships to themselves?

This question had two parts. (1) Can children acquire an appreciation of the differences between the surface and dynamic approaches to behavior and apply the dynamic approach in their relations with their parents, teachers, other adults, in their relations with their associates, and in guiding their own development?

(2) If they can learn and can be motivated to apply, will that reduce the emotional conflicts and increase the amount of mutually satisfying interaction in these relationships?

This question, with varying emphases on the several aspects, was studied in the investigations by Morgan (1942), McCandless (1941), Bate (1948), and Stiles (1950). In summary, these investigations showed that children in the elementary and secondary grades can learn the beginnings of the dynamics of behavior, that they can learn to apply this knowledge in their relations with others, and that the process of learning about human behavior can be greatly extended on the school level.

THE PLACE OF EDUCATION IN HUMAN RELATIONS IN THE SCHOOL

When it became fairly clear that children can learn to approach behavior in terms of its causes, considerable thought was given to the next problem that suggested itself, namely, how can the material about behavior be inserted into the school curriculum?

Two approaches could be made. One would be to introduce a separate course on human relations. This is perhaps the first suggestion that occurs. When we studied the problem, however, several questions arose.

When we looked over the various "core" areas in the school curriculum we noted several that dealt rather directly with human behavior. Examples are social studies, English (human behavior in literature and writing), home economics (family relationships), and guidance. How did it happen that in spite of these opportunities to study human development people grew up with a surface approach to behavior as in the case of the parents and teachers we had observed? Why is the surface approach so apparent in our culture?

A careful study of this question led to an examination of the content and method of the several subjects as now taught in school, and this revealed an interesting situation. It can perhaps best be described by an example from community civics. When we examine the discussion in the ordinary civics book of such a problem as crime, for example, we find a discussion of how the police force is organized, its function as prescribed by law, methods for detecting and apprehending the criminal, and the system of courts, training schools, and prisons that have been developed. We may find a short discussion of the fact that crime is somewhat associated with economically underprivileged conditions.

But all of this approaches crime as a "surface" phenomenon. We can show this by considering the questions we would ask if we approached criminal behavior in terms of its causes. If we do that we would ask such questions as these: Are the ways in which the police and the courts handle a criminal such that after they apprehend him they try to find out what caused the behavior and then take the causes into account in their reactions toward him? Do they try to find out in a given case whether the causes are such that the criminal can be rehabilitated into a self-respecting co-operating citizen and not be a constant threat to other members of society, or if he cannot be rehabilitated is he then effectively isolated? In other words, do the present systems that society has set up study the criminal to find out the causes of his behavior and base their treatment of him on those findings?

Furthermore, if criminal behavior is caused, then real protection from the criminal requires that the community find out and change those conditions that produced him. Real protection—both in the sense of protection from direct damage to life and property which the criminal may inflict and also in the sense that taking care of criminals is a drain on the other citizens—comes when people in the community are aware of the forces that tend to produce crime and seek to change those forces.

In considering what the forces are we will have to go beyond the observations that poverty and similar conditions are somewhat correlated with crime and ask the more penetrating question: How does it happen that some persons living in a given environment become criminals, while other persons living in the same home and same neighborhood do not? But these questions are not considered in the usual text. The treatment is largely surface in character.

We could give other examples illustrating the same point. In short, much of the treatment of human problems in civics teaches the "surface" approach. What is true for civics also tends to hold true for the other social studies. Stiles (1947), for example, found in analysis of the material on human behavior in 15 social studies readers used in the elementary school that less than one percent of the selections treated human behavior in the dynamic way. Much of the treatment is of the surface variety.

The question now becomes: Under what arrangement do we have the most effective learning conditions? Do we have it if (a) we have a surface approach to behavior in the usual school subjects and a dynamic approach in a separate course on human behavior, or (b) if we have a dynamic approach wherever human behavior is discussed?

It is well known from studies on learning that changes are made most effectively when that which the child learns is applied consistently in a variety of situations. This suggested to us that we may profitably experiment further with the possibility of changing the content of school subjects from a surface to a dynamic treatment. Accordingly, studies were undertaken to determine how the material on the dynamics of behavior could be integrated into such areas as social studies, English, guidance, home economics, and others. Also, studies were undertaken to see how and to what extent the child could apply the dynamic approach in his relations with his associates and in guiding his own development.

In addition to school influences, there are the home influences. A child learns from the way his parents act toward him. Just as in the case of the teacher, the parent can work with the child using a surface approach or a more causal approach. If he uses principally a surface approach he is demonstrating to the child a non-causal method of working with others which the child will also tend to adopt. We have evidence (Ojemann, 1946) that children learn early in life a surface approach to behavior.

Such an analysis of the problem indicated to us that if we wanted to develop causally-oriented children, we needed classrooms equipped with teachers who both teach causally-oriented content materials and practice the causal approach in their daily relations with pupils. It would also help if the home environments of these children encouraged the causal approach at least in some measure. We have attempted to develop such classrooms and homes.

Under our general plan, the program, by arrangement with a school system, provides summer fellowships so that selected teachers can attend an intensive training program. This program is designed to familiarize the teacher-students with the differences between surface and causal approaches, to help them apply the causal approach to the daily activities in the classroom, and to develop skill in teaching causally-oriented materials.

A supervisor of teachers, on the Preventive Psychiatry staff, works with the teachers throughout the year, holding a series of conferences with each. During the summer training program, each teacher assists in the preparation of teaching materials for his own classroom. With the supervisor's help he continues this adaptation of materials for classroom purposes throughout the year. We thus obtain a group of classrooms for our laboratory, each equipped with a causally-oriented teacher and appropriate curricular content.

EXAMPLES OF CURRICULAR EXPERIENCES

To provide a more detailed picture of the integrated program as presently conceived, it may be helpful to examine some of the actual learning experiences that are provided at several age levels. Examples for this purpose will be drawn from two age levels, namely, primary and intermediate.

1. Examples of experiences at the primary level.

A. *Demonstrations furnished by the teacher's behavior.* At each age level, as has been indicated, the child is influenced by the behavior of the teacher as well as by what he hears or reads. How the teacher handles the day-to-day social situations that arise in the classroom and on the playground, the extent to which the teacher seeks to know the child's ambitions, concerns, and abilities and makes use of this information in planning his program of work and understanding his behavior before dealing with it, are examples of experiences that affect the growth of a causal orientation.

This training of the teacher to practice the causal approach is an important part of the program at all age levels and the primary level is no exception.

Furthermore, as soon as the child has some appreciation of why a situation has to be understood before it can be reacted to logically, the teacher can take the simpler situations that arise and work them out with the class to involve the children in a practical application of a causal orientation. It is important that the teacher choose only the simpler situations at the beginning, for a careful grading as to difficulty is as important in learning human behavior concepts as it is in learning other concepts.

B. *Use of narratives.* To help the primary child develop an appreciation of the differences between the non-causal and causal approaches (at the primary levels the teachers have labeled the approaches the "non-thinking" and "thinking" ways), a variety of materials have been developed which can be read to the child and discussed with him. One type of material consists of stories in which the non-causal and causal procedures are contrasted. Listening to the narratives and discussing them provide vicarious experiences for learning the differences between the two ways of living.

Each narrative describes some behavior situation. After the situation has been set forth, some character in the story begins to make a surface approach to it, then rethinks his proposed reaction and makes a more causal approach. Some of the ways in which the behavior may have developed come out and one of the characters in the narrative acts in the light of these data. The situation has a reality about it in that someone begins to make a surface approach which children in our culture experience quite frequently. But, it also introduces a new way of living—a way that takes account of the meaning of the causes of behavior instead of their overt form.

For example, in one situation a boy gets into so many fights that something has to be done. The teacher in the story is about to deal with this in the usual way when he recalls that such things do not occur of their own accord. He does a little probing and before long it comes to light that this boy has been teased a great deal because he had to go home immediately after school each day to help take care of his baby sister and didn't have time to play with the other children. When the teacher learns this, he takes measures to work out this basic problem.

To help the child develop a more generalized conception and to prevent him from thinking only of incidents involving himself, situations were developed involving children older and younger than himself and children from quite different environments. There is some observational evidence that situations involving people different from the child tend to be less emotionally charged and therefore less difficult for the child to consider causally in the early discussions.

Each narrative is preceded by a short introduction for use by the reader. After the reading of the story there is a discussion. The purpose of this discussion is not only to recall the incidents of the story, but also to bring out the differences in procedure when one thinks of causes as contrasted with principal attention to the overt form of behavior. The discussion is also designed to consider alternative ways of meeting situations and some of the probable effects of these alternatives.

It is suggested to the teacher that this material furnish part of the offering in the regular "story period." Under usual school conditions, the material read in the story period deals with various objects and events in the child's environment. Some of it deals with physical objects, some of it deals with people. It is suggested that material dealing with people be heavily weighted with the causally-oriented materials described. The causally-oriented stories are thus part of the primary child's story period content.

C. *Use of expositions to help understand and appreciate the work of the teacher and other persons with whom the child interacts directly.*

An example of this type of material is a leaflet entitled "The Work of the Teacher." This is a simplified discussion contrasting the conception of the teacher as "someone whose main job is to check up on you" with the conception of "a guide to help you learn." This material is designed to be read by the teacher to the class and talked over with it. The logical implications of the "guide to help you" concept are described, including what alternatives are available to the child and their respective probable consequences when he finds his learning experiences not challenging. Included also is a discussion of how it may help the teacher to "tell her when something is worrying you."

The purpose of the material is to help the child gain some understanding of the behavior of the teacher, her feelings, and her methods. It is also designed to help the child begin learning that he has a part in arranging his social environment.

Similar material has been prepared to help the child gain some appreciation of the work of parents and other adults in his social environment.

2. Examples of experiences at the intermediate level.

A. *The behavior of the teacher.* Since pupils at the intermediate levels can read syllabi, work sheets and other material to be read by pupils can be prepared. However, at this level as at the primary level, the pupil also learns from what he observes of the behavior of the teacher in the daily interactions with the class. Hence, it is recognized in the integrated program that the teacher's daily behavior is an important part of the learning experience at the intermediate level as well as at the primary level, and the plan includes training of teachers at this level also in practicing the causal orientation. A pamphlet prepared for the National Education Association for use by teachers reflects this recognition.[1] In its full development, the integrated plan expects that all teachers will apply the principles of human development in their daily classroom work.

At this level there is also the opportunity to help the pupil take some responsibility for his own development. The discussion of the work of the teacher, referred to in the description of sample materials at the primary level, is extended to include a consideration of how the pupil can help to build up his cumulative record for the school, in what areas he can keep the teacher informed about his attitudes and feelings, and how he can apply what he is learning to his own behavior.

At this level also there is the possibility of using the room council as a laboratory in which the child can apply the causal orientation in a real life situa-

---

[1] R. H. Ojemann. Personality adjustment of individual children. #5 *What Research Says to the Teacher*, National Education Association, October 1954.

tion. Since in the integrated plan the subject matter areas of social studies, health, and reading incorporate material designed to enrich a pupil's conception of the dynamics of behavior, and since he is encouraged to apply the enriched conception to situations arising in the room council, it will be helpful to indicate how the subject matter areas make their contribution before describing the use of the room council in detail.

B. *Teaching causally-oriented social studies.* In elementary social studies each of the major topics can be developed in terms of the basic factors operating in the behavior of the people involved.

The following examples will illustrate this. As an introduction to fifth grade social studies, two teachers[2] prepared the following introduction:

*I. Introduction
to
Fifth Grade Social Studies*

This year we are going to try to look at Social Studies in a little different way. In Social Studies we discuss problems about people. It will help us to understand these problems more fully if we know something about why people act as they do.

This little booklet is to be used with your textbook in Social Studies to make it possible for you to learn more about the behavior of people and what the effects of their behavior are.

We will want to find out how situations come about that cause people to act the way they do.

1. What are the needs the people are trying to satisfy?
2. What methods are they using to work out their feelings?
3. What are the effects on other people as a result of the methods chosen to work out those needs or feelings?
4. What might happen if other methods were used?

These questions are then developed in the discussion of historical events in subsequent units.

ATTITUDES OF PARTICIPATING TEACHERS

Our program brings up two groups of questions. The first group relates to procedures: How does the plan work? What is the attitude of the teacher toward it? Can teachers be interested in cooperating in such an enterprise? Do the teachers resist training in mental health principles?

Thus far, we have worked with primary, intermediate, and secondary school teachers. At the present writing, we have a group of fifteen primary, fifteen intermediate, eleven secondary teachers, and three counselors drawn from three school systems. They have participated in the summer program and have helped to revise various aspects of the curriculum to develop in the child a sensitivity to the

[2] Appreciation is expressed to Ann Pavlovsky and Marian Kennedy.

causes and consequences of behavior. For instance, instead of being content with the usual textbook statement that, unlike boundaries between many European countries, the United States-Canadian border has never been fortified, they prepared a discussion, based on available studies of conflict and cooperation, on some of the probable underlying factors in producing the United States-Canadian relationships. The counselors have helped the secondary teachers extend their knowledge of the children in their classes.

The fact that we have had more requests for inclusion in the program than we can accommodate indicates that the teachers on the whole have a positive attitude toward it. Those who have been accepted have cooperated enthusiastically.

Something we learned in our early work may provide a clue to at least part of this cooperation. While most presentations of mental health for teachers today stress the motivating forces operating in the child, little emphasis is given to the problem of how these forces can be expressed constructively under classroom conditions and how the teacher can accept her past mistakes. One of the hypotheses underlying the approach in our program is that much of the resistance appearing in work with teachers arises from the frustration a teacher feels when she learns about a child's needs but does not see how she can meet them under classroom conditions. In our work with teachers we point out these problems early in the program, on the theory that if the teacher realizes we are aware of his problems and are interested in helping him resolve them he will feel less frustrated. As the program has progressed we have found this to be true. Always we attempt to increase the security and self-respect of each individual member of the program by working *with* the teachers rather than telling them.

Can a teacher help children in elementary and secondary schools take a more understandable approach to social situations? If so, what effect does this have on the children? Does it make them more, or less, secure? More, or less, able to develop satisfying relations with others? We have evidence that significant changes have been produced throughout the primary and intermediate grades. This evidence has been reported in several studies (Levitt, 1955; Ojemann, Levitt, Lyle and Whiteside, 1955; Snider, 1957).

A typical example may be found in some of the data obtained from our experiments with the fourth, fifth, and sixth grades. At each level a causally-trained teacher was matched with a teacher without such training from a nearby school, who served as a control. The matching was according to sex, age, training, and years of experience. Similarly, the children in the respective classes were equated as to intelligence. The experimental group was like the control group, except that the control teacher did not participate in the summer training program and did not use causally-oriented curricular materials.

At the beginning of the school year all the children were given two causal-orientation tests. In one of the tests, the child was presented with a series of social situations to which he was asked to suggest a solution. The possible reactions ranged from arbitrary, judgmental, and punitive, such as: "It serves him right—

he should be made to stay in"; to an awareness of possible complexity, such as: "The teacher should find out more about this."

In the second test, another series of social situations was presented, each followed by a series of statements with which the pupil was asked to indicate agreement or disagreement. Some examples are: "It wouldn't make much difference what method the teacher used to make him stop (bothering others) so long as he stopped bothering others." "Since these boys do the same things (described in the situation) they are probably all alike in most ways." "If another boy disobeyed his father the same way, his reason would be the same as Jack's."

The children were given tests again in the spring and the results of the experimental and control classes compared. In all grades a statistically significant change appeared in the experimental group but not in the control group.

Thus it appears that our laboratory, which consists of a teacher trained to be sensitive to the dynamics of behavior and to demonstrate this sensitivity in the daily living in the classroom, and using a curriculum which incorporates these principles, is producing a degree of causal orientation among children.

Does the new orientation help causally-oriented children make more satisfying adjustments to their environment? We have various kinds of data to throw light on this question. For example, children from both the experimental and control groups were given the anti-democratic tendency scale test developed by Gough, Harris, Martin, and Edwards (1950). This is essentially a measure of authoritarianism.

A detailed analysis of the results (Levitt, 1955) obtained from the experimental and control groups showed a significant difference between the two groups on both scales. The causally oriented children showed significantly less authoritarianism. It thus appears that as children become more aware of the dynamic complexities of human motivation and behavior, their attitudes toward others begin to change from an authoritarian relationship to a more democratic relationship. In all of the analyses the effects of intelligence were eliminated by various statistical procedures.

ROLE OF CAUSAL ORIENTATION IN MENTAL HEALTH

A great many questions need answering before we can determine what role a causal orientation toward behavior plays in the prevention of mental illness and development of mental health. For example, we want to know what happens in later years to the child oriented causally through his school experiences. We want to know what kinds of behavior disturbances an "inoculation" with a causal orientation will prevent, if any, both during school age and in later years. Already, our laboratory enables us to study the relationships that develop between teachers and pupils in the causally-oriented classroom as compared to the relationships in a non-causally-oriented classroom. It also points the way for a study of a host of questions that arise in the investigations of the causes of emotional breakdowns and the avenues by which mental health in its full measure may be achieved.

ASSUMPTIONS UNDERLYING THE PROGRAM

As we look over the whole program, what are the assumptions that underlie it? It seems that there are two or perhaps three. The first is that we can describe the differences between a surface and a causal approach to behavior. From the numerous occasions in which we have attempted to communicate the meaning of these concepts, it appears that it is possible to distinguish these approaches in their major aspects. We expect that a gradual refinement in meaning will take place (Levitt and Ojemann, 1953).

A second assumption is that a careful study using methods that can be duplicated and repeated by others so that the results can be checked is the only way in which we will be able to discover what degree of causal orientation can be developed at the various age and intelligence levels and what the effect is when a thoroughgoing causal orientation appears. It will be noted that we are not assuming that a causal orientation will relieve all mental strains or prevent all mental breakdowns. Rather we are asking the question, to what extent will an "inoculation" with a causal orientation prevent various types of mental illness and increase the amount of emotionally satisfying and creative uses of human energy? In our tests of the effects of the causal orientation, we are interested not only in measuring the degree or extent of prevention, but we are also interested in measuring the degree or extent to which human energies are released in "creative" and "satisfying" achievement.

Finally, in the early stages of our work we had to assume that learning a causal orientation was not so incompatible with the individual goals of the teachers, children, and parents with whom we worked that it produced long-enduring conflict and frustration. Both observation and test result have indicated that this is no longer entirely an assumption but may be considered a generalization that has a degree of support.

Our program, which goes by the title of The Preventive Psychiatry Research Program, is an example of teachers, guidance workers, and other school personnel joining hands with research investigators to study not only whether changes in learners can be made, but also what the effects are of these changes in the lives of the learners. Teaching is viewed as a way of creating a new pattern or way of living, the effects of which can then be studied (Ojemann, 1948).

REFERENCES

Bate, Elsa B. 1948. *The effect of especially prepared materials in a learning program in human growth and development on the tenth grade level.* Iowa City, Iowa: State University of Iowa. Unpublished doctoral dissertation.

Gough, H. G., D. B. Harris, W. E. Martin, and M. Edward. 1950. Children's ethnic attitudes: I. Relationship to certain personality factors. *Child Develpm., 21*, 83–91.

Levitt, E. E. 1955. Effect of "causal" teacher training program on authoritarianism and responsibility in grade school children. *Psychol. Rep., 1*, 449–458.

———, and R. H. Ojemann. 1953. The aims of preventive psychiatry and "causality" as a personality pattern. *J. Psychol., 36*, 393–400.

McCandless, B. 1941. *A study of selected factors affecting radio listening behavior.* Iowa City, Iowa: State University of Iowa. Unpublished doctoral dissertation.

Morgan, Mildred I., and R. H. Ojemann. 1942. The effect of a learning program designed to assist youth in an understanding of behavior and its development. *Child Develpm., 13*, 181–194.

Ojemann, R. H. 1948. Research in planned learning programs and the science of behavior. *J. educ. Res., 42* (No. 2), 96–104.

———. 1946. The effect on the child's development of changes in cultural influences. *J. educ. Res., 40* (No. 4), 258–270.

———, E. E. Levitt, W. H. Lyle, Jr., and Maxine F. Whiteside. 1955. The effects of a "causal" teacher-training program and certain curricular changes on grade school children. *J. exp. Educ., 24* (No. 2), 95–114.

Snider, B. C. F. 1957. Relation of growth in causal orientation to insecurity in elementary school children. *Psychol. Rep., 3*, 631–634.

Stiles, F. S. 1947. *A study of materials and programs for developing an understanding of behavior at the elementary school level.* Iowa City, Iowa: State University of Iowa. Doctoral dissertation.

———. 1950. Developing an understanding of human behavior at the elementary school level. *J. educ. Res., 43*, 516–524.

Wilkinson, Frances R., and R. H. Ojemann. 1939. The effect on pupil growth of an increase in teacher's understanding of pupil behavior. *J. exp. Educ., 8*, 143–147.

Chapter 7

COUNSELING THEORY
AND PRACTICE

This chapter will consider the importance of counseling theory for the elementary school. Factors unique to the elementary school setting and purposes of counseling in the elementary school are set forth. The counselor's personality is discussed as a central concern of counselor education. Principles basic to counseling children are detailed.

Some educators might question the importance of studying counseling theory and suggest that it is more important to be familiar with the process rather than with theoretical considerations. Experience at the secondary school level has shown that some school counseling has been handicapped because of a lack of careful consideration of the applicability of counseling theory to the school setting. In elementary school guidance and counseling, there is an urgent need to analyze the contributions of existing counseling theory to the counseling process.

Historically, it has been difficult to find materials in guidance textbooks which deal with specific methods of counseling children. The need for a counseling service for all children was expressed in 1950 by Wilson, whose article is included in Chapter 2 of this book. In "Dimensions of Elementary School Guidance Report" (1964), Meeks strongly advocated child counseling. The report of the ACES-ASCA joint committee on the elementary school counselor, in April 1966, viewed counseling as one of the three significant functions of guidance.

While authorities in the field of guidance have increasingly recommended counseling in the elementary school, the particular theory that would be appropriate for child counseling is still a controversial issue. A recent book, *Guidance: An Examination* (Mosher, Carle, and Kehas, 1965) surveys a variety of theories, including behavioral, Rogerian, existential, ego-counseling, and social reconstruction. This book provides an excellent background of some of the basic issues in counseling theory. Another valuable text in this area, edited by Stefflre (1965), is *Theories of Counseling.*

Allport (1962a) says that the counselor always views the counselee through his "professional spectacles," that is, theory affects the way in which the counselor perceives the counselee. Allport (1962b) suggests three basic images of man: "man seen as a reactive being . . . man seen as a reactive being in depth . . . and man seen as a being in process of becoming." Each counselor evaluates the various images of man and functions on the basis of his assumptions about man's nature.

Research on counseling in the elementary school is limited (Biasco, 1966; Kranzler, Mayer, Dyer and Munger, 1966; VanHoose, 1966). Students should approach counseling theory with the recognition that it is constantly changing. Theobald and Stefflre have both commented on this state of flux:

> Since they are bound by space and time and the present level of our knowledge, the best of theories will not long serve. If we should accept this limitation, we should teach our students not only presently held theories, but ways of building new ones. (Theobald, 1961, p. 100)
> Theory building will need to be a constant process for those who remain in counseling. (Stefflre, 1965, p. 11)

Theory cannot be avoided, and the counselor will have to be constantly making decisions about it.

COUNSELING DEFINED

Counseling is a personal relationship between a professionally trained counselor and a child which assists the child to communicate and to meet immediate and future needs. This process facilitates growth through changes in perception, conviction, attitudes, and behavior. The process should be differentiated from therapy, which puts a greater emphasis on personality reorganization.

Counseling is a form of learning. It puts an emphasis on the learner as a responsible, choice-making individual whose decisions reflect the sort of person he wants to be (Stewart and Warneth, 1965).

Guidance theory for the elementary school must differ from guidance theory for the secondary school because of the basic differences between the child and the adolescent. The elementary school child is more able than the adolescent to integrate various forces from home, school, and peer relationships which form the foundation for later development. Farwell and Peters (1957) were perhaps the first to point out some of these differential factors. They indicated that the child is usually more genuinely congruent with himself and what he expresses than the adolescent. There is less differentiation between outer behavior and inner feelings in the child than in the adolescent. This is often not noticed, because the child's reasoning processes are not fully developed, and he is therefore less able to verbalize his feelings. Also, children are not anxious about advanced education or careers; their problems relate to acquiring basic skills and becoming socialized.

The elementary school counselor is in a situation where he must meet the varied expectations of administrators, teachers, parents, and children. Counseling may occur in a setting in which the significant adults expect the counselor to "straighten out the student so that he sees things my way." The counselor must deal with the child's confused feelings about himself and his significant adults. The child has learned that the school system is judgmental and evaluative. It may be difficult for him to function in a situation which is nonjudgmental and which emphasizes self-evaluation.

Peters (1959) stated that the different choices and decisions, the relationship between teacher and pupil, the dependency relationship with parents, and the general lack of self-referral by children to the counselor all have an important effect on the nature of the counseling service. Elementary school guidance and counseling must consider the implications of these developmental differences and build an appropriate counseling program.

DEVELOPMENTAL FACTORS IN CHILD COUNSELING

The contributions of the early elementary school years to the forming of the child's basic attitudes, goals, and values is highlighted in a longitudinal study released by the Fels Research Institute (Kagan and Moss, 1962). This report stresses that increasing emphasis must be given to the years between the ages of six and ten, since adult personality is initially forming during these years. Childhood achievement of boys, for example, has shown to be extremely highly correlated to adult male achievement. The child's concept of himself as an academic achiever and his attitude toward school tasks are formed early in life. In preadolescence, when he begins to develop a concept of himself (Piaget, 1929), the child can benefit from clarification of his feelings and concepts.

Individual differences in developmental patterns, caused by variances in rates of development, can create adjustment problems for the child both in school and out. Mussen and Jones (1958) demonstrated variance in the self-concepts and motivations of early- and late-maturing boys.

Research points to the significance of individuality (Chess, Thomas, and Birch, 1965). The counselor must be able to identify individuality and help each child learn to use his individuality for himself and society.

It is important that the counselor be familiar with basic needs of the child: love, security, belonging, acceptance, and independence (Dinkmeyer, 1965a and b). These needs provide guidelines for the guidance and the counseling processes in the elementary school.

The child's dependency upon adults tends to restrict him from changing certain aspects of his environment. His choices are comparatively limited when contrasted with those of adults; the child can not decide to change parents or drop out of school. However, he should be encouraged to make decisions when the situation permits.

Conceptual development in the child is not as advanced as in the adolescent. This is due to the understandable fact that children have relatively limited experiences and vocabularies which affect their ability to comprehend certain concepts.

Counseling children necessitates extensive work with parents and teachers. This work is mainly concerned with improving the adult's capacity to relate to the child so that the child's perception of human relationships can be modified.

DIMENSIONS OF ELEMENTARY COUNSELING

Child counseling seems to fall into two definable approaches: developmental counseling, which is not always problem-oriented but focuses on the over-all development of self-understanding and methods for solving the developmental tasks; and counseling for the modification of behavior and attitudes, which is often problem-oriented and which attempts to change a child's faulty and confused convictions, percepts, attitudes, and behavior. Although principles and processes are similar, there may be differences in emphasis between the two counseling approaches.

Developmental counseling is usually short-term and places a much greater emphasis on collaboration with the child. The developmental problem is investigated and analyzed in order to help solve it. This type of self-help results in developing a sense of personal worth and a feeling of competence and adequacy in coping with the school's expectations.

Counseling for the modification of attitudes and behavior has as its goal a change of attitudes, feelings, or specific behavior. In this type of counseling, the counselor is more active; he may use behavioral modification techniques or confront the individual directly. This counseling may help the child understand the purpose of symptoms and the reasons for his failure to deal with problems.

The articles by Peters and Dinkmeyer that appear in this chapter are examples of the developmental approach to counseling. The articles by Dinkmeyer on Adlerian theory and practice and the article by Krumboltz and Hosford on behavioral counseling are examples of modification counseling.

PURPOSES OF CHILD COUNSELING

The counseling service in the elementary school is based upon specific objectives and purposes. Most important among the purposes of child counseling in the elementary school are goals that help the child as an individual, for example:

1. To know and understand oneself, one's assets and liabilities, and through this self-understanding develop a better understanding of the relationship between one's own abilities, interests, achievements, and opportunities.

2. To develop self-acceptance, a sense of personal worth, a belief in one's competence, and self-confidence, and, with this, an accompanying trust and acceptance of others.

3. To develop methods of solving the developmental tasks of life with the resultant realistic approach to the tasks of life as met in the areas of work and interpersonal relations.

4. To develop increased self-direction, problem-solving and decision-making abilities.

5. To accept responsibility for one's choices and actions, that is, awareness that behavior is a result of certain consequences.

6. To modify those concepts and convictions that do not "work," to accept wholesome attitudes and concepts, and to perceive reality as defined by others.

Counseling is part of the educative process directed toward the development of self-understanding. It assists the child to explore and deal with feelings, attitudes, values, and purposes.

THE ROLE OF THE COUNSELOR
IN THE COUNSELING PROCESS

To work effectively the counselor must be a certain kind of person. Fullmer and Bernard (1964) state: "There is an increasing body of evidence to support the proposition that the counselor's personality development should be the central focus of counselor education." The counselor must be able to understand and accept the child and relate to him as an equal. It is particularly important that the counselor be honest, sincere, and able to command the child's respect. Counseling, then, involves the development of empathy, the ability to understand the feelings of others.

PRINCIPLES AND PROCESS
OF CHILD COUNSELING

In child counseling a mutual alignment of goals must exist between the counselor and the child. They must not only be on friendly terms, but they both must be involved in matters of real concern to the child.

The child frequently is not a volunteer for counseling services. He may be referred by a teacher, and the teacher's reason for referral may not be something the child himself perceives as his problem. Counseling may be more of a problem with the referred child than with the more mature counselee who seeks out the counselor on his own volition. The counselor must be able to respect the child's negative feelings. A good relationship begins with the problem that the child perceives as important, for he will be ready to discuss it. There are times, of course, when the child can not on his own choose to drop counseling, when he wishes to, and this has an obvious effect upon his cooperation with the counselor.

The counseling experience is a new and unique area for the elementary school child. He therefore does not have any past experience which enables him to know what to anticipate in counseling. The role of the counselor and counselee must be clarified so that the counselee can be ready for the counseling experience. Although the counselor may be ready to counsel, nothing of value will occur unless the child understands the nature of this relationship.

A child counselee may require more verbal interaction from the counselor than the more mature counselee. The counselor must be ready to be active in the interview, encouraging the child's own expression rather than eliciting responses of "yes," or "no" (Schulman, Kaspar, Barger, 1964). The counselor must be an active listener, aware of things that might provide clues to the personality of the counselee, even though nothing may be stated directly. An insightful counselor will realize the need for a sharper sensitivity to non-verbal factors, such as facial expressions, gestures, and body movements, which offer clues to the true personality of the child.

Reflection of feeling can be an effective procedure in counseling. However, some children have limited affective vocabularies and little ability to relate their feelings. With such children, the counselor may be more successful if he himself described what he thinks the child is feeling. Perhaps he might say, "Could it be you feel that no one cares?" Or, he might put the feelings in the child's words: "Does it sometimes seem that nobody likes you?" These interpretative statements provided in a tentative hypothesis (Brammer and Shostrom, 1960) can help convince the child that the counselor really cares and understands him, and at the same time accelerate the development of the child's self-understanding.

Traditionally, one of the devices used to work with children in counseling situations is play materials, the theory being that a child will be more relaxed and less hostile to the counselor. This would seem to be a successful practice, since the attention span of a child is so limited and since the troubled child might not be able to accept the presence and intrusion of a strange adult. Recently, however, there has been evidence to prove that very young children can engage in productive counseling without play materials(Schulman, Kaspar, and Barger, 1964). Many counselors, in spite of this finding, tend to rely on play materials to help reduce pressure on the child and the counselor. Counseling time is used constructively to establish the trusting relationship between child and counselor. The child can experience acceptance and respect without being forced to participate in verbal behavior (Nelson, 1966).

A major therapeutic technique that the counselor provides is encouragement (Dinkmeyer and Dreikurs, 1963). The counselor's encouragement is apparent by his interest in and concentration upon the child and his assets, thus enabling the child to recognize and accept his faults. Encouragement is an indication to the child that the counselor *is* listening to him and does understand him.

The article by Combs recognizes that counseling is a learning process designed to assist the individual to learn more effectively and efficiently. However, Combs cautions against general acceptance of learning theory and instead advocates perceptual theory, which assumes that all behavior is a function of the individual's field of perception at the instant of behavior. Combs believes that the goal of counseling should be to assist the troubled child in changing or adjusting his perception. He presents six variables of perception which are significant in the counseling process.

Krumboltz and Hosford also believe in the application of learning principles to the counseling process, but differ from Combs in the theory from which they operate. They believe that the counselor should be judged by the degree to which he helps pupils engage in more appropriate types of behavior. Their article includes specific illustrations of the application of learning principles to the child's problems emphasizing the development of techniques that are specific to the unique problems of the child in contrast to reliance on a set of counseling procedures. A systematic analysis of the reinforcing consequences associated with behavior is also presented.

The article by Dinkmeyer on Adlerian theory and practice emphasizes the holistic nature of behavior. The counselor is encouraged to focus on the total pattern of psychological movement in the social setting. Adlerians are more concerned with purposes and goals than with causes. Responsibility for understanding resides first with the counselor and is transferred to the counselee. The article details the dynamics of behavior. While theoretically the Adlerian approach to behavior is similar to that of Combs, the Adlerian emphasis on the importance of consequences is similar to behavioral counseling theory.

Peter's article develops a rationale for the importance of counseling in the elementary school, suggesting that the central purpose is developmental, not remedial or therapeutic. Developmental counseling is a service that helps pupils understand themselves, others, and what is expected of them in the school. Peters presents ten techniques useful in developmental counseling with children.

In "Developmental Counseling in the Elementary School," Dinkmeyer offers some of the components of a theory of this type of counseling and some of the contributions of child development research to the counseling process. Unique factors of his counseling include a short-term service with a basically collaborative relationship, in which the child learns to investigate, analyze, and deliberate. The goal here is to help the child become more self-directed in dealing with developmental tasks.

Nelson adds to the counselor's repertoire by providing a succinct discussion of play materials. He believes that the omission of play materials from counseling may result in a lack of communication. His opinion differs from Schulman's position on the use of play materials (Schulman, Kaspar, and Barger, 1964). Nelson provides some simple criteria for selection of play materials, stressing that when used in counseling, they rarely require highly interpretive remarks, and he instead emphasizes the importance of accepting remarks which reflect and summarize.

The use of play materials in counseling the school child is still a controversial issue. The materials may be useful to the counselor in establishing communication with the child, but play should not make the counselor negligent of his major responsibility which is to develop the child's understanding of himself and facilitate changes in attitudes and behavior.

REFERENCES

Allport, G. 1962. Psychological models for guidance. *Harvard educ. Rev.*, *32*, 373–381.

Biasco, F. 1966. *The effect of individual multiple counseling and teacher guidance upon the sociometric status of children enrolled in grades four, five and six.* Oswego, N.Y.: New York State University. Mimeographed.

Brammer, L. M., and E. L. Shostrom. 1960. *Therapeutic psychology.* Englewood Cliffs, N.J.: Prentice-Hall.

Chess, Stella, A. Thomas, and H. Birch. 1965. *Your child is a person.* New York: Viking.

Dinkmeyer, D. 1965a. *Towards a theory of child counseling at the elementary school level.* Moravia, N.Y.: Chronicle Guidance Publications.

———. 1965b. *Child development: the emerging self.* Englewood Cliffs, N.J.: Prentice-Hall.

———, and R. Dreikurs. 1963. *Encouraging children to learn: the encouragement process.* Englewood Cliffs, N.J.: Prentice-Hall.

Farwell, Gail, and H. Peters. May 1957. Guidance: a longitudinal and a differential view. *Elem. Sch. J.*, *57*, 8.

Fullmer, D., and H. Bernard. 1964. *Counseling: content and process.* Chicago: Science Research Associates.

Kagan, J., and H. Moss. 1962. *Birth to maturity.* New York: Wiley.

Kranzler, G., G. Mayer, C. Dyer, and P. Munger. 1966. Counseling with elementary school children: an experimental study. *Personnel guid. J.*, *44* (No. 9).

Meeks, Anna. 1964. *Dimensions of elementary school guidance* (tentative draft). Mimeographed.

Mosher, R., R. Carle, and C. Kehas. 1965. *Guidance: an examination.* New York: Harcourt.

Mussen, P., and M. Jones. 1958. Behavior inferred motivation of late and early maturing boys. *Child develpm.*, *29*, 61–67.

Nelson, R. 1966. *Elem. Sch. Guid. Counsel.*, *1* (No. 3).

Peters, H. October 1959. Differential factors between elementary and secondary school counseling. *Sch. Couns.*, *7* (No. 1), 3–11.

Piaget, J. 1929. *The child's conception of the world.* New York: Harcourt.

Schulman, J. L., J. C. Kaspar, and Patricia M. Bargar. 1964. *The therapeutic dialogue.* Springfield, Ill.: Charles C. Thomas.

Stefflre, B. 1965. *Theories of counseling.* New York: McGraw-Hill.

Stewart, L. and C. Warneth. 1965. *The counselor and society.* Boston: Houghton Mifflin.

Theobald, A. 1961. *The challenge of abundance.* New York: New American Library of World Literature, Inc.

VanHoose, W. 1966. *Dimensions of counseling in the elementary school.* Paper presented to the American Educational Research Association, Chicago.

Wilson, Frances. 1950. Guidance in elementary schools. *Occupations: Voc. guid. J., 24* (No. 3).

Counseling as a Learning Process*

Arthur W. Combs

There can be little doubt that counseling is, in essence, a learning process. When counseling is successful, the client learns a new and better relationship between himself and the world in which he lives. Counseling badly done may, equally well, result in learning a poorer, less effective way of living. Whatever happens in counseling, the client learns something from the experience, even if it is nothing more than the idea that counseling is not much help to him. In this respect, counseling is no different from any other life experience. Counseling, however, should be a situation expressly designed to assist the client to learn more effectively and efficiently than is possible in most other life experiences. If not, counselors had better close up shop.

Assuming that counseling is fundamentally a learning experience, it would appear logical that our existing theories of learning should apply to the problem. Unfortunately, this does not turn out to be the case. The fact that counseling is a learning process does not mean that existing theories of learning automatically become useful in solving the problems of counseling. The writer has been forced to the conclusion that traditional learning theories seem to have little to offer for the improvement of counseling. Indeed, the attempt to apply those theories to the problem of counseling may even be fraught with considerable danger.

Our existing learning theories, for the most part, are concerned with small bits of the problems encountered in counseling. They seem to have little application beyond the simplest behavior, while the behavior of clients is complex and involves entire personalities. Most of our traditional theories apply to the *process of learning* rather than to *people who learn.* Counseling is unquestionably a proc-

* *Journal of Counseling Psychology,* February 1954, vol. 1, no. 1.
  By permission.

ess of learning, but a much broader process of learning than we have usually considered under that heading. What appears to happen to clients in counseling is a matter of personality reorganization calling for much broader concepts of learning than most present theories of learning even attempt to deal with.

This discussion does not mean to suggest that existing learning theories have no application to learning in counseling. They *do* apply, but to such small and isolated aspects of the problem of personality organization as to make them almost useless for any practical purpose.

THE EXPERIENCE OF EDUCATION WITH LEARNING THEORY

Educators have been dealing with problems of learning for a long time. Modern education has taken as its goal "the optimum development of the individual" and that objective could serve equally well as a goal for counseling. Counseling, like education, is a learning process. Perhaps we can learn something about our problem by observing the contributions traditional learning theory has made to education.

If there is any place where one would expect learning theory to have proved of value, it would be in the field of education. Yet, interestingly enough, learning theory has provided little or no leadership in solving problems of educational method. Leadership in education, almost exclusively, has come, not from learning theorists, but from educational philosophers. One looks in vain to find any great educational movement arising from learning theory. As a matter of fact, learning theory in some instances has even had a regressive effect on education. At the very time when education is moving to a holistic concept of teaching, many educators are still hammering away at methods of drill and rote learning growing out of the Ebbinghaus experiments of three generations ago. Because such learning theory seems to be "scientific," furthermore, many teachers find great comfort in continuing to teach by methods long since outdated.

Modern education has shifted its emphasis from subject matter to children, from processes to people. As a result, the theory of greatest use to educators is not learning theory but personality theory. The mental hygienists have taken over a very large share of the former functions of learning theorists in many a school of education. The unpleasant fact of the matter is that modern schools of education find little that is helpful in the average course on learning for the training of beginning teachers. Teachers have discovered long since that children are people with feelings, beliefs, attitudes, personal meanings, and convictions. Learning theory, which does not help to deal with these facets of child behavior, seems to the average teacher far out of touch with reality. She needs a broader, more inclusive approach to her problems. Education tried to gear itself to learning theory but found it to be a mistake. It would be unfortunate were we to make the same error in counseling. Counseling, too, is a problem of people rather than processes. Perhaps we have something to learn from the experience of education.

THEORY LEVEL AND APPLICATION

There is nothing sacred about theory. Theory in any field of endeavor is nothing more than a systematic explanation of events useful to the purposes one has in view. Theory, which holds for one frame of reference or one problem, may be totally inadequate, even misleading, in another. Theory can be constructed on many levels and for many different purposes, but is maximally efficient only for those levels and purposes for which it is designed. Atomic theory is useful in dealing with problems of atomic energy. At that level and for those purposes, it is relevant and essential. Theories of organic and inorganic chemistry are useful and pertinent for the pharmacist when he makes up a doctor's prescription. He knows little or nothing about atomic theory, however, and carries on his job quite effectively without it. This is not to imply that atomic theory does not hold for the chemicals with which he deals. Indeed, they do, but the pharmacist does not need to know them to carry on his profession adequately. On still another level, colleges of home economics have developed theories of cake baking quite without reference to chemical or atomic physics. While it is true that chemical and atomic theory is at work in the batter along with the hands of the cook, the cook does not need to guide her behavior by them, or even to know they exist. This is as it should be. Society needs its atomic physicists to make atomic bombs, but most of us would rather our cakes be baked by cooks!

This same relationship of theory to function is true of learning theory as well. The learning theory one finds useful for his purposes depends upon the number of variables one attempts to control in studying a process. For example, theory may be constructed for purposes of understanding what happens to a client in the counseling situation. To do this, it is necessary to deal with people as they are—with a large number of variables left uncontrolled. Nevertheless, it is quite possible to construct effective theories extremely helpful for our purposes. This is the kind of study many educators carry on in the classroom to discover better methods of inducing learning-in-life situations. Such studies, however, make some people very uncomfortable. Too many variables remain uncontrolled. Accordingly, one may seek to study learning on a level wherein more of the variables may be controlled. He can, for instance, study learning in the laboratory instead of the classroom, where theories of learning can be developed from experiments using tachistoscopic exposures. One can go further and control the material being learned by removing all meaning from it as in the use of nonsense syllables. In short, one can repeat the Ebbinghaus experiments and find new theories of learning applicable to the "purer" situations constructed under such laboratory conditions. It is possible to eliminate even more variables and study a single stimulus-response unit as Pavlov did with his dogs. Here, too, it would be feasible to construct learning theories applicable to the kind of situations studied. Unfortunately, when learning is examined under these restricted conditions it is no longer people who are being studied but an isolated process.

Dynamic personality theory is expressly designed to aid our understanding of behavior outside the laboratory, in free situations where few, if any, variables are likely to be in the control of the observer. The fact of many variables left uncontrolled makes some psychologists feel that such investigations are somehow less "scientific." This is an unfortunate attitude which equates science with minuteness rather than understanding. Teachers have long since discovered how inadequate minute theories are in providing guides to classroom learning. In the writer's experience, such theories have proved equally fruitless as approaches to understanding what happens in the counseling process.

The major problems of our time are problems of human relationships. In solving these problems, psychology must, of necessity, play an ever more important role. To do this effectively, we need theories about behavior at every level which help us understand behavior. It is difficult to conceive, however, how we can live up to our tremendous birthright by an atomistic approach to holistic problems. Too great an insistence upon such an approach may make it difficult or impossible to contribute significantly to the great social problems of these times.

Although the writer's basic training in psychology was thoroughly behavioristic, he has been increasingly disappointed in traditional approaches to learning theory as they apply to the counseling process. Though these theories have explained certain isolated aspects of what seems to be happening to clients, they have generally failed to explain the kinds of changes any counselor observes daily in the course of his practice. Even more disappointing, they do not offer much help in improving practices or in providing guides to behavior when problems arise for which no ready answers are available. The counselor must live and work in a world where variables can seldom be controlled or held constant. Theory which applies only under laboratory conditions is of little help in solving his practical problems.

PERCEPTUAL FIELD THEORY AS A GUIDE TO COUNSELING PRACTICE

More and more the writer has been forced to adopt a field theory of personality organization based upon our growing understanding of the nature and function of perception and the concept of self. Perceptual theory seems eminently more satisfactory in explaining what we can observe about human behavior. It seems more helpful, too, as a personal guide to behavior in our never-ceasing attempts to become effective individuals, whether it be in counseling or any other aspect of human relationships. This theory has been stated on several other occasions. The writer would certainly not presume to claim that it is the answer to all our counseling problems. It is only an approach to personality which has proved satisfying, logical, and helpful in organizing thinking and guiding practice. That, after all, seems to be the purpose of any theory—to give meaning to the events we observe and to make possible the prediction and control of events still in the future. There is not room here for an exposition of this theoretical position. Let us, therefore, look only at its fundamental assumptions and point out a few of its implications for counseling theory.

Briefly, this theoretical position begins with the assumption that all behavior is a function of the individual's field of perceptions at the instant of behaving. In other words, people behave according to how things *seem* to them. If a man believes oysters can be eaten only in months with an "R," he will avoid eating them in June and July. If he does not know about this concept, or if he does not believe in the "R" fiction, he will eat them anytime. How each person behaves at any moment is a function of the organization of his perceptual field at the moment of behaving—or misbehaving.

This perceptual field has the feeling of reality to the individual and is always organized with respect to the concepts he holds of himself. As the field of perceptions changes, so, too, does behavior. When we perceive differently, we behave differently. When perceptions are vague and indistinct, behavior is correspondingly vague and inexact. When perceptions are clear and accurate, behavior is similarly precise and efficient.

This is the frame of reference within which an increasing number of psychologists are placing their thinking and research. It is a broad frame of reference capable of integrating and giving meaning and order to a large amount of our accumulated research and thinking. It is consistent with client-centered therapy and much of psychoanalysis. It seems to apply equally well to the problems of vocational and educational counseling and to the problems of classroom teaching. Many of the seemingly diverse points of view, such as those of Freud, Rogers, Murphy, Allport, Snygg and Combs, Frank, and a host of others interpreted in this framework, fit into a meaningful and useful theoretical structure. A tremendous amount of recent research also finds effective interpretation within this general framework. Research on perception, for example, is directly applicable to such a theoretical position. So, also, is a large amount of current research on such problems as threat, rigidity, discrimination, and the whole field of research on projective instruments.

If it is true that behavior is a function of perception, then the goal of counseling must be to assist the client to change his perceptions. Effective, efficient, and satisfying behavior both from the viewpoint of the client and of society requires a maximum freedom of perception. Rogers, for example, has described the adjusted person as follows: "It would appear that when all of the ways in which the individual perceives himself—all perceptions of the qualities, abilities, impulses, and attitudes of the person and all perceptions of himself in relation to others—are accepted into the organized conscious concept of self, then this achievement is accompanied by feelings of comfort and freedom from tension which are experienced as psychological adjustment."

In perceptual terms, the goal of counseling thus becomes one of aiding the client to achieve a perceptive field as rich, varied, accurate, and free of distortion as possible. If the perceptive field is organized about the concept of self, this theory would imply, further, that counseling must concern itself with helping clients gain clearer, more accurate perceptions of self and the relationship of self to the world in which each lives.

If it is true that behavior is a function of perception, it follows that to change behavior it will first be necessary to find ways of changing perception. The perceptual field of the client is, however, a personal, internal organization not directly open to manipulation from outside. This means that counseling must be seen, not as a place where something is done *to* the client, but as providing a situation in which the client can be helped to change his ways of seeing. Counseling in this sense becomes a process of assisting, facilitating, and encouraging change in perception. It seems, furthermore, to reverse the usual doctor-patient role in which the doctor is the one who knows and the patient does not. In counseling, it is the client who knows and the counselor who does not. The counselor in this frame of reference is a catalyst in a process of growth. His task is to create a special kind of experience for his client that will help him to explore and perceive a more adequate relationship of self to life.

VARIABLES OF PERCEPTION
AS THE FACTORS OF COUNSELING

Finally, if it is true that behavior is a function of perception, then the variables of the process of counseling become the factors affecting perception. To understand and control the process of counseling, it becomes necessary to understand and control the factors that encourage or impede perception. Once these factors are well understood it would seem possible to design the counseling process in the light of these understandings. There is much yet to be learned about the variables of perception, but a fine start has been made. The literature already includes a considerable body of knowledge about some of these variables and every day brings new understanding about some further aspect of perception.

To this point there are at least six variables of perception about which a good deal is already known and which have immediate bearing upon the counseling process. Applying what is known about these variables opens up possibilities of improving the counseling process. These are:

1. Perception is a function of the state of the physical organism in which the perception ocurs. Perception both affects and is affected by the physical organism which serves as the vehicle for perceiving.

2. Perception takes time. Effective perception requires sufficient exposure to make perceiving possible.

3. Perception cannot occur without opportunity for experience. This opportunity for perceiving may be of a concrete character or may be purely symbolic. In any event, there must be some form of opportunity provided for perceiving to happen.

These first three variables of perception are already well known and understood. They have been more or less intensively studied for a number of years. The last three have been far less subjected to experimental study but continue to grow in importance every day. They are:

4. Perception is a function of the individual's values and goals. The values and goals of the individual have a selective effect upon the individual's field of perceptions. Other factors being equal, people perceive more sharply and effectively those aspects of themselves and of life which have greatest value for them.

5. Perception is a function of the self concept of the perceiver. The concept of self has a selective effect on the perceptual field. People perceive that which is appropriate for persons with their concepts of self to perceive. Children who perceive themselves as poor readers read poorly. We are only beginning to understand the tremendous importance of the self concept upon every aspect of human behavior. It appears to be the very core around which all the rest of our perceptions of reality are organized.

6. Perception is seriously affected by the experience of threat. These effects seem to be of two kinds: (a) When a person feels threatened his field of perceptions is reduced to the object of threat producing the well-known effect of tunnel vision; and (b) when threatened, the individual seeks to defend his existing self-organization. Both of these effects seem to have extremely important bearings upon the counseling process.

A good deal is already known about these six important variables. Much of this information has a direct bearing upon the kind of counseling situations we need to construct. What is already known of these variables is highly useful in guiding the counselor in his task. These seem like fruitful fields for further experimental exploration. It is conceivable that there are a number of other important variables affecting perception with equally important implications for the counseling process waiting to be uncovered.

Counseling is indeed a function of learning. Learning in counseling, however, is never an isolated process. It is *people* who learn in counseling. Counseling could not exist without them. A theoretical position which can help us very effectively in improving our understanding of the processes the counselor sets in motion or the methods he devises to help his clients must be a theory that deals with people.

Learning theory applies to some parts of the problems of counseling. We cannot afford, however, to jump to the conclusion that because it is partly applicable it is a sufficient or an adequate avenue of explanation or exploration. Nothing is more dangerous in human thought than ideas which are partly true. The danger of theory partly right is that by providing partial answers it encourages people in the vain hope that with a little more effort, a little more trying, they can find answers to the whole problem. Sometimes this works but sometimes, too, it is better to find a better premise as a framework from which to evaluate and improve our practices. An adequate theory for counseling must *include* learning theory but must also go beyond it. This seems to require a personality theory in which traditional learning theory would play but a very minor role. The writer of this article has here indicated the direction of his own bias, but the fact of the matter seems to be that *almost any* personality theory is a more effective guide to practice than the best our traditional learning theories have so far produced.

Behavioral Counseling
in the Elementary School*

John D. Krumboltz / Raymond E. Hosford

"Same ol' run-around again," said Miss Ford as she returned from her conference with the school counselor.

"What's the problem?" asked Joe Peterson, a fellow teacher.

"You remember that I referred Don to the counselor because he would go into a terrible rage and kick and scream whenever he didn't get his own way. Everyone was afraid of him. I didn't know what to do. I had tried everything from sending him to the principal to standing him in a corner. Nothing seemed to work."

"Well, what did the counselor suggest?"

"Nothing, really. That's the trouble. The counselor said that Don's responses on the various tests indicate he is a very anxious and aggressive child who has a low self-concept. So what? I already know that."

"Didn't the counselor have any ideas of what to do?" insisted Mr. Peterson.

"The only real suggestion I got was that Don needs to learn how to get along with others. But that is precisely why I referred him—I want to help him learn to get along with the other boys and girls, but I don't know how. I guess I was hoping for something more from the counselor," said Miss Ford with more sadness than anger.

"I know what you mean," Joe said. "Early in the year I referred Mickey, you know, the shy little girl who clams up whenever she is asked to give a report in front of the class. The counselor told me that she has an inferiority complex as the result of a fixation at a premature level of development. If knowing those words does any good, it sure doesn't show. Mickey, poor scared kid, is just as mousy as ever. I wish I knew how to help her."

"Maybe the counselor would like to be more helpful but doesn't know either," suggested Miss Ford thoughtfully.

* *Elementary School Guidance and Counseling*, 1967, vol. 1, no. 1.
  By permission.

"Maybe so. But just once I'd like to see the counselor produce some results."

The complaints of these two teachers certainly do not apply to all counselors. But they do have one important implication: *A counselor's success is judged by the degree to which he can help pupils engage in more appropriate types of behavior.* When a teacher refers Don to a counselor because of his frequent temper tantrums, she hopes in some way that Don will decrease the frequency of these tantrums. She is not asking the counselor to improve Don's self-concept or to reconstruct his personality. If a teacher wants to help shy, withdrawn Mickey to learn how to participate in class, he eventually expects Mickey to talk more in class. He is not asking for the counselor's opinion about the origin of the problem or to hypothesize about the inner state of the child's mind. The success of the counselor's work, regardless of the intervening processes used, will necessarily be judged by the observed improvement in the child's behavior.

In this article we propose that a behavioral approach to elementary school guidance offers counselors an effective way to specify and accomplish the purposes of counseling. We will first show how a behavioral counselor would handle the problems of Don and Mickey by applying some principles of learning. We will then consider some broader implications and problems of behavioral approaches to counseling.

APPLYING SOME LEARNING PRINCIPLES

The two problems described here are based on actual cases referred to an elementary school counselor who applied learning principles to resolve them. Though names and identifying data have been changed, these cases will be used to illustrate how actual behavior problems can be solved through systematic attention to the reinforcing consequences associated with different kinds of behavior.

POSITIVE REINFORCEMENT
OF SUCCESSIVE APPROXIMATIONS

Mickey, a bright sixth-grade girl, was referred to the counselor because she became extremely anxious when asked to give an oral book report before the class. Because Mickey had sometimes participated in class discussions, the teacher was surprised to see her become too nervous to continue. He quickly suggested that she give her presentation another time.

In talking with the counselor, Mickey explained that she wanted very much to talk in front of the class but had never been able to do so. Her cumulative record showed that her past teachers seldom asked her to give oral reports because of the anxiety she developed when speaking before a group. The counselor thought the best approach would be to help her learn gradually the behaviors necessary in giving a report. Thus, a program of counseling activities was formulated to accomplish this goal of counseling.

A combination of procedures was used by the counselor in helping Mickey learn the behaviors necessary to solve her problem. In the counseling setting, Mickey met with the counselor once a week for six weeks and practiced getting out of her seat, coming to the front of the room, and saying a few words. The counselor suggested she begin with brief reports and gradually build up to longer presentations. Mickey was always free to stop and sit down whenever she felt anxious about talking. During each session the counselor smiled, said "very good, Mickey," and gave other types of reinforcement as Mickey successfully role-played the part of giving a report.

The counselor also worked closely with Mickey's teacher in setting up a program for gradually increasing Mickey's ability to speak before a group. The teacher agreed to progressively include Mickey in a social studies committee which was giving oral presentations on various countries. At first Mickey was asked to help only by pointing on a large map to the city, river, or area that was being discussed by other members of the committee. Members of the group, at the suggestion of the teacher, gradually involved Mickey more in the discussions. Each week Mickey was asked to tell a little more about the location and terrain of a country while the other members of the committee covered the political, social, and economic aspects. At the end of the two and one-half months, Mickey's presentation was about the same length as that of other members of the committee.

Mickey was often thanked for helping out and was given praise and approval by the teacher and members of the committee each time she participated with the panel. The two co-chairmen of the committee were also encouraged to tell Mickey she did very well as she increased her participation, thus providing for peer reinforcement. Mickey gradually became more comfortable while in front of the class and eventually was able to give reports on her own. She was also among the students who volunteered to give an oral presentation at the end of the year when a few parents attended the completion of the social studies unit.

The role-playing allowed Mickey to practice the behavior under low-stress conditions. When an individual role-plays a behavior enough times, the role becomes part of his repertoire of behavior. He is then better able to perform the behavior in other situations. In this case, the role-playing also gave the counselor an excellent opportunity to reinforce and encourage Mickey as she made increasingly better approximations to the desired behavior.

The counselor helped to arrange a program of systematic positive reinforcement in the classroom as well as in the counselor's office to help Mickey learn how to talk before a group. Behavior that is reinforced or rewarded is more likely to occur again (Skinner, 1953). Thus, to increase the occurrence of a particular behavior (in this case Mickey's oral reports), it is often only necessary to insure that reinforcement be given soon after the behavior occurs.

A grades, approving gestures, and verbal remarks such as "very good" and "well done" are a few of the reinforcing stimuli effective for encouraging most school children in our society. The important aspect in Mickey's case was that reinforcement was given for any *improvement* in speaking before a group. She did not need to make a polished speech before receiving the approval and attention of her teacher, counselor, and peers. Each gradual step toward improvement was reinforced.

Several studies in counseling (Johnson, 1964; Krumboltz and Schroeder, 1965; Krumboltz and Thoresen, 1964) have shown that reinforcement procedures can be used very effectively in school counseling to promote or change a particular behavior. The annotated bibliography contains references which may suggest other principles and examples, as well as theoretical formulations derived from research in learning.

Absence of Reinforcement after Undesired Behavior

An effective technique for eliminating undesired behavior is "extinction"— arranging for *no* reinforcement to follow the inappropriate behavior. The use of this procedure can be seen in the case of Don. Don was a third-grade boy who often had rather violent displays of temper on the playground whenever he did not get his way. Since he was relatively new to the school, his teacher, Miss Ford, thought the tantrums would decrease as Don adjusted to the school situation. Rather than decreasing, Don's tantrums became more frequent.

After talking with Miss Ford and the boy's mother, the counselor arranged to be on the playground to observe Don. He noticed that when Don began to scream and pick fights with others, the teacher would quickly respond and attempt to quiet him down. Don usually calmed down when Miss Ford sat on the playground bench with her arm around him. Miss Ford said that she felt Don needed a feeling of security since he responded very quickly to words of reassurance from her.

The next day when Miss Ford came to see the counselor, she asked what was causing the tantrums and what she should do about them. The counselor felt that in this case the increase in the tantrums resulted from the reinforcement Don received from Miss Ford whenever he kicked, screamed, or picked a fight. In effect, Don had more tantrums because he had learned that such behavior usually gave him the undivided attention of the teacher. The tantrum behavior apparently had been learned at home and generalized to the school situation.

The counselor explained to the teacher that behavior previously learned through reinforcement can often be eliminated by permitting it to recur without any reinforcement. Thus, a program for the extinction of the behavior was formulated with the specific goal of decreasing the number of Don's tantrums. In this case, the principal of the school and the child's mother were included in the process. It was agreed that when Don began a display of bad temper on the playground, Miss Ford would busy herself with the others and in general ignore his behavior. The same procedure was used in the classroom. In those instances when the class was disturbed too much, Miss Ford would quietly escort Don to the hallway, and the principal would take him to the nurse's room where he would remain until he calmed down.

The conference with Don's mother revealed that the same type of behavior was manifested at home. After considerable effort on the part of the counselor, Don's mother also agreed not to provide him with reinforcement for the tantrum behavior. It was agreed that Don would be left in his room to "cry it out" each time he resorted to displays of temper. In a very short time Don stopped having tantrums both at home and in school—the tantrum behavior was extinguished.

By providing for no reinforcement after the tantrum, Don's counselor, teacher, and parents were able to eliminate the undesirable behavior. Extinction procedures as used here, as well as other procedures (e.g., Wolpe, 1958), have been shown to be effective counseling techniques for weakening or eliminating deviant behaviors. It is possible that other methods could have helped Don learn to control his temper. However, a warm understanding approach would not only be ineffective in this case but, as used here, was actually partly responsible for maintaining and promoting the undesirable behavior.

Variety of Techniques

The behavioral counselor does not rely on any one set of counseling procedures but instead tailors specific techniques to specific problems. The techniques the counselor uses are employed to aid the student in learning those behaviors necessary to the solution of his problem. If the underachiever, for example, is referred for counseling, the behavioral counselor would not devote his time and energy trying to determine what is "abnormal" about the individual's personality by administering various personality tests. Rather, he would attempt to devise techniques and procedures that would be effective in helping the individual to improve his achievement. He would seek ways of providing more encouragement for constructive efforts at improving his school work.

Specific techniques for specific problems are not readily available but must be devised by the counselor to fit each individual problem. Procedures described in various research studies, however, may be suggestive. The use of systematic, positive reinforcement (Johnson, 1964; Krumboltz and Schroeder, 1965), tape recordings of students modeling a desired behavior (Bandura, 1965; Krumboltz and Thoresen, 1964), programmed instruction (Bruner, 1965), video-taped presentations and films (Krumboltz, Varenhorst, and Thoresen, 1965), "behavior contracts" and role-playing (Keirsey, 1965), and systematic desensitization of anxieties (Lazarus, 1961; Wolpe, 1958) are some examples of procedures counselors might try to help students learn the behaviors necessary for the solution of their particular problems.

THE PURPOSES OF COUNSELING

The central purpose of counseling, and the main reason for its existence, is to assist each student, teacher, or parent with the specific problem for which he is seeking help. The main task then for counselors is to assist the individual in *learning* those behaviors that will result in a solution to his problem.

From a behavioral approach, all relevant goals and objectives of counseling must be focused on behavior. Thus, the counselor would state his counseling goals in terms of observable behavior rather than in discovering or changing some abstract inner personality process (Krumboltz, 1966). Since students' problems are different from each other, the goals of counseling would be stated differently for each individual. Broad general goals for all individuals, e.g., self-understanding or increased ego strength, are deemed by the behavioral counselors as too abstract to be useful in specifying the purposes to be accomplished.

The goals of the behavioral counselor may be organized under three categories: (1) altering maladaptive behavior, (2) learning the decision-making process, and (3) preventing problems. In each category the objectives of the counselor are specific changes in behavior sought by or for the student and agreed to by the counselor.

Altering Maladaptive Behavior

The situations of Mickey and Don provide good examples of goals the behavioral counselor would use in instances of maladaptive behavior. For Mickey, the goal of counseling was an increase in the skills necessary for giving oral reports before the class. For Don, the counselor's goal was to decrease the number of tantrums he was displaying at school. For both problems, observable changes in behavior were the explicit objectives of the counseling process.

The advantages of this approach can be easily seen. By avoiding ambiguous abstract terms, e.g., to increase Mickey's ego strength, the counselor was able to communicate with the teacher and Mickey as to what they were trying to accomplish. Thus, the counselor, teacher, and Mickey had a clear understanding of the goals of the counseling; all were able to take active roles in the process; and all could see progress being made toward the goal.

Learning the Decision-Making Process

A second major category of objectives in behavioral counseling is aiding students in learning how to make good decisions. Many personal and educational problems can often be solved when individuals know how to go about making a decision. Counselors can be effective in aiding elementary school children in learning how to (1) construct alternative behaviors, (2) seek relevant information about each alternative, (3) weigh the possible outcomes and values of each alternative, and (4) formulate tentative plans of action.

Consider Frankie and Brian. Frankie blurts out incorrect answers without taking sufficient time to think through a problem. Brian, on the other hand, vacillates from one side of the question to the other and can never make up his mind. Both boys could benefit from some systematic help in learning how to make decisions wisely.

Research studies have shown that presenting information on probable outcomes (Gelatt, 1964) and reinforcing either deliberation or decision type responses (Ryan and Krumboltz, 1964) influence the decision-making process. By aiding students to learn how to use the steps involved in the decision-making process, counselors and teachers are in effect providing students with problem-solving skills and attitudes that will aid them in meeting new problems in the future.

Preventing Problems

The third type of goals for counseling is that of preventing problems. By setting up educational programs which help students learn the behaviors necessary in the decision-making process, counselors can be effective in assisting students to solve some of their future personal, educational, and vocational decisions. But counselors must also be concerned about other educational practices.

Students who are discouraged because of harsh punishment for low grades, or feel inadequate because of a constantly dissatisfied teacher or parent, are all too often seen by a counselor after the damage is done. By asking for and taking an active role in the curricular and extracurricular programs of the school, counselors can help prevent educational practices which stifle the desire for learning and create serious emotional maladjustment.

STUDENT PROBLEMS SEEN AS PROBLEMS IN LEARNING

The way we conceptualize a student's problem will determine our goals and procedures in counseling. It is important, then, that school counselors conceptualize student problems in ways that suggest steps for solving them. As we have seen in the cases of Mickey and Don, the behavioral counselor does not view deviant student behaviors as symptoms of pathology but as inappropriate behaviors that have been learned in the same way that any other behavior is learned. The counseling process is a learning situation in which the counselor aids the counselee in learning those behaviors necessary to the solution of his problem. How behavior is learned and how it may be unlearned or altered become central issues for the behavioral counselor.

Since most learning is a function of environmental consequences, effective procedures for producing behavior change depend on the arrangement of the student's environment. In reality, environmental modification is the only channel open to counselors for influencing human behavior. The behavioral counselor thus looks at the student's environment to see what is maintaining the behavior and what changes in the environment would significantly aid the individual to learn those behaviors necessary for solving his problem.

Conceptualizing the problem as one of learning guides the counselor in the steps that must be accomplished and allows him to monitor progress objectively. Since counseling is seen as a learning process, the counselor becomes an integral part of the educational system and joins with teachers, administrators, and parents to help children learn how to lead fuller, richer lives.

SUMMARY

A behavioral approach to counseling offers elementary school counselors an effective means for helping students with specific problems. This approach has several unique characteristics:

1. Since most human behavior is learned, it treats the counseling process as a learning process.

2. It assumes that effective procedures for producing desired behavioral change lie in arranging the student's environment to promote the desired learning rather than in manipulating hypothetical processes or entities within the individual.

3. The outcomes and goals of counseling are stated and assessed as specific changes in behavior shown by the student.

4. The counseling interview itself is only a small part of the total process of helping the student learn to solve his problems. Teachers, parents, and peers are all seen as important persons in providing an environment conducive to new learning.

5. Counseling procedures vary for different individuals and are specifically designed for the particular problem of each individual.

6. Counseling procedures and techniques are derived from scientifically based knowledge of the learning process.

Some counselors have said that the behavioral approach is just good common sense. Parents, counselors, and teachers frequently use effective learning principles without realizing the application they are making. However, it is important for the counselor to know why certain procedures are used, when to apply them, for what types of students, for what specific problems, and to accomplish which goals. The counselor can thus become an integral part of the educational process.

ANNOTATED BIBLIOGRAPHY

Bandura, A. 1961. Psychotherapy as a learning process. *Psych. Bull.*, *58*, 143–159.
Surveys many experimental and clinical studies using behavioristic psychotherapy. Relates many types of deviant behavior that have been treated successfully by direct focusing on the behavior itself.

Krumboltz, J. D. (ed.). 1966. *Revolution in counseling: implications of behavioral science.* Boston: Houghton Mifflin.
Chapters by Krumboltz, Bijou, Shoben, and Wrenn explore the possibilities and problems arising from application of learning principles to counseling.

————. 1965. Behavioral counseling: rationale and research. *Personnel guid. J.*, *44*, 383–387.

Asserts that the goals of counseling must be in terms of some end condition and not the means to achieve that end. Rationale for the behavioral approach, counselor limitations, and useful counselor activities are discussed.

————. 1964. Parable of a good counselor. *Personnel guid. J.*, *43*, 118–123.

This article provides a comparison of behavioral and client-centered approaches to a counseling problem. The similarities and differences in the assumptions and procedures of the two approaches are discussed.

Krasner, L., and L. P. Ullmann (eds.). 1965. *Research in behavior modification*. New York: Holt, Rinehart and Winston.

Fifteen articles of research in personality, child, clinical, social, general, and experimental psychology are presented. Such areas as learning principles, the interview, vicarious reinforcement, verbal conditioning, modeling, small groups, and hypnosis are covered.

Magoon, T. 1964. Innovations in counseling. *J. counsel. Psychol.*, *11*, 343–347.

Magoon presents possibilities in using audio-visual materials in career counseling.

Michael, J., and L. Myerson. 1962. A behavior approach to counseling and guidance. *Harvard educ. Rev.*, *32*, 382–402.

A behavioristic model for counseling is presented as an approach for the development of a scientific approach to guidance. The phenomena of conditioning is discussed in terms of the experimental learning psychologist.

Ullmann, L. P., and L. Krasner (eds.). 1965. *Case studies in behavior modification*. New York: Holt, Rinehart and Winston.

The writers present a variety of behavioral problems in which psychotherapeutic procedures derived from social learning theory are applied. Cases are drawn from a wide variety of clinical and non-clinical settings.

REFERENCES

Bandura, A. 1965. Behavioral modifications through modeling procedures. In L. Krasner and L. P. Ullmann (eds.), *Research in behavior modification*. New York: Holt, Rinehart and Winston.

Bruner, Fern. 1965. The effect of programmed instruction on information-seeking behavior in tenth-grade students. Palo Alto, Calif.: Stanford University. Unpublished doctoral dissertation.

Gelatt, H. B. 1964. The influence of outcome probability data on college choice. Palo Alto, Calif.: Stanford University. Unpublished doctoral dissertation.

Johnson, C. J. 1964. The transfer effect of treatment group composition on pupils' classroom participation. Palo Alto, Calif.: Stanford University. Unpublished doctoral dissertation.

Keirsey, D. W. 1965. *Transactional casework: a technology for inducing be-*

havior change. Paper presented at the Annual Convention of the California Association of School Psychologists and Psychometrists, San Francisco. Mimeographed.

Krumboltz, J. D. 1966. *Stating the goals of counseling.* Monogr. no. 1. California Counseling and Guidance Association.

———, and W. W. Schroeder. 1965. Promoting career exploration through reinforcement. *Personnel guid. J.,* *44,* 19–26.

———, Barbara B. Varenhorst, and C. E. Thoresen. 1965. *Non-verbal factors in the effectiveness of models in counseling.* Paper presented to the American Educational Research Association, Chicago.

———, and C. E. Thoresen. 1964. The effect of behavioral counseling in group and individual settings on information-seeking behavior. *J. counsel. Psychol.,* *11,* 324–333.

Lazarus, A. A. 1961. Group therapy of phobic disorders by systematic desensitization. *J. abnorm. soc. Psychol.,* *63,* 504–510.

Ryan, T. Antoinette, and J. D. Krumboltz. 1964. Effect of planned reinforcement counseling on client decision-making behavior. *J. counsel. Psychol.,* *11,* 315–323.

Skinner, B. F. 1953. *Science and human behavior.* New York: Macmillan.

Wolpe, J. 1958. *Psychotherapy by reciprocal inhibition.* Stanford, Calif.: Stanford University Press.

Conceptual Foundations of Counseling:

Adlerian Theory and Practice*

Don C. Dinkmeyer

Rogerians, Freudians, trait and factor theorists—the exponents of personality theories that have influenced current counseling practice—are numerous. The school counselor should be familiar with the fundamentals of a variety of theoretical formulations.

Among those who have made noteworthy contributions to the conceptual foundations of counseling is Alfred Adler. Adler had much experience with children in school, and his experiences provide us with many insights into the counseling process.

* *The School Counselor,* March 1964, vol. 11, no. 3. By permission.

Adlerian therapy is characterized by an uncovering, analytical, and interpretive emphasis. While close to Rogers in its philosophy of the nature of man, it is quite divergent from the Rogerian school in practice and technique. Adlerians place more emphasis on counseling as a cognitive process than do the Rogerians. There is a greater concern for acquiring certain types of information.

Adlerians are interested in the family constellation of the client, the psychological position of the individual among his siblings, and the ages, sex, and roles of the various siblings as viewed by the counselee. The general family atmosphere is explored as to certain relations within the family.

Counseling is seen as a learning process in which the individual learns about himself and his interpersonal relationships. It is educational in the sense that it serves as a re-educative bridge to better self-understanding and better relationships.

PURPOSIVE BEHAVIOR

Man is perceived as an indivisible social being whose every action has a purpose. This is differentiated from mechanistic-deterministic theories in that it places a stress on the holistic nature of behavior and points to both freedom of choice and purposiveness of behavior as central in understanding the individual. Social striving and the individual's functioning in his social setting are important.

The Adlerians believe that all behavior is purposive and that actions are directed toward goals. They feel it is more important to recognize the purpose than the cause or genesis of the symptom. While not failing to take causes into account, they add a dimension to our understanding of an individual by viewing the purposes.

Although the causes of many problems cannot be changed by either counselor or client, the client's use of his situation and his purposes are subject to change.

Counseling is directed toward developing an understanding of client goals, an understanding that first resides in the counselor and then in the client. However, all hypotheses about purposes and goals are set up tentatively and become effective therapeutically when accepted and internalized by the counselee.

All behavior has social meaning. Man is best understood when viewed in terms of his social setting. Social striving in this system is seen as primary, not secondary. The counselor looks at the functioning of the individual and explores his adjustment in the life tasks of work, social and sexual roles.

For the student he investigates adjustment relative to school tasks. Does the individual participate in the work of school; does he seem to enjoy his work?

The area of social adjustment is explored also. The counselor is interested in how the counselee gets along with peers and with adults. Both the quality and quantity of friendships are explored.

Finally, the feelings of adequacy in the male or female roles are investigated in order to determine both how the counselee feels about himself in this area and how he gets along with members of the opposite sex. This provides a handy overview of the major areas of interpersonal difficulty.

LIFE STYLE

To understand the individual, one must know the pattern of his life—his life style. The style of life, the evaluation of self and society, is the key to understanding the individual. It tells us why he acts as he does and enables us to predict behavior in the future with a fair amount of validity. It serves as a guide in the planning of counseling.

Awareness of the basic assumptions of the client enables the counselor to understand client behavior. Successful counseling will provide the client with insight and facilitate the change of his behavior.

Each individual has the creative power to make biased interpretations of all that he experiences, and to assign personalized meanings to his experiences. This emphasizes for the counselor the importance of determining the subjective view of the client. Adlerians are vitally interested in how the patient sees the situation. They are not there to establish the facts, but to establish how the client sees the facts.

All of the psychological processes can be understood in terms of a self-consistent organization, and understanding the goals provides insight into the life style.

Neurotic symptoms are seen as safeguards which help maintain self-deception. The symptoms have a purpose. They may enable the individual to defend the self, gain attention, show his social power and control over others, get even or confirm his already present faulty views. The client is guided to see and use new solutions to his problems.

On the basis of the foregoing assumptions, it becomes important to see the purpose of emotions and symptoms. Emotions are not seen as some type of mystical driving force, but instead as movements that serve the individual's purposes (Dinkmeyer and Dreikurs, 1963). Emotions can be seen as social tools that facilitate the achievement of goals.

MALADJUSTMENT

A criterion for maladjustment is found in the lack of social interest. Insofar as the client lacks the ability to cooperate and to be concerned about others, he lacks interpersonal adjustment.

Psychopathology is a result of mistaken concepts and inadequate psychological movement. Overambition, discouragement, and the striving from a felt minus to a plus position are crucial elements in understanding the dynamics of behavior.

The discouraged individual lacks confidence in himself. He anticipates failure. He has a mistaken evaluation of his situations and functions as if things were hopeless (Way, 1962).

Overambition comes from the concern to be better and more than one is. An achievement never leaves this individual satisfied; he only desires to excel. As one might predict, when he cannot be the most successful in an area, he gives up and becomes the least, because this also serves to draw attention to him.

Thus, an important ingredient of any counseling situation is encouragement. The counselor is more than acceptant. He values the individual as he is and focuses on his assets. This faith enables the client to build faith in himself. In the counseling process any positive effort is recognized, not only successes. The client is enabled to build his self-confidence and self-respect (Dinkmeyer and Dreikurs, 1963).

Maladjustment in this model is interpersonal, not intrapersonal. The client must solve life tasks and develop his relations with people. More time is spent in discussion of the current stream of life than in extensive review of the past.

FOUR-PHASE APPROACH

There are four phases of counseling for this orientation: the relationship, the investigation of dynamics, interpretation to the client, and reorientation.

The *relationship* sought in therapy is a cooperative one. It is vital that the counselor and the counselee establish a common goal. Counseling is conversation with a purpose, and if it is to be effective it should be a common purpose. The relationship is one of mutual trust and respect. This is more than mere rapport; it implies collaboration and requires the already mentioned alignment of goals.

The relationship in counseling requires close cooperation, and for many individuals it is the first good human relationship. The individual should feel understood and should anticipate success from the counseling relationship.

The *investigation* explores the current life situation as it is viewed by the individual. Here is where the counselor investigates the complaints, problems, and symptoms. The objective situation and the functioning of the individual in the three major areas of life—work, social, and sex—are investigated and discussed.

An understanding of the dynamics of the individual gives us access to the personality or life style. This is obtained by an investigation of the formative years. The counselor is interested in the early family atmosphere, the relationship between the parents, and the client's relationship with the parents.

The client's position in the family constellation is significant. Modern Adlerians are not concerned merely with ordinal position, but instead with psychological position. While it is important to learn if the client is oldest, second, youngest, middle, or the only child, one also should determine the sex of the siblings and the variances in ages in the constellation.

The client's feelings about his relative position among his siblings in a variety of traits must be obtained. Recollections of early childhood are consistent with the pattern of life as seen by the client. The early recollections as taken from the client provide another method of seeing the goals and mistaken assumptions.

Adlerian *interpretations* characteristically put an emphasis on goals. They confront the client with not only his feelings but the purpose of these feelings. The individual's purposes, intentions, and private logic are pointed out. The basic premise of the life style is regularly referred to. While the client may not be told what to do, he is informed about the purpose of his behavior, and then he can draw his own conclusions.

There is a direct and deliberate exploring of values. The mirror technique, whereby the individual sees himself, is used. In this technique the counselee is confronted with his goals and intentions. This is used to stimulate change by making the individual aware of his part in the decisions he makes relative to his psychological direction.

In the *reorientation* phase the client gives up his mistaken concepts and beliefs in favor of more accurate evaluations. One of the more important changes during counseling is the change in the self-concept. Adlerians are interested in changing the faulty value systems insofar as they cause the client to function ineffectively in his interpersonal relationships.

ADLER'S CONTRIBUTION

What, then, can Adlerian theory contribute to the conceptual foundations of counseling? It presents a model that reveals man as purposive and goal-directed, one whose behavior can best be understood subjectively and in terms of its social meaning. This goal becomes the final cause and, for the counselor, the working hypothesis.

Motivation is understood in terms of pulls instead of pushes. Knowledge of the life style helps one to see the dynamic unity and pattern in all psychological movement. Many confusing, contradictory cases take on meaning when viewed systematically.

In this technique the counselor is active in the sense that he explores the interpersonal relationships and conducts the investigation. He analyzes and seeks understanding in terms of the present purposes of the client. The counselor listens in order to pick up the theme and the direction of psychological movement. He will also interrupt to point out self-deceptive tendencies. He may interpret and suggest, but it is up to the patient to decide.

EXAMPLES

Some of these principles can best be seen through case illustration.

A boy of 11, Steve, comes for counseling. Though of above average IQ, he has not produced as the teacher expects in the classroom. The counselor discusses what things they might do together to help Steve, and they eventually focus on the school problem.

Steve talks about an eight-year-old sister, who does exceptionally well in school. She is seen as a bother and someone who restricts his movements.

After developing an awareness of the client's feelings, the counselor formulates a tentative hypothesis. He asks, "Could it be that you want to show Miss Wilson that you can't?"

The first response is a hesitant "No," but his smile shows a recognition of his purpose. Further discussion brings Steve to greater awareness of how he demonstrates his inadequacy and how it excuses him from certain school tasks.

This counselee has some interesting early recollections including: "When I was five my friend could ride a two-wheeler, but I could only ride a tricycle. I tried one day to catch up with him, but couldn't. I felt bad."

Also, "I remember when I was in first grade, the teacher told me I would have to do the work over. My parents felt I was too small; I felt unhappy."

He operates on the faulty assumption that: (a) I am not as much as others my age; (b) I can get people to serve me; (c) People don't believe I can function as well as I ought to.

Future discussions were directed at helping Steve to see his assets and build faith in himself.

Jane, 13, is a child who demonstrates continuous interpersonal difficulties. She has strong oppositional tendencies and does not get along well with peers, teachers, or parents.

Her early recollections can be interpreted to tell us she feels, "People don't treat me right," and, "I am not as much as I should be."

Here the relationship is more difficult to establish. The counselor must show that he is not easily discouraged and doesn't expect too much.

In a discussion about her home Jane demonstrates strong negative feelings toward parental management. She admits she is determined to get even and frequently is successful. Here is where parent conferences are of value, and a discussion of new ways in managing Jane is held.

In the counseling sessions Jane tried to prove she is vicious. The counselor offers the tentative hypothesis, "Could it be you feel you have to get even?" Jane replies, "Yes, sort of." A discussion ensues regarding revenge.

Some of the following sessions were used to encourage Jane by showing she was trusted and is a person of value.

SUMMARY

Adlerian theory, then, adds a dimension to the counselor. He may study causes, but he goes beyond to an awareness of purposes. Thus, he gains insight into some really significant factors in understanding and treating the individual. The well-educated counselor will want to become familiar with the formulations of the Adlerians as he develops his personal theory of counseling.

REFERENCES

Dinkmeyer, D., and R. Dreikurs. 1963. *Encouraging children to learn: the encouragement process.* Englewood Cliffs, N.J.: Prentice-Hall.

Way, L. 1962. *Adler's place in psychology.* New York: Collier.

Counseling Children
in the Elementary School*

Herman J. Peters

The interview is a technique particularly well adapted to uncovering subjective definitions of experiences, to assessing a child's perceptions of the significant people and events in his environment, and to studying how he conceptualizes his life experiences (Yarrow, 1960).

It is interesting to note that counseling as a distinct guidance function is given minimal treatment in the early literature on elementary school guidance. When it is mentioned, it refers to teacher counseling. In speaking about guidance activities for intermediate and junior high school pupils, Bryant (1928) gave three phases of the junior high school program. These reflect the final stages of elementary school guidance. The first phase stressed contact with each seventh grader for personality development and educational achievement. The second phase emphasized "the individual conference" with each eighth-grade student for vocational purposes. The third was an individual conference with each graduating (ninth-grade) student for vocational purposes. Bryant made no mention of counseling but only implied it through "the individual conference" method.

Allen (1930) reported that guidance functions in the elementary school were classified under three headings: (1) personnel records and research, (2) counseling, and (3) orientation. Under "counseling," Allen referred only to the room teacher as having counseling functions in the areas of: (1) personal and social adjustment, (2) attendance and health, (3) discipline—school citizenship, as well as with (4) parents, physicians, nurses, home visitors and (5) the special teachers for music and drawing, auditorium, nature study and science (the homeroom teacher puts the picture together if she has time to study the child).

In 1950, Wilson emphasized "a counseling service for all children from the kindergarten through the eighth year, recognizing that guidance is not a privilege accorded the maladjusted, but that it is a necessity for every normal child."

COUNSELING CHILDREN—
CAN IT BE DONE?

The question often arises whether counseling is a workable guidance function with children, especially with those in the early grades. Segar (1952) states

---

* Paper prepared especially for this book of readings.

that, "With very young children the interview can be used effectively for increasing pupil-teacher understanding. On the playground, after school, at lunch, the teacher may informally talk alone with the child. . . . Interviews may assist the child: (1) to understand certain cause and effect relationships, (2) to make more desirable choices of behavior, (3) to solve a specific problem, and (4) to develop a personal plan of action . . . (p. 414).

Bakwin and Bakwin (1960) state that, "It should be emphasized that every child who has some fluency in speech (i.e., age 3 years and up) can express his inner, hidden mental processes as well as his conscious strivings and desires at a verbal level, without necessarily resorting to highly specialized techniques of play therapy, puppetry, projective testing, and the like" (p. 236).

In 1963, Meeks pointed to a county elementary school guidance counseling program in which the counselor spent much of his time counseling individual pupils and small groups of pupils. She stated, "It is our firm conviction that children with poor self-concepts do not learn. Counseling has as its chief goal helping pupils gain a more realistic self-concept."

Eubanks (no date) cites differential developmental factors of children from those of secondary school students as bases for stating that ". . . the elementary child is not ready for a formal counseling program. . . ."

Boy and Pine (1963) present role descriptions of pupil personnel specialists for the Lexington Public School in Massachusetts—in outlining the elementary school counseling consultants' duties. There is a pinpointing of counseling responsibilities both with children and parents. In working with children, the elementary school counseling consultants, "engage in counseling with individual students and groups of students when it is deemed that such counseling will be educationally helpful" (pp. 103–104). The reader should be alerted that "educationally helpful" is not defined. Counseling, if it is effective, will be educationally helpful—directly or indirectly—will it not?

Today, counseling children in the elementary school is a topic that invites polemics in the guidance field. Shertzer and Pruett (1961) emphasize the importance of counseling in the elementary school. Hart (1961) reported that holding conferences with parents, counseling pupils with learning, physical, social, and emotional problems ranked high in both teachers' ratings and authority ratings as to the relative importance of selected duties for the elementary counselor to perform.

Counseling is the key activity in any guidance program. Most guidance experts agree on this. However, the unique nature of the counseling process at the various school levels has received scant attention. Curran (1962) states that, "Generally speaking, there seems to be comparatively little difference between the interview process with children and that of adolescents or adults. Often a small child talks freely and the interview follows the paths described. The same skills and responses are necessary for counseling children as for adolescents or adults and if properly used, favorable results can follows" (p. 296).

Although counseling is recognized as a definite part of the elementary school guidance program, two points are emphatically apparent: (1) There is no careful analysis of counseling with children in the elementary school setting. More emphasis seems to be on counseling parents and interpreting data to staff members. (2) Most literature on counseling in the elementary school assumes a transfer of principles and procedures from college and clinical counseling. Brammer and Shostrom (1960) state that, "The goals of counseling are similar for children and adults, but because of the child's immaturity and dependence on others, modifications of techniques are necessary" (p. 332). Further, the available literature is oriented to those children in need of special assistance from other branches of the helping profession, e.g., from the staff at children's mental health centers. The key question is: What basic factors should be considered in counseling children in the elementary school guidance program?

Many of the skills and procedures of clinical and college counseling can not be transferred without modifying them to fit the counseling situation in the elementary school. We can only assume that variations of them will be applicable, but that is all. We have little or no research to substantiate such a contention. The purpose of this paper is to examine, from another vantage point, the process and some of the factors necessary to an understanding of counseling children in the elementary school.

WHAT IS THE CENTRAL GOAL OF COUNSELING IN THE ELEMENTARY SCHOOL?

The central goal of counseling children in the elementary school is developmental in nature, not remedial or therapeutic: that is, it is for those individuals in the classroom who have at least a fair degree of psychological inner harmony. True, some boys and girls need remedial or therapeutic counseling. However, this service should come from a specialist other than the school counselor because the needed treatment requires the precise prescription of the specialist. The argument that no other specialist is available in many of the schools does not give license to the school counselor to go beyond his competencies.

However, the school counselor works in a counseling relationship with those who can profit at this time from a continuity of harmonious relationships in the classroom. There may be some disturbed children who cannot continue as regular classroom participants. Their discontinuities of self-integration are such that, with the help of a specialist, other than the school counselor, they can learn to cope with the learning situation. The emphasis here is developmental. Others in need of special counseling are referred to the appropriate school or community resource. The Educational Policies Commission (1960) in *Contemporary Issues of Elementary Education* stated the developmental concept well when it said, "To learn well the things a school attempts to communicate, a child must feel a sense of personal worth. This derives not only from the home, but from the school. It requires a feeling of adequacy to cope with the school's expectations" (p. 8).

Developmental guidance seeks to help the individual know his competencies and adequacies, what is expected to him, and how he is meeting his own self-expectations. Counseling focuses on the individual and his totality and is not a piecemeal bit of information incidentally acquired about the subject in the learning situation of the classroom. Developmental counseling requires the effort of a counselor skilled in assisting the pupil in the assessment of his potentiality at a level he can understand. In other words, the concern of individual counseling services in the elementary school should be to aid the pupil: (1) to achieve self-understanding, (2) to learn to deal with complicated interpersonal relationships, (3) to attain appropriate academic achievement, and (4) to alleviate special personal or emotional problems. This is well summarized by Ruth Richards (1943): "The elementary counselor's chief goal then is to awaken in the child the understanding that all persons differ widely in their aptitudes and interests, that there are a thousand other jobs, and that our school system is offering opportunities for each individual to discover and use his natural abilities, so that he will later function in his chosen field of work" (pp. 109–110).

SOME PERTINENT CONCEPTS

The elementary school counselor must understand the developmental process of growth of the childhood years. The nature of the child as a personality distinct from infant, adolescent, youth or adult must be clearly delineated. The topic of "child development" is comprehensive. Excellent books are available.

The boy or girl in the elementary school is dependent on adults. By his very nature he cannot accept full responsibility for his behavior. He is learning little by little that he is responsible, but he cannot accept the full consequences of his behavior because our culture does not permit children to make important final choices or decisions. At the elementary school level the child is beginning to learn the choice-making process, but his dependency on adults means that most counseling must be done within the framework in which the pupil lives.

It should also be kept in mind that the fears of the child enter into the counseling relationship. In general, many children look to some adults with insecurity and fear of rejection. To be sure, they are looking for love and affection, but they are also alert to any kind of adult behavior that indicates non-acceptance of them. The elementary school counselor has the unusual opportunity to create a climate of acceptance between himself and the child. This may be one of the few experiences a child has to be in a non-threatening atmosphere with an empathic adult. His image of the adult world may then begin to be more positive.

Counseling by its very nature is an effort to help the individual gain more integrity as a person, achieve a greater sense of identity, and give purpose and direction to one's life. This implies the ability to reason, comprehend, and understand. Implicit in the physical development of the child, is the on-going developmental process of the child's growth in his ability to reason. For some children counseling will not be too effective because of their difficulty in reasoning. Piaget found that the growth of logical thinking in the adolescent differs radically from that of the child. Although he emphasizes logical structures, his explanation applies to the total reasoning faculties of the child. Here again, it is not a black and white transition from non-reason to reason but is rather a *gradual* development of the reasoning faculty as part of the maturation process. In the counseling process this must be kept in mind as one tries to think through with the child his concerns of daily living.

Building Oneself for the Foundation of Adolescence and Adulthood

The counseling experience for the child in the elementary school can be a significant experience or a series of significant experiences in his school career. It will continue to focus attention on him as an individual, as a person of worth and dignity. It will help him to think through, albeit gradually, his progress in development. The importance of peak experiences in one's life is well documented by Maslow (1961). Counseling can often be a high point in a child's life. Maslow has listed a number of results that have been produced in a person through effective counseling. Some of these are: "The person in the peak experiences feels more integrated (unified, whole, all-of-a-piece) than at other times. He usually feels himself to be at the top of his powers, using all of his capacities to their fullest. The person feels himself, more than at other times, to be the responsible, active, creating center of his activities and perceptions" (pp. 59–67).

Certainly the key to successful living is to be fully integrated as a person. Integration suggests "integer," a oneness. If the child has the self-confidence and assurance that come of knowing and accepting himself as a person, he will respond more easily to life's demands. If not, he is more apt to become disturbed and agitated, thus preparing the way for mental breakdown or ineffective functioning in adolescence and childhood. But as the child begins to feel his creativeness and the legitimacy of his experiences, he will form a sound foundation for a successful adulthood. Counseling should help the child to understand himself more clearly.

TECHNIQUES

The techniques of developmental counseling hinge on the counselor-counselee relationship. The counselor should stand as a model of the fully integrated adult. This is far more crucial in this type of helping relationship than in others. The counselor is in an educational setting and does form part of the total learning situation for the pupil. The pupil is learning, directly and indirectly, to find avenues that will promote his developmental progress. How the counselor conducts himself in the school setting can be a subtle way of pointing out to the pupil possible courses of direction for his own self-development.

Some of the particular techniques to be emphasized in developmental counseling with elementary school children would include: (1) appraising, (2) information-alerting, (3) encouraging, (4) collaboration on self-study, (5) analyz-ing, (6) interpreting, (7) clarifying, 8) evaluating, and 9) reinforcing. These techniques should be used within the conceptual framework of developmental counseling for children as presented earlier in this paper. Other aspects of coun-seling derived from other theories need to be studied to determine their proper place in the scheme of the helping relationship. From the current progress of the school counselor movement, however, we can obtain some cues about counseling techniques from those used in other than school settings, but these techniques must be carefully translated to the school situation and their effective-ness must be pragmatically tested in the school environment.

Appraising

If a pupil is to grow and develop, he must have a reasonable understanding or appraisal of himself that is consistent with his intelligence and maturity level. The person is both the means and the end, the vehicle and the destination, the structure and the process. One of the chief objectives of the counseling interview is to stimulate self-awareness in the individual through the give and take of the counseling relationship. The extent to which an individual manifests self-knowl-edge based on an accurate appraisal of self can be determined in the counseling interview (Williamson, 1959).

The proper use of tests as a means of helping youths better understand them-selves is an essential part of the appraising process. Rothney (1952) stated in his research that, "The tentative conclusion is simply that telling sophomore, junior and senior high school students their test scores and interpreting these scores to them during counseling interviews does not seem to cause significant negative nor disturbing reactions" (p. 332). The careful analysis of test results to children in a general but intelligent way can also contribute to the child's understanding of himself.

Guidance Information-alerting

The information which the person communicates about himself in the guid-ance situation is the raw material used by the counselor to further increase the child's insight into the dynamics of his own behavior, as well as to deepen his knowledge of the world in which he lives. Primarily, information-alerting is the liberally-educated counselor's endeavor to give the counselee an attitudinal base for making wise educational and career decisions by providing him with in-teresting information about the world of education and work.

In developmental counseling, information-alerting is not an end in itself. Information is given to initiate favorable attitudes for later years, as well as to encourage positive avoidance of the pitfalls resulting from ignorance. Today's world demands this kind of guidance. Both the chance approach or the delayed-until-high-school thinking lead to ineffectiveness in living.

Encouraging

The literature on counseling seems to frown on encouraging the counselee for fear it be directive, usurpation of authority for oneself, or judgmental in nature. Yet the counselor's wise use of encouragement can become a significant factor in the counselee's life space. Open encouragement of the counselee may be the best way for the counselor to demonstrate his carefully understood appraisals and information, but it can also serve as a means of reinforcing the counselee's ego strength by demonstrating concern by significant others.

Flanders (1959) reported on teacher-pupil contacts and mental hygiene. He emphasized the place of teacher sensitivity and rapport in successful classroom teaching. Applicable to counseling are the findings on encouragement. "It is a bit shocking to realize that the best prediction for approximately 100 social studies classrooms in Minnesota is that the teacher uses less than three percent praise and encouragement, or less than five percent of his talking time reacting to and using ideas that students initiate" (p. 38). For growing, shaping, searching youth, encouraging in counseling is a needed technique. The process of encouraging reflects one's value of the child and the faith in the child. The encourager is acting as if he does have confidence in the child. Encouraging means that the counselor recognizes and capitalizes on a child's strengths, assets, and interests (Dinkmeyer and Dreikurs, 1963).

Collaboration on Self-study

Developmental counseling includes the active encouragement of the counselee in the counseling process. The counselee is not a passive participant or subject of experimentation. He is not merely a test-taker, an emotional cathartic dispenser, or case to be studied. The counselee must be involved in re-searching himself. The Hawthorne effect of one's participation in self-examination is observable in reports of counseling successes. The literature shows that one grows to the extent one is involved and that motivation arises out of intrinsic needs. As the reader has probably experienced greater development out of direct and deeper participation, so the counselee has more opportunity for optimal growth in self-fulfillment to the extent he is involved and participates. Esther Lloyd-Jones' (1954) writing on student personnel work as deeper teaching emphasizes the possibilities for more growth where the focus is on "me," not on a group. The implementation of the concern for a person as a particular, very special *individual,* is the ultimate concern of good counseling.

Analyzing

Analyzing oneself for full development is the crux of developmental counseling. Analyzing oneself is to explore self-meaning. The counselor assists the counselee in this self-exploration, based on the counselee's perceptions of himself based on his total life space situation. Combs and Snygg (1959) stated that the accuracy of a description of one's total self depends on: "(1) the clarity of the counselee's awareness, (2) the adequacy of symbols for expression, (3) the social expectancy, (4) cooperation of the subject, and (5) freedom from threat and the degree of personal adequacy and the change in field or life space perception as a result of looking at oneself" (Combs and Snygg, pp. 439–464).

The counselor has the difficult task of attempting to place himself in the perceptual field of the counselee. This he does by observation, inference-making, and by the testing of inferences. The counselor uses the tools and techniques discussed elsewhere to assist the counselee to analyze his total life situation. "The key to understanding behavior, whether it be our own or other people's, lies in large measure in the skill we develop in the exploration and understanding of the nature of people's perceptions" (pp. 439–464).

Interpreting

If analyzing oneself is the exploration of self-meaning, then interpreting is the attempt to understand the philosophical significance of that exploration. Interpretation utilizes knowledge of guidance tools and techniques and of child and adolescent development.

Goldman (1961) discusses four kinds of interpretation: (1) descriptive, (2) genetic, (3) predictive, and (4) evaluative. Descriptive interpretation describes a person's past and present life situation. Predictive interpretation emphasizes what the future holds. Evaluative interpretation involves the "should" or "should have"—a value judgment. Goldman points out that there are two methods of deriving data for interpretive purposes—mechanical and non-mechanical. The main sources of data are test data and non-test data (pp. 143–160).

The developmental counselor does not leave to chance or to possible misinterpretation the meaning of the counselee's behavior as often happens with other techniques. Neither does he force upon the counselee *an* interpretation. Nevertheless, the counseling process does give added assurance, in contrast to an instructional or group approach, that the counselee is making proper use of the insights counseling affords by striving for self-integration and optimal self-development at an appropriate maturity level.

Clarifying

Clarifying is part of the interpreting function. Either counselor or counselee may request the other for more appraisal, information, or analytical interpretation. Clarification is not used to show the counselee that he was "wrong." It is used to give precision to an interview or to simplify transactional analyses. In good developmental counseling the counselor not only takes the initiative in attempting to clarify problems, but he also carefully respects the counselee's *need* for clarification and understands that with children the need for clarification is paramount and concomitant with cognitive development.

Evaluating

Evaluating is part and parcel of the other techniques of developmental counseling. It is a process that permeates the interview. However, a time comes when there is need for a clearly defined evaluation of one's development. Ideally this should occur two or three times each year throughout a pupil's school career. The counselor assists the counselee in examining congruences between his potential and actual performance. Discrepancies between expectancies of self and others and one's aspirations are essential content for the evaluative process as well as an examination of the presses of inner needs and environmental demands and limitations. A careful examination of one's relationships with others is part of developmental counseling.

Reinforcing

Reinforcing the "good" that is derived from the other aspects of the counseling process is fundamental to developmental counseling. Ways of implementing the strengths serve as a fertile source for handling weaknesses. Too often, pupils have periodic moments of successful development only to be at loss in a "sea" of overwhelming routine. The emphasis, however, upon living up to one's capacities—a part of the prescriptive, consultative process—should help the pupil tailor his behavior to future needs. "Educators generally hold today, in line with the pioneer work of Thorndike, that learning takes place when a motivated child is rewarded (reinforced) for responding discriminately to an environmental stimulus" (Pressey, Robinson, and Horrocks, 1959, p. 222).

Developmental counseling uses evaluative procedures and tools to assist the counselee in interpreting behavior and consequences with the other techniques providing accuracy and clarity, e.g., analyzing and interpreting. The counselor must take initiative because the pupil has not had enough experience in developing awareness of the full implications of his actions. Developmental counseling aims at assisting the individual to sharpen his discriminative responses. Such counseling focuses on the individual in his singularly unique self and life situation.

WHERE WE ARE

Counseling with children depends a great deal on the attitudes and understanding of the adults with whom children live and do their school work. The school counselor is in a strategic position to counsel elementary school children because of his preparation, the kind of person he is, and the contribution he has to make to the total school program. The developmental approach offers the best basis for helping all boys and girls to understand themselves and reach toward their own self-fulfillment—the achievement of their optimum capabilities. The counseling function with elementary school children is, indeed, future oriented; it is a gradual, evolving process. The components of elementary school guidance and counseling need to be studied.

The effectiveness of elementary school counseling processes is, however, an area where we have little research to back up our practices. The mere inclusion of a chapter on counseling in a book on elementary school guidance does not mean that it actually happens the way the authors would have you believe. Too much is superimposed from other unlike settings. However, in 1965 there were signs of more research in this area. Van Hoose (1965) found that one can have and analyze counseling sessions with elementary school children.

Counseling children is one of the key topics for study in guidance in the larger educational world. Perhaps many of the growing problems of personal and social upheaval could be better handled if persons had the opportunity to develop a sound foundation of responsible personhood during the elementary school years. Experiencing one's development through counseling offers one of the best means for achieving this sense of responsibility with freedom.

REFERENCES

Allen, H. C. February 1930. The functions of guidance in the elementary schools (grades 1–6) and the organization necessary for efficient service. *Voc. Guid. J.*, 8 (No. 5), 220–221.

Bakwin, H., and Ruth M. Bakwin. 1960. *Clinical management of behavior disorders in children*. Philadelphia: Saunders.

Boy, A. V., and G. J. Pine. 1963. *Client-centered counseling in the secondary school*. Boston: Houghton Mifflin.

Brammer, L. M., and E. L. Shostrom. 1960. *Therapeutic psychology*. Englewood Cliffs, N.J.: Prentice-Hall.

Bryant, Edythe K. February 1928. What commendable guidance activities are now provided for intermediate and junior high school pupils. *Voc. Guid. J.*, 6 (No. 5), 207.

Combs, A. W., and D. Snygg. 1959. The exploration of meaning. In *Individual behavior*. Revised ed.; New York: Harper & Row.

Curran, C. A. 1962. *Counseling in Catholic life and education*. New York: Macmillan.

Dinkmeyer, D., and R. Dreikurs. 1963. *Encouraging children to learn: the encouragement process*. Englewood Cliffs, N.J.: Prentice-Hall.

Educational Policies Commission. 1960. *Contemporary issues in elementary education*. Washington, D.C.: National Education Association.

Eubanks, C. W. (no date.) *Guidance services in Louisiana*. Baton Rouge, La.: State Department of Education Bulletin No. 969.

Flanders, N. A. 1959. Teacher-pupil contacts and mental hygiene. *J. soc. Issues*, 15 (No. 1), 38.

Goldman, L. 1961. *Using tests in counseling*. New York: Appleton.

Hart, R. N. December 1961. Are elementary counselors doing the job? *Sch. Couns., 9* (No. 2), 70–72.

Lloyd-Jones, Esther, and Margaret R. Smith. 1954. *Student personnel work as deeper teaching.* New York: Harper & Row.

Maslow, A. H. January 1961. *Personality theory and counseling practice.* Paper prepared for the University of Florida conference on personality theory and consulting practice.

Meeks, Anna R. 1963. *Comprehensive programs in elementary school guidance.* Mimeographed.

Pressey, S. L., F. P. Robinson, and J. E. Horrocks. 1959. *Psychology in education.* New York: Harper & Row.

Richards, Ruth. March–June 1943. *Counseling the elementary school.* Baltimore, Md.: Baltimore Bulletin of Education, *20* (No. 3), 109–110.

Rothney, J. W. M. 1952. Interpreting test scores to counselees. *Occupations, 30,* 332.

Segar, W. B. March 1952. Beginning steps in guidance in the elementary school. *Occupations, 30* (No. 6), 414.

Shertzer, B., and Rolla F. Pruett. September 1961. *Guidance in the elementary schools.* State of Indiana, Department of Public Instruction.

Van Hoose, W. 1965. *Counseling elementary school children.* Columbus, Ohio: The Ohio State University. Doctoral dissertation.

Williamson, E. G. September 1959. The meaning of communication in counseling. *Personnel guid. J., 38* (No. 1), 6–14.

Wilson, F. M. December 1950. Guidance in elementary schools. *Occupations, 29* (No. 3), 168.

Yarrow, L. J. 1960. Interviewing children. In Paul H. Mussen (ed.), *Handbook of research methods in child development.* New York: Wiley.

Developmental Counseling

in the Elementary School*

Don C. Dinkmeyer

With the greatly increased extension of counseling and guidance services to the elementary school level, counseling theorists have become aware of a greater need for a theory of developmental counseling with children. This theory must take

* *Personnel and Guidance Journal,* November 1966, vol. 45, no. 3.
By permission.

account of such basic factors as the nature of the child, the elementary school setting, and the goals, techniques, and process of the counseling. Furthermore, those who would counsel in the elementary school must become aware of the research in the broad area of child development and child psychiatry.

NATURE OF THE CHILD

The most obvious difference between secondary school and elementary school counseling stems from the nature of the child. The elementary school child is still in the process of becoming—physically, socially, emotionally, and as a total personality. He is in a process of unfolding and there are still certain developmental changes that will come about as the result of this growth process.

Research in child development points to the importance of considering developmental changes. Thus, the counselor would need to be aware of "normal developmental problems" as contrasted with serious adjustment difficulties. He should know that there are wide individual differences in developmental patterns that are due to basic differences in rate of development. These developmental differences create adjustment problems for the child both in the tasks of school life and social life.

The counselor, therefore, should have available developmental data that tell him about individual rates of development and enable him to infer something about the child's feelings about himself in the peer group.

Mussen and Jones (1958), in their study of the self-concept in late and early maturing boys, have indicated a variance in the self-concepts and motivation of these two groups.

It is important that each counselor be familiar with the basic needs of the child. The child has specific needs that relate to the guidance process. He needs to mature in self-acceptance, in his understanding of self, and in his comprehension of his assets and liabilities. The child needs to develop a more realistic self-evaluation and the counselor can help in this process. The counselor can also assist the child to develop, to mature in social relationships, to belong, and to identify. The child needs to develop independence, to take on responsibility, to make choices, and to be responsible for these choices. He needs to mature in his ability to plan. The counselor provides an environment in which the child is independent, makes choices, and becomes responsible for his decision. The child also needs to mature in understanding the role of work in life as it first appears in educational achievement and then as it appears in the environment as related to jobs and employment opportunities. The child needs to develop a realistic self-appraisal of his capacities, interests, and attitudes as they relate to the work tasks.

The counselor, at the elementary school level, will recognize that he needs to work with the significant adults in the child's life. This includes the teacher and the parents. With the teacher he will encourage intensive child study that takes into account developmental information and the developmental factors significant in comprehending the way in which the child approaches the developmental tasks of living. He will help the teacher to have available cumulative records that provide information about rate instead of status, dynamics of behavior instead of descriptions of the past. The cumulative record should show the pattern of development both physically and psychologically.

Behavior is purposive, and acquires its meaning in the social setting. Beyond the understanding of need, the counselor must understand the purposes of behavior in specific children. Purposes are the directive forces in the child's life, even though the child may not be aware of these goals and purposes. We need to look at the purposes of misbehavior as they are illustrated in attention-getting, and seeking to be powerful, to get even, or to demonstrate inadequacy (Dreikurs, 1957). As we become cognizant of the individual's purposes, we are able to deal with the child's private logic, and become aware of the basic style of life and concept of self and others. Psychological growth is patterned, and we must focus on the unity of behavior and the style of life, avoiding the collection of fragmentary data and instead looking at the direction of psychological movement.

Recent research tends to indicate that the early elementary years are much more significant than any of us have been truly able to determine prior to now. The research of Bloom (1964) indicates the significance of the first three grades in predicting the total pattern of achievement. Kagan and Moss (1962) at the Fels Research Institute recently released a study indicating that many of the behaviors exhibited by the child during the period from six to ten years of age, and a few during the period from three to six, were moderately good predictors of theoretically related behavior during early adulthood. This study indicated that the child who was achieving well early in school will generally continue to achieve well. There is a need to provide early encouragement for the academic achiever, and to identify those who are not meeting the academic tasks at this stage of life.

The elementary counselor should also be aware of the developmental task concept as first formulated by Havighurst. He needs to recognize that the pertinent tasks of middle childhood involve learning to get along with age-mates, and participating in the give and take of social exchange.

Most human problems are interpersonal problems and these problems increase as the child moves into a peer society. The research of Piaget (1929), which has increasingly attracted the attention of American psychologists, shows that during preadolescence the child begins to develop a concept of self quite distinguishable from the outer world. This is the time when the clarification of feelings, concepts, attitudes, goals, and an understanding of self would be most significant.

The development of conscience, morality, and values begins early in the elementary school. The child is in the process of developing this internal moral control and set of values. The child learns that rules are necessary and thus develops what Piaget calls the morality of cooperation. Piaget believes that middle childhood is a crucial period for the development of this cooperation. The counselor could be available to help the child through this stage as an awareness of values and goals emerges. The child will frequently need help in reconciling his values, his ideal self, and his actual performance. However, the child needs to learn to make plans, and to act in the present and immediate future independent of other parents and other adults. Counseling can provide the opportunity to assist in the making of choices, planning, and deciding.

C. Tryon and J. Lilienthal (1950) have provided an interesting presentation of the developmental tasks and their importance for the counselor. They indicate that these might be used as guideposts that permit us to assess the rate at which the child is developing in regard to the tasks of life. They suggest that the counselor might be aware of some of the following pertinent tasks:

a. achieving an appropriate dependent-independent pattern;

b. achieving an appropriate giving-receiving pattern of affection, learning to accept self as worthwhile, learning to belong;

c. relating to changing groups, establishing a peer group, and learning to belong and behave according to the shifting peer code.

COUNSELING IN THE ELEMENTARY SCHOOL SETTING

The counselor cannot counsel without an awareness of the elementary school setting, and the fact that he is part of an educational team. He should be aware of the philosophy, objectives, and practices of the school. He should be familiar with the curriculum and the opportunities within the curriculum for the student's development. He must be cognizant of the teacher's crucial role in classroom guidance. The teacher should be encouraged to provide regular guidance activities, to identify problems, and to provide guidance through the teacher-counselor role.

Developmental counseling, which can be contrasted with adjustment, or crisis counseling, is not always problem-oriented in terms of assuming that the child has some difficult problem. Instead, the goals are the development of self-understanding, awareness of one's potentialities, and methods of utilizing one's capacity. Developmental counseling truly focuses on helping the individual know, understand, and accept himself. This type of counseling, then, becomes personalized learning, not individualized teaching. The child learns not only to understand himself but to become ultimately responsible for his choices and actions.

UNIQUE FACTORS

The type of counseling we are considering Hummel (1962) has referred to as ego counseling. This implies that it may be a short-term service in which the relationship is basically collaborative and the child works on problems that are of concern to him. The counselor helps the child investigate, analyze, and deliberate to solve more effectively certain developmental problems. Thus, exploration, examination, and resolution are basic techniques. There is mutual survey of the facts, clarification of feelings, consideration of alternatives, development of problem-solving techniques, and arrival at decisions.

The counselor provides a non-evaluative relationship and offers his collaboration. His job is to clarify, to reflect, to restate as precisely as possible the meanings he perceives to be implied in the counselee's statements. However, the counselor, at times, will interpret, confront, question, and thus facilitate the child's capacity to solve his own problems.

The elementary school child is in the process of formulating a style of life and self-concept. There is a considerable body of evidence that indicates that the child with a poor self-concept, compared with those who have more positive self-concepts, will be more anxious, less well-adjusted, less popular, less effective, less honest, and more defensive (McCandless, 1961). One of the tasks of the school counselor is to assist each child to feel accepted as he is. The counselor seeks to help the child discover his potentialities, to acquire a realistic appreciation of his assets and limitations, and to set certain goals. This should enable the child to accept himself rather than seek to conform to standards that are out of harmony with what he is or would hope to be.

PRINCIPLES IN CHILD COUNSELING

What, then, are the fundamentals we need to be aware of in child counseling?

1. Counseling is a learning-oriented process carried on in a one-to-one social environment. It must utilize the best that we have available from learning theory.

2. The relationship is crucial in the counseling process. It should be one in which there is mutual trust and mutual respect, enabling the counselee to become more open to communication and more motivated to change. Change is always more possible in a non-evaluative, non-judgmental atmosphere.

3. The counselor helps the client to understand and accept what he is, and to use his newly acquired knowledge about self to realize his potential, to change in attitude, behavior, and, eventually, style of life.

4. The child is frequently not a volunteer. There is a real need for common purpose and a motivation for counseling. It is important that the goals of counseling be mutually aligned between counselor and counselee. It is important to understand the individual's objective viewpoint, to be emphatic, to recognize his private logic.

5. We need to listen not only for the words, but to what is behind the words. We need to become skilled in guessing the child's psychological direction. Behavior is purposive and has social implications. We need to make the child more aware of his purposes, goals, convictions, and attitudes. As the child becomes aware of his faulty assumptions, he can "catch" himself.

6. There are certain dependency factors that will restrict the child from

changing certain things in his environment. His choices may be limited in terms of restrictions placed upon him by adults such as parents and teachers.

7. There is a necessity for working intensively both with parents and teachers if we are to change the child's environment. Contact with the significant adults is directed at changing the adult's behavior and thus the child's perception of self and human relationships. The counselor most of all must become aware of the goals and the unity in the pattern of the counselee's behavior. Maladjustment is characterized by increased inferiority feelings, underdeveloped social interest, and uncooperative methods of striving for significance (Dreikurs, 1950). These dynamics help the counselor to explain and understand the child's behavior.

8. Because the child may not be as verbal as the adult, there is need for sharper sensitivity on the part of the counselor in working with non-verbal cues and non-verbal factors. We need to listen with the child's ears and observe to determine what is behind the total psychological movement. Our observation of a recognition reflex in his facial expressions sometimes enables us to comprehend his goal. Disclosure of the child's goals and purposes when given in appropriate fashion can be a most significant technique.

9. The counselor provides encouragement as a major therapeutic technique. He enables the client to accept himself so that he has the courage to function (Dinkmeyer and Dreikurs, 1963).

10. Some children have a minimal ability to relate their feelings. They may not always be sensitive to reflection, and they need a tentative statement in regard to feelings such as: "Could it be you feel the children are against you?"

11. The individual's perceptions are more important than the objective reality of the situation.

12. People will move in positive directions when they are really free to choose. We need to provide the atmosphere that permits them to make these choices.

13. The feeling of basic trust between counselor and counselee opens the channels of communication. The mutual alignment of goals also assists this development.

14. Counseling is looked upon as a re-eductative process directed toward the development of self-understanding, the changing of convictions, and the development of increased social interest. It is not heavily oriented toward vocational guidance; instead it deals with the developmental tasks, problems, and needs of the child. Through self-understanding, self-acceptance, and clarification of feeling the greatest growth can occur.

15. The cognitive and conceptual development of the child is not always as advanced as we might hope and, hence, the counselor must be certain communication is meaningful. Children have limited experiences and, hence, will have a limited ability to comprehend certain concepts.

16. The counselor becomes aware that he needs to empathize so closely that he can guess what it is that the client is thinking, and that he can put this into the

client's words. The effective counselor is one who understands the way in which the individual strives to be significant and who helps the individual to accept himself. He sees the developmental problems as interpersonal problems. His communication with the client helps the client to understand new ways of relating to others.

Developmental counseling provides the child with an opportunity to explore his feelings, his attitudes and convictions. The counselor starts with the problems that the child perceives and helps him to solve them. The counselor in this situation provides a relationship that accepts, understands, and does not judge. It provides the counselee with constant clarification of his basic perception of life. This relationship enables the counselee to become increasingly self-directed so that the goal is one of enabling him to deal with both the developmental tasks and the general problems of living. This type of developmental counseling suggests that counselors would not only be problem-oriented, but would be concerned about all students in the school population.

The goal is to take certain grade levels and offer assistance to each student by providing an opportunity for some four or five contacts devoted to the specific objectives of counseling as they have been presented. When we can provide this form of counseling at the elementary school level, we can probably insure a greater productivity academically and, hopefully, much more effective social relationships between children and between children and the significant adults in their atmosphere. Thus, we can see that elementary school counseling may need a new theory and a new set of practices. Developmental counseling might provide a direction quite different from that of typical secondary school counseling.

REFERENCES

Bloom, B. 1964. *Stability and change in human characteristics.* New York: Wiley.

Dinkmeyer, D., and R. Dreikurs. 1963. *Encouraging children to learn: the encouragement process.* Englewood Cliffs, N. J.: Prentice-Hall.

Dreikurs, R. 1957. *Psychology in the classroom.* New York: Harper & Row.

———. 1950. *Fundamentals of Adlerian psychology.* New York: Greenberg.

Hummel, R. 1962. Ego-counseling in guidance: concept and method. *Harvard educ. Rev., 32,* 463–482.

Kagan, J., and H. Moss. 1962. *Birth to maturity.* New York: Wiley.

McCandless, B. R. 1961. *Children and adolescents: behavior and development.* New York: Holt, Rinehart and Winston.

Mussen, P., and M. Jones. 1958. The behavior inferred motivation of late and early maturing boys. *Child Develpm. 29,* 61–67.

Piaget, J. 1929. *The child's conception of the world.* New York: Harcourt.

Tryon, C., and J. Lilienthal. 1950. Developmental tasks: the concept and its importance. *Fostering mental health in our schools.* 1950 Yearbook, Association for Supervision and Curriculum Development, Washington, D.C.: The Association.

Play Media

and the Elementary School Counselor*

Richard C. Nelson

The elementary school child is a flexible, learning being who utilizes play to test his theories of getting along in his world, who learns of his status and acceptance level through playing with other children, who may attempt to alter his social position through experiences he tries out in a play setting, and who finds an outlet for his energy, anxiety, joy, and other feelings through play activities. Play fulfills the role for the child that work fulfills for adults. Play is the child's work. As the adult finds his way of life through work, so the child finds his way of life through play.

THEORETICAL CONSIDERATIONS

The view taken here of counseling is that it is a vehicle for the individual to explore his thoughts and feelings and evoke courses of action, behavior patterns, or attitudes which might serve him well. At the same time, the nature of the child as an activist rather than as a verbalizing being makes it clear that this exploration may be done on a verbal or a non-verbal level. Thus, it is assumed that play media may be used in counseling as an essential tool of the counselor for facilitating this self exploration.

PLAY IN COUNSELING

Play is more than a child's fun and games. It is the child's learning, testing, communicating, and expressing media and as such provides most appropriate material for counseling. Ginott (1961) states that ". . . the child's play is his talk and the toys are his words." This suggests that the omission of play materials

* *Elementary School Guidance and Counseling Newsletter,* 1966, vol. 1, no. 3. By permission.

in counseling may well result in a lack of communication. Allen (1942) comments that ". . . it would be difficult to establish a relationship with a child without play activity." Axline (1964) through her report of counseling with a disturbed child in *Dibs: In Search of Self*, provides a model for the elementary school counselor of an effective type of accepting, reflecting, clarifying relationship with a child.

It may be contended that the major aspect of Axline's approach, which is not applicable to work by the elementary school counselor, is her willingness to work with severely disturbed children. This is to say that the relationship desired in counseling is basic to the well-being of both disturbed and non-disturbed children.

While the above writers and many others, who write concerning counseling with children, refer to play therapy and psychotherapy, many of the techniques in these sources may be used by the elementary school counselor. This generalization is supported by Moustakas' (1959) inclusion of a chapter on play therapy with "normal" children and by Axline's discussions in a section entitled "Implications for Education."

So much is play needed by the young child in counseling that the counselor may well be asked, as was one counselor-in-training, "You got a pencil and some paper?" Or as has also happened, another child may pick up an imaginary telephone to facilitate his expression of feelings or thoughts.

PLAY MEDIA SELECTION

Nearly any piece of equipment has expressive possibilities in the eyes of a child, but three key criteria for selection of play media for elementary school counseling should be (1) materials that may be used in a variety of ways, such as clay, paints, and pipe cleaners; (2) materials that promote communication, such as toy telephones and a typewriter; and (3) materials that encourage expression, such as a toy gun, hand puppets, or a bounce-back toy.

Generally, the more flexible the materials used in the counseling office, the better; the more readily the imagination of the child can let this or that piece of equipment be what he needs it to be, the more desirable it is. Structured games, fancy dolls, models, and other such toys have limited adaptability, are limited in expressive and communicative possibilities, and should probably not be used.

USING PLAY MEDIA

The child smashes things when he is angry, fights when his toy is taken, hugs his mother when he is happy, and hands a child a toy when he wants to show he likes him. The child is a doer, not a talker. Asking a child to tell you about his problem may produce results the equivalent of those obtained when an unartistic adult is asked to draw an expression of his difficulty. While it is possible to contend that the adult may profit by expression through art, puppetry, or clay, few young children could profit by verbal expression alone.

One possible advantage in utilizing play media is that it reduces pressure on the child and counselor. The time is being utilized, so the urge to "fill the unforgiving minute," to which Kipling refers, is less often felt by the counselor and counselee. Thus, instead of the counselor feeling a need to probe or the counselee feeling a need to fill an embarrassing silence, each may contemplate the object being constructed when discussion wanes, and the object may become secondary when the discussion resumes. This should not be construed as license for the counseling sessions to wander continually into unprofitable lanes. The need for the counselor to understand the counselee's feelings about the objects he creates, or the events or persons he mentions, is not lessened, nor is the need for the counselor to consider whether the counseling sessions are worthwhile for the counselee over a period of time.

In utilizing play in a public elementary school setting the counselor should maintain sight of his major responsibility, that of assisting with the everyday concerns of normal youth. Play in counseling with normal youth rarely requires highly interpretive remarks or probing on the part of the counselor. Accepting remarks which reflect and summarize either behavior or statements are more appropriate.

The child who has named a toy soldier Daddy and then tosses him aside to play with something else should be met with reflection of the specific behavior rather than interpretation. "You're through with the Daddy-soldier and now you are going to play with something else," is more reflective of the actual occurrence than "You're tired of Daddy and you want to play with something else." The latter interpretation may well be verbalized by the child and it should be his right to do so. Since children can make the same object do for a gun, a flagpole, and a mud-stirrer in a matter of a few moments, allowance should be made for the soldier to have lost or changed identity before being cast aside.

The child's imagination is probably already working as he picks up an object and wonders aloud what it might be. A response such as, "What would you like it to be?" is more appropriate than, "It could be a post or a gun or. . . ."

A child who breaks an object finds more help in a response such as, "It bothers you because you broke the doll," than "That's all right, we have plenty more." The latter response unlike the former does not allow for the child to learn to live with his feelings, accept them, and understand them.

Feelings, then, are encountered and dealt with in counseling elementary school children, but interpretation and probing are limited or eliminated.

SUMMARY

This article expresses the position that counseling should occur in a setting that is comfortable for the child. Since the child tends both to learn through play and to express himself through play, the use of play media in counseling elementary school children is well warranted. The literature on playing in counseling, though mainly related to play therapy, is replete with models which can be emulated by the elementary school counselor in working with normal children.

Well selected materials allow for flexibility, expression, and communication. The counseling itself should rely more on accepting responses, reflection, and summarization than upon questioning and interpreting. The elementary school counselor should seek training in the use of play media in counseling and avail himself of the advantages of working in media familiar to the child.

REFERENCES

Allen, F. H. 1963. *Positive aspects of child psychiatry*. New York: Norton.

———. 1942. *Psychotherapy with children*. New York: Norton.

———. 1947. *Play therapy*. Cambridge, Mass.: The Riverside Press.

Axline, Virginia. 1964. *Dibs: in search of self*. Boston: Houghton Mifflin.

Dorfman, Elaine. 1951. Play therapy. In Carl R. Rogers (ed.), *Client-centered therapy*. Boston: Houghton Mifflin.

Ginott, H. 1961. *Group psychotherapy with children*. New York: McGraw-Hill.

Moustakas, C. E. 1959. *Psychotherapy with children*. New York: Harper & Row.

Chapter 8

GROUP COUNSELING

During the past decade, the use of group counseling in the elementary school has increased considerably, and, along with it, there has been a huge increase in the amount of literature on the subject (Biasco, 1965; Munger, Winkler, Teigland, Kranzler, 1964; Stormer, 1967). This chapter will establish the rationale for group counseling and describe the unique factors in the role of the group counselor. Attention is given to selection of group members, size and composition of group, and other practical administrative considerations.

Group counseling has been defined as:

> . . . a dynamic, interpersonal process through which individuals within the normal range of adjustment work within a peer group and with a professionally trained counselor, exploring problems and feelings in an attempt to modify their attitudes so they are better able to deal with developmental problems. (Cohn, Combs, Gibian, Sniffen, 1963, p. 355–356)

Group counseling involves two or more people working by means of their interpersonal relationships to discover alternative solutions to problems. The relationship of the individuals within the group is the important factor.

Group counseling is part of the educational process and should be developed by the pupil personnel services within the school. Group counseling must be clearly distinguished from "mass" therapeutic procedures and group guidance. Mass procedures may be time-saving, but they do not use a group process (Pearson, 1966). Group counseling can be distinguished from group guidance by its content, procedures, and the role assumed by the leader (Goldman, 1962). For more detail on this matter, the reader is directed to Goldman's article, appearing in Chapter 9.

RATIONALE FOR GROUP COUNSELING

Group counseling's major therapeutic effect stems from its recognition that most problems are primarily social or interpersonal. The child must learn to interact effectively within the group. Group counseling satisfies this condition by providing direct experience in social interaction.

The child's character is expressed through social movement and interaction. Group counseling provides the child an opportunity to reveal personal convictions and develop self-understanding. The child benefits from the corrective influences and encouragement of the group. Members of the group come to understand their own behavior by observation of and identification with the behavior of others. The process gives them an opportunity to consider alternative behavior and test reality.

The process of group counseling enables members of the group to feel a genuine sense of belonging, regardless of any individual's shortcomings; indeed, the child often acquires a sense of belonging because of his deficiencies.

Group counseling helps the child develop social interests. In the group situation he can show his concern for others and participate in the give and take of life (Dinkmeyer, 1967). In his position as a member of the group, the child has an opportunity to see that other children may have problems similar to his own (universalization). In this way, he may lose the feeling of being different. Within the safety of this socially accepting group, the child can approach his problems at his own speed.

Group counseling considerably enhances the corrective process. The counselee experiences feedback from his group peers regarding his behavior and is thus given an opportunity to develop new behavioral approaches to social problems.

Group counseling recognizes that the child is an indivisible, decision-making being whose actions have a social purpose (Dreikurs and Sonstegard, 1965). It recognizes that belonging is a basic need and that man is therefore not self-actualized until he belongs. In the classroom, children who already feel adequate tend to establish the social atmosphere and benefit most from social interaction. In group counseling, on the other hand, those whose needs are greatest are able to derive the most help (Sonstegard, 1958). The group thus provides the opportunity to develop a feeling of equality, confidence, courage, and adequacy; to release negative feelings; to work out role identities; and to be loved.

Group counseling is of particular value to school counselors. The counselor has the opportunity not only to hypothesize about social behavior but to *observe* social interaction. Psychological movement and social purposes can be seen, understood, and modified. The counselor can use children in the group to help each other. Although group counseling obviously provides a chance to help more children at one time, it should not be chosen as a guidance method merely because it is expedient. It should be used, rather, because of the inherent advantages of the group setting and group procedures.

ADMINISTRATIVE CONSIDERATIONS

The organization of groups for counseling in the elementary school involves selection of members, composition and size of the group, physical setting, and length of sessions. Each counselor must develop policies which best fit his own school setting.

Members of the group are selected because at the start they have common problems and they are motivated to work on the solution of the problem. They must be able to communicate their problems, feelings, and attitudes to others. The counselor selects members that he believes will have a therapeutic effect on each other. Members should not only profit from the counseling but be able to contribute to the development of the other members. The child must be emotionally ready for the group experience and must be permitted to choose whether he wishes to join. He should understand why he has been asked to participate and what the group will expect of him.

The size of the counseling group will vary with the age or maturity of the counselees. Optimum group size for effective elementary school counseling should probably not exceed five or six children (Mayer and Baker, 1967). Definitive data on the precise size for effective group work is not yet available.

Group counseling ideally is conducted in a setting which provides enough distance between members of the group so they can readily communicate and observe other members of the group without being so close as to become involved in diversional activity. Counseling can be successfully conducted in regular classrooms, locker rooms, storerooms, cafeterias, stages of auditoriums, conference rooms, and small offices (Combs, Cohn, Gibian, Sniffen, 1963). Eventually, school buildings will probably provide counseling offices or auxiliary rooms large enough for at least six students.

The elementary school group usually meets for one session per week, with sessions effective at from thirty to forty-five minutes in length. Students must recognize that there is a limit on the time available to the group. At the time the group is established, it may also be desirable to set a definite termination date.

As with all phases of the guidance program, it is important that all the people concerned with the school—students, teachers, parents, and administrators —understand the purposes and methods of group counseling. It is vital to clarify the objectives with all concerned to avoid misconceptions about the type of children enrolled, the activities, and the expected gains.

THE ROLE OF THE LEADER

Since an understanding of personality dynamics and characteristics of the helping relationship are fundamental to group work, it is important that the leaders be experienced in individual counseling.

There are some real differences between individual and group counseling. In group counseling, while the counselor concentrates on understanding the speaker's feelings and assisting him to communicate, he must also observe how the comments of each member affect other members of the group. He must give members the opportunity to test tentative solutions and to provide each other with feedback (Ohlsen, 1960).

Group counseling requires certain unique skills of the counselor. He must be capable of telling the children what they cannot do and establishing limits to their behavior. At the same time, he must be continually helping them to discover their own direction. For this, he will have to relinquish his own personal preferences and refrain from enforcing his authority on such matters. Obviously, group counseling will require greater emotional stability on the part of the counselor than most other counseling work.

Lifton (1966) describes the leader's job as follows:

> Basically, the leader's initial job is to help the members of the group learn to direct their attention on each other rather than on a leader. He achieves this by continually focusing on:
> 1. The meaning of an idea to the group.
> 2. The issues that the group seems to be in disagreement over and that they feel a need to resolve.
> 3. The feelings they are expressing through their behavior rather than their spoken words.
> 4. The ways they are forcing others into roles or behaviors.
> 5. The actions or problems which the group raises and needs to solve.
> 6. The continuity between group sessions and themes raised. (p. 117–118)

The group leader exists to facilitate the growth and development of the group. He should always keep in mind that the group is one of the primary instruments of assistance to its members.

MECHANISMS OF GROUP COUNSELING

This section presents the dynamic processes of group counseling. The group provides a feeling of belonging and acceptance. The child learns that he can share his experiences with others and still be socially approved. He is given opportunities to test reality by means of the feedback from other group members. Often, upon experiencing feedback from the group, a child will say, "I had never thought of it that way before," and an idea will then take on completely new meaning to him. In this way, interaction produces insight.

Altruism—exerting oneself for the benefit of others—is encouraged in the group. The child has the opportunity to give love and to assist others. The group provides a unique opportunity to demonstrate social interest and cooperation.

In group counseling, the child comes to realize that thoughts which he believed were unique to him are often common to others. This realization helps him develop the courage to face his difficulties.

The group serves an important function by providing what has been termed transference, providing an opportunity for a continual flow of emotional support.

Group counseling increases the child's receptiveness to new ideas. He becomes more open to the thinking of others and sometimes may even come to accept ideas which were previously unacceptable to him.

The group plays an important part in personality development. Social interest and cooperation are more important than personal elevation and egocentric action. The group gives opportunities for catharsis. There is a chance to expose self-derogatory and hostile inner feelings without punishment.

STRUCTURE AND PROCEDURES

Group counseling is therapeutic when group members have common purposes and values and have established norms, roles, and rules for their group. To be therapeutic, counseling groups must be cohesive. The more cohesive the group is, the greater its therapeutic value for its members. This cohesiveness leads to a willingness of group members to help each other.

The opportunity to choose is a major element in growth. The first choice the child must make is whether to be in the group or not. Even more important, in each meeting he may decide to participate or to withdraw (remain silent) if the feeling of threat is too strong for him.

The dynamics of group counseling can be broken down into four phases: relationship, understanding, interpretation, and reorientation.

Group relationship must be based upon mutual acceptance and respect. It is less personal but also less authoritarian than the individual counseling relationship, and frequently it is easier for the child to accept criticism from his peers than from the counselor. Ideally, the counselor should be just one member of a democratic group.

The counselor's understanding of each child can be enhanced by the group situation. In individual counseling, the counselor is dependent upon the child's report, whereas in group counseling, he has an opportunity to observe interaction in which the child's real attitudes, convictions, and perceptions are revealed more reliably. Some children gain the courage to talk in the group situation and thus provide the counselor with a better understanding of what they are experiencing.

Group interpretation presents the child with unusual opportunities to see himself in others. Children can also learn by recognizing the validity of interpretations which have been given to other children. Frequently, the child will report that recognizing the dynamics of someone else's behavior has helped him to understand his own actions.

Reorientation provides an opportunity for the child to test new perceptions and attitudes. The group permits the child to be himself without fear of losing status (Dreikurs, 1960). It breaks down some of the feelings of social isolation and encourages participation.

The group leader uses a variety of tools and techniques, depending upon the situation. In some instances disclosure and confrontation can be used, preferably on a tentative basis, such as "Is it possible . . .?" This procedure may accelerate the individual's or the group's understanding of the dynamics of a given behavior.

Group counseling may use the mirror effect of not only the counselor but also the peers. The child is often able to observe himself in others. In some instances, he may even say something like "I remember when I used to think that way," or "When I used to do that. . . ."

The counselor can help the child examine his feelings. He may describe a feeling which the child, until this time, had not been aware of, and in this manner help clarify for the child how he experiences the world.

Group counseling provides a unique opportunity for social learning. For the retiring child, it may dissolve the wall of social isolation which he has experienced. It may enable the aggressive child to experience the benefit of group interaction.

IMPLICATIONS FOR COUNSELOR EDUCATION

Counselor education should comprise course work in the dynamics of group behavior. However, in order to serve as leader of a group and to be effective in human relations, the counselor should have a group experience himself. This type of group experience could enable the counselor to become more sensitive to himself and his own purposes. Practicum experiences in counselor education should provide for supervised group counseling experience. With the development of specialists' degrees and extended graduate training, a practicum devoted solely to group counseling is considered essential.

As developed by Dreikurs and Sonstegard, the social nature of human beings is basic to a rationale for group counseling. Dreikurs and Sonstegard view man as an indivisible, social, and decision-making being whose actions have a social purpose. Man's personal characteristics are expressed through social movement and interaction with others. Maladjustment and failure to function are the result of mistaken approaches to finding one's place in the group. Feedback, disclosure, and psychological confrontation are parts of group procedure. The group increases the child's receptiveness to new ideas and tends to help each member develop a feeling of belonging. These authors describe the structure of the group counseling process in terms of: the relationship; the examination of the purpose of each group member's action; psychological disclosure; and reorientation and redirection. Their group counselor is active within the group.

The group relationship is described by Ohlsen in terms of the permissiveness, acceptance, and understanding of the counselor. He makes it clear that group counseling requires treatment by the group as well as the individual relationship with the counselor. Criteria for the selection of clients are presented, with self-selection and personal readiness considered essential. The group process is adapted with the elementary school child to provide more structure and limits, more active participation on the part of the counselor, and smaller groups which meet for shorter periods of time but more frequently each week. Ohlsen makes a unique contribution by adapting the process to children. He strongly recommends that teachers be trained to utilize group techniques.

Combs, Cohn, Gibian, and Sniffen discuss the advantages of group counseling in the school. They report on their own experiences in the public schools and consider the practical problems of size, meeting time, physical setting, and initiation of a group. In structuring the group, some of the authors found it useful to distribute mimeographed materials entitled "Rules of the Game" which are included in their article.

Boy, Isaksen, and Pine consider the counselor's relationship to group members as a depth relationship, in contrast to other authors in this section. The limits and values of group counseling are examined. Multiple counseling is perceived as the basis for establishing an effective individual counseling relationship. The authors have a unique perception of the role of group counseling in the guidance program.

REFERENCES

Biasco, F. 1965. *The effects of individual counseling, multiple counseling, and teacher guidance upon the sociometric status of children in grades four, five and six.* Bloomington, Ind.: Indiana University. Unpublished thesis.

Cohn, B., C. Combs, E. Gibian, and A. M. Sniffen. 1963. Group counseling: an orientation, *Personnel guid. J., 42* (No. 4).

Combs, C., B. Cohn, E. Gibian, A. M. Sniffen. 1963. Group counseling: applying the technique. *Sch. Couns., 11* (No. 1).

Dinkmeyer, D. 1967. Theory and principles of group counseling in the elementary school. *Guidelines, 5* (No. 2).

Dreikurs, R. 1960. *Group psychotherapy and group approaches.* Chicago: Alfred Adler Institute.

———, and M. Sonstegard. 1965. Rationale of group counseling in the elementary school. *Readings in Guidance in the Elementary School.* New York: Selected Academic Readings.

Goldman, L. 1962. Group guidance: content and process. *Personnel guid. J., 39* (No. 6).

Lifton, W. 1966. *Working with groups.* Second ed.; New York: Wiley.

Mayer, G. R., and P. Baker. 1967. Group counseling with elementary school children: a look at group size. *Elem. Sch. Guid. Counsel., 1* (No. 2).

Munger, P., R. Winkler, J. Teigland, G. Kranzler. 1964. *Counseling and guidance for underachieving fourth-grade students.* Report of Cooperative Research Project No. 2196.

Ohlsen, M. April 1960. Counseling within a group setting. *J. Nat. Ass. Women Deans Couns., 23,* 104–109.

Pearson, R. November 1966. Group versus "mass" procedures—for what? *Sch. Couns., 14* (No. 2).

Sonstegard, M. March 1958. Interaction processes and the personality growth of children. *Group Psychother., 11* (No. 1).

Stormer, G. E. 1967. Milieu group counseling in elementary school guidance. *Elem. Sch. Guid. Counsel., 1* (No. 3), 240–254.

Rationale of Group Counseling*

Rudolf Dreikurs / Manford Sonstegard

The fact that human beings are social beings is basic to the rationale for group counseling. Each man's personal characteristics express his social movement and interaction with others. Children, as social beings, live and grow in groups. The family is the first group in which the child seeks to find his place. Later, he struggles to find his place in his peer group. Each child develops his own unique approach to integration within the group. The method he chooses is in keeping with his concept of himself and his interpretation of life. On this basis, he assumes a unique role within each of the groups to which he belongs.

The impact of the group on each child is readily observed whenever he participates within it. The use of the group to influence the child not only constitutes an effective way to teach but also an effective means of exerting corrective influences. Group techniques are more imperative in a democratic society where the authority of the adult has been replaced by the authority of the group. The group is the reality in which the child operates.

Group methods in one form or another have been in vogue since the beginning of time. Socrates used a form of group counseling with youth which consisted essentially of reorientation by well-formed questions. For his pains, Socrates

---

* *The Teleoanalytic Approach To Group Counseling* The Alfred Adler Institute, Chicago, 1967.

was accused of corrupting the youth. Effects of group methods were noted by others. Aristotle was aware, for example, of the cathartic effect of the theatre.

However, group methods for corrective purposes are essentially the product of the Twentieth Century. The great interest in group therapy and group counseling parallels man's advance toward political freedom and equality. It had its beginnings in Europe at the beginning of this century, and reached its peak during the decades following World War I. Group methods in Europe, however, were perverted into mass performances as Europe regressed into totalitarianism. It spelled the end of group therapy and group counseling. Such approaches did not revive on the Continent until after World War II, for group methods depend on democracy and equality. Group therapy and group counseling with their need for free expression of each member are democratic procedures and do not flourish in an autocratic atmosphere, they in turn create one.

Since group methods thrive only in a free social and political environment, it is not surprising that group techniques developed rapidly in the United States. They had their beginning in private practices by psychiatrists and later were adopted in the field of education.

A Viennese psychiatrist, Alfred Adler, appears to have been one of the first to use group methods deliberately and systematically in his child guidance clinics. They were not clinics in the strict sense, for Adler met with groups of teachers in the schools of Vienna and then with groups of parents outside the schools. The procedure consisted of counseling children and parents in the presence of other parents and teachers. In this way, group counseling became part of educational practices.

While group therapy, like a barometer, was rising and falling with political trends, group counseling has shown a steadily increasing trend. There would naturally be some opposition to group counseling by those who favor individual counseling. We cannot at one stroke point out the heritage of early psychological thinking, considering "privacy" as essential for counseling and therapy. We inherited the concept that mental ills and maladjustments stem from inner conflicts of the individual and are his private and intimate affair. If this were true, there would be no place for group counseling. It would have no effect. Indeed, it might even be harmful.

The concept that maladjustment means mistaken approaches to finding a place among one's fellow men replaced the deterministic explanation of maladjustment as a consequence of pathological processes within the individual. Adler postulated an "ironclad logic of social living" and "the unity of personality" as the basis of his Individual Psychology. This new psychology was in tune with the forward surge of democratic principles. It recognized man's ability to decide for himself, and provided a formula for democratic living by considering social equality as the basis for cooperation and social harmony. In this light, the tremendous intrinsic power and strength of each individual becomes recognized. A child may appear weak and deficient when he becomes discouraged and loses self-confidence. Actually, he is merely using wrong methods to find his place. The teleological perspective of Individual Psychology regards behavior as being purposive; it emphasizes the creative ability of every individual who is good or bad, "strong" or "weak," as *he* determines his actions towards self-directed goals.

The realization that the problems of all children are essentially social gives group counseling its special significance both for the diagnosis of the child's difficulties and for their solution. In the action and interaction between the members of the group, each expresses his goals, his social attitudes, his intentions. Looking for deep psychological processes in the child and his parents is not needed, even frowned upon, as such "introspection" usually loses sight of their real problems.

To visualize man as an indivisible, social, and decision-making being, whose actions have a social purpose, is not always easy. We have behind us a history of mechanistic explanations of behavior, explaining it either by physiological processes and heredity endowment or as a result of environmental influences. Behavior was, for instance, understood as being based on habits, mechanistically developed through responses to stimulations. Or one assumed an interplay between hereditary endowment and environmental stimulations. The answer to the question of which played the more dominant role in determining behavior, heredity or environment, depended on political leanings. In an autocratic society the first was considered as decisive; man was born good or bad, high or low. With the democratic evolution, the emphasis shifted to environmental influences. But in either point of view, man was considered a passive victim of forces within him and around him. Personality was thought of as a product of the struggle between heredity and environmental forces. Later modifications pictured either biological instincts and drives being in constant conflict with the demands of society, or physiological processes distinguishing each organism.

In contrast to these concepts, we see man's behavior not as a result of the impingement of environment upon his psycho-physical makeup; it is rather his personal response to his hereditary endowment and environmental experiences as he perceives them, his interpretation of what he sees and the conclusion which he draws. Man formulates his own individual goals and purposes in life, and molds both his hereditary makeup and environmental experiences according to his self-created "private logic." This holistic, socio-teleologic concept of man is the basis for our counseling as an educational and correctional approach toward a change in behavior and personality.

In an autocratic society, all human relationships are those of superiority and inferiority, dominance and submission. In a democratic society, everybody reaches a state of equality. In the development of democracy, the power of adults to "make" a child perform, behave, or study decreases; it becomes increasingly more difficult and often impossible. As the individual achieves a status of equality, inner motivation becomes more important than pressure from without. When the authority of adults diminishes, the group of peers gains in importance.

The problems of our children are primarily social. Each child tries to find his place in society. His behavior expresses his social orientation and intention. In this light, behavior is a movement toward a goal. It is not sufficient to know what a teacher "feels" toward a child, or the child toward the teacher. It is more important to discover what the pupil *does* to the teacher and how she responds to his misbehavior. Usually *her* reactions are in line with *his* intention, which she does not recognize. The counseling approach must serve to clarify the nature of their interaction, and, if necessary, improve it. We need to deal with their common problem, i.e., their relationship. Either teacher or student can change it.

Group counseling is a natural tool to deal with relationships. Through group counseling we can experiment with interactions and produce changes in the mistaken goals which the student is pursuing. Heretofore, the element of privacy was an indispensable requirement of counseling. Willingness to air intimate feelings and conflicts in front of others was considered a sign of exhibitionism or of other abnormal needs. It has been our experience that this need for privacy is often a neurotic reaction, prevalent in a highly competitive era. "People live a life of quiet desperation," as Emerson stated, and reside in an atmosphere of emotional isolation, ever fearful that deficiencies will be discovered. It is this fear which clamors for privacy. The lack of mutual trust, of the all-important feeling of belonging, keeps people at a distance. This is less true of young children, but becomes more pronounced as they advance up through the grades.

The spread of group counseling is not only the consequence of the dearth of sufficiently trained counselors, but also reflects public interest in and request for new and more effective methods. The social values promulgated in group counseling are in line with man's search for equality and cooperation. It teaches each member to deal with each other as an equal. Group counseling implies more than assistance to individuals; it becomes a social force in a culture which is in a transitional stage from an authoritarian to a democratic society. Thus, it is more than counseling, more than education. It promotes a new social concept and fortifies definite cultural trends. Group counseling is a product of the democratic evolution and a tool to meet its needs.

What are the dynamics of group counseling? Any attempt to formulate a theory for the effectiveness of group counseling is encumbered by historical antecedents. Counseling is still looked upon in many circles as a form of dealing with the problems of individuals; therefore, it is only natural that attempts are made to transfer theoretical concepts formulated in individual counseling to group approaches.

The first to formulate a theory of group dynamics was probably J. L. Moreno. He developed his theory of "tele"; sociometry was the method devised to evaluate the group structure. Subsequent studies and observations have pointed up a number of mechanisms that are germane to group counseling and explain its effectiveness.

Counseling is learning. If learning is to take place, there must be action. Kelly (1947) points out, in the Hanover study, that a subject could look upon objects in a compartment, but was unable to "see" what he was looking at until

he took action by touching one of the objects with a pointer or stick. Then everything fell into place and he could "see" the object. In the group, participation is
the action that is necessary for "seeing." Without participation in the group by
the members, no correction can result. The participation may be of a non-verbal
nature. The writers have experienced group sessions when a youngster who is
extremely withdrawn would have withdrawn still further and perhaps left the
group if pushed to interact verbally. Permitted to participate more passively on
the non-verbal level as by a smile, movement of the lips, twinkle of the eye, or
other reactions to the interaction of the other group members, the withdrawn
youngster, after a period of time, forgot himself and began to participate verbally. Most people have observed that talking to someone about a problem is often .
beneficial. Even though the other person may merely listen, without any comment,
the one who talked may go away with a better understanding of his problems.
Disclosures of goals are similar, except that the group has the added advantage of
providing a "feedback" from the other members of the group guided and stimulated by the counselor. The effectiveness of psychological confrontations is sometimes expressed by, "What you say is not new, but I had never thought of it that
way before."

Insight, and thereby an understanding of our own problems through listening to someone discussing his, is another advantage of group counseling. Let us
take as an example a parent who came for individual counseling. It became clear,
after a number of interviews, that the necessary reorientation was going to be
slow. It was suggested that the mother attend the parent group counseling sessions. During the second group session, she interrupted the discussion with
another parent with, "Now I know what I am doing wrong." A remark by the
other mother struck a chord which the counselor, in individual sessions, was
unable to achieve. Each group member identifies himself with others, comes to
understand his own problems, changes his ideas, and in turn encourages others
through his participation. Universalization is the cementing element in achieving
group cohesiveness. This is true for adults as for children as well.

Some youngsters develop negative concepts of themselves which no amount
of effort on the part of teachers or counselors can alter. In such cases, the group
appears to exert two unrelated influences. The group increases one's receptiveness
to new ideas, to new concepts. In individual counseling we find a frequent defense mechanism, the individual denying or rejecting them. A more important
outcome of the group process goes beyond the intellectual acceptance of ideas;
the interactions in the group tend to help each member develop a feeling of belonging. Learning and the growing of insight is facilitated by group discussion.
Children and parents are often more influenced and encouraged by their peers
than by the teachers or counselor. As an example: Bruce, a bright boy, made
little progress in school, despite the efforts of both his teachers and parents.
Bruce was invited to join a peer group for counseling. One day, after attending
a number of sessions, he remarked, "Before I joined this group, I thought I was
dumb." Another youngster who was a member of a group said to his mother,

"You know, I am not so stupid." "What makes you say that?" she asked. "The kids who meet with Mr. ——— to talk about things think I am smart." "We have told you this before," she answered. "Yeh, but these guys mean it."

Group counseling not only helps the individual parent or child to help himself, but the members begin to help each other, for participating in a group almost automatically evokes mutual help. The majority of the classrooms are competitive with each student interested, for the most part, in his self-elevation or giving up altogether. Under these conditions, there is little possibility to assume responsibility for one another to counteract the social isolation in which each lives. It is generally assumed that children in the same classroom know each other. On the contrary, many are as socially isolated as a hermit. This was brought to our attention in a conversation with Karen who was interested in horses and riding. Karen did not own a horse, and therefore had no opportunity to ride. "Well, Karen, if you're interested in learning, Alice would be happy to let you ride her horse and even teach you to ride. Why don't you talk with her about it?" "Oh! I couldn't do that." "Why not?" "I don't even know her." "I thought Alice said you were in the same class with her." "Yes, I am, but I don't know her."

These were not isolated or rejected youngsters. What must life in the classroom be like for them? Group counseling helps to dissolve the social wall in which most children live. When a group member says, "I'll help you with it if you like," we immediately know two things: (1) the child who has offered help has found his place in the counseling group and is likely on his way to finding his place in a large group—the classroom, and (2) the help will be offered to a peer because of social interest and not merely to elevate himself personally.

The group provides a social situation with real meaning. Some youngsters have never had an opportunity of testing themselves in a real social situation. They may never have felt belonging in the family group and have never been assured of their place in the school group. In group counseling each member feels soon that he has a place, despite his shortcomings and deficiencies. Under the guidance of the counselor he learns how to contend with conflicts of ideas and interests which he encounters in the group and develops coping devices when he returns to the family and classroom group. The problems of each youngster reveal themselves in a group, at home or in school; therefore, they must be solved in a group. It is in group counseling the youngster finds he is equal with others. In the counseling groups, deficiencies lose their stigma. Paradoxically, deficiencies may be the necessary qualification for membership in a counseling group; let us say, in group counseling for underachievers. Thus, in the group, deficiency does not lessen social status, but serves as a basis of equality for all.

In a democratic setting, as contrasted with an autocratic society, an atmosphere of equality is necessary to obtain the cooperation of all participants. Integrated efforts help all individuals attain greater fulfillment of their potentialities. It has been pointed out that the poteniality for establishing positive social attitudes is usually limited or absent in the community or the school; it exists in a well conducted counseling group. The group becomes a value-forming element. Individual counseling does not lend itself as well to bring about necessary value changes. Group counseling cannot avoid dealing with values. All values present group consensus; group participation in one way or another affects the value system of each member. The normal family and classroom experience of a youngster is usually not conducive to shaking his already well established and set value systems; they usually fortify his wrong values. School and home are not reference groups with which the child identifies himself. The impact of experiences in group counseling is bound to have a beneficial effect on the value systems of each participant.

This can be illustrated by the interaction in a group of third graders. Larry did not get up in the morning to have breakfast with his parents. He would not eat solid foods. None of these facts were known to the counselor. The group interaction went something like this:

Larry: This morning I woke up at the sound of the mixer.

1st child: The mixer!

Larry: Yes, my mother was making my milk shake for me.

2nd child: A milk shake for breakfast?

Larry: My mother always fixes a milk shake for me. Then she brings it to bed for me.

1st child: You eat in bed?

Larry: While I am drinking the milk shake, my mother draws the water for my bath. She is a regular servant to me.

Counselor: How many of you have breakfast brought to you in bed?

3rd child: Oh, I haven't eaten in bed since I was a baby. I always get up for breakfast.

4th child: I always get up.

5th child: I never heard of milk shakes for breakfast. I take my own bath, usually before going to bed, now that I am big.

The interchange went on for a short time concerning responsibilities of getting up in the morning, getting dressed, and eating what the family had for breakfast. Larry listened silently. After a while the discussion turned to other topics. Soon after, Larry's mother related in the parent group that he was now getting up in the morning, and for the first time ate the same kind of food as the rest of the family. Larry's family experiences maintained the faulty goals he was pursuing, and reinforced his goal of getting service. The counseling group became a means for effecting a change for the better.

Counseling must have structure. This is easily discernible in individual counseling. In group counseling, because of the interaction of the members, the structure which the counselor provides is not always so easily observed. It is there, nevertheless. Without structure, the group interaction becomes confused and chaotic. In keeping with the dynamics of counseling in general, the group counseling process consists of: (1) the establishment and maintenance of proper relationships; (2) an examination of the purpose of each group member's action or behavior; (3) revealing to each student the goals he is pursuing, called psychological disclosure; and (4) a reorientation and direction.

1. Developing an effective counseling relationship requires more than mere good relationships. The counselor has to establish himself as the leader of the group, even though a democratic atmosphere must prevail. An effective group counseling relationship is based on mutual respect. It does not mean that each member may do anything he pleases. Firmness and kindness is necessary in all group counseling, as illustrated by the following incident. Jeff, a fifth grader, attempted to maneuver the counselor into a power struggle during each group session. Although the counselor recognized what Jeff was trying to do and refused to become involved in a fight, it became evident that Jeff's disturbing behavior would disrupt the entire group. The counselor asked the group, "Do you see what is going on?" The members pointed out that Jeff wanted to be the boss. His behavior, they said, disrupted discussion. They indicated their disapproval of his behavior. The counselor made it clear that he did not intend to fight with Jeff. But Jeff continued disturbing. The counselor then told Jeff he would either have to go along with the group so the discussion could continue, or he would have to leave. Jeff persisted. The counselor then asked Jeff if he was leaving by himself or if he had to be removed. Jeff made no move to leave. The counselor then insisted, firmly but kindly, that Jeff leave the room with the understanding that he could return when he felt able to participate. Jeff returned to the group after an absence of one session. The change in his behavior was dramatic, not only in the counseling group, but also, as reported by the parents, at home and in the classroom. The redirection of Jeff's mistaken goals could not be attributed to this one action alone; the parents had been counseled in a group with other parents, and the teacher attended a teachers' seminar, and they began to understand Jeff's behavior and what to do about it. However, the counselor established himself as a leader of the group and a man of his word.

2. The goals which the child is pursuing underlie his behavior. The method of examining, of discovering these goals, can be applied in individual counseling as well as in a group situation. However, the child's goals and movements become more obvious in the interaction between him and the counselor in individual sessions. Secondly, the counselor no longer depends exclusively on the student's verbal reports of his outside interactions with others. He sees him in action during the session. Often the child acts differently in a group than when alone with the counselor. Much of the veneer which the child uses as a cover-up may be stripped away in the group, and his true personality is openly revealed. As an appropriate illustration let us take Gale, a bright, charming, fourth-grade girl. Most of the teachers were impressed with her; she was aggressive, but she caused no trouble. In Gale's group, and from the same classroom, was Jim, who was a bright boy also, but a disturbing element in the classroom. At the beginning of one group session, with Gale and Jim present, the school principal came into the room. Gale immediately invited him to participate in the group session.

He accepted, but had to leave to answer a phone call. Gale informed a late arriving group member that the empty chair beside her was reserved for the principal, and he should locate another chair. The group discussion shifted immediately after the principal returned. Gale took the initiative and began subtly to push Jim down, and to put herself in a favorable light. This disturbed Jim, and he began to act up, whereupon other boys also began to act up. Gale had achieved her goal and could sit back with a feeling of "see how badly they behave and see how good I am." The expression on her face vividly revealed her triumph. The principal indicated his disapproval of the boys by his non-verbal reaction. Gale had given the principal the most adroit "snow job" that could be imagined. The group was well on the way to getting out of hand when the counselor began to change the course of the session with, "I wonder how many of you know what happened to get the boys started acting up?" The techniques which Gale used to push the boys down and build herself up, thus creating a classroom disunity, couldn't have been discovered by counseling Jim and Gale individually. It could only be revealed in the group situation.

3. The group helps more effectively than individual counseling to gain insight and to redirect each child's mistaken goals. The group facilitates the process of insight. Many would not be able to learn about themselves but for the interaction taking place in the group. The child comes to see himself in others. Thus, the psychological disclosures and the interpretations during the group sessions are not only valuable for the child to whom they are directed, but to other members of the group who learn from these disclosures. A sixth-grade girl recognized herself when we counseled one of her peers. "I used to be like that, always helping the teacher, being good and doing the right things, not because I wanted to, but because I would get in good."

Mistaken goals and erroneous motives among members of the group are similar enough so that each member can see himself in others. It appears that this factor should be considered in selection of group members. In other words, the more similar the group, the stronger the mirror effect. Thus, there is the greatest possibility of learning from each other when members are selected on the basis of their common problems, for example, groups of underachievers, parents, teenagers, drop-outs, and the like.

4. The statements and opinions of group members often carry more weight than anything the counselor tells them. In a parent group, a father was relating how neither he nor the mother could make their son Butch, a sixth grader, come home after school to change from school to play clothes. Butch had been spanked, had privileges removed, and had been subjected to numerous punitive actions. He still persisted in going with the boys right from school to play, rather than coming home first, to change clothes. The father said, "I told him tonight that the next time he goes to play with the boys without first coming home to change, I am going to take his model airplanes from the ceiling in his room and trample them to bits."

The counselor, being human first and professional second, reacted in a characteristic manner, but fortunately not quickly enough. Another father fairly shouted, "You can't do that. That's just being revengeful." Another member pointed out that there was good reason for Butch's behavior. "How would you like being left out just because you had to go to change clothes?" The counselor had recovered sufficiently, professionally, to say, "What do you think of that?" The father admitted that he had not thought of it that way before, but it made sense because Butch had been having trouble making friends. The counselor recommended what the father could do and asked him what he thought of the recommendations. "Well, if they (the parents in the group) say it will work, then it will work."

The reactions of the group members and what they told the father was much more significant than what the counselor might have said. Group members accept each other more in redirective efforts because they sense the equality that exists among them. In the above case, the counselor was able, later in the session, to develop more insight and exert more corrective influence because he had won the active support of the group.

The insight that a counselor helps to develop in the group sessions is not always a matter for the individual alone. Very few, if any, human beings understand their own behavior. Even though Socrates admonished people to "know themselves" centuries ago, man still does not "know himself" and may never in reality be able to understand himself. But he can and will likely learn about human behavior in general. So children and parents in groups learn something about themselves, but more about people. With the understanding of human nature, they begin to understand themselves. Group counseling is in reality a learning process. Research indicates that the group enhances learning and that counseling, as a learning process, is enhanced by the group.

The development of insight often becomes an end product in individual counseling. It could also become an end product in group counseling as well, and sometimes does. However, insight is not an end in itself—it is merely a means to an end. It is not often a basis for behavioral change, but always a step in that direction. The end product is reorientation and redirection. The children are helped to redirect their mistaken goals, and the parents to give up erroneous concepts about dealing with children and to make a change in their approaches and relationships. The change becomes evident in the child's improved relationship with his peers, with his teachers, with his siblings and parents, and in a more realistic concept of self. The group becomes an agent in bringing about these changes because of the improved interpersonal relationship in the group, a greater possibility for each group member to see himself as he is, and the realization that his concept of himself and the goals he is pursuing are faulty.

REFERENCE

Kelley, E. 1947. *Education for what is real.* New York: Harper & Row.

Counseling Children in Groups*

Merle M. Ohlsen

The counseling of school children in groups has become more frequent with recent developments in elementary school counseling. As consultants to teachers, elementary school counselors also have been encouraged to help teachers adapt group techniques for the teachers' use. Though this paper is primarily concerned with introducing group counseling to children, the selection of clients, and with adapting group counseling methods for children, the writer will discuss briefly some of the possibilities for helping teachers to use group techniques.

The writer assumes that the readers of this journal understand the counseling process, including the kinds of interaction that occur within a group of normal adolescents as they talk about the problems that bother them and try to help each other learn to behave more effectively (Ohlsen, 1964). Clients must learn to help others as well as to obtain help for themselves. All of the competencies required of the counselor in individual counseling are required here, and more, too. Besides trying to understand the client who is speaking, to capture his feelings, and to help him express his feelings and change his behavior, the counselor must help clients to learn to help others and to observe how the speaker's comments, as well as the various members' nonverbal behavior, influence each of the other members. He must also select clients with care, taking into account their possible impact upon each other and he must enlist their assistance in developing a therapeutic atmosphere.

The setting for group counseling meets the optimal conditions for learning described by Seeman (1963): "It is a safe environment; it is an understanding environment; it is a caring environment; it is a participating environment; and it is an approving environment" (p. 8). Clients also see counseling as providing an opportunity to be open, honest, and frank—or a situation in which it is safe to test ideas and solutions to problems and where frank evaluations of efforts to change can be obtained. As a consultant to teachers, the elementary school counselor can also use his knowledge of group behavior to help teachers develop Seeman's optimal conditions for learning within their classrooms.

INTRODUCING GROUP COUNSELING

As a regular member of the school staff rather than a specialist functioning out of the central office, the elementary school counselor has many opportunities to get to know the pupils and the staff and to describe his services for them. When he wishes to introduce group counseling, therefore, he will be able to de-

6 *School Counselor*, May 1968, vol. 15 (in press). By permission.

scribe group counseling both to teachers, either in informal contacts or at a faculty meeting, and to pupils in their classrooms. He can explain how pupils may be helped in groups, and can answer questions on what will be expected of clients in groups. Such presentations encourage self referrals and help teachers to understand the nature of the treatment process.

When pupils ask to join a counseling group or are referred by their teachers, individual interviews are scheduled. The purpose of the individual interview is to answer any questions a client may have about group counseling; to help the counselor get to know the child better in order to determine how he can best be helped and with whom he would best fit in a counseling group; to give the child a chance to discuss the problems with which he hopes to obtain assistance in the group, and thereby increase his readiness to discuss these problems in the group; and to assess his readiness for group counseling and commitment to change his behavior. The counselor often supplements the information obtained in the individual interview with a teacher or parent conference and by carefully examining the child's cumulative record.

Since only a few individual sessions are required to help many school children, not all children who refer themselves, or who are referred by their teachers, will be assigned to groups. If the counselor decides that a few sessions with the child or his teacher or parents best meets the child's needs, he is not assigned to a counseling group. Thus, the intake interview may become the first in a series of several individual counseling sessions. Sometimes a counselor will decide to work with a child on an individual basis and later decide to assign him to a group.

SELECTING CLIENTS FOR GROUPS

Children who seem to profit most from group counseling include shy children, children who have difficulty participating in class discussion, children who want to make friends, and children who have better ability than their performance indicates. Usually the last type needs help in accepting his ability before he can improve his performance. Rarely is it advisable to include only one type of client in a single group—e.g., gifted underachievers. Usually such children can best be treated along with some other children who can accept their ability and are concerned about why they are not doing better than they are. Ohlsen (1964) reported that best results were obtained when, after describing group counseling to children, more children volunteered than could be included in the next group to be begun. Under these circumstances prospective clients tried harder to convince the counselor in the intake interview that they were ready for counseling and that they really had something to talk about in the group. As they tried to convince the counselor that they should be included in the next group, they increased their own readiness for counseling.

For every group a counselor must carefully select clients. He must be permitted to accept only those clients whom he feels reasonably certain that he can help, and preferably only those who want to join a group after they have learned what will be expected of them and what they can expect from others in their group. Even after a group is organized the counselor must feel free to take an unproductive member from the group or reassign anyone who does not seem to fit into the group. Both Fiedler (1949) and Broedel, Ohlsen, Proff, and Southard (1960) found that even a single blocking client can sometimes take such an anti-therapeutic stance that its members never establish a therapeutic climate.

For group counseling to be effective with even upper-grade elementary school children Ohlsen and Gazda (1965) concluded that both pupils and parents must understand and accept what will be expected in the counseling groups. Sonstegard (1961) obtained significant results with similar clients, but he also provided group counseling for the pupils' parents and teachers. Where this is not feasible, or possibly not even necessary, Ohlsen and Gazda suggested that at least regular consultations with parents and teachers are essential. Their under-achieving fifth graders discussed many situations in which they felt that they had been treated unfairly and there was nothing that they could do about it. A fifth-grade boy described his feelings as follows: "We're just kids and don't count for much; even our dogs are treated nicer than we are." Whereas adolescents are able to help a peer convey to the person who has hurt him how he has been hurt and to help him do something about his situations to improve it, fifth graders feel trapped. They lack the independence and the adolescent's repertoire of social skills to cope with life's problems. Hence, the important adults in their lives must accept considerable responsibility for helping them cope with problems and improve their environment (Ohlsen and Gazda, 1965, p. 81).

ADAPTING GROUP COUNSELING METHODS FOR CHILDREN

The writer's counseling experiences and research with groups indicate that though the same basic principles of counseling apply to all ages, the counselor must adapt his techniques to his clients' social and emotional maturity, their previous experiences in groups, and the development of their communication skills. Work with fifth, sixth, seventh, and eighth graders clearly suggests that the discussion type of counseling that is effective with high school and college students also works well with seventh and eighth graders, but certain changes are recommended for fifth and sixth graders (and these probably apply to fourth graders):

1. These younger children need more structure and more carefully defined limits. Even when they are carefully selected for a group, they have difficulty defining limits and enforcing them as the committed older children do. They must understand what is expected in group counseling and how this differs from what is expected in their classrooms.

2. Associated with the need for more structure, Ohlsen and Gazda (1965) concluded that there seemed to be a need for more active participation on the counselor's part than was required in the adolescent group. These younger chil-

dren did not seem to be able to detect and reach beyond mere talk to respond to significant therapeutic material as Ackerman (1955) indicated that his adolescents were able to do. Though their ability to do this increased over the treatment period, and they were able to gradually accept more responsibility for helping develop a therapeutic climate, fifth and sixth graders required more time to learn to do this than did adolescents. Furthermore, when the counselor failed to participate enough, especially during the early sessions, the clients became restless, were easily distracted, and often competed for the counselor's attention.

3. Though these children do have some ability to empathize with peers, as Lerner (1937) reported, they have difficulty maintaining a sustained interest in another's problem. Consequently, Ohlsen and Gazda (1965) concluded that these children should be treated in smaller groups (perhaps five or six instead of seven or eight) and for shorter periods of time (perhaps forty- to forty-five minutes instead of an hour). They also recommended three meetings a week instead of two.

4. Ginott (1961) reported that prevailing practice in clinics is to separate boys and girls for treatment during the latency period. Ohlsen and Gazda noted that in their group girls were more mature, exhibited more interest in boys than boys did in girls, tended to threaten boys with the discussion of topics related to sex, were more verbal, and tended to dominate discussions. Hence, though they generally favor the treatment of mixed groups, they conceded that it may be wise to treat girls and boys of this age in separate groups. On the other hand, they had some strong reservations concerning this recommendation: the counseling group may be the best place for boys and girls to deal with these antagonistic feelings and to learn to relate to each other.

5. Within the group, clients often need to act out as well as talk out their problems. Role playing is effective whenever a client has difficulty describing a situation or conveying to others how he feels about it; or when he wants to obtain others' reactions to his way of meeting a situation; or when he feels he needs practice in meeting a situation (Ohlsen, 1964, p. 174). Puppets also may be used with them effectively, especially when the group develops the skits to be portrayed by the puppets. Other play materials such as family dolls, finger paints, and sketching paper may be used with these children, but care must be taken in selecting the materials lest the children perceive use of these materials as "kid's stuff."

Finally, the writer would like to consider briefly how a counselor may work with primary school-age children in groups. Though this writer believes that the normal children with whom he has worked can put their feelings in words better than many authors have indicated, special attention must be given to communicating with these children. Since this is discussed in another paper it will not be discussed again here (Ohlsen, 1965). It will suffice to say that more use should be made of play materials than was suggested above for fourth-, fifth-, and sixth-grade children. A short description of a counselor working with five first and second graders illustrates how children who had difficulty talking to each other can be helped in groups. All of them tended to be shy and two were having difficulty learning to read. Before they entered the room, the counselor had laid out sheets of brown wrapping paper, finger paints, modeling clay, and various sizes of dolls—some dressed as adults and others as children. When they came into the room, each selected the materials of his choice and sat down to play. Provision was made for the children to sit around a long table in a large office which was used as a playroom. One of the girls and two of the boys chose to play with finger paints. The third boy played with clay and the remaining girl played with dolls. As the children played the counselor moved about, responding first to one child, then to another. As he watched a child play he would try to determine what the child was trying to express and respond to him in the child's medium—e.g., if the child was playing with finger paints he would respond to him with finger paints. The children were also encouraged to interact with each other. Occasionally, one would speak to the entire group—a sort of show and tell. When necessary the counselor helped such a client get the attention of the entire group. He also tried to convey to his clients that not everyone was expected to speak to the entire group just because one wanted to do so. Although normal children do seem to express themselves verbally better than disturbed children, counselors are urged to take note of Ginott's warning: "Many serious mistakes in child therapy are committed by adults who try to give verbal insight to children whose language is play. Forcing them to verbalize is like compelling them to converse in a foreign language" (Ginott, 1958, p. 413).

TEACHER'S USE
OF GROUP TECHNIQUES

Most elementary school teachers are interested in their pupils as individuals, and many are already using group discussion techniques. They exhibit this interest in their pupils by listening to them when they bring problems to school and by encouraging them to talk about their interesting experiences—e.g., by show-and-tell sessions and by giving them a chance to role play situations that trouble them.

The teacher's guidance responsibility is to listen and to try to understand—to let his pupil know that he cares about them and that he will set aside time to give them a chance to discuss special topics that concern them. When his pupils begin to discuss topics that the teacher feels should not be shared with the entire group, he arranges private conferences with individuals or small groups. On the other hand, the teacher should not be expected to do counseling. It should be reserved for persons who are qualified to do it. With the help of a counselor, however, the teacher can encourage normal social, emotional, and intellectual development of children with effective use of group techniques.

Recently Rogge (1965) did an excellent demonstration to illustrate how a teacher can use group methods to motivate learning. What he did was to set aside a time when pupils were given a chance to ask any questions they wished. Rather than to merely answer their questions, he helped them explore where they could find the answers to their questions and helped them talk about how they felt about each other's questions. In order to further excite learning when one pupil has answered a question, the teacher may ask them still further questions.

Since some teachers doubt their ability to field such questions, and to deal with the embarrassment associated with some questions, they often need help in learning to apply Rogge's methods. Rogge usually begins with a demonstration in the teacher's classroom. After they have discussed it, and sometimes even critiqued his tape recording of it, he encourages the teacher to try it, with him observing. Usually he encourages the teacher to make a recording of the discussion so that he will have specific responses to discuss when helping the teacher critique his own session. Teachers also can help each other critique tape-recorded sessions of such discussions.

Role playing (some call it sociodrama) is another group technique that the teacher can use. It differs from "playing house" or "playing school" in that it is an organized effort to teach pupils to cope with specific problems. It provides the pupil who requests assistance with an opportunity to relive a specific problem, to express his feelings about it within a safe emotional climate, to test his ideas for coping with the problem, to obtain his classmates' and teacher's ideas for solving his problem, and to practice these solutions while interacting with people whose reactions he values. In fact, when a child describes a situation and the people involved in it, tells how he feels and how he thinks they feel, directs and participates in the scene role played, and answers his classmates many and varied questions before playing the scene, he usually better understands himself and the whole situation even before he role plays the scene.

For example, Robert, a second grader, was beaten up by Mike, a fifth grader, during the lunch period. After helping Robert clean up, Miss Pickens suggested that perhaps the class could help Robert figure out how to cope with Mike. Since Mike had been picking on several of the small boys in the neighborhood, this idea appealed to the pupils. They set the stage for the sociodrama by having Robert describe what happened during the incident. Then members of the class volunteered for the various roles; several children volunteered for their own roles. The others in the scene were briefed by Robert. Finally, Miss Pickens pointed out that though they should try to reenact what happened, they should not worry about saying precisely what was said before—instead they should try to say and act as they felt their characters would. When Miss Pickens thought they had gone far enough into the scene to help Robert, she interrupted and asked Robert to tell what he would have done differently and suggested that he ask questions about the issues which concerned him. Then she gave the other players a chance to comment on how they felt about what happened and to make suggestions to Robert. Finally, she gave the rest of the group a chance to express their feelings about the scene and to offer Robert suggestions. Not only did Robert get many good suggestions, but all of them obtained ideas for coping with bullies (Ohlsen, 1959, p. 640).

Thus, group techniques can be used effectively by teachers too. Though there are many questions for which no one has answers at this time, much can be done to help children in groups. Lack of qualified personnel is probably the most serious problem facing school counselors who want to initiate group counseling programs. These personnel are needed to counsel pupils and to help teachers improve their competencies in working with groups.

REFERENCES

Ackerman, N. W. 1955. Group psychotherapy with a mixed group of adolescents, *Inter. J. Group Psychother.*, 5, 249–260.

Broedel, J., M. M. Ohlsen, F. Proff, and C. Southard. 1960. The effects of group counseling on gifted unachieving adolescents. *J. Counsel. Psychol.*, 7, 163–170.

Fiedler, F. E. 1949. An experimental approach to preventative psychotherapy. *J. abnormal soc. Psychol.*, 44, 386–393.

Ginott, H. G. 1961. *Group psychotherapy with children.* New York: McGraw-Hill.

————. 1958. Play group therapy: a theoretical framework. *Inter. J. Group Psychother.*, 8, 410–418.

Lerner, E. 1937. The problem of perspective in moral reasoning. *J. Sociol.*, 43, 294–299.

Ohlsen, M. M. 1965. *The elementary school counselor.* College of Education, University of Illinois. Mimeographed.

————, and Gazda, G. M. 1965. Counseling underachieving bright pupils. *Education*, 86, 78–81.

————. 1964. *Guidance services in the modern school.* New York: Harcourt.

————. 1959. *Modern methods in elementary education.* New York: Holt, Rinehart and Winston.

Rogge, W. M. June 10, 1965. *A demonstration on elementary school teachers' use of group discussion methods to motivate learning.* Mount Zion Conference.

Seeman, J. 1963. *Motivations to high achievement.* Guidance summer lecture at the University of Colorado.

Sonstegard, M. 1961. *Group counseling methods with parents of elementary school children as related to pupil growth and development.* Cedar Falls, Iowa: State College of Iowa. Mimeographed.

Group Counseling:

Applying the Technique*

Charles F. Combs / Benjamin Cohn
Edward J. Gibian / A. Mead Sniffen

The authors have recently conducted a series of experimental projects designed to demonstrate the values of group counseling as a technique in the public school. They worked in practical situations in regular school buildings and within the limits of the usual school curriculum. From these experiences certain common patterns of procedure relating to the use of group counseling have become apparent.

Group counseling is often the most feasible tool available to the counselor in reaching the difficult or troubled student. It seems to be especially effective when applied to adolescents. Many studies have emphasized the importance of a peer group to the adolescent; the concept of group counseling capitalizes on this peer group identification.

Group counseling is a social process. The persons involved approach problems at their own speed within the safety of a social setting. Here they may explore problems that are important to them within the security of a group of peers who share their problems and with whom they identify. Moreover, they may do this without fear of external direction or the pressure of adult coercion. The adult whom they experience within the group is an adult in a new role—the helpful, non-judgmental, non-threatening adult.

In addition to these advantages, group counseling offers to the school the attractiveness of an efficient use of the counselor's time, energy, and influence for dealing with personal problems. Thus the counselor may work with greater numbers of those students who need help most or present the greatest threat to smooth school operation.

The counseling pattern to be used in any particular school must be tailored to the school system in which it is to be applied. A counseling program must always meet the needs of the framework within which it exists. If it does not meet these needs, it will soon cease to exist.

Counseling must be experienced, then, as helpful not only to the students but also to the administrators and, particularly, to the teachers of the students who are being counseled. Involvement of administration and faculty will avoid the hazards of a counseling program that may otherwise be viewed by these

* *The School Counselor*, October 1963, vol. 11, no. 1. By permission.

people as capricious or threatening. They should be drawn into the formation of the group counseling program, and there should be continual feedback in order to maintain a high level of involvement.

SELECTION OF STUDENTS

The classroom teachers must be made to feel that they are active participants in the selection of candidates for the group. The opinions and reactions of the faculty and administrators are extremely valuable to the counselor in identifying the disruptive student, the gross underachiever and others who are of deep concern to the school.

Likely candidates for group counseling may also be identified by studying school records. For instance, if the purpose of the proposed group is to deal with the disruptive or disorderly, school records will often give valuable indications of such previous difficulties. If the basic presenting problem is underachievement, candidates may be identified in terms of differences between measured capacity and achievement, or teachers' recorded comments of classroom difficulty.

FORMING A GROUP

It is important in a new or formative program that the groups be carefully balanced. The members of a group should have a common presenting problem, but they should also have different levels or degrees of the problem. The counselor who tries to establish a group composed only of the most severe and recalcitrant persons who present a particular problem is almost assuredly foredoomed to disappointment. Members of the projected group should present mild as well as severe evidence of a particular problem.

The composition of a group will also be determined by the maturity of its members. It must be borne in mind, in this respect, that groups having both boys and girls will present certain special types of problems. For instance, on the junior-high-school level, in the same age range, there may be wide variations in maturity of the two sexes and in their psychosocial readiness to discuss certain issues.

In the final analysis, of course, the composition of the group will, to a larger extent, be predetermined by the period of the day that prospective members will be available.

Since group counseling is, insofar as possible, non-coercive, the composition of the group will depend upon the identification of the members with each other and with the counselor. As groups are instituted and as members experience success and satisfaction, other students will hear of them and will volunteer for these and for future groups.

SIZE OF GROUP

The size of the group will depend on several major factors: the maturity of the students who are being considered for the projected group, the level of adjustment that they present, and the topic to be discussed.

Elementary school children seem less capable of deferring their actions and reactions than are older children. The elementary-age child seems to be neither as verbal nor as group-oriented as the junior-high or secondary-school student. Therefore, a small group of four to six seems to afford these younger children a better opportunity to interact with their peers and to gain social experience than they would find in a larger group. The counselor must also be a more active group member with this age child than with older students.

At the junior-high and secondary-school levels, the optimal size seems to be six to eight students, depending upon the students and the topic or purpose for which they will be meeting. The more antisocial or antischool the attitudes of the group members, the lower the number that can be easily handled within the group. In a group of eight, each member seems to have an opportunity to talk and yet also to listen or to be less active when he wishes.

As the group size increases, the number of its interactions seems to increase geometrically. Beyond ten members the number of interactions definitely hampers the progress of the group. In counseling with aggressive students, even a group of eight is often too large. Six seems to be a more practical size.

PHYSICAL SETTING

Group counseling in regular school buildings must, of necessity, use existing facilities. One of the appeals of this technique is that it does not require a glorified setting and can be easily adapted to what is available. The authors have successfully conducted group counseling sessions in regular classrooms, locker rooms, store rooms, cafeterias, stages of auditoriums, conference rooms, and small offices.

Ideally, the room where the students meet should be as plain as possible. The optimum room size for a group of six to eight students seems to be about 15' x 15', with a round or square table having a seating capacity of approximately ten people.

There should be enough room between members of the group so that, while they can readily communicate with all of their neighbors, they are not so close to others that they are tempted into diversionary activity. It is also highly desirable to have a soundproof or isolated room, so that any noise of the group will not disturb the rest of the school.

With students having academic difficulties it is also important that there be as little distraction as possible. The room should be small enough that the individual cannot readily back away from the group or walk about the room in a manner that would be distracting. While groups are meeting, the central office should be requested to cut off the public address system and telephone calls to the room.

LENGTH OF SESSION

At the junior-high and secondary-school level, the length of group counseling sessions will usually be determined by the length of the class period. In the elementary school, the class periods will not present so great a complication. Group counseling sessions seem most effective when they are of thirty-five to forty-five minutes' duration. Sessions lasting less than thirty to thirty-five minutes do not seem to allow a group to approach and develop topics. On the other hand, sessions that last longer than forty-five minutes may result in boredom.

INITIATING COUNSELING

There are certain techniques that may be of help to the beginning group counselor who is concerned about the important step of initiating the counseling sessions. A sample of an initial structuring might go somewhat as follows:

"I think we all know each other. We are going to meet during this period, in this room, every week for the next two weeks. We're going to be getting together to try to solve problems that we all share. Everyone in this group, for instance, seems to have a lot more ability than is actually being used. Somehow, something is getting in the way and keeping each one of us from being all that we can. We are going to be meeting together to try to find out what some of these reasons are and what we can do to solve them.

"While we are here in this group we are going to talk about anything that is of concern to us. We can say anything we want in any way that we want. Obviously there are going to be some limits. We don't want to disrupt the rest of the school, and of course we can't destroy any of the equipment in this room—or each other, for that matter. But other than these limits, I want you to feel free to express yourselves in any way you like.

"What we say in this group is our business. Nothing we say here is to be told to anyone outside of the group by you or by me. No one else is going to know what goes on here—that's our business. I am here to work with you and perhaps help you to work through the problems, but together we may be able to work something out which will help us all. We must all work together; we must all try to understand each other.

"Okay, who would like to begin?"

Very definite "Rules of the Game" can assist group members in adjusting to the new situation. Certain of the authors, for instance, have found it useful to distribute mimeographed material to the members of the group, somewhat as follows:

RULES OF THE GAME

1. Group counseling is a cooperative job. We must all work together to help each other solve problems.

2. We can't solve problems if we refuse to look at them honestly. Let's try not to let our previous ideas get in our way.

3. Try to really listen to what the person next to you is saying. Don't just try to convince him that you're right. Listen to what he says, just as you expect him to listen to you when you have something to say.

4. Stick with a topic; don't get side-tracked. Wait until the rest of the people seem to be willing to let a topic rest for a while before you try to change it.

5. Speak whenever you have something to say. Don't be afraid to speak up even if what you have to say isn't particularly clear in your own mind. But on the other hand, be careful not to cover up what you mean to say by saying too much.

6. One of the best ways you can help the others is to let them know that they are not alone in what they feel. If you have experienced the same feeling, tell them. You may be surprised to find that you will be able to understand more about the way you feel as you find yourself talking to others about how they feel.

7. Don't feel that you have to come to a group solution or agreement. The purpose of the group is to explore problems together. The decision that you as a person come to must be your own. The only solutions that are good for you must be those that have a personal meaning for you. Someone else's answer may not apply to the way you feel.

8. A group discussion goes along best when everybody trusts each other. Be careful that the others don't feel that you are making fun of them. If you are going to work together and solve problems, you're going to have to trust each other. The more quickly you get to know the others and they get to know you, the more quickly this group is going to "pay off" for you.

ATMOSPHERE

The group counseling situation must be a permissive one. There must be an openness to all of those experiences that can and should be explored within the framework of the educational setting. The counselor must be experienced by the students as an accepting and facilitating adult. However, he must also remember that he is operating within a school framework and that there are certain limits and restrictions by which the group must abide. Permissiveness does not mean anarchy.

The limits observed must be those which are really necessary to the functioning of the group. Children and adolescents find that the security of limits is very important. They are in formative social periods and find security in the periodic restructuring of the group and its aims. This often enables them to abandon courses of action which they may have already begun to experience as largely unrewarding.

The control of the topics to be explored should be in the hands of the students. It should be their decision to change the subject of discussion and, if necessary, to reorganize the group. The problems presented by the group should be explored where possible in terms of generalized, rather than specific, situations. The boy who presents the group with a specific problem about one certain teacher should find the group discussing behavior of teachers and pupils in general. The counselor must be careful when clarifying a specifically presented problem to re-present it in its more general framework.

The counselor must continually attempt to draw out the members of the group, to be aware of the feelings of the counselees and to reflect these feelings to the group. The counselor serves as a catalyst. He clarifies the statements that the group makes and the feelings expressed. He reflects these sentiments in a way that allows each member to examine his own feelings and the group to explore their feelings together. Thus he crystallizes feelings and meanings.

The authors have found that members of the group seem to have built-in controls for the depth of problems they are willing to explore. A topic will be handled only if the group feels it can actually deal with and solve the problem. When the group or particular members feel beyond their depth or not yet prepared to deal with a subject, progress may be effectively blocked by their lack of participation or by their changing the subject. Restlessness, resistiveness, aggression or hostility often appear at this point.

If the counselor pushes the group too fast toward a particular solution or even toward a particular problem, the group will usually try to stop him and will give indications that he is losing them. If he responds to these signs and slows down or stops and allows the group once again to assume control and catch its breath, psychologically, the group will usually move ahead rapidly.

The counselor must always seek to respond to the true feelings underlying the statements that the counselees make. He must not fall into the trap of responding to the content of what the students say or, worse yet, to his own needs and attitudes toward these problems.

The members of the group will often test the sincerity of the counselor (who is, after all, a representative of the adult society) and the other members of the group. Before they will reveal themselves or explore problems of deep meaning to them, they must have faith in the integrity of the other members of the group.

As they become able to express their pent-up feelings and needs within the safety of the group, they test and reorganize their perceptions of themselves and of the world around them. Essentially, they are groping toward greater self-adequacy and greater self-acceptability. As they work through group problems, they will be able to see new relationships and will thus become more effective individuals.

DURATION

It is very important to establish at the beginning of a series of counseling sessions a definite duration for the group counseling experience. This seems to give structure to all members of the group so that they can more readily judge the available time remaining. That is, each group member can assess the gains already achieved at any point in the series and the time needed to reach a goal.

Group counseling seems to be most effective on a one-period-per-week basis, running approximately fifteen to twenty weeks. Of course, the needs of the particular school will largely dictate the initiation and duration of counseling.

The timing of the start of a series of group counseling sessions is important. Members of the group seem to be more able to tolerate interruptions in counseling after the group has been well established rather than in the formative period, when consistency seems to be very essential. Members often feel rejected if they experience a break in the group pattern in the early periods. It is important that group sessions not be started shortly before Christmas or Easter vacations or semester breaks, for if the formation of a group is thus broken the members may return rather coldly to the group.

The greatest gains from group counseling will take time. The counselor should not be too concerned if there is a lack of observable difference in behavior or attitude early in the counseling process. Counseling often seems more effective if the groups terminate after the designated period and reopen at a future date.

It may be that the group will decide to close prior to the originally decided length of time. The counselor should be aware of becoming so personally involved with the group that he feels that an expressed desire for closure is a rejection of himself. If the counselor is unthreatened by the request for closure, the problem of closure will be a rather simple one.

If the counselor is informed by the group that they feel they have discussed all they want to at this time, he should begin structuring for closure. However, he should also leave the door open for them to return. He might say, for instance:

"Okay, some of you seem to feel like stopping. Let's take a vote on it and decide. If as a group we decide to quit at this time, let's begin to taper off over the next few sessions. We'll review what we've discussed and what conclusions we've come to. If in the future we as a group or as individuals want to come back, we can resume this group or start a new one."

It is often in the discussion of closing that many problems not previously discussed will come up. This gives additional material for the tapering-off sessions. Two to five sessions should be used for closing. However, the control should be entirely in the students' hands. If the group decides on four sessions for tapering off, and then later decides to stop after two sessions instead, this is their prerogative.

During the tapering-off sessions, the counselor should assist members of the group to summarize, clarify, and restate the problems that have been covered. He should help them discuss the various solutions they have previously explored. It is very important that all members of the group have the opportunity to express themselves on the various problems and their own unique solutions.

The tapering-off sessions are exceedingly important since some students may be deeply threatened by the idea of the closure of the group. They may find it quite difficult to give up the relations formed in the group.

CONCLUSIONS

Group counseling is an exceedingly valuable tool, far too seldom used within the regular school framework. Its advantages are manifold:

1. In dealing with several students simultaneously, it spreads the effect of the counselor and at the same time preserves his effectiveness.

2. It seems to be more readily accepted by students in that, since it occurs within a peer group, it is not as "different" or as threatening to them as individual counseling.

3. It makes effective use of the social setting and the peer identification.

4. The adult experienced by students in group counseling is unique in that he is accepting of them and facilitating their experiences, rather than imposing an external judgment. He is a resource, a catalyst, and, perhaps, a new kind of adult.

5. Often the establishment of counseling groups within the school may facilitate individual counseling and other new opportunities to meet the needs of the students.

The authors would like to emphasize that group counseling is not an art known only to a few practitioners who possess unique skills and talents. Group counseling is a technique that is effective and highly efficient of the counselor's time and energy. Most important, it is a technique which lies well within the capabilities of the perceptive school counselor.

Multiple Counseling:

A Catalyst for Individual Counseling*

Angelo V. Boy / Henry L. Isaksen / Gerald J. Pine

The counselor with adequate background in personality theory can use multiple counseling to make the process of working with individuals more effective.

Multiple counseling is a process in which one counselor is involved in a relationship with a number of clients at the same time. Froelich (n.d.) suggests that multiple counseling is a term that describes a specific counseling situation

* *The School Counselor*, October 1963, vol. 11, no. 1. By permission.

involving more than one counselee. Slavson (1947) indicates that in effect multiple counseling is a special application of the principles of individual counseling to two or more persons simultaneously.

The number of clients may vary. From her work with maladjusted students, Driver (1954) recommends six as the optimum number of individuals in a group. As a result of experimentation in this area, Froelich recommends four to eight members as a possible optimum number.

Multiple counseling is psychologically a deep relationship between the counselor and the group to the end that group members have the opportunity to explore the causal factors that have influenced the growth of their particular problems. Because of the depth of the relationship, the process demands that the counselor be well versed in the dynamics of behavior. The beginner who engages in multiple counseling without due recognition of his limitations may expose his subjects to unwarranted danger.

Group members exist in a free atmosphere in which they are able to express their emotions and sift over the circumstances of life that have caused them concern. The counselor enables group members to involve themselves in the process of self-discovery essentially through an empathic attitude that encourages group members to untangle the reasons why they are what they are. Group members proceed with ease since they have a positive reaction to the acceptant and understanding atmosphere which characterizes the counseling relationship (Hobbs, 1951).

FORMING A GROUP

In an effort to provide group members with a maximal growth situation, there are certain principles that should govern the formation of a group for multiple counseling.

The group members should be somewhat alike in their problem area. For example, all may have difficulty relating to parents, all may be overly tense in normal testing situations, or all may have personality conflicts with one or more teachers (Froelich, no date).

The group members should be voluntarily involved in the process of counseling. A student's membership in a group should not come because of any coercion. The student should be involved in the counseling relationship because he has a desire for counseling assistance rather than because it is merely the parent's, principal's, teacher's, or counselor's desire (Hobbs, 1951; Ohlsen, 1955). Each of the group members should have the freedom to drop out at any time. In other words, the probability is little that a client will make any sort of progress if he is compelled to continue against his wishes (Ohlsen, 1955).

THE COUNSELOR

The creation of a growth-producing atmosphere depends largely upon the counselor's ability to communicate empathically with members of the group.

Since a deep relationship is more dependent upon the counselor's genuineness in the association, this relationship cannot be accomplished merely by the use of certain techniques. Such an approach to counseling usually results in a superficial relationship between client and counselor rather than in the meaningful relationship achieved only by the embodiment of a wholesome attitudinal structure that is a genuine and integral part of the counselor's person.

If we can accept counseling as a depth relationship between client and counselor, it would seem that the law of diminishing returns would set in when we attempt to relate to a group of individuals. A sensitive counselor finds it difficult to relate deeply to even one individual, and when he attempts to relate to a group, it becomes even more difficult to involve himself deeply with any one member of the group. Multiple counseling cannot provide for each pupil the full attention of the counselor that individual counseling can give (Ohlsen, 1955).

The larger the counseled group, the more difficult it becomes to relate to each individual within the group. As the counselor attempts to establish a significant relationship with client A, client B expresses himself and the counselor must switch his involvement to client B. If he has been deeply entwined with client A, however, his involvement with client B cannot be quite as meaningful.

When clients C, D, E and F become involved in the process, the counselor is constantly pulled away from a significant relationship with one, toward a more superficial relationship with all.

If the counselor were going to maintain a significant relationship with client A, this could be accomplished only by sacrificing, to some degree, relationships with clients B, C, D, E and F. A truly professional counselor, deeply interested in the effectiveness of his work, will want ultimately to dissolve his relationship with the group and work with each member of the group on an individual basis.

For the competent counselor it is often easy to establish a deep and meaningful counseling relationship with an individual client. A skilled counselor can give his full self to this one client in an attempt to bring about a relationship that will result in the client becoming an independent, freely functioning individual who can handle his own life.

But when the counselor attempts to "give of himself" to many, he finds that although each may have a part of his involvement, his involvement is not as complete with any one as it should be, since he cannot become fully and effectively involved with more than one client at a given time.

The counselor cannot relate deeply to any one member of the group since the other members are seeking "pieces" of his involvement. The group members, although able to function with comfort and ease, still verbalize at a somewhat superficial level because they do not perceive the counselor as relating to them individually and deeply.

They also do not have as much time to talk about their problems in the multiple counseling session as they would in an individual session (Ohlsen, 1955).

The deep and innermost feelings of individual members of the group are seldom brought out since the individual has to deal not only with his own feelings but with the reactions of the group members. They cannot always move with safety in the revelation of certain feelings. These feelings are acceptable to the counselor but perhaps not to other members of the group. For some students multiple counseling is inappropriate because of the disturbing effect these students may have upon the group, or because of the disturbing effect the group may have upon them (Ohlsen, 1955).

Even though the group affords a form of safety and protection in the opportunity for the client to conceal his feelings, the group member is not apt to explore himself thoroughly in depth. As someone else speaks, he can only be fractionally involved with his own feelings and growth.

VALUE

On the other hand, multiple counseling should be an important aspect of a school's counseling program. Although multiple counseling presents communicative limits for the empathic school counselor, the relationship does provide the hesitant client with a beginning point. It should not serve, though, as a replacement for the one-to-one relationship between client and counselor.

Some believe that the principal value of multiple counseling is that it enables the counselor to help more pupils each day and, therefore, results in more economical use of the counselor's time.

However, Ohlsen warns that multiple counseling is not a substitute for individual counseling:

> This (group counseling) should not lead to the elimination of individual counseling; educators must be more concerned with the best service for each individual than with cost. The eventual cost to society of a permanently maladjusted person far exceeds any saving which could come from eliminating individual counseling in the school (pp. 294–325).

Some contend that the results of multiple counseling by itself approximate those of individual counseling. Wolberg (1954) questions the validity of this notion, contending that multiple counseling is a valuable *adjunct* to individual counseling. Driver (1954) looks upon multiple counseling as an enrichment of individual counseling and not as a substitute for it. Super (1949) feels group work can accomplish much if it is preventive in nature, but it is not a replacement for individual counseling.

The primary value of multiple counseling lies in the opportunity it affords the counselor to establish contact with individuals who may need a different kind of help from that of an individual counseling relationship.

There is the strong possibility that some students will find it easier to relate to a group of their peers in the presence of a counselor than to establish a one-to-one relationship directly with the counselor. There is some supportive value to a client in an experience that causes him to realize that he is not alone in his feelings.

As indicated earlier, there is a certain degree of safety and protection in a group. A given member of the group may be more inclined to recognize and express his feelings toward teachers or parents, or his inadequacy to cope with the demands of the school atmosphere.

He may also be encouraged by the experience of having other students accept his feelings without criticism. Finally, he may find it easier to arrange an appointment with the counselor when he discovers that other members of his group are doing so.

Multiple counseling should serve as a basis for establishing a good individual counseling relationship with students who have need of it.

A group can be formed for multiple counseling with a stated time limit of, say, six one-hour counseling sessions. During these six sessions the counselor proceeds to penetrate the feelings of members of the group as deeply as possible and creates, to the best of his ability, a growth-producing atmosphere. Members of the group understand the structure before they begin and accept the limit of six sessions.

Near the end of the series, group members are invited to meet with the counselor on an individual basis. Those members of the group who are not in need of, or who are not yet ready for, the individual counseling will undoubtedly profit from the experience of participating in the six group counseling sessions. On the other hand, those who are more deeply troubled will want to continue the relationship. They will have had the opportunity to begin the process of self-exploration and they will desire an opportunity to go even further.

Multiple counseling can serve as a meaningful beginning point in establishing an effective counseling relationship with individual students. Viewed in this perspective, multiple counseling can serve as a process of readiness for individual counseling but never as a substitute for an effective one-to-one relationship between client and counselor (McDaniel, 1956).

REFERENCES

Driver, Helen I. 1954. *Multiple counseling: a small group discussion method for personal growth*. Madison, Wisc.: Monona Publications.

Froelich, C. P. (no date). *Multiple counseling—a research proposal*. Berkeley, Calif.: University of California. Mimeographed.

Hobbs, N. 1951. Group-centered psychotherapy. In C. R. Rogers (ed.). *Client-centered therapy*. Boston: Houghton Mifflin.

McDaniel, H. B. 1956. *Guidance in the modern school*. New York: Holt, Rinehart and Winston.

Ohlsen, M. M. 1955. *Guidance: an introduction*. New York: Harcourt.

Slavson, S. R. (ed.). 1947. *The practice of group therapy*. New York: International Universities.

Super, D. E. 1949. Group techniques in the guidance program. *Educ. psychol. Measmt, 9,* 496–510.

Wolberg, I. 1954. *The technique of psychotherapy*. New York: Grune & Stratton.

Chapter 9

VOCATIONAL ORIENTATION
THROUGH GROUP GUIDANCE

Group guidance has proved to be one of the most effective ways of dealing with vocational problems. This chapter will present the rationale and specific objectives of the vocational orientation of group guidance and its various theories. The most common method of presenting vocations in the elementary school is analyzed and a program of vocational development through group guidance is recommended. The procedures described may be carried on by either the teacher or the counselor. However, if guidance is to be developmental in nature and reach all children, the teacher, of necessity, will take a major share of the responsibilities in this area.

The educational and vocational guidance of children requires a planned program with attention to the developmental process that begins in early childhood. Children can be helped to plan for a life in which change is expected in the individual as well as in the world of work (Borow, 1964).

GROUP GUIDANCE AND
GROUP COUNSELING

Group guidance and group counseling are differentiated in terms of content and process. Group guidance involves more structure and planning by the group leader than group counseling. It may deal with school-related topics or topics that originate with the student. While group counseling involves small groups of four to six in number, group guidance may involve the entire classroom. Group counseling is usually led by the school counselor while group guidance more often will be a function of the classroom teacher.

Glanz (1962) reviews the many catastrophic failures in the early attempts at group guidance. Often, in the past, teachers were merely informed that they were to be responsible for group guidance, and without further preparation in the group process, were then expected to proceed in supplying children with educational, occupational, or social information. This situation brought resistance from both teachers and students. Successful group guidance requires readiness on the part of teachers as well as students. Group guidance focuses on those common needs and interests which evolve when members of the group share in the planning of activities. The group guidance approach provides a series of sessions that aid pupils with personal, social, educational, and vocational problems. The general objectives of group guidance are: preventive, insofar as it provides students with assistance for normal, everyday problems before they develop into crisis situations; and developmental, insofar as it helps children share and solve many of their common developmental problems.

Group guidance helps children understand a wide range of information about themselves, their values, and the world in which they live. A complete group guidance program includes material in the personal, social, educational, and vocational areas. Some of this material—such as that developed by Ojemann —has already been referred to in Chapter 6.

Group guidance objectives may also be applied to regular instruction. The child can gain considerable experience in understanding himself, others, and the world of work in the regular subject-centered classes if teachers are cognizant of the objectives of classroom guidance (Schmidt, 1966).

THE VALUE OF VOCATIONAL INFORMATION

Advocates of the vocational orientation in the elementary school believe that work is a way of life, one of the fundamental tasks of all human beings, and that the most adequate human adjustment occurs when the nature of the work task is congruent with the aptitudes, interests, and values of the individual in question. A person's vocation is an important and unavoidable aspect of his life. Super (1952) stated:

> We believe that vocational development is the development of self-concept, that the process of vocational adjustment is a process of implementing a self-concept, and the degree of satisfaction attained is proportionate to the degree through which the self-concept has been implemented.

Choices and decisions are the products of a long-time process; they are not the inspirations of isolated moments.

The objectives of the vocational aspects of guidance in the elementary school are:

1. To increase the child's understanding of his abilities.

2. To provide the opportunity for the child's exploration of the aptitude, interest, and personality factors necessary on certain jobs.

3. To make the child aware that his self-image will determine his choice of work and way of life.

4. To assist children to develop realistic attitudes and methods in dealing with school achievement as an aspect of vocation.

5. To help pupils understand that rapid changes taking place in the world of work will necessitate advanced specialized training.

6. To help the child understand that all legitimate occupations are worthwhile.

These broad objectives must be a part of the total group guidance program and can be implemented directly by the classroom teacher (with the help of the counselor).

Hill (1965) questions the rationale for vocational information in the elementary school. He suggests that the emphasis is no longer on exact prediction of vocational choice, but that "vocational development is an ongoing, continuous, and generally irreversible process" (Super and Bachrach, 1957). Productive vocational development is thus the result of the formulation, clarification, and acceptance of realistic self-concepts. Since the forming of the self-concept starts early in life, Nelson (1962) has suggested that counselors should assist children in vocational planning early in the elementary grades.

Attitudes toward vocation and education obviously do start early in life. The children in a study by Simmons (1962) exhibited a high degree of awareness of occupational prestige. Elementary school children may be far more prepared for vocational information than had been previously assumed. Nelson (1963) demonstrated that children as low as grade three have well-developed attitudes regarding occupation and levels of education. Nelson found that children as early as ages eight or nine tend to reject some occupations as of no interest to them. The vocational thinking of children by grade six has been shown to be quite realistic (Davis, Hagan, Strouf, 1962).

THEORIES OF VOCATIONAL DEVELOPMENT

Ginzberg, Axelrod, and Herma (1951) believe that occupational choice is a developmental process taking place over a series of approximately ten years. The child's values and goals provide the basis for occupational choice. Ginzberg's findings indicate that men who made early career decisions were most successful in their vocations when they were middle-aged (Ginzberg and Herma, 1964). In Ginzberg's theory, the child is helped to explore the difference between fantasy and reality in his occupational choice.

Hoppock (1957) believes that occupations are chosen to satisfy basic needs. Choice begins as soon as the child becomes aware that occupations may meet some of his needs. In this theory, unrealistic choices result from the child's lack of information about himself and his occupational opportunities.

Super (1952) believes that the choices a person makes are means of implementing his self-concept. From this point of view, the child needs opportunities to explore, assume a variety of roles, and thus clarify his self-concept. Super has a number of vocational developmental tasks which could serve as a basis for the program.

Anne Roe (1956) has utilized the concept of a hierarchy of needs, which was originally developed by Maslow. She believes that vocational choice is based on needs that are determined by our early experiences. When a person's needs change so will his occupational preference. This information would tend to help the child understand how occupations may satisfy his needs and the advantages and disadvantages of various occupational requirements.

Vocational choice is a process rather than a single act. It occurs developmentally and is most successful when one has available knowledge of one's abilities, aptitudes, and interests. Thus, if the child understands the kind of person he is, he should be able to see his relationship to vocational opportunities.

VOCATIONS AS TRADITIONALLY PRESENTED IN THE CURRICULUM

Tennyson and Monnens (1965) investigated the way in which the world of work is presented to children by the medium of the elementary school textbooks. They found that only a small fraction of the many existing types of work were given any consideration in elementary school texts. In general, the workers presented were engaged in the principal professions and service occupations; clerical workers were seldom mentioned. Clyse (1959) also illustrated the biased picture of the world of work that children get from basal readers.

Most school teachers are more acquainted with professional, clerical, and sales work than with skilled and semiskilled work. Lifton's study (1960a) of 400 elementary school teachers showed that teachers knew most about professional fields of work. When these teachers were asked to choose occupations for which they knew educational requirements, salary, and opportunities, they listed the greatest number of occupations in the professional field, while barely mentioning skilled trades. Lifton indicated that the distribution of teachers' knowledge about jobs was almost the exact reverse of the actual distribution of jobs as listed by 1950 census data.

Lifton's (1960b) investigation of textbooks indicated that primary grade texts stress service occupations while upper grade texts emphasize professions. Little attention is given to skills or trades. Lifton calls attention to the distortion that occurs in early ideas about careers. Teachers, because of their own limited backgrounds, frequently present distorted concepts about the working world which ultimately lead to vocational maladjustment.

THE VOCATIONAL DEVELOPMENT PROGRAM

Hill (1963) indicated the importance of helping children begin early to understand the role of education and employment in their lives. He believes in systematic orientation to the role of work through instruction, individual study, and exploratory experiences. The school counselor helps teachers develop units and find materials which help to establish a developmental sequence of information in these areas.

Wrenn (1962) made the following recommendations:

In the elementary school the identification of talents and of early patterns of development is a joint responsibility of teacher, counselor, and other pupil personnel specialists. . . . Clearly also it is the responsibility of the counselor to provide realistic social and vocational orientation in the elementary school, particularly for the students who terminate their formal education at this level (p. 138).

Career and educational planning are important aspects of elementary school guidance. The actual program in the school should begin with an evaluation of the current attitude toward educational and vocational materials in the elementary school curriculum.

Units of instruction in educational and vocational areas should begin in the primary grades and present a sequence of recurring kinds of experiences related to a variety of vocations. Instruction should provide for field trips, interviews with workers, viewing of audio-visual materials, and similar experiences. The counselor might arrange for PTA meetings, group parent conferences that help parents to understand their child's problem in planning for education and vocation. The program would involve the early identification of children with special talents or special needs. A varied curriculum also permits the child to explore and discover his talents and needs.

The guidance counselor should demonstrate group guidance techniques and provide the teacher with resource material. This will require the development of a resource center which contains guidance material in the vocational, educational, personal, and social areas.

Goldman discusses the potential advantages of group guidance. He explains that the lack of success with group methods at present is due to the failure to recognize the importance of content and process. Goldman presents the approaches of three different group leaders to the same topic. Special training and supervised practice are prerequisites for effective group guidance.

Lyon summarizes the new vocational theories of Holland, Roe, Ginzberg, and Super, and notes the importance of childhood experiences in determining vocational choice and accomplishment. Vocational development is part of the child's self-concept and identification in the adult world. Lyon discusses the nature of the crucial decisions and commitments that are required at a relatively early age. She indicates that possibly children who are exposed early to occupational exploration become vocationally mature sooner than children who are not exposed, and approach education with a greater commitment even in grade school. Specific suggestions are made for programs that promote vocational maturity. Lyon also discusses the importance of the child's knowing himself and his abilities, his feeling of pride in doing a job well or exercising a talent, and having a sense of dignity in his work.

Lifton describes the failure of teachers and textbooks to meet the child's interests and informational needs. Both teachers and textbooks present a distorted picture of the world of work. He describes several new and promising developments in this area.

Arbuckle establishes that there is a paucity of material dealing with vocational guidance in the elementary school. He reviews theories of vocational development in an attempt to determine the place of occupational information in the elementary school, questioning the stress on prognosis, prediction, and the matching of a child's abilities to someone else's plan. The elementary school teacher and guidance counselor are to help the child utilize his capacity to make choices. Arbuckle believes that the best use of occupational information is exploration and that the vocational unit in the elementary school should be directed at helping children to work toward the goals of critical thinking, respect, and understanding. Occupational information is important insofar as it is able to serve to help a child become involved in the learning process.

REFERENCES

Borow, H. 1964. *Man in a world of work.* Boston: Houghton Mifflin.

Clyse, Juanita. May 1959. What do basic readers teach about jobs? *Elem. Sch. J., 59,* 456–460.

Davis, D., Nellie Hagan, and Judie Strouf. 1962. Occupational choice of twelve-year-olds. *Personnel guid. J., 40,* 628–629.

Ginzberg, E., S. Axelrod, and J. L. Herma. 1951. *Occupational choice: an approach to a general theory.* New York: Columbia University Press.

———, and J. L. Herma. 1964. *Talent and performance.* New York: Columbia University Press.

Glanz, E. 1962. *Groups in guidance.* Boston: Allyn and Bacon.

Hill, George. 1965. *Management and improvement of guidance.* New York: Appleton.

———. 1963. Guidance in elementary schools. *Clearing House, 38,* 111–116.

Hoppock, R. 1957. *Occupational information.* New York: McGraw-Hill.

Lifton, W. 1960a. Introducing the world of work to children. Teachers manual for *What could I be?* Chicago: Science Research Associates.

————. 1960b. *The elementary school's responsibility for vocational misfits.* Chicago: Science Research Associates.

Nelson, R. 1963. Knowledge and interest concerning sixteen occupations among elementary and secondary school students. *Educ. psychol. Measmt, 23,* 741–754.

————. 1962. Early versus developmental vocational choice. *Voc. guid. Quart., 11,* 23–27.

Roe, Anne. 1956. *The psychology of occupations.* New York: Wiley.

Schmidt, W. 1966. Group guidance in the elementary school. *Counsel. guid. J.,* 5 (No. 2).

Simmons, D. December 1962. Childrens' rankings of occupational prestige. *Personnel guid. J.* (No. 4).

Super, D. 1957. *Vocational development: a framework for research.* New York: Bureau of Publications, Teachers College. Columbia University.

————. September 1952. *A theory of vocational development.* Presidential address given before the American Psychological Association.

————, and P. Bachrach. 1967. *Scientific career and vocational development.* New York: Columbia University Press.

Tennyson, W., and L. Monnens. 1964. The world of work through elementary readers. *Voc. guid. Quart., 12* (No. 2).

Wrenn, C. G. 1962. *The counselor in a changing world.* Washington, D.C.: American Personnel and Guidance Association.

Group Guidance:

Content and Process*

Leo Goldman

Group methods of guidance and counseling have been at once a great hope and a great disappointment. Counselors have hoped that group methods would make it possible to use their time more efficiently for transmitting commonly-needed information and interpretations. This would be especially valuable in schools, where case loads almost universally are too large. But economy of time was only one of the hoped-for advantages. It seemed logical to expect that boys and girls, and adults too, could benefit from sharing experiences with others and exchang-

* *Personnel and Guidance Journal,* February 1962, vol. 39, no. 6. By permission.

ing ideas about the handling of their problems. For some it should be helpful just to know that their problems are not unique. From the counselor's point of view, enriched understanding of his counselees should result from the opportunity of seeing how each of them functions in the group setting. For these and other anticipated values, counselors in many settings, but especially in schools, looked to group methods for valuable contributions to a total guidance and counseling program.

Despite these presumed advantages, group methods of guidance and counseling seem to have experienced many failures, perhaps most notably in schools. Repeatedly one hears of group activities that were tried and abandoned: homeroom guidance, occupations units in classes, and special guidance and counseling groups. The reasons given for failure are many: lack of interest or ability on the part of teachers, inadequate supervision of group leaders, too large groups, and others. Some have reached the conclusion that group methods are just not suitable for the attainment of guidance goals. Yet there are several books which contain guidelines for effective work with groups and at least some evidence that group methods are useful (Bennett, 1955; Forrester, 1951; Hoppock, 1949; Warters, 1960).

Why then have there been so many unhappy experiences with group methods of guidance and counseling? In the observation of the writer, there seems to have been in many instances a lack of understanding of the roles of *content* and *process* (Goldman, 1954). The crux of the position being taken here is that too many group guidance activities have been guidance only in their contents; the process has often not been suitable.

CONTENT AND PROCESS

Table 1 shows the two dimensions: content across the rows and process down the columns. In each instance, the total range is divided for convenience of discussion into three parts, but this is arbitrary. Each dimension should be seen as a continuum which could with equal logic be divided into two parts or ten.

Content. Going down the rows, we move from the usual academic subjects—mathematics, literature, and all the others which are universally accepted as school curricular content—to topics at the other extreme, which are in many places considered to be off-limits, topics such as dating behavior or parent-child relations. Between the extremes are the school-related topics such as educational and vocational opportunities, which, though not academic subjects, are usually accepted as belonging somewhere in the school's total curriculum.

Process. Moving from left to right we go from the more traditional, teacher-directed methods to those which give pupils more responsibility for planning and conducting classroom activities. Also, as we go across the columns, there is decreasing emphasis on cognitive elements and increasing emphasis first on atti-

TABLE 1/ INTERACTION OF CONTENT AND PROCESS IN GROUP
GUIDANCE, GROUP COUNSELING, AND GROUP THERAPY

	PROCESS		
	Level I	Level II	Level III
	Leader plans topics	Leader and group members collaborate in planning topics	Topics originate with group members
Content	Lecture and recitation	Discussions, projects, panels, visits	Free discussion, role-playing
	Facts and skills emphasized	Attitudes and opinions emphasized	Feelings and needs emphasized
	Units in regular classes	Separate guidance groups meet on schedule	Groups organized as needed, meet as needed
Type A Usual school subject-matter mathematics, English, etc.	1	4	7
Type B School-related topics: the world of work, choosing a college, how to study, etc.	2	5	8
Type C Non-school topics: dating behavior, parent-child relations, handling frustrations, etc.	3	6	9

tudes and opinions, and later on deeper feelings. The manner of forming the groups is also seen to differ. Finally, perhaps the best indicator of differences among these processes is the kind of evaluative questions one asks. At Level I, the questions are likely to be: How much does he know? How much skill has he developed? At Level II, the questions are more likely to be such as these: Does he have well-developed and well-substantiated opinions? Have his attitudes changed or developed? And at Level III the questions would be: How does he behave in relation to peers or parents? How realistic a degree of self-acceptance does he have? It seems clear that Levels II and III contain more of the elements of guidance and counseling, while Level I has more of those which are appropriate to instruction.

INTERACTION OF
CONTENT AND PROCESS

To illustrate the interaction of the two dimensions, we will see how three different group leaders might handle the same guidance topic: choosing a high school course of study.

1. Mr. Jones includes a unit on choosing a high school course of study in his eighth-grade English classes. He decides early in the school year which week he will devote to this unit. He introduces the topic one day, pointing out its importance and asking questions to see how much thinking the pupils have already done. Then he assigns some readings in a series of guidance publications. During the next few class meetings he makes sure that the class understands what each of the courses of study consists of—academic, general, commercial, and vocational—and for what kinds of occupations each is suitable. He urges the boys and girls to be realistic in their choices. In particular he points out that pupils sometimes make poor choices because they are too concerned with prestige or doing what their friends do. (This approach would seem to fit most closely the content-process interaction of cell 2, a combination of Type B content with a Level I process.)

2. Mr. Smith meets each eighth-grade class one period each week to discuss various guidance topics. The problem of selecting a high school course of study almost always comes up naturally in each group as they discuss their future plans. At that point Mr. Smith helps the class to decide what information they need and how they will go about collecting it. The specific methods vary somewhat from class to class, but generally the pupils divide among themselves a variety of readings, visits, and interviews in order to learn about the courses of study they are thinking about. Then they bring their various findings to class and discuss both the facts and their opinions about the advantages and disadvantages of different courses for different people. Usually each one tells about his own preferences and the reasons for them, and the others comment or raise questions. Mr. Smith tries to get each pupil to think about his educational plans in the light of his previous school history, his parents' values, and other factors. He will often raise thought-provoking questions and will sometimes correct inaccurate information. (This approach seems to be a combination of Type B content and a Level II process and therefore would be a cell 5 interaction.)

3. Mr. Brown sets up groups for multiple counseling whenever he recognizes common needs among several of his counselees. He has just organized a group of youngsters who are indecisive or in conflict about their high school course of study. They have worked out a schedule to meet twice a week for as many weeks as necessary. During the meetings Mr. Brown encourages each pupil to describe his own problem to the group and to explore it in some depth. Some of the youngsters tell about parental pressures, and others describe their feelings of inadequacy. Sometimes two or three find that they have very similar problems. Together they try to understand the factors that are operating and then try out

on each other suggestions for dealing with their problems. Sometimes a boy or girl finds reassurance just in the knowledge that someone else faces a very similar problem. Mr. Brown makes occasional interpretations and reflections, and sometimes he suggests that they role-play a problem situation or a solution that someone has proposed. When the pupils or Mr. Brown feel that information is needed regarding the courses of study or related occupations, they decide how to obtain the information. The group disbands whenever it appears to the pupils and Mr. Brown that their purposes have been fulfilled. (This approach would seem to belong in cell 8 or 9, since it involves Type B or perhaps C content, with a Level III process.)

FROM TEACHING TO GUIDANCE ACTIVITY

The illustrations used show how three different kinds of process might be applied to one of the common group guidance topics. Similar illustrations could be developed for other topics such as dating behavior, study habits, or career planning.

The thesis here is that for a group activity to move from the teaching of a school subject to a guidance activity requires changes both of content and process. Referring to Table 1, the movement is diagonally from upper-left to lower-right. In cell 1 would be found the kind of classroom that is probably typical at the college level and that decreases in frequency of occurrence as one moves backward through secondary and elementary schools. At the other extreme, in cell 9, is the kind of activity that is usually referred to as group therapy. Somewhere around cell 5 is what the writer would call group guidance; in cells 6 and 8 are the activities that he would identify with the label "group counseling" or "multiple counseling." Others prefer to define these terms differently and would therefore place them differently among the cells.

In the writer's observations, group guidance and group counseling have in many instances gone awry in schools because they have been cell 2 and 3 kinds of operations, such as those conducted by Mr. Jones in the first of the three illustrations. The group leaders have usually been classroom teachers, many of them without any special training in guidance, who spend only a fraction of their time in this so-called guidance activity, be it in a homeroom, a unit of an academic subject, or a once-a-week "guidance" or "occupations" class. It should not surprise us, then, that they use much the same approach in their guidance activities as in the classroom: assigning readings in textbooks, asking pupils to recite in the class, doing much explaining, advising, and exhorting, and even giving grades at the end of a unit or course. Imagine, a grade in "Guidance!"

Even well-trained guidance counselors often find it difficult to depart from Level I in their group guidance work. They too have had their group leadership experience as teachers in subject-matter classrooms. Unfortunately, they receive little preparation for group guidance activities in most counselor-education programs; supervised practice in group guidance or group counseling is almost unheard of. It is understandable, then, that even professional, full-time counselors find it difficult to shift to Level II and III approaches.

What seems to happen in many schools, then, is that "group guidance" becomes merely another academic subject. Yet counselors, teachers, and administrators sometimes expect Level II or III outcomes, such as more realistic planning, changes of attitude, and even changes of observed behavior. When these outcomes are not obtained, too often "group guidance" is denounced as the culprit.

TEACHING AT LEVELS II AND III

To complete the analysis of Table 1, we should note that not all teachers use Level 1 methods exclusively. There are English teachers who use a novel or play to help pupils to understand their own motivations and problems. There are home economics teachers who use a variety of methods to sharpen and develop children's understandings of the roles of various family members. There are social studies teachers who stimulate youngsters to explore opinions, attitudes, and prejudices regarding political and economic matters. One might say that all of these teachers are performing guidance kinds of functions. The writer would prefer to regard these rather as a variety of teaching—an excellent variety indeed. The term Guidance, with a capital G, might better be reserved for those activities which are guidance both in content and process.

The purpose here is not to segregate teaching from guidance but simply to maintain a meaningful distinction between the *major* functions of teachers and guidance specialists in today's schools. Admittedly, the distinction is not perfect, since good teachers sometimes operate at Levels II and III, and good guidance workers sometimes operate at Level I. When one compares the work of teachers as a whole with that of guidance workers as a whole, however, the distinction has validity and serves a useful purpose.

SUMMARY AND CONCLUSIONS

Group methods in guidance are differentiated from teaching both in their contents and in the processes by which the contents are handled. Too often guidance groups seem to differ from subject-matter classes only in their contents. This may be one of the major reasons for the failure of so many homeroom and other group guidance enterprises. It seems clear that group guidance, group counseling, and group therapy, as these terms are used here, require special training, including supervised practice. Even with such training, it seems doubtful that many classroom teachers will be able to make the transition from the processes that are appropriate to teaching to those that are more appropriate to guidance. Instead it would appear to be necessary that group guidance and group counseling be done only by those who do not concurrently have normal classroom teaching responsibilities.

REFERENCES

Bennett, Margaret E. 1955. *Guidance in groups*. New York: McGraw-Hill.

Forrester, Gertrude. 1951. *Methods of vocational guidance*. Boston: Heath.

Goldman, L. 1954. Counseling: content and process. *Personnel guid. J., 23*, 82–85.

Hoppock, R. 1949. *Group guidance*. New York: McGraw-Hill.

Warters, Jane. 1960. *Group guidance*. New York: McGraw-Hill.

Vocational Development
and the Elementary School*

Rhee Lyon

In 1962, Ruth Barry and Beverly Wolf, of Columbia University, wrote an *Epitaph for Vocational Guidance*. In that slender volume with a strong title the authors argued vigorously that vocational choice could not be adequately handled by a visit to a specialist who matched person to occupation by way of tests. Vocational guidance conducted in that way is presumed dead, although we know that in reality it still flourishes, and lucratively at that. In its place, however, Barry Wolf, and many others interested in vocations, have advocated an integrated concept of counseling which would be available to individuals throughout their lifetime. Vocational theories now view occupational choice as a long process interwoven with life as a whole. New vocational counseling uses developmental psychology, self-theory, and motivational psychology as well as tests, labor market statistics, and job descriptions.

I would like to summarize the new vocational theories and to indicate their implications for those who work with elementary school children, for interestingly enough, the more these theories are explored through research, the greater the indications are that childhood experiences have an important impact on vocational choice and accomplishment.

HOLLAND: OCCUPATIONAL ENVIRONMENT

On first inspection, the work of Holland (1959) appears to resemble the old vocational guidance because of his interest in developing tests that will help

* *Elementary School Journal*, April 1966, vol. 66, no. 7. Copyright 1966 by The University of Chicago Press. By permission.

to match people to the most compatible jobs. Although his approach is in line with the use of vocational interest tests such as the Kuder Preference Record and the Strong Vocational Interest Blank, it is far more comprehensive in scope.

Holland has classified "occupational environments" into six major groups: motoric, intellectual, supportive, conforming, persuasive, and esthetic. He believes that people have adjustive orientations to life, distinctive life styles characterized by preferred methods of dealing with daily problems, and that these orientations correspond to the major occupational environments. Although Holland does not explain how a person develops the life style, childhood experiences must certainly play a major role. His description of the supportive orientation illustrates how strongly Holland relies on a motivational psychology of careers:

> Persons of this [supportive] orientation prefer teaching or therapeutic roles, which may reflect a desire for attention and socialization in a structured, and therefore, safe, setting. They possess verbal and interpersonal skills. They are also characterized as responsible, socially oriented and accepting of feminine impulses and roles. Their chief values are humanistic and religious. They are threatened by and avoid situations requiring intellectual problem-solving, physical skills or highly ordered activities, since they prefer to deal with problems through feeling and interpersonal manipulations of others. Persons of this class are best typified as orally dependent in the sense of being verbal, feminine and dependent (pp. 35–45).

Vocational choice is bounded by the occupations available to the individual in his preferred orientation, by his ability to perform adequately, by his self-evaluation, and by a host of other factors such as his knowledge of occupational classes, social pressures from family and peers, and limitations imposed by the environment. Holland has put forth a number of hypotheses on how adequate choices are made. In particular he believes that self-knowledge and occupational knowledge increase the accuracy and adequacy of choices. External influences such as opportunity and social pressures operate most strongly on people who have no clear orientational preference. Social influence seems to be most crucial in early adolescence because preferences have not yet been well integrated. Holland's theories provide a rich source for research ideas, but he appears to be most concerned with the development of inventories which will more accurately assess occupational choice. He does acknowledge, however, that research on aspects of childhood is ultimately necessary if we are to learn how interests and life styles grow.

ROE: ORIGIN OF INTERESTS

Using Maslow's theory that a hierarchy of needs exists within each of us, Roe (1956) has observed that occupation can be the channel for achieving not only what she calls "lower-order" needs, such as safety and security, but also higher needs such as self-esteem, independence, and self-actualization. Roe has not undertaken research to test this theory, but recent studies by Hertzberg

(1959), an industrial psychologist, have produced data linking Maslow's hierarchy of needs to levels of job satisfaction. Hertzberg's respondents indicated that certain aspects of their employment (for example, low pay, lack of security, incompatible social environment) could produce dissatisfaction. These aspects relate directly to elements in Maslow's lower-order needs. Yet, even if conditions causing dissatisfaction are remedied, the respondents could not be counted on to rate themselves as satisfied. Satisfaction could come only from the more intrinsic response to job content, degree of involvement, and the nature of recognition given to the worker. These conditions closely fit the higher-order needs of esteem and self-actualization (Hertzberg, Mausner and Snyderman, 1959).

Roe's (1957) major interest recently has been in discovering how occupational interests are formed. In 1957 she postulated that family environment and the quality of child care would make a difference in whether a person in his adult life would choose a people-centered or a thing-centered occupational field. This carefully specified theory has been tested with largely negative results. Roe and Siegelman (1964) have recently published the latest of the findings which indicated that, contrary to expectations, men engineers reported warm, loving memories of home life, while men social workers reported impaired parental relationships. Women engineers identified with their fathers and differed from their male counterparts in having an unusual amount of childhood difficulties to surmount. Despite these interesting findings which point to family influence, Roe seems to have despaired of deriving a theory based on early childhood experiences. She writes:

> Does our data offer any suggestions for a psychology of occupations? It is a plausible guess that in a reasonably good labor market an individual with the modal socio-economic background and education and with abilities, interests and other factors within the middle range of the population, will make his occupational choices well within those occupations that are most typical for his sex. Chance may play a major role. . . . In the case of socio-economic factors, membership in upper or lower classes practically precludes certain (different) occupations unless other factors are so extreme as to outweigh the influence of the background (Roe and Siegelman, 1964).

Not all motivational theorists have felt obliged to turn to sociological explanations, however. We have seen that Holland relied heavily on the concept of interest reflecting deep psychological needs. Many of his examples are couched in terms coined by Freud, Adler, Horney, and Fromm. Nachman (1960) is representative of a group which seeks to test Freudian concepts concerning the sublimation and expression of basic needs through work. She reports interesting findings on apparent links between family disciplinary measures and the choice of law, dentistry, and social work.

It certainly would be safe to say that childhood experiences do contribute to differentiations in capacities and motives for vocations and that these in turn are crucial in vocational choice. The relative strengths of various factors—genetic, familiar, social, and cultural—remain a puzzle, however.

GINZBERG: VOCATIONAL COMPROMISE

The decade of the 1950's was a period of great activity in the growth of vocational counseling concepts. Eli Ginzberg and his associates were among the earliest writers to report on research indicating that vocational choice is a long process, involving a series of decisions and following a discernible developmental pattern (Ginzberg, 1952; Ginzberg, Ginsberg, Axelrod, and Herma. 1951). Ginzberg also noted that the process is largely irreversible unless the individual is prepared to exert great efforts, and that it is characterized by compromise as the individual learns about occupational demands.

Three stages of choice have been generalized from research by Ginzberg: First, until a child is about eleven years old, his choices are characterized as being in the realm of fantasy; that is, he believes that he can become whatever he wants. Second, the junior high and senior high school period, encompassing ages eleven through seventeen, finds a number of students making tentative choices, using such guides as interests, capacities, and values, in that order of maturity. Finally, after age seventeen, the period of realistic choice is thrust on the adolescent, for he is made most keenly aware of limitations as his ambitions connect with such realities as opportunity for higher education and the evaluations of employers. He must explore alternatives, crystallize a general choice, and then eventually make even more minute specifications in this age of specialization.

Ginzberg has found that the time of crystallization will vary according to how early an individual finds a talent which becomes a vehicle for occupational choice. Some young people achieve a singleness of purpose at an early date, while others move gradually through the pattern of vocational compromise. Certain deviations from the pattern can be construed as danger signals, however. If, for instance, a seventeen-year-old is still operating on the fantasy level or interest level common to younger children, one may expect trouble because his actual situation will be demanding mature decisions. Some individuals will seem unable to make choices, a condition which Ginzberg attributes to a pathological passivity or a pleasure orientation that makes any work discipline distasteful.

Ginzberg and Herma's latest report (1964) compiled from records and replies of past fellowship holders at Columbia University indicates that those men who had made early career decisions concerning field of entry were the most successful in their jobs at mid-life. While it is wise to remember that premature vocational commitments may produce unsatisfactory results, Ginzberg's report does serve to remind us that an early adequate commitment can be most advantageous. Getting the individual to the point where his self-knowledge and occupational knowledge insure adequacy of choice is, of course, a central problem.

SUPER: VOCATIONAL MATURITY

Donald Super has found a similar pattern in vocational development; however, his theory is perhaps more psychological than that of economist Ginzberg. Whether we call it ego psychology or self-theory, for Super (1963) vocational development theory is related to a general development theory of the emerging self. Although Super has elaborated on career stages and patterns through the complete life span, his analysis of the early years is quite similar to that of Ginzberg: the fantasy period during the years from four to ten, and capacity taking meaningful shape from eleven to fourteen, and the period of exploration ranging from fifteen to twenty-four (Super, 1956–1957).

More recently Super (1960) became interested in investigating the earliest "post-fantasy" stage and undertook a study on the vocational maturity of ninth-grade boys. The indices he established for judging vocational maturity were the boys' concern about making vocational choices, their acceptance of responsibility for choices and planning, specificity of information about preferred occupations, specificity of planning for preferred occupation, and use of resources in orientation to vocational choice. Super found that the ninth-grade boys did not rate very high on maturity or even logical consistency. He sounded this as a warning to counselors who might be trying to promote vocational choice at this early age and indicated that the best policy was to keep vocational objectives general and a variety of avenues open for exploration.

THE TASK OF THE ELEMENTARY SCHOOL

If a child is in the fantasy stage of vocational development during the elementary school years, and if the quality of his family relationships is the true channel to occupational orientation, what possible role does the elementary school teacher or counselor need to play in vocational choice? Would it be best to let vocational pressures wait and concentrate on developing academic and social capacities? Are immediate developmental tasks, such as forming friendships or developing appropriate sex identification, more pressing? Why should vocational developmental tasks be anticipated in the elementary school if it is true, as Super indicates, that at age fourteen the best policy is still one of keeping many avenues open?

Questions such as these remain pertinent and valid, and yet it is obvious that genetic and family background do not operate unmitigated by such social conditions as educational requirements, unemployment rates, and knowledge of "the ropes" to a career. Furthermore, it should be emphasized that the new developmental theories concerning vocation are not tied to physical maturation; vocational interest does not suddenly arrive at puberty along with interest in the opposite sex. From the start, vocational development is part and parcel of the growing child's self-concept, his identifications in the adult world, his expectations concerning the rewards of work, and even the clarity of his perception of American society.

There is another reason for early concern: Our modern society has not carefully geared its educational system to fit the vocational maturation rates of individuals. It is exceedingly difficult for young people to move in and out of high school or college, approaching the educational experience when they are ripe to use it vocationally. Crucial decisions and commitments are required at a relatively early age; and if a child sees his education as a burden to cast off rather than as a ladder leading somewhere, he is not likely to use the resources at hand when they are most conveniently offered. We know, for example, that the pattern of underachievement which for boys begins in third grade is an accelerating one, difficult to break (Shaw and McCuen, 1960). Yet these boys are faced with the choice of entering the college preparatory program at age fourteen, one of those almost irreversible decisions that determines one's social and economic positions as an adult. It is possible that children who become vocationally mature through earlier contacts with occupational exploration would approach education with a greater commitment, even in the grade schools.

When we consider again Super's findings on the vocational maturity of fourteen-year-olds, we discover that not everyone emerges from the fantasy period at the same time or at the same rate. Certain boys in his study proved to be more vocationally mature than others. Maturity appeared to be associated with the following background characteristics:

> The boy lived in an intellectually and culturally stimulating environment.
>
> He had the mental ability essential for responding to that environment.
>
> He responded with aspirations to higher rather than lower socioeconomic occupational levels.
>
> He was achieving well in his current activities.

At what point in this chain of factors vocational maturity enters is not clear. That is, we do not know whether it is a cause or an effect of the last two factors listed. Nevertheless, the boys who are vocationally mature at age fourteen are at a distinct advantage in being able to use the school's resources. Not surprisingly, the intellectual quality of their home life seems to have speeded maturity, although it had not pushed them into a premature decision.

Super has noted that children tend to enter occupations at the same socioeconomic level as that of their parents. Leaving that level and moving up seems to depend on the parents' resources, contacts, information, and values. To put it another way, some boys are able to plan for themselves in the world of work at an earlier age because they are more knowledgeable about that world. They see adults actively pursuing careers. If they do not intend to follow in their father's footsteps, they are ready to take responsibility in formulating their own alternatives. In short, their approach to careers is an active, inquiring, knowledgeable one. The point to be made here is that programs in the elementary school could simulate the guidance processes that occur in the homes of advantaged boys.

The problem is most severe, of course, for slum dwellers, rural or urban, who may not know intimately a working adult who is engrossed in his vocation. While their knowledge of slum culture may be extensive, this hardly serves them in selecting an optimum vocation and planning to make it a reality. For the upper socioeconomic classes, the choice of the college preparatory track is almost automatic, compelled by class expectancies. This is certainly one major advantage because the vocationally immature upper-class boy automatically keeps many avenues open while he moves through the academic program. Krippner (1965), in his study of upper-middle-class students attending junior high school, found parental and class expectations so pervasive that even pupil dislike of school and poor achievement did not deter college planning. Yet those of us who have worked with economically advantaged youths recognize that many are listless in their approach to high-school learning and vocational choice; economic advantage does not guarantee a culturally and intellectually stimulating home. The amount of vocational information held by these advantaged children (a number of whom may be even too apathetic to take responsibility for finding a suitable college for themselves) is often severely restricted. It is not difficult to find sons of wealthy men who do not know what their fathers really do on the job, or what it is that makes an occupation fulfilling. If they spend time with adult men, it is most often in the pursuit of leisure activities, and most of the jobs they can hold or observe are meant for minors or offer no career possibilities. One discovers that such boys, like many a lower-class youth, do not know how to translate their interests into an occupational image and that their understanding of the rewards of work is limited to money. Thus, the economically advantaged youth can exhibit a vocational immaturity surprisingly similar to that of the lower-class youth—although we know that somehow the advantaged youth usually manages to find something that will allow him to retain class membership.

What, then, is to be done for the many adolescents who lack aspirations and commitments or believe vaguely in the American dream but are confused about the means for moving toward it? For these young people vocational information files, labor market statistics, and even test results are so inadequate as to be almost useless.

Super (1957) has written, "To know oneself, what one has to sell, is important; it is also important to know the world of work, to know what one can do that employers will pay for." To that we might add, perhaps even more basic is to feel the integrity involved in doing a job well and exercising a talent; to comprehend the dignity of work; to discover how vocation can be a route to self-actualization. Such knowledge and attitudes cannot be handed out in lectures and brochures shortly before each important vocational decision. It is even quite possible—as longitudinal studies seem to indicate—that by adolescence the attitudes we have discussed must already have been incorporated into the self-concept if they are to operate effectively in later life.

SOME PROGRAM SUGGESTIONS

It should be said again that the purpose of vocational concern in the elementary school is not to speed a definitive occupational choice. The purpose may well be to foster self-knowledge, particularly in relation to the world of work. As the child emerges from the fantasy period, he can begin to use his preferences as springboards for discovering how his orientation to life might be translated into vocation.

Academically, programs to explore vocations can be sound, although assembling such programs depends on the teacher's ingenuity. The lack of material and the logic of deferring concern until a more "appropriate age" have produced a situation in which it is easier to learn about the historical, geographical, and natural world in the elementary school than it is to understand the economic, sociological, and psychological aspects of the world of work. The study of biographies and industries is an obvious example for even a traditional curriculum. A less conventional approach might focus on social problems such as automation or equal opportunity. An introduction to the scientific method might include attention to the occupational demands of scientists and the many fields and levels of responsibility encompassed by the term *scientist*. Field trips and guest speakers can also be effective, particularly if the speakers are not limited to high-status professional men.

Possibly the easiest areas to cover are in the realm of general information, but as we have seen, vocational theories rate psychological aspects such as interests, abilities, work attitudes, and personality types as extremely important. These aspects are less easily integrated into the regular curriculum and are more often placed in the domain of group guidance. We are not sure when and how work attitudes grow, and we seem to feel that values are more easily "caught" than systematically analyzed in the classroom. Certainly mouthing values such as "the dignity of work" will not cause a child to incorporate them into his personal make-up. The difficulty in getting at values and self-exploration is pointed up in a report by Kaback (1960) on a program designed to introduce occupational information to children in elementary school. The children were told to investigate jobs in their community, and the list of questions, while commendable, will indicate how easy it is to avoid values and evaluation. The reports were to compile the following data:

How many different jobs are there in the community?
How many people are employed in each job?
What is the nature of the work done?
Are certain jobs declining or expanding?
What are the educational and training requirements?
How does one get the jobs?

What opportunities are there for advancement?

What are the weekly or monthly earnings, the vacation time and health insurance benefits?

Missing from the report are such questions as: Why do people work? Do different people give different reasons? What do people in different occupations say they like best about their jobs? What do they like least? Would they choose something different if they could start again? What is an interest? How does it differ from a talent? Why would you work? Are there any jobs you are sure you would not like? Why? Are there any occupations you would like but think you cannot enter?

One excellent series devised by Lifton (1962) has managed to combine a variety of approaches in a program for Grades 6–9. This program includes a workbook with sections that require thought on such questions as: Who are you? What do you like to do? What is a job? What are job families? What good is school? Three hundred occupational briefs are available; each devotes two pages in story form to the worker, ranging from the unskilled to the professional. Another section is devoted to job facts, including projections into the future. Specialized bibliographies are also provided.

Occupational interests are an uncharted course in the curriculum of the elementary school. Those who are interested in the developmental approach to childhood education may agree that it is time to concern ourselves with the promotion of vocational maturity.

REFERENCES

Barry, Ruth, and Beverly Wolf. 1962. *Epitaph for vocational guidance*. New York: Bureau of Publications, Teachers College, Columbia University.

Ginzberg, E. April 1952. Toward a theory of occupational choice. *Occupations*, *30*, 491–494.

————, S. W. Ginsberg, S. Axelrod, and J. L. Herma. 1951. *Occupational choice: an approach to a general theory*. New York: Columbia University Press.

————, and J. L. Herma. 1964. *Talent and performance*. New York: Columbia University Press.

Hertzberg, F., B. Mausner, and B. Snyderman. 1959. *The motivation to work*. New York: Wiley.

Holland, J. L. Spring 1959. A theory of vocational choice. *J. counsel. Psychol.*, *6*, 35–45.

Kaback, Goldie R. 1960. Occupational information in elementary education. *Voc. guid. Quart.*, *9*, 55–59.

Krippner, S. 1965. The educational plans and preferences of upper-middle class junior high school pupils. *Voc. guid. Quart.*, *13*, 257–260.

Lifton, W. M. 1962. *Work (widening occupational roles kit)*. Chicago: Science Research Associates.

Nachman, Barbara. Winter 1960. Childhood experience and vocational dentistry and social work. *J. counsel. Psychol.*, 7, 243–250.

Roe, Anne. Fall 1957. Early determinants of vocational choice. *J. counsel. Psychol.*, 4, 212–217.

———. 1956. *The psychology of occupations.* New York: Wiley.

———, and M. L. Siegelman. 1964. *The origin of interests.* Washington, D.C.: American Personnel and Guidance Association.

Shaw, M. C., and J. T. McCuen. June 1960. The onset of academic underachievement in bright children. *J. educ. Psychol.*, 51, 103–108.

Super, D. E. 1957. *The psychology of careers.* New York: Harper & Row.

———. Winter 1956. Vocational development: the process of compromise or synthesis. *J. counsel. Psychol.*, 3, 249–253.

——— et al. 1963. *Career development: self concept theory.* New York: College Entrance Examination Board.

———, and P. L. Overstreet. 1960. *The vocational majority of ninth-grade boys.* New York: Bureau of Publications, Teachers College, Columbia University.

Vocational Guidance

in the Elementary School*

Walter M. Lifton

The swell in the number of textbooks written for people involved in guidance in elementary schools is but one indication of the increasing concern of professional workers with their responsibility for providing help at this level. Counselor Trainers find that an increasing proportion of their classes contain students working in the elementary schools. This article is devoted specifically to a discussion of the role and use of vocational guidance in the elementary grades.

THE GROWING CONCERN

For some time now writers in the field have pointed out the marked discrepancy between children's concerns and the manner in which the textbooks and teachers meet them. Specifically, Bennett (1955, in evaluating the results of the

* *Vocational Guidance Quarterly*, Winter 1959. By permission.

Midwest Conference of State Supervisors of Guidance Services and Counselor Trainers held in 1950, as well as the results of the SRA Junior Inventory, points up the real and growing concern of youngsters over their academic and vocational future. She documents clearly the fact that, based on SRA Junior Inventory responses, their answers to the question "I'd like to know what I'm going to be when I grow up" remained approximately the same from grades 4 through 8, accounting for 38, 41, 38, 36, and 40 percent, respectively, of responses for each grade.

Hoppock (1957), beyond suggesting ways occupational concepts could be introduced into the schools, points up the need to integrate the presentation of the material into the existing curricula of the schools. Certainly the incorporation of any data into the curriculum today is dependent on both parent and teacher attitude. With this in mind, two studies are worth reviewing.

Shores and Rudman (1954) surveyed 270 communities to see how closely parents', teachers', librarians', and children's evaluation of children's reading interests and informational needs (grades 4-8) coincided. A few of their results are cited. They found that girls more frequently than boys wanted to ask about horses, dogs, vocations, boy-girl relationships, ethics, values, and religion. Parents show a particularly strong desire for children to ask questions about vocations. Teachers are more concerned with social skills. It is also possible that teachers consider the elementary school years as inappropriate for serious concern with vocations. They also found that children are not necessarily interested in asking about the same things that they wanted to read about.

AN EXPLORATORY STUDY

The second study was conducted by the author. It was concerned with the implication that teachers might not be aware of the early age at which attitudes and values about the world of work begin to crystallize. It was also concerned with the emphasis on vocations, in terms of career planning, rather than utilizing the elementary grades as a place where curiosity about the world might help broaden a youngster's perspective.

Two beginning classes in guidance provided subjects for the survey. The students in these classes were primarily teachers in the elementary schools and did not plan on professional guidance careers but wished instead to increase their classroom effectiveness. Each teacher was asked to consider which occupations they could use as illustrations of classroom concepts. To insure real occupational sophistication they were restricted to only those jobs for which they knew training requirements, salary levels, and job opportunities. Using the Dictionary of Occupational Titles categories their responses were tallied. Professions led the list by far, followed by sales and clerical tasks, with skilled trades barely showing. The job distribution was almost the exact reverse of the distribution of jobs resulting from census data.

The teachers were then asked to go through all of the books used in their classes and to make a list of any occupation used as an illustration. Again the results were fascinating.

In the primary grades there was a heavy emphasis on service occupations. There was then a rapid shift in the upper grades to the professions, with the skilled trades again being barely represented. In other words, from both their teachers and their texts youngsters were receiving a distorted picture of the importance and types of jobs available.

Realizing that these teachers could not help youngsters secure a true picture of the world of work if their own experiences and textbooks did not offer help, the author then began a survey of books available in the area of occupations to develop a list teachers could use to supplement their background. Again the results were surprising. From a series of books for the early primary grades published by Children's Press there appears to be a complete vacuum until books for junior high school youngsters like the Dodds Meade series occur. To verify this finding, the author approached several major book publishers to explore their interest in books describing the world of work and designed for grades 3–6. Repeatedly, the answer given was that they did not have, nor did they plan to publish, books of this type because "children are not interested in vocations."

SERIOUS QUESTIONS ARISE

All of these results raise for guidance counselors several serious questions. If these results based upon small samples hold true, in more controlled studies several avenues are available to the profession to improve the situation. Guidance supervisors might encourage teachers to engage in more field trips where the emphasis of both pupils and teachers would be directed on the workers and the skills they utilize. Parents might be encouraged to come to school and share with the children information about their jobs. Teachers could be encouraged to seek different types of employment during summers. Publishers could be encouraged to put out materials which they then could be sure of selling.

The above material suggests a rather negative picture. There are several recent advances, however, worth noting. Several of the leading encyclopedias have completed major revisions of their entries on careers and vocations. In almost all cases the number of pages allotted has been vastly increased. At least two publishers utilize a guidance consultant to insure that all articles in their encyclopedias present a more realistic picture of the world of work and job opportunities. One anthological encyclopedia, *Our Wonderful World*, has introduced a vocational game, which appears throughout the volumes. The game is designed to help children see how their interests persist from one industry to another. They also are given a chance to think about work activities on several hundred jobs. Recently, a social studies series (McIntire and Hill, 1954) on the third-grade level, focused on "working together," utilized skilled trades among their many examples. There is a book on the world of work for use in grades four to five now being given a pilot run in three cities to test children's interest and the correct placing of this kind of material. One city system has developed a course (Burack, no date) for use in grades seven to eight to help children who may not be continuing on to high school.

It is obvious that many questions requiring research have been raised. Equally necessary is the development of texts to meet the developing needs of schools for vocational guidance materials. If the age-old concept of guidance as a lifelong process is to remain true, greater attention to the role of the elementary school can no longer be delayed.

REFERENCES

Bennett, Margaret. 1955. *Guidance in groups.* New York: McGraw-Hill.

Burack, M. (no date). Unpublished course materials for City of Chicago elementary schools course on vocations, grades 7–8.

Hoppock, R. 1957. *Occupational information.* New York: McGraw-Hill.

Lifton, W. M. 1960. *What could I be?* Chicago: Science Research Associates.

———. 1957. Ask yourself. In *Our wonderful world.* Chicago: Spencer Press.

McIntire, Alta, and Wilhelmina Hill. 1954. *Working together.* Chicago: Follett.

National Association of Guidance Supervisors and Counselor Trainers. 1953. *A national study of existing and recommended practices for assisting youth adjustment in selected elementary schools of the United States.* Ann Arbor, Mich.: Ann Arbor Publishers.

Rudman, H. C. 1954. *Interrelationships among various aspects of children's interest and informational needs and expectations of teachers, parents, and librarians.* Urbana, Ill.: University of Illinois. Doctoral dissertation.

Shores, H. J., and H. C. Rudman. 1954. *What children are interested in.* Champaign, Ill.: Spencer Press.

Occupational Information
in the Elementary School*

Dugald S. Arbuckle

At first sight, this appears to be a rather dull and pointless topic, a topic about which a person could write little. I could, of course, indicate that we must integrate occupational information into the elementary school curriculum, that

* *Vocational and Guidance Quarterly,* Winter 1963–1964, vol. 12, no. 2. This paper was presented at the 1963 APGA Convention in Boston. By permission.

teachers must be less occupationally naïve, that textbooks should be more occupationally realistic, and that we need to have work experiences at the elementary level so that children may learn that it is just as honorable to be a garbage man as it is to be a teacher, even though no teachers want to be garbage men, and don't even associate with garbage men. But everyone seems to know this, for this is about all that is found in guidance and counseling literature.

The *Review of Educational Research* for April, 1960, contains 73 references to occupational and educational information with only one reference to the elementary school. Perhaps the author of the chapter was guilty of inner frame of reference reading, or perhaps there wasn't really much to report. In the last eight years of the *Vocational Guidance Quarterly*, there were only four articles dealing with vocational guidance in the elementary school. There was an equal paucity of material in ten years of *The Personnel and Guidance Journal*, where only two articles dealing with vocational guidance in the elementary school were found.

Nor is there much to be found in representative textbooks. In 84 articles in a book of readings by Farwell and Peters (1960), there were five articles dealing with elementary school guidance, but nothing on the place of occupational information in the elementary school. This was also true of a book by Johnson, Stefflre, and Edelfeldt (1961). Gilbert Wrenn's (1962) recent opus paid little attention to the elementary school counselor in a changing world. In Willey's (1960) book there were no references whatsoever, and a blank was also drawn in a book by Bernard, James, and Zeran (1956). Cottingham (1956), Barry (1958), and Crow and Crow (1962) made only the most fleeting of references to the place of occupational information in elementary school guidance in their books. All of these, it should be noted, are books dealing specifically with guidance in the elementary school.

At this point, one might wonder if this indicates that all these writers were missing something, or is it just that there is not much to write about when it comes to the place of occupational information in a program of elementary school guidance? From my reading, however, I did get some impressions.

SPECIFICS ARE EASY

Specific answers to specific questions about the place of occupational information at the elementary level seem to be answered fairly briefly and fairly easily. One of the two best examples I found occurred in Mathewson's book (1962) where he described the stages of a child's development, beginning in the early grades. He stressed identification of aptitudes and potentialities as

> . . . fundamental appreciations of conditions of social living, including common occupational pursuits being followed in the community and their meaning in fulfilling social needs (p. 229).

More specifically, Norris, Zeran, and Hatch (1960) indicate a need for information in early elementary grades to develop wholesome attitudes toward all fields of work, to make children aware of the wide variety of workers, to help children answer questions about occupations, and to bring out the varying rewards of work. They suggest that in upper elementary levels, occupational information will help a child learn about workers at the state, national, and international level; it will aid him in seeing the interdependence of workers, and it will acquaint him with the abilities and qualities needed for successful performance on the job. In addition, they suggest occupational information will help him to know the areas of information important in making vocational choice; it will acquaint him with the problems of choosing and holding a job, and it will acquaint him with the fact that it is necessary to give careful study to making a choice of a future career.

SUGGESTIONS ARE DEBATABLE

The specific suggestions of "what to do" are more debatable than they appear to be, however, particularly in light of current personality theory, learning theory, and theories of vocational development. The "how-to-do-it" cookbook suggestions are easy to understand, and worthwhile, to a point. The only trouble is that the cookbook often only makes sense to the person who wrote it. When someone else tries a recipe, it just isn't the same. In fact, the cake often comes out quite flat, even though the cookbook was followed to the letter.

A good example of this is a reference by Hoppock (1957) to a social studies program built around occupations where stress was on the study of man rather than the study of environment. It sounds wonderful, but it can probably serve only as a springboard for other creative teachers and counselors who will develop something of their own. Those less creative individuals who try to copy it will have a rather pallid version of what Hoppock describes, since the vital ingredient, the people who worked out the original plan, are not there.

THEORIES ARE CHALLENGING

More vague, but much more challenging, is the question of the place of such a seemingly drab subject as occupational information in the elementary school, when considered in the light of various theories of vocational development. Webster gives plenty of leeway in the various definitions of a "theory." One definition states a theory as being "a more or less plausible or scientifically acceptable general principle offered to explain phenomena," while another, "a hypothesis; a guess." Too frequently, however, theories become viewed almost as facts. They develop a sort of halo that enables one to excuse almost any act, as long as one is following some theory.

Even better, of course, is developing one's own theory of vocational development or choice. The pages of the *Journal of Counseling Psychology* abound with such theories. Often the educated people who develop these educated guesses are the first to agree that this is all they are. Unfortunately, however, sometimes theories become viewed as cause rather than effect, and studies are undertaken to show that what is true is true.

Empirically and existentially, one might question a situation where a theory becomes an acceptable reason for a certain action or movement that one human makes toward another. At least it seems reasonable to question those counselors who deter the future direction *of others* on the basis of someone else's guess as to where they should go and what they should do. Theories should not be viewed as determiners of human action.

One might assume that theories relating to vocational development should show some relationship to the actions proposed by some writers regarding what might be done about occupational information at the elementary school level. Unfortunately, they are often contradictory. With nearly all theories, at least in the area of human behavior, there is usually much evidence gathered on both sides. Theories which are more specific are more vulnerable, while generalized statements or guesses are more subject to modification according to the direction of the wind.

Roe (1957), for example, comes forth with a fairly definitive statement when she theorizes that certain kinds of family atmospheres create a psychological climate depending upon whether they satisfy or frustrate the early needs of a child. On this basis, she predicts particular and specific career groups toward which a child will move. The specific hypothesis, however, is not supported in such reported studies as those by Grigg (1959), Hagen (1960), Switzer, Grigg, Miller, and Young (1962), and Utton (1962). On the other hand, a study by Kinnane and Pable (1962) confirms the general hypothesis that family influences are critical in the development of work values.

We find a somewhat similar contradiction of a more specific hypothesis when we note a study by Davis, Hagen, and Strout (1962). This study tends to support the more specific aspect of the Ginzberg theory that tentative choices are made between ages 11 and 17, over the fantasy choices of earlier years. Small (1953) reports a study in which no evidence was found to support the theory of fantasy choice prior to eleven, or a movement toward tentative choices from 11 to 17. On the other hand, O'Hara's study tends to indicate that the normal upper limit of fantasy choice should be 8 or 9 rather than 11.

We also note that in 1962, sociologist Lipsett (1962) commented that "If the thesis is accepted that social factors are of great importance in the vocational development and career planning of an individual, it follows that a counselor needs to understand these social factors and their influence upon an individual" (pp. 432–437). It is interesting to find that Super (1956) anticipated him by some six years when he said, ". . . although social action is important in understanding the development of the self, it does not satisfactorily explain the selection and synthesizing process which leads to the development of a self picture" (pp. 249–253).

Most of what might be called the rather broad and general, and thereby safer, theories of vocational development tend to reflect the generally acceptable behavioristic, middle class views and values of the authors.

Holland (1959) for example, discusses his theory, which ". . . assumes that at the time of vocational choice the person is the product of the interaction of his particular heredity with a variety of cultural and personal forces including peers, parents, and significant adults, social class, American culture, and the physical environment. Out of this experience the person develops a hierarchy of habitual or preferred methods for dealing with environmental tasks" (pp. 35–45).

Segal (1961) reports on an attempt ". . . to demonstrate that psychoanalytic theory can be utilized to predict personality differences in individuals choosing one of two vocational outlets. . . . These hypotheses were derived from information about the kinds of activities each of the professions required of an individual, and the interaction of such activities with the satisfaction of the individual's need" (pp. 202–212).

Hadley and Levy (1962) refer to a "reference group theory"—the influence of groups on an individual's attitudes and behavior, and under what circumstances this influence is most effective, and the manner in which the influence is exercised.

All of these statements tend to point in a similar direction, in that they all reflect . . . a somewhat . . . deterministic, behavioral science view of man as being a creature *of* destiny, rather than the creator *of* his destiny. And while, at this point, one might say: what in the world has this got to do with the question of occupational information at the elementary school level, I would think it has a good deal to do with it, since much of the current writing and thinking on the "what to do" regarding this question tends to reflect the various theoretical postulates. Let us now take a questioning look at some of the thoughts and ideas that have been reflected in these past few pages.

ENVIRONMENT REFLECTS MAN

Current occupational literature tends to operate on the assumption that man lives in an outside-of-himself determined world, and in this sense accepts the general view of empirical science. Super (1962) voices this as well as anyone when, in defining his concept of vocational counseling, he refers to it as ". . . the process of helping the individual to ascertain, accept, understand, and apply the relevant facts about himself to the pertinent facts about the occupational world, which are ascertained through incidental and planned exploratory activities" (p. 2).

While we talk of "freedom" and "development" and "choice," Super's statement, and others like it, carry a strong implication of understanding in the sense of accepting and adjusting to what is. The environment becomes the center of life rather than the individual. The "world of work" becomes some vague outside-of-the-person force to which man must learn to adjust. It becomes a sort of fixed field without people. It would seem, actually, to differ very little from the fitting of a certain shaped human to a similarly shaped occupational hole.

There is, however, another existential view of man which is somewhat different. Man is not seen as the victim of deterministic forces outside of himself but rather as the creator of his world. "Environment" is not something outside of me to which I must, in order to get along, learn to adjust, but it is, rather, a reflection of me. I have a responsibility, not to adjust to a fixed environment, but as a result of my living, to do something to modify and change both it and me. Indeed, one may question whether one could actually say "it" and "me," since they are both entwined with each other.

However, in this case the *me* is the essential ingredient, and the *it* something which is the product of the *me*. The reality of the Mississippi environment of James Meredith is not the same as that of another Mississippi Negro who numbly accepts his fate as a member of an inferior race. The James Merediths are the creators and the movers of their culture, not the passive victims of it.

To the child the occupational world, the much talked about world of work, does not become a dark outside bogey man to which he must adjust some sad day. Rather, it is a world of people, just as work is people. In this sense, it is no different than the world of work which is currently a part of him, whether he is eight or eighty.

The stress on prognosis, prediction, and the matching of a child's abilities, to someone else's plans implies a high level of the imposition of one human on another. It is restrictive. The implication is that one is bound by one's boundaries, and that the taking of a chance, the risking of possible failure in doing something to challenge those boundaries, is to be avoided at all costs.

Failure is only deadening when an individual feels and believes that there is nothing he can do about it. However, failure need not be traumatic if an individual feels there is a chance for movement, that there is another direction where he may go. I do not accept the concept that it is always better to move a child away from a venture where the odds are that he will fail, as long as the direction he is going in is the direction where he wishes to take a chance, to take a plunge.

In our culture, color of skin, religion, level of intelligence, physical deformity, may, of course, be restrictions to movement. However, they only chain an individual when he confuses his inner freedom-to-be with the restrictions on his outside freedom. One always has an inner freedom. It cannot be taken away. One can use this inner freedom to widen gaps and cracks in those outside forces which restrict outer freedom. Socrates was a freer man than those who offered him the cup. Christ was a freer man than those who nailed him to the cross.

These men have always been with us, and without them there would be no James Meredith is freer than the white students who spit at him.

forward movement. The child can learn that is is the way he can be too, that actually this is the way he *is*. Surely the elementary school teacher and counselor can help the child to move in the direction of being what he is, to live in a world of his making, unless they too, of course, have accepted the numb, secure, and deadening comfort of the world of Mr. Orwell, which is not unlike that of Mr. Skinner.

INFORMATION IS UNREAL

If we at least consider the possibility that people and work are irrevocably related; that one does not learn how to best fit into the other; that to a high degree, one is the other; then we may raise the question of the part occupational information plays in the life of a young child. Certainly we can assume that occupational information, per se, has as little personal meaning as the vast majority of information which is poured, shoved, and ground into a child during his years of formal education.

Talk about the dignity of all jobs, including that of garbage man, probably means as little to a child as the suggestion that there is a relationship between that strange ingredient we call intelligence and successful performance as a surgeon. Both are quite unreal in the living world of a child. The garbage man, incidentally, must be getting a bit sick of being used as the occupational example of a fellow who is really doing an honorable job, usually by teachers or writers who would rather be dead than be a garbage man!

We might wonder if most occupational information must continue to be somewhat unreal to children and to all of us in a personal sense. I agree with Hatch (1951) on the need for stress on occupational exploration in the elementary school, as indeed there should be the element of exploration in all learning and education. However, we should emphasize the use of information only as a vehicle and a means for exploration. What children remember specifically and didactically about a trip to a glue factory seems to me to be of no point whatsoever. What is important is the process and the involvement of the individual in the glue factory.

I question what seems to be a general assumption that an increase in the amount of information about anything will somehow result in a broader learning by the student. Learning, after all, is a process. It does not come with an automatic piling on of more and more information. Also, I agree with Lifton (1959) when he says ". . . from both their teachers and their texts youngsters were receiving a distorted picture of the importance and types of job activities," and with Kowitz and Kowitz (1959) who say, "On the elementary level the selection is too often limited to about a dozen service occupations such as the milkman, postman, and policeman" (p. 154).

Only, however, when this distorted picture is assimilated as a part of the person will it have a negative effect. We might assume that meaningless, distorted pictures are as hard to digest as meaningful, undistorted pictures. I have a hunch, too, that real distortion depends on the attitude and the value system of the teacher as she presents the information, valid or not, to the children. I applaud Kaye (1960) when she says, in describing the results of an occupational unit in Grade 4, that it ". . . helped the children to work toward the goals of all good teaching; critical thinking, respect, and understanding" (pp. 150–152). If this happens, it is more likely to be because of the teacher and her ability to get children involved in an exciting and exploratory journey of learning, rather than because of the information she used.

WORDS ARE RESTRICTIVE

There also seems to be some unfortunate implications in the use of the words *fantasy* and *choice*. Choice is very much like freedom in that it is a relative, changing, moving concept. Restrictions on choice, like those on freedom, may come from the outside as well as from the inside. Outside restrictions regarding choice that continually face the child are bad enough. Even worse, however, is the implication that choice, like freedom, is an outer-decided matter, rather than an inner-determination. The child may grow to believe that he has no choice. Unfortunately teachers and counselors often teach him this lesson.

Choosing is not finding the "right" thing, but is rather the ability to move within restrictions, modifying and changing them. The real lack of choice that faces many adults today is not due to overt circumstances, but rather to their acceptance of the concept that their ability to choose depends on something outside of themselves. It is a belief in their inability to have any choice that makes the lack of choice real.

The word fantasy as it is related to choice usually carries a negative connotation and is considered to be something that is not really real. In the field of occupations, fantasy choices are usually defined as translations of simple needs and impulses into occupational goals. Tentative choices, on the other hand, are decisions based upon capacities, interests, and values.

This again, however, suggests outer determination of individual movement, and implies that unless we move in an occupational direction, where, according to the data, we "fit," we are being unreal and guilty of fantasy. This, I assume, is why Ginzberg would consider early occupational choices as fantasy, since the child has not yet had time to discover what his shape might be, and thus cannot fit himself into an appropriate niche.

The life that a young child in the elementary school is living, however, is very real to him. For him, his current life is his "world of work." Because he is involved in it day by day, I sometimes wonder if the so-called fantasy of his occupational dreams is possibly a good deal less fantastic than the occupational future that certain concerned adults are planning for him. While we consider fantasy to be akin to the discrepancy between the ideal self and the operating self, they are both a real part of real living. Ife we aim at reducing them to nothing, we may reach that unhappy stage of complete adjustment when we no longer are alive.

This real world of children was illustrated in a recent conversation I overheard between four eight- and nine-year-olds. They were talking about religions, and one of them said, "Well, I don't think I'd want to be a Jew," to which another replied, "Of course, if you were a Jew you'd feel different about being a Jew." The others all agreed. It might be better if we were to stop talking about preparing a child for the world to come, and help him to do the best he can in living the life he is living. The only real life that he can know is the life he lives. In all the rest there must be an element of fantasy and dreaming.

In occupational literature, the terms fantasy and choice are usually used in a behavioristic sense. They both smack of a concept where one spends a part of his life preparing to fit into something that will be best for him, and then after he is cozily fitted, that is that. However, since the life of a child differs only in degree from the life of an adult, the only way a child can "prepare" for the years ahead is to live the present years, which we hope would include an element of what the more prosaic adult might consider fantasy.

Occupational information, then, has a claim to a place in the elementary school curriculum just as any other information and knowledge. Like any other information, however, it is important only to the extent that a teacher or counselor is able to use it to help a child become involved in the learning process. I know of no evidence to indicate that memorizing that the salary of a mailman is less than that of a high school principal will have any bearing on the vocational development of a child.

We might hope, too, that teachers and counselors, using information that is representative, valid, and accurate will help children see that they may always have freedom of choice, no matter what the restrictions placed upon them may be. This freedom of choice implies that there will be no guarantee of success and happiness; even that the choice they make may turn out to be wrong. They may even feel more certain about being uncertain and fantasize about the adult world of tomorrow, because it is simply an extension of their very real world of today.

REFERENCES

Barry, J. A. 1958. *The elementary teacher and guidance.* New York: Holt, Rinehart and Winston.

Bernard, H. W., J. C. Evans, and F. R. Zeran. 1956. *Guidance services in elementary schools.* New York: Chartwell House.

Cottingham, H. F. 1956. *Guidance in elementary schools.* New York: McKnight.

Crow, L. D., and Alice Crow. 1962. *Readings in guidance.* New York: McKay.

Davis, D. A., Nellie Hagen, and Judie Strouf. March 1962. Occupational choice of twelve-year-olds. *Personnel guid. J.*, *40*, 628–629.

Farwell, Gail F., and H. J. Peters. 1960. *Guidance readings for counselors.* Skokie, Ill.: Rand McNally.

Grigg, A. E. Summer 1959. Childhood experiences with parental attitude: a test of Roe's hypothesis. *J. counsel. Psychol.*, *6*, 153–155.

Hadley, R. B., and W. V. Levy. Summer 1962. Vocational development and reference groups. *J. counsel. Psychol.*, *9.*, 110–114.

Hagen, D. Winter 1960. Careers and family atmospheres: an empirical test of Roe's theory. *J. counsel. Psychol.*, 7., 251–256.

Hatch, R. N. 1951. *Guidance services in elementary school*. Dubuque, Iowa: W. C. Brown Company.

Holland, J. L. Spring 1959. A theory of vocational choice. *J. counsel. Psychol.*, 6, 35–45.

Hoppock, R. 1957. *Occupational information*. New York: McGraw-Hill.

Johnson, W. F., B. Stefflre, and R. A. Edelfelt. 1961. *Pupils' personnel and guidance services*. New York: McGraw-Hill.

Kaye, Janet. Spring 1960. Fourth graders meet up with occupations. *Voc. guid. Quart.*, 8, 150–152.

Kinnane, J. F., and M. W. Pable. Winter 1962. Family background and work value orientation. *J. counsel. Psychol.*, 9, 320–325.

Kowitz, G. T., and N. Kowitz. 1959. *Guidance in the elementary classroom*. New York: McGraw-Hill.

Lifton, W. M. 1959–1960. Vocational guidance in the elementary school. *Voc. guid. Quart.*, 8, 79–81.

Lipsett, L. January 1962. Social factors in vocational development. *Personnel guid. J.*, 40, 432–437.

Mathewson, R. H. 1962. *Guidance policy and practice*. New York: Harper & Row.

Norris, Willa, F. Zeran, and R. Hatch. 1960. *The information service in guidance*. Skokie, Ill.: Rand McNally.

O'Hara, R. P. October 1959. *Talk about self*. Harvard studies in career development (No. 19). Unpublished.

Roe, Ann. Fall 1957. Early determinants of vocational choice. *J. counsel. Psychol.*, 4, 212–217.

Segal, S. J. Fall 1961. A psychoanalytic analysis of personality factors in vocational choice. *J. counsel. Psychol.*, 8, 202–212.

Small, L. 1953. Personality determinants of vocational choice. *Psychol. Monogr.*, 67 (No. 1).

Super, D. E. Winter 1956. Vocational development: the process of compromise or synthesis. *J. counsel. Psychol.*, 3, 249–253.

————, and J. O. Crites. 1962. *Appraising vocational fitness*. New York: Harper & Row.

Switzer, D. K., A. E. Grigg, J. S. Miller, and R. K. Young. Spring 1962. Early experiences and occupational choice: a test of Roe's hypothesis. *J. counsel. Psychol.*, 9, 45–48.

Utton, A. C. Spring 1962. Recalled parent-child relations as determinants of vocational choice. *J. counsel. Psychol.*, 9, 49–53.

Willey, R. D. 1960. *Guidance in elementary education*. New York: Harper & Row.

Wrenn, C. G. 1962. *The counselor in a changing world*. Washington, D.C.: American Personnel and Guidance Association.

Chapter 10

PARENT CONSULTING
AND PARENT EDUCATION

Although parent consulting has not been an important function in secondary school guidance, elementary school guidance and counseling practices may produce a new era of family counseling and family education.

Since guidance work with parents is relatively unexplored, there are a number of fundamental questions to consider, for example, how much counseling of parents should be done by school personnel? What percentage of time in the total guidance program can be appropriately spent with parents? Counselors will need to know the nature of their contact with parents and the extent to which they should become involved in parents' personal problems which, of course, affect their children. Educators and counselors must consider the best process for developing communication between parents and counselors and between teachers and counselors regarding parent contacts. Policies must be established concerning what information is to be shared with parents and what is to be kept confidential among school personnel.

RATIONALE FOR PARENT CONSULTING
AND PARENT EDUCATION

The family situation is significant for the child's development. It is in the family that the child first acquires a culture and develops his unique approach to the tasks of life. It is here that he learns the primary social skills. The family affects the child's feelings about personal adequacy and provides the first models

341

for his behavior. Parents are the first teachers: The child learns not only from what they say but from observing their behavior.

Parent consulting can be a tremendously productive area of elementary school guidance. It is true that parents and teachers observe different aspects of the child's behavior. A sharing of observations can develop a better over-all understanding of the child. Teachers will have the opportunity to develop sensitivity to the child's family life.

The school can and must help parents play a more integral part in their child's education. The parents of the elementary school child are usually eager and receptive to school contacts; they earnestly seek information and assistance in raising their child. Poorly planned and executed parent-teacher relationships will discourage parents about the ability of professional educators to be of assistance to them. From the guidance point of view, improved communication with parents is necessary. Communication typically occurs only through the report card or written notes that tend to focus on the weaknesses or liabilities of the child and rarely permit mutual understanding of the child's difficulties. Personal contact, however, can help clarify both the teacher's and the parent's ideas about the child.

The objectives of parent consulting are:

1. To give parents an understanding of family relationships and the setting in which the child is raised.

2. To enable parents to understand the school program and its objectives.

3. To have parents report to and share with the school personnel the child's reactions to the school program.

TEACHER AND COUNSELOR ROLES IN PARENT CONSULTING

The teacher and the counselor both have important roles to play in parent consultation. It is vital that they understand each other's responsibilities and maintain contact with each other regarding any parent conferences. A brief summary of notes acquired at any parent conference should be made available to those concerned school personnel—counselor, teacher, and principal.

The teacher should have definite responsibility to parents for securing and presenting certain types of information. The counselor and the teacher can decide before a parent conference what the school needs to know about the child in order to serve him best.

Developmental guidance is interested in serving all children, and the teacher is therefore the logical person to initiate a contact with parents. The first contact with parents should occur during the early weeks of the school year. At this contact, the teacher meets with all parents to discuss the curriculum and his philosophy of child development and discipline. Within the first two months of school, the counselor should meet with parents to provide information regarding the child's progress in school. At the first report period, the teacher should have made available samples of the child's work, the child's evaluation of his progress, the cumulative record, and other pertinent school information. The purpose of this contact is to share information about the child's goals, interests, attitudes, and feelings regarding school. It is imperative that adequate time be allowed for this contact, perhaps thirty minutes—allowing sufficient time to develop communication while still staying within realistic time limits. Parent conferences might take place over a two-day period and would necessitate either hiring substitute teachers or providing vacation days for children. A second teacher-parent conference might routinely be scheduled at the third marking period of the year. This conference should be brief and directed at reporting the child's development.

As indicated by this model, counselor-parent consultation would be concerned with different content than teacher-parent contact. The counselor should be available to all parents in parent-education sessions which might meet as often as twice a month. These sessions would focus on imparting general knowledge of children and specific knowledge regarding effective parent-child relationships.

The counselor should be available for appointments with parents regarding special learning difficulties of children, problems in social and emotional development, and general problems in child rearing and discipline. Solutions for such problems could be dealt with in the planned family counseling and parent education sessions which should be available to all parents.

Through in-service education, the counselor demonstrates parent interview techniques for the teacher. Such programs would present opportunities to role play parent-teacher interviews and to hear taped sessions which illustrate some of the problems in parent-teacher contacts.

THE PARENT INTERVIEW

The basic purpose of any parent interview is communication. It should develop a closer working relationship between parents and school professionals and should adhere to the fundamental principles of interviewing. Parent interviews should avoid random generalizations or "social talk." Time and contact is valuable and should not be used inappropriately.

Preceding the parent conference, parents should be sent a printed explanation of the conference that indicates the amount of time that will be available and the issues that concern the teacher or counselor. The explanation should provide extra space for the parents to list questions which they will want to ask at the conference.

The teacher should prepare for each interview individually, focusing on the child, not on the curriculum. It will be important to begin by discussing the child's assets, interests, and things he does well. Early in the interview the parents should be asked how they feel about the child and his progress.

Teachers may discuss ways of stimulating learning, parents' relationship to homework, and information that the parents may need about the school's program and policy. The interview could also be an effective means to discuss the understanding and accepting of the child's uniqueness. With adequate training, teachers can provide parents with methods and techniques of stimulating the child's development (Grunwald, 1955).

Prerequisite to the interview is the teacher's ability to build a relationship of trust, respect, and goal alignment. The teacher must be careful to talk the parent's language and avoid educational jargon in his attempt to communicate. He must be a good listener, letting the parents talk so that he can perceive their feelings and interpretations of school situations.

During every interview, the teacher should keep those confidences which have been shared by children or parents. Professional ethics should decide the kinds of things that could be revealed. A simple standard might be: How will sharing this information help the child?

At the conclusion of the interview, the parents should be asked to summarize what they have learned. The teacher then clarifies any misunderstandings. Sufficient time should be permitted between interviews so that the teacher can briefly summarize in writing the results of a completed interview before beginning preparation for a new interview with other parents.

PARENT EDUCATION

The counselor can have his most extensive effect upon children through parent education. The goal of parent education is to help parents learn to relate more effectively to their children. There are a number of methods that can be employed in the development of parent education.

The counselor might form a discussion group in child development which would meet during the day or after school to discuss general problems of child rearing. This group might develop a list of topics of particular concern to parents and discuss both general and specific procedures for working with children. It might profit by organizing study groups to consider the ideas presented in books such as: Bettelheim's *Dialogue with Mothers* (1962); Dreikurs' *The Challenge of Parenthood* (1958); Dreikurs' and Soltz' *Children: The Challenge* (1964); or Ginott's *Between Parent and Child* (1965).

Examples of dynamic discussion groups are community parent-teacher education centers which have been formed in various sections of the country. These centers usually meet once a week to focus on the development of knowledge about children in general and to consult with individual parents regarding typical developmental problems. This approach has been found to help personalize the learning process to parents in terms of specific situations. Through open family consultation, the community centers help parents understand the dynamics of their child's behavior while recognizing that their problems are much like the problems of other parents. They help parents to establish policies and a consistent plan of action in dealing with their children. In broad terms, the community centers attempt to formulate a philosophy of human relationships within the family (Dinkmeyer, 1967). In the past, model centers have been conducted at Quincy, Illinois (Stormer, 1967), and presently are part of the work at the University of Oregon (Christensen, Merten, and Mead, 1966).

Eleanore Braun Luckey indicates that parents of elementary school children may be eager for help and receptive to education. Counselors and teachers, however, must be well trained for parent education. She emphasizes the importance of goals and counseling procedures for the conference. Values, procedures, and content in parent education are included.

Kowitz and Kowitz propose that home-school relations can be improved by improving four types of communication: flow of information about the child to the school; flow of information about the school to the home; periodic reports from the school; and handling of special problems. They discuss the importance of collecting information pertinent to the educational process rather than routinely and purposelessly collecting large amounts of data. They stress the importance of establishing communication with parents early and maintaining it constantly. They clarify the counseling relationship and process in the parent conference.

Sonstegard discusses the importance of a goal for the parent conference. While there are generally accepted procedures for counseling and interviewing, the parent interview has unique factors which require different purposes and techniques. Sonstegard describes four distinct steps in counseling the parent and includes an outline and flexible methods of adapting these steps for the parent interview.

REFERENCES

Bettelheim, B. 1962. *Dialogues with mothers*. Glencoe, Ill.: Free Press.

Christensen, O. C., F. T. Merten, and D. E. Mead. 1966. *A guide to parents*. Eugene, Ore.: School of Education, Division of School Psychological Services, University of Oregon.

Dinkmeyer, D. 1967. A study of Adlerian child guidance counseling. *Indiv. Psychol.*

Dreikurs, R. 1958. *The challenge of parenthood*. New York: Meredith Press.

———, and Vicki Soltz. 1964. *Children: the challenge*. New York: Meredith Press.

Ginott, H. 1965. *Between parent and child*. New York: Macmillan.

Grunwald, Bernice. 1955. The application of Adlerian principles in a classroom. *Amer. J. indiv. Psychol.*, 11 (No. 2).

Stormer, G. E. 1967. Milieu group counseling in elementary school guidance. *Elem. Sch. Guid. Counsel.*, 1 (No. 3), 240–254.

When the Elementary School
Counselor Deals with Parents*

Eleanore Braun Luckey

With the advent of the elementary school counselor, a new era of family counseling and education appears on the social horizon. Guidance personnel have long been aware that pupils have parents and that parents often have to be reckoned with in one way or another as the school carries on its task of educating the individual child, but for the most part, dealing with parents has been a peripheral and often neglected function.

Few junior or senior high schools have developed any kind of extensive program of family counseling or parent education. As a matter of fact, it is at the secondary levels that parent interest and participation (even in the PTA) become little more than assenting nods, disgruntled grunts, or raised eyebrows. Parents of adolescents are often reluctant to bring their problems to the school or to have the school bring it to them. When a child is on his way to being a young adult, parents are aware that their influence is waning; they are no longer "new" parents who can appropriately seek guidance, and they are, for the most part, terribly fearful of what they have "already done" to their offspring. Their need for self-protection is not an easy barrier for the teacher, counselor, or principal to break through. The adolescents, themselves, discourage the parental-teacher alliance. A busy school schedule with many and diverse demands on the faculty tends to make all the possibly interested parties pretty inaccessible.

The elementary school picture is different. Partly because the primary school child is younger and still very much a part of the family's protective circle, the counselor will find himself drawn more and more into the vortex of family affairs. Also pulling the counselor to the family is the readiness of the parents for this involvement—their eagerness for help and their receptivity to education.

Parents have been bombarded by child-rearing authorities, newspaper columnists, feature-writing journalists, child psychologists, and psychological novelists and scenario writers. They have been confused by a succession of "best methods" for child training and are neurotically conscious of all the "do's" and "don'ts" for children *in general*. But in the elementary school counselor they will see not only "the" authority on children generally but one who knows and understands and can advise about *their* children. Parents want to know about their

---

* Paper prepared especially for this book of readings.

progeny, not only in the school situation, but in social situations and at home. Few parents know enough other youngsters or have enough knowledge of child development to know whether or not their own children are "normal for their age," and most parents are overly concerned about having offspring who fit the expected social pattern.

Mothers, and fathers too, want help with their own roles. In our generation parenting has become a terribly confused issue, and mothers often no longer know what is expected of them as mothers. Fathers—currently being accused of abdicating their manly responsibilities—have often given up entirely or are rigidly sticking by their grandfathers' muskets!

Regardless of whether he would or no, the elementary school counselor is destined to become the family counselor and the parent educator. The only questions that remain are, "How well will he be prepared?" Until he is in "full swing" and well bolstered by background courses in family dynamics, child development, and conjoint therapy some interim suggestions may be pertinent.

THE PARENT CONFERENCE

The situation in which the counselor currently finds himself most frequently "working with" parents is in the conference. Usually there is little opportunity for what most counselors would term "counseling" with the parent—although this will be determined by the problem that is to be dealt with, the attitude of the school authorities, the needs of the parents, and most importantly, the orientation and philosophy of the counselor.

It could more appropriately be said that the counselor offers *guidance*. The effectiveness of this guidance is largely determined by the relationship existing between the counselor and the parent, and this, in turn, is largely determined by the counselor's knowledge of himself, of the situation, of the child and his parent, and by the counselor's ability to use himself as an effective instrument to bring about the goals he is working toward.

Counselor Self-Awareness

Working with parents necessitates a special self-awareness in terms of one's own feelings and prejudices regarding family situations. For example, the counselor who himself has had a nagging, dominant mother may well have a hard time dealing with Johnny Jones' nagging, dominant mother! The capable, career-gal counselor may find herself punitive toward and resentful of pretty Mrs. Dinkle who is "only a housewife" to handsome Mr. Dinkle and a mother to four little Dinkles. Or, she may find herself combing her hair overly long before her appointment with Mr. Dinkle. If the counselor hasn't worked through quite all of his own problems with authority figures (and few of us have!) he may quake in his boots when confronted with a father who reminds him of his own. The counselor who for years waged the battle of the siblings around his own family table may be overly empathetic with the youngster who is at the bottom of the family pecking order.

No matter how "normal" or "mature" the counselor may be, or how well he has worked through his own family problems, nor how accessible his feelings are to his palpations and manipulations, he will tend to interpret all families on the basis of what he has experienced in his own family. On this basis he may make many erroneous assumptions, especially when he is dealing with families in a socio-economic stratum different from his own. He may jump to conclusions and overshoot, or fall short. He may be carrying around a lot of stereotypes and misinformation about families that he has never examined. For example, he may really believe that children from homes of working mothers are likely to have more problems than children of non-working mothers. He may believe that children with no siblings have more relationship difficulties and that most of the children from large families were surely unwanted and unloved! He may believe that divorce is inevitably bad for children, and that cleanliness is next to godliness!

The counselor needs, too, to examine his own feelings with regard to his position on matters of school policy. In working through some problems, he may find himself having to defend school rules, the superintendent's attitudes, the English teacher's classroom procedure. He will want to know just how he does feel about these matters himself, how far he can compromise himself, how staunchly he can support "the system." He will try to remember that he and the school are all teammates on the same side working for the welfare of the student; one of his functions is to convey this spirit of cooperation and concern to the parent.

Perhaps the most difficult pressure the counselor must deal with comes from the demands that parents put upon him because they overestimate him. Like most people who have problems, parents want someone to give them the solution. They come expectantly, asking to be *told*. The counselor who doesn't have that ready answer is likely to seem pretty stupid to the parent; and when he is perceived as stupid, the very least he can feel is embarrassment! It is a great temptation to filibuster, to think up a good pat answer, or to be defensive and apologetic. Only the counselor who knows that he doesn't have the answer, and knows that it is quite all right for him not to have it, can avoid falling into the trap of giving advice and sounding important.

Understand the Goals

Successful parent conferences demand a considerable amount of preparation. Only in cases of emergency should a counselor go into a session with parents without having his goals well defined. He should ask himself (particularly if it is he who has asked for the conference) just *why* he is seeing the parent and what he expects to accomplish. Is he reporting the child's progress—or lack of it? Is he seeking information about the child, or the family, or the child's living conditions? Is he seeking the parent's cooperation toward better academic or social adjustment for the child?

If the conference is being held at the parents' request, the counselor will want to know *before* the parents arrive what they want of him or of the school, or of the child. Parents sometimes may not *really* know why they want to see the counselor; it may be that the basic problem will not emerge for two or three sessions. When this is the case, the counselor must rely on his own sensitivities to help him explore and on his ability to *wait for* the parent. Often the parent needs to talk about himself more than he needs to talk about his child. Whether the counselor can permit this or not depends on the counselor's own sense of adequacy, the attitude of his administration toward his functioning as a family counselor, and priority demands on his time. In any case, the elementary school counselor needs to be very familiar with all of the possible agencies and individuals within the community to whom he can refer parents for marriage or family counseling. He almost certainly will need to call on them.

Children are sometimes caught almost as helpless victims in the complex relationship of a warring husband and wife. When this is the case, the school counselor will usually want to be straightforward in stating the sources of the child's difficulty, but will prefer to remain uninvolved in the marriage squabble. Referral to a family social agency, to a capable minister or priest, a marriage counselor or psychiatrist, may be the only real avenue to help for the child.

No matter how well defined the goals may be at the beginning of the conference, the counselor must be prepared for them to change—and sometimes rather suddenly—during the conference. Such was the case when the Browns were asked to come in to talk about Bill. The counselor's intention had been to discuss a persistent theft problem the school had been having with Bill, but it veered considerably when Mr. Brown appeared—a big, burly, gruff fellow who stated at the outset that "if you want to see me 'cause that brat of mine's in trouble, I'll break every bone in his body." Although Mr. Brown and the counselor spent that hour talking about Bill and some of his problems, the counselor was content to discover for himself why Bill might be stealing and chose not to reveal the difficulty to the parent.

There are several legitimate goals for the counselor-parent conference. One of the most important is the exchange of information about the child. Children are largely a "home-made product" (or better, a home-made process!) and by understanding the parents and the home in which the youngster lives, the counselor comes to his keenest insights about the child.

From the parents the counselor comes to know the expectations they hold for the child, the concept they have of him, and the way they interact with him. Most counselors would agree that when one deals with a child, the most important aspect of him is his own self concept. When the counselor meets the parents, he begins to understand where that self concept came from. A most important clue to any child's difficulty lies in the perception of that child by his parents who are the two most important persons in his world.

It is from them that he has learned most about what adults are. He has learned that they are to be trusted or feared, to be catered to or avoided, to be manipulated, to be fooled, to be admired and emulated. It is from them that he learned which behavior in our society is rewarded and which is punished; which feelings are to be shown and which hidden. He has learned that life is a joyous adventure, a treacherous drudge, or something somewhere between these two. And most of all it is from them he has learned who and what he is—as well as he knows—primarily whether or not he is himself a valuable person to be loved and cherished.

Because parents, too, are human and their children are a kind of extension of themselves, the counselor will want to learn how the parents "use" the child in meeting their own needs. Some children are scapegoats; some are status symbols. Some children are glorified, some are cut-down to size daily by a parent who can't stand competition. Some are excused; some are blamed. Attitudes and values that parents exhibit toward their children usually become a hard-and-fast part of that child. The counselor needs to ask himself, "What must living day in and day out with this parent mean to his youngster?" When that question is answered, much of the child's behavior becomes understandable.

It is not infrequently that the school and the home have quite different views of the same youngster. The teacher has a different point of vantage and also has less invested in a given individual, but in addition to this, youngsters behave differently in a school setting than in a home setting. They try out different kinds of behavior and test the results. A most profitable interchange is one in which these perceptions can be shared so as to make more complete those held by both parent and teacher.

Sometimes it may be necessary for a counselor to help the parent see his child in a new or different perspective. The mother who insists on seeing her twelve-year-old son as "her baby" needs to be brought up to date. The counselor can present the boy as an able, independent little hustler who can no longer appropriately be kept in swaddling clothes. The youngster who is uncooperative around home and who is seen as "naturally lazy" may be a "real go-getter" at school. A counselor can help a puzzled parent account for these discrepant reactions.

Human beings always help each other most by adding to one's self-respect. This is true with children and it is true with adults. The elementary school counselor must not only show respect for the child and for the parent but must indicate to each of them that he has respect for the other. A parent grows in his own stature when he sees that the counselor respects his offspring! The offspring grows in that parent's stature when the counselor demonstrates his own respect for the child. No matter how rough the relationship between parent and child may be, some smoothing takes place as the two learn to respect each other.

Parents especially often have a hard time looking at their children as "people." It is good for them to talk to an adult who knows their child and who accepts and respects that child. One of the greatest contributions a counselor can make to the relationship between parent and child is to demonstrate his own acceptance of and interest in the child and in the parent. This means that in cases where there is conflict, the counselor must not "take sides," he must be genuinely concerned for the welfare of *both* sides.

In setting goals for the conference, the counselor needs to be realistic. If this is to be a single contact, he shouldn't expect too much. Not much sharing takes place between comparative strangers in an hour; not much listening can be done. A one-shot conference may accomplish little else than to establish a little warmth and trust between school and home. It can, however, do that, and a successful initial contact is not to be underestimated.

Know the Child

One of the complaints that elementary school counselors often have is that they have little opportunity to know many children very well. It tends to be only the problem child that they become well acquainted with, and often they are familiar with him more as a set of test scores and teacher's complaints than as an effervescing, malevolent personality and a warm body.

Little can be accomplished without the counselor's knowledge of the child, his problem, the extent and duration of it, and a hypothesized prognosis. Those dimensions necessitate knowing the child himself and before this is accomplished, a parent conference is destined to be dismal. Not all conferences are concerned with problems. When the concept of guidance for the non-problem child becomes a reality, the counselor's job will become unbelievably complex unless the student ratio is drastically reduced.

Know the Parent

Knowing a specific parent before a conference is usually unlikely, but keeping in mind some of the things that are generally true about all parents can be helpful.

When parents come to the school about their child, it is usually because something is "wrong" either at home or at school. This stacks the cards from the beginning and means that the parent is carrying a load of anxiety and fearful anticipation. How bad is it going to be, he wonders. Is it his fault? What can be done to help? One of the earliest interview tasks for the counselor is to help the parent to be more comfortable; and in doing this, the counselor himself is likely to become more at ease. The opening moments of the conference often determine how the whole conference will go. These are the moments in which both the counselor is likely to be somewhat afraid of the unknown adult opposite him, and the unknown adult is likely to be very afraid of the knowledgeable counselor. So long as defenses are up, litte communication takes place.

The first move is the counselor's. It's his "house" in which he is host and he sets the scene. If he has asked for the conference, he needs to present its purpose; if the conference is being held at the parent's initiative, the counselor needs to indicate his willingness to listen. In both cases he will be attentive and sensitive to the parent; he will see him as an individual—often fearful, sometimes aggressive, and always anxious.

Counseling that is done with a parent is often based on the assumption that the parent loves his child and wants what is best for that child's development. This may be placing too much faith in human nature. Many parents have not reached a stage of maturity in which they are able to love anyone—even their progeny. It is probably more real to assume that what the parent wants for the child is that which will make the parent show up to good advantage as a parent and a successful, social individual. This need not be evaluated as "bad." It just *is*.

The counselor cannot be expected to do away with his own hierarchy of values and judgments regarding those conditions that are or are not "good" for children, but he does need to be aware of his own values and recognize that some families may have quite other standards. Because it is generally very difficult for a middle-class counselor to empathize with and appreciate the values of a parent who is in a different class (especially the lower class) he will want to beware of his own strong feelings of what is "right" and what is "wrong."

Counselors must be mindful of the fact that many parents, perhaps most, carry a fair-sized load of guilt about their children. This feeling of guilt may or may not be rational; the reality is that it exists. When a counselor criticizes a child, he is also criticizing the parent. In reporting inadequacies or social transgressions of a youngster, the counselor will need to be especially objective, yet understanding and sympathetic.

In most cases parents appreciate a straightforward, honest approach, but the counselor must always assume the responsibility of assessing precisely how much and what information they can be given. He should be cautious of tossing the parent more of a package than he can handle, and he should be cautious about giving the parent a weapon with which he can bludgeon his young.

Confidence should not be betrayed. The counselor should not allow himself to serve as a channel of communication between parent and child; his function is to facilitate direct communication between them, not to serve as a go-between. Neither can he permit himself to be caught arranging conferences on the sly or seeming to ally himself with any one faction against the other.

It is difficult not to think of Mr. and Mrs. So and So as a unity and treat them as if they were *one* factor; this is especially so if both of the couple participate in the conference and one acts as the spokesman for the pair. A father and a mother, however, may have very different perceptions of their children and hold expectations that are in conflict. In spite of the fact that the parents are a dyad, over and above that relationship they are individuals, and must be considered as such.

With all these things to keep in mind, the counselor has to constantly remind himself that to the parent, a school counselor is a very important person and what he says carries a tremendous amount of weight. Accepting this much responsibility is frightening, and any good counselor is likely to be a little bit scared, and he should be! When one touches the family, one is likely to rock the cradle of humanity.

PARENT EDUCATION

Until now the public school has assumed little responsibility for anything that might be called "parent education." This has been delegated to the PTA—if to anyone. Some community agencies, foundations, and churches have had short courses from time to time that might qualify for this classification. For the most part, there has been little provision for groups of parents to get together to discuss their experiences in parenthood. With the school's extension into elementary school counseling, parent education may well become an integral part of the school program—if for no other reason than self defense.

The demands and needs of parents will increase to proportions that will make it impossible to meet them through the conference or individual counseling session simply because there will not be enough time or staff. It is not only the parent of the problem child who wants to know about his child; *most* parents want to know about their children. If the school is going to offer a service for the problem child, why not, also, for the gifted? And if services are available for these two groups, why should the great middle range be neglected?

Getting a group of parents together, killing several birds with one shot, as it were, will conserve time, put the least strain on faculty time, and show greatest gains. The purpose will not be social, nor will it be a p.r. stunt for the school administration. The goal is to help the parent learn to work with his own child so that the school will have less of it to do.

A well-trained teacher or counselor can't deal with the child as effectively as a well-trained parent. Teachers and counselors are human and subject to the same fallibilities that parents are and, in addition, have twenty or thirty children to be concerned with instead of the family's three or four. The teacher isn't as ego-involved with any one child and can't possibly be as concerned about any given child as his parent is. Although a teacher comes to know his students very well, a parent can know his offspring even better. It is customary for a child to change teachers and counselors fairly frequently, but even with our current divorce rate, the turnover in mothers and fathers is pretty low.

Generally speaking, however, the parent needs some assistance in knowing his child, and in acquiring some of the information that is pertinent to this child's growth and development. He could usually use some help with developing insights into himself as well and into the relationship that exists between him and his child.

Parents, for the most part, are not too stupid to learn—especially if they are well taught. High among the things that they *want* to learn is something about normal growth and development patterns of children, about social and emotional maturing, sibling rivalry and strife, nutrition, family recreation, values and standards. They want to know especially about discipline and its relationship to punishment and reward. They want to know about sex education and how to answer their children's questions about sex. They want to know what they can do now to help their child as an adult to live successfully in a future time that will have so many social changes that it will be quite different from their own. They want to know, too, how to live themselves with the stresses and strains of modern life and not "take it out on" their children. Essentially, they want to know more about how to be *good* parents. They need help in knowing *how*.

There are many things they want to know, too, about the school and their child's achievement in school. Many school systems are still taking the easy way out and telling the parent very little about the child at school on the basis that the "average parent" doesn't understand. The "average parent" *can* understand if he's given the opportunity. He can understand achievement tests and I.Q. measures and the difference between the two. He would probably even enjoy taking these himself. He can understand percentiles and distributions and norms. When parents know what these terms mean—and how little and how much they mean!—the school no longer will need to treat such records as if they were a high state secret. Parents themselves can interpret scores to their children, and in most cases wouldn't do a much worse job than a lot of counselors do. The school has operated long enough on the assumption that parents are too dumb to interpret anything but A-B-C grades.

If parents begin to know as much about our sacred cows as the professionals do, the test score and the inventory results will be more likely to assume more realistic proportions and less damage be done with them. If parents are given the responsibility of some of this interpretation, a great deal more meaningful sharing and communication will go on between parent and child.

Better coverage of occupational information can be made by a group of parents than by teachers who are occupationally pretty homogeneous. Trends, developments, and local occupational situations can often be supplied by many of the "experts," who are themselves a part of the parent group. If parents are properly stimulated, they will begin to think about Johnny's vocational guidance; and who is in a better position to assess Johnny's personality, his ability, and his opportunity than his interested parent? Who is in a better position to question their own motives in favoring one kind of work for Johnny over another? And while this process is going on, the parent will learn—as will Johnny and possibly even the counselor—what kind of preparation is necessary to qualify for such a job, where, and at what cost.

Perhaps it is time that the school shared with the home what it knows about drop-outs. If the school has shared enough information previously, it may well be that the home will take the drop-out problem off the school's worry-list.

If small groups of parents meet fairly frequently to talk over children's problems and to learn more about children, under skillful leadership they will soon begin to talk over their own problems and learn more about parents. When that happens, the elementary school counselor will have accomplished the goal of every good counselor and will have worked himself out of a job. For with fewer parent problems, there will be fewer student problems.

But not entirely, for no matter how much time and effort the school may decide to put into parent education there will be as many parent failures as there now are student failures. There will always be those who need individual attention over an extended period.

In most communities this kind of parent education under the auspices of the school administration is not presently feasible nor contemplated, but as the elementary-school-counselor concept begins to reach parents, their demands will make some kind of group work imperative. An hour of a counselor's time spent with a group of twenty parents for several weeks might well save twenty or more individual counseling sessions extended over a much longer period. The counselor's time spent in this way benefits not only the child and school system but the whole of the community and, in time, the world community.

Be it by conference or by group, the elementary school counselor will be the instrument that will make possible the alliance between school and family that both have so long wanted and hoped for.

Improving Home-School Relations*

Gerald T. Kowitz / Norma G. Kowitz

Our country is experiencing a series of significant social changes which mandate changes in our schools. The current status of our nation, as a world leader and as the most affluent society history has known, may not have been a direct result of excellence in our schools; certainly, there were other forces. However, there can be no doubt that our ability to sustain progress is directly related to the quality of education provided our youth. Unless they are prepared to begin at the apex of our achievements, the trend of social progress will become one of social deterioration.

It is no longer enough to insure a child a basic, minimum education. Programs are needed which will support the maximum development of individual talents. Academic achievement will, of course, be one major goal, but we will also need a high level of personal development—the ability to live with the anxieties of the times and to strive toward a future which often is frightening.

* *The National Elementary Principal*, April 1964, vol. 63, no. 5.
By permission.

The school cannot do the job alone. It must have the support and, at times, the active cooperation of the home. Communications between the school and the home, while an integral part of the educative process, are also often seen as a source of problems. The long and embarrassing history of problems between the school and the home makes it evident that there is no easy solution. On the other hand, as a school moves toward a quality program, there are some things that can be done to improve the relationship.

Many of the problems between the home and the school can be studied in terms of four types of communications:

1. Flow of information about the child to the school

2. Flow of information about the school, its policies and operations, to the home

3. Periodic reports

4. Special problems.

As we shall see, each of these types of communication is requiring more specialized techniques. Guidance workers have a growing responsibility in each.

INFORMATION ABOUT THE CHILD

If the school is to do a job of quality education, it must have information about the child. In fact, quality in education can be defined in terms of providing opportunities for the child to develop his talents. Among other things, this means that the home must help the school to understand the child and also the aspirations his parents have for him. When parents are expected to provide the school with information, much of it of a personal nature, they have a right to know how it will be used to advance the education of their child.

As in the past, parents will continue to provide information for administrative and legal purposes. Additional information will be needed for guidance purposes. The frustration of parents who are asked to provide the same information over and over again or to provide data that seem irrelevant is rivaled only by the dilemma of the school: What is to be done with the growing heaps of information? There is little point to collecting large amounts of data on a routine basis with only a vague hope that some day it may be helpful. Studies of data processing indicate that excessive data usually confuse the issue and always overburden the processing system, whether human or electronic. The identification of information that is pertinent to the educative process is a difficult task. Just what must the school know about the child to serve him best? Specification of information that will be useful and its collection and efficient handling will be a major guidance problem for elementary education in the next decade.

As the role of information expands from that of a simple administrative requirement to a necessity for proper educational guidance, the procedures for handling it must change. The importance of good relations with the home suggests that the guidance worker may devote a major part of his time to visiting homes with the dual goal of securing information about the child and giving information about the school and its program.

But what about the teacher who has carried this responsibility? It is probably impossible, and certainly unrealistic, to expect teachers to develop a high level of competence in the many content areas and also be trained guidance workers. Already, many elementary schools have teachers who specialize in reading, art, science, music, mathematics, and foreign languages. There are also specialists in personal development—the nurse, the psychologist, and the guidance worker. The growing number of specialists denies a continuation of present practice: communication with the home only through the teacher. The report card has been obsolete for some years, and it is not realistic to expect parents to confer periodically with three or four teachers and as many specialists. As specialization increases, the classroom teacher will see less of the child, and each teacher will see different aspects of his development. The specialists will have still other views. The guidance worker who is trained in personality development and in educational theory and who is familiar with school practice appears to be the logical person to carry the responsibility for gathering the pertinent information and communicating with the home.

INFORMATION ABOUT THE SCHOOL

Many of the problems in home-school relationships emerge from the fact that the school is a social institution. As such, it functions with an institutional value system. At the same time, the goal of the school is to serve the individual child as he matures. This requires a very personal, individualized set of values. It is inadequate to assume that what is good for the group will be good for each individual in the group. Nor is it reasonable to verbalize the doctrine of individual differences but to expect all children and their parents to respond alike or to assume that a rule will be equally applicable to all.

Since the school is a large and complex institution, it must have rules and regulations in order to operate. Very few of these rules have ever been evaluated or even thoroughly studied, especially in terms of their educational implications. Many guidance problems arise because of the incompatibility of several policies. For example, while the school may recognize that the development of each child is unique and continuous, decisions on his promotion are traditionally made only once a year. Furthermore, if the child is judged inadequate for promotion, he must repeat the entire year, even though he may lack only a few specifics. In fact, he may have made remarkable progress if we accept the notion of judging his achievement in terms of his own developmental pattern.

Policies on homework are also a source of recurrent problems between the home and the school. An important goal of education is to train the child to work on his own. However, busy work is no more profitable at home than at school. On the other hand, if assignments are so difficult that the child must be tutored by his parents, they may soon begin to wonder why the teacher is employed. With the trend toward introducing new materials and new methods into the curriculum —a trend which must continue if we are to have quality education—parents are finding themselves increasingly inadequate as teachers. The goals of homework and the policies for achieving these goals require careful planning and continual study. Adequate communication with the home is a vital element in the program of homework.

A related policy, the expectation of parental participation, is a frequent source of problems which usually need not exist. If the school expects parents to participate, parents must know and understand what is expected of them. If, on the other hand, the school has a "hands-off" policy for parents, this should be made clear. Only conflict can be expected if school policy requires the child to work alone, but the evaluation of that work assumes extensive parental help. Similarly, if the parent-teacher organization exists solely as a fund-raising corporation, this should be made clear. If its purpose is better communication between teachers and parents, a different structure is needed.

Where the goals of the school are not clear or where the preservation of traditions or defense of arbitrary policy are more important than the development of the child, the problem is not communication with parents but manipulation of them. In the case of attempted manipulation, the process of parent-school relationships is no longer one of solving mutual problems but rather one of coercion, conflict, and cold war.

PERIODIC REPORTS

Education is unique among the professions in that it is a continuing activity and not dependent upon a special problem or project. Because it is continuous, periodic reports will be expected by those who support it.

Many problems can be avoided by communicating expectations at the beginning of the year. It is usually inadequate to inform only the child. In fact, parents will expect more information and explanation than the child.

While in the past some believed that children could be frightened into working harder, there is no place in the quality school for a psychology of fear. A climate of fear in the classroom is as unreasonable academically as it is mentally unhealthy. An attitude of enthusiasm, or at least expectation, is far more useful than one of fear or apprehension.

Any time of evaluation may be a time of anxiety. Evaluation—that is, a judgment on the progress a child has made—is an important function. Without assessment, effective guidance and sound planning for the future are impossible. The school occasionally reneges on the matter of judgments. It seems easier to say, "Teachers do not give grades; pupils earn them," or, "The school did not make the decision." Of course, teachers give grades and schools make decisions, and both of these are judgments upon the child which will affect his future. Furthermore, all children cannot receive favorable reports. No teacher or school can guarantee this. However, a minimum requirement of an unfavorable report is that it must be a judgment of the child's work, not a condemnation of the child. It must, in the case of an inadequacy or deficiency, report how the situation can be corrected. It is not enough to say that the child must work harder or that he is careless. These are innocuous statements that neither clarify the problem nor suggest how the child may be helped.

When parents are kept informed of the progress of their child in relation to the expectations of the school, and when they know that the school has made a concentrated effort to help the child, the likelihood of conflict is lessened. Nevertheless, even with newer innovations such as the ungraded unit, there will be moments of truth—a time when some parents must be told that their child is not able to move ahead with his peers. Here is a growing role for the elementary guidance worker. The decisions which must be made require data from many sources. Unification of data, like counseling with parents, requires special skills.

Periodic reports suggest report cards. Although simple grading schemes are known to be inadequate, some parents continue to demand them. One reason for this persistence is that most adults were taught when they were pupils, perhaps unintentionally, that grades are the most important thing about school. What they learned to feel about grades is far more important to their present attitudes than what the school may have attempted to convey by the grades. Along with attitudes about grades, some parents also acquired strong negative feelings about teachers and school. There can be no doubt that an important part of establishing good relations with the home is planning a generation ahead. Unless children gain a reasonable perspective of the school as pupils, they will not have one as parents.

Semantic confusion—that is, a failure to establish common meanings—is fatal. Adequate definitions cannot be found in dictionaries nor can a school write enough specifications to define the terms used in reporting. Since the school works with children in human relationships, the emotional connotations of terms are usually more important than specific denotations. As we learn more about the process of communication, it becomes increasingly clear that the goal of purging terms of their emotional loadings is a foolish one; communications with parents about their children will always carry an emotional cargo. The goal cannot be to remove it, only to insure an appropriate loading.

SPECIAL PROBLEMS

No area of guidance shows the need for special training more than counseling with special problems.[1]

A fundamental principle in solving problems is to establish communications

---

[1] For an extended discussion of techniques for counseling with parents, see: Gerald T. Kowitz, and Norma G. Kowitz. *Guidance in the Elementary Classroom*, New York: McGraw-Hill, 1959, pp. 293–307.

early and maintain them constantly. While this is easy to say, is it reasonable to expect a teacher to establish and maintain a close relationship with thirty or forty sets of parents? Perhaps a more pertinent question is whether we should expect a teacher to provide quality education to such a large class.

Actually, each year will bring only a few serious situations in which a counseling relationship will be needed. When such problems arise, it is often too late for the teacher to begin to develop the relationship of trust and confidence that is needed. Involving another person, such as a guidance worker, who is not in an administrative position, can sometimes provide a neutral and accepting situation.

In any decision-making conference the goals must be made clear to all parties. To the extent that one party is coerced or forced to accept the goals of the other, the decision will be unacceptable and the subsequent actions will fail for lack of wholehearted support.

In any relationship that approaches the complexity of the education of the child, it is inevitable that there will be problems. Regardless of the nature of the problem, there are some general rules that can be used.

A child who has a problem needs all the friends he can muster. He needs friends among the professionals at school as well as the backing of his parents. In most cases, the parents will support the child. He is a physical and ego extension of themselves, and they will defend him just as they would defend themselves. This may mean that they will fail to see the problem.

A first step is to define the position of the child and his parents. This should be done without apology or negative implications. Such phrases as, "I know you may not agree, but . . ." or "Well, I suppose you think . . ." set the stage for conflict and failure. A first goal is to demonstrate an open mind and place the school in the role of an ally rather than an antagonist.

A second step is to develop mutual agreement on the problem. This flows quite naturally from the first. Where the school and the parent can agree on what the problem is, the stage is set for a solution. In fact, until this is done, any progress toward a solution is an illusion.

A common obstacle to defining the problem, one that is usually disposed of easily, is school policy. In some cases, the policy is such that an exception can be made to support the well-being of the child. In others, where the policy is so important that it must be inflexible, the reasoning behind the policy should be presented rather than just a statement of what must be done. It is important to remember that the goal is understanding and eventual agreement, not just enforcement.

Another obstacle, not so easily overcome, is the concept of the child held by the parent. This concept too often corresponds more closely to the idealized image the parent has of himself than to a real image of the child. When this is the case, it is essential to have the best possible working relationship with the parent before attempting to solve the problem. Again, an accepting relationship, established and maintained in the past, will be far more useful than a few rapport-building moments at the beginning of the conference.

Where the concept the parent holds of the child is at variance with the one held by the school, a useful approach is to point out that a child may play a rather different role in school than he does at home. After all, the requirements and expectations are very different, and the child adjusts by developing alternate roles. Somewhere in the maturational process, usually in adolescence, the child tends to unify his roles. Integration is never complete; all of us play somewhat different roles in various situations. By recognizing the need for different roles, and the requirements of each, both the home and the school can gain a better understanding of the child. The goal is not to blame or condemn the child but to understand his position in the educative process and help him cope with the educational encounter. With the parents allied behind the school, chances for success are increased.

Guidance is an essential component of quality education. Like other innovations in elementary education, it requires specialized training.

A major function of guidance in the elementary school is communicating with parents. The goal is neither a grudging compliance nor an armed truce. The goal is to provide guidance for the child so that he may receive maximum benefit from his education.

A Rationale

for Interviewing Parents*

Manford Sonstegard

People interview each other constantly. There is hardly anyone who, if he communicates at all, does not engage in interviewing someone. Therefore, kinds and types of interviews are unlimited.

Much of the interviewing that takes place is spontaneous and unlearned as illustrated by this humorous exchange:

"Would you tell me, please, which way I ought to walk from here?"

"That depends a good deal on where you want to get to," said the Cat.

"I don't much care where—," said Alice.

"Then it doesn't matter which way you walk," said the Cat.

"So long as I get somewhere," Alice added.

"Oh, you're sure to do that," said the Cat, "if you only walk long enough!"

Interviewing, as part of counseling, requires special skill, knowledge,

* *The School Counselor*, December 1964, vol. 12, no. 2. By permission.

creativity, and special techniques—all of which have to be learned. A counselor should get results if only he keeps on long enough. But for the counseling to be effective, the counselor must know where he is going. Once proper knowledge and technique are acquired, the professionally growing counselor improves and perfects his interviewing skill through continuous practice.

There are general techniques or principles of interviewing which are applicable to any counseling situation. However, the adroit counselor adapts his interviewing techniques to each individual he counsels while adhering to fundamental psychological principles. The particular techniques he applies at the moment are governed by a number of factors. The reason for the individual's need for counseling is one of the primary factors to be considered. Interviewing a high school student presents a situation different from that involved in interviewing an elementary school child, for example. There are still other differences when a parent is interviewed; the pattern has to be unique for this particular kind of interview.

A parent interview is unique for at least two reasons. First, in his initial contact, the parent does not come, except in unusual cases, for psychological help for himself; he comes because he is baffled by the behavior of one or more of his children. Thus, the counselor is confronted with an adult who comes to ask for counseling for someone else. Second, the parent is generally not concerned with the "why" of the child's behavior, but rather with "what can be done about it."

The counselor cannot help the parent find out what he might do to improve the deficiencies or misbehavior of his child until he is able to discover the reasons for the child's behavior. To attempt to counsel a parent who seeks help without first ascertaining the meaning of the child's behavior would be comparable to a doctor's prescribing a drug without diagnosing the individual's illness. Since the behavior of the child is causatively related to his interpersonal relationship with his parents, counseling the child without simultaneously counseling the parents would be comparable to the struggle of Sisyphus.

Counseling the parent may be characterized by four distinct steps. First, the counselor has to establish a proper relationship with the parent. Next, he has to understand the parent and his problem. After the counselor understands the problem, he must help the parent understand himself and his interaction with the child. The last step involves reorientation of the parent.

The interview with the parent should reveal the reason for the child's behavior. An interview with the child follows; if he has difficulties in school, the teacher should also be interviewed. The first interview, if properly conducted, establishes a solid and constructive counseling relationship between counselor and parent.

A carefully structured first interview is essential for successful counseling of parents. The counselor first encourages the parent to describe the nature of his problem. "Please tell me why you are here," or "Why did you come to talk to me?" may be a good opening statement. Or one can ask, "What is your problem?" or "What are you concerned about?"

Since the parent has come for a specific purpose, an uninhibited narration of the child's deficiencies usually ensues: how he behaves, what he does wrong, his conflicts with sibling(s), or eating problems, for example. Some troubles in school may also be disclosed. Because of the parents' spontaneous response, the counselor may fall into the error of letting him ramble on indefinitely. The information may be interesting but not helpful for an understanding of the child.

During the initial phase of the interview, the counselor asks the parent to elaborate when statements are of a significant nature. For example, the parent relates that the child has begun to lie. Lying means one thing to one person and something else to another. Whether the lying is pathological or merely a defense against the parents' insurmountably high standards, criticism, nagging, and fault-finding, for example, cannot be ascertained without encouraging the parent to amplify. This may be done by asking, "What happened before this? What did you say? What did you do when—? What did he do when you—?" The basic and primary objective of the interview with the parent is to discover why the child behaves the way he does. In other words, what purpose does the child have in doing what he does?

The behavior of a child does not just happen. Because he is a rational being, he does not merely react to environmental stimulation, but he acts as well. Action is movement, and it is movement toward something which the individual wants. The objective for which he strives, then, becomes his goal. The goal seeking becomes related to his perception of the relationships between himself and the people with whom he interacts. Thus, the child is not predictable; his behavior depends upon the decision he makes, although he may not be aware that he is deciding what he is doing. Consequently, the initial report of the parent is followed by specific questions to discover the reason for the child's doing what he does.

The nature of the child's interpersonal relationships with persons with whom he interacts is fundamental to an understanding of his behavior. This is almost never covered spontaneously by the parent. The counselor will of necessity guide the parent in relating pertinent information so that he may gain clear insight in certain pertinent areas. One of these is the child's position in the family and his interpersonal relationships with siblings. Who is the eldest? Next in line? How does he get along with the other children in the family? Whom does he protect? Who protects him? With whom is he in conflict?

SUGGESTED OUTLINE

In order to get some insight, one should ask, whenever the parent reports some kind of misbehavior, "What did you do about it?" Knowing that, one can see the field in which the child operates and the purpose of his disturbing behavior. Then one can ascertain the following significant facts:

I. Under what conditions did the complaint or problem arise?
   A. At what age?
   B. What has been its duration?
II. What is child's relationship to siblings?
   A. Position in sibling sequence.
      1. Distribution of males and females?
      2. How siblings are different?
      3. How siblings are similar?
   B. With whom is child compared?
      1. Who is child most like?
      2. Who is child least like?
   C. Nature and extent of
      1. Conflicts?
      2. Rivalry?
      3. Competition? (Explain)
      4. Submission?
      5. Rebellion?
         a. Active?
         b. Passive?
III. Environmental influence
   A. Relatives
      1. Grandparents
      2. Other relatives
   B. Other people living in house
   C. Neighbors
IV. What are you doing about it?
   A. Relate in detail the interaction.
   B. Clarify if necessary by: What do you mean by that?
V. In what other way does the child stand out?
   A. Conditions under which he functions adequately?
   B. In what way is he successful?
VI. What is the nature of the daily routine?
   A. How does the child get up in the morning?
      1. Who awakens him?
      2. Is he called more than once?
      3. What about dressing?
      4. What about breakfast?
   B. What happens as he gets off to school?
   C. Describe the lunch hour—the dinner (each mealtime)
   D. How does the child get off to bed? At what time?
VII. What happens when the family goes out together?
   A. Preparation for going out and special efforts
   B. What happens when away?
VIII. How are the child's social relationships?
   A. Ability to make friends with others
      1. Neighborhood children
      2. Adults
      3. Children at school
   B. Does he have pets, and does he take care of them?

  C. Attitude toward school
     1. School work
     2. Relationships with teachers
     3. How does he deal with people in authority?
  D. What impressions has he gained from the family situation?
     1. Has there been any tragedy in the family?
     2. Who is boss?
     3. What methods of discipline have been used?
     4. What kind of punishment?
     5. What kind of supervision?
  IX. What does the child think about his future?
     A. What does he want to be when he grows up?
     B. What is the occupation of other members of the family?
  X. Does the child have nightmares, bad dreams?

Follow-up or Responses

The suggested outline is merely a frame of reference. Rigid adherence to the form will result in a merely mechanical interview, devoid of the subtlety through which the counselor discovers the nature of the interpersonal relationships existing between parents and child. An inflexible dependence upon the outline may block sensitivity to the parents' reactions to the interview. For example, the parent may become apprehensive when asked to elaborate upon his response to the child's behavior. Even though, "What do you do about it (the behavior)?" is an essential part of the interview in providing the counselor with valid insights into the parents' relationship with the child, he may accept the parents' actions without either verbal or non-verbal approval or disapproval. He may, however, point out the parents' faulty methods as the interview progresses. Thus, unsound psychological approaches the parent may be using are interpreted and reoriented during the interview or during the counseling process, whichever approach the counselor considers most suitable.

Even though the counselor is mindful of establishing a good relationship with the parent during the interview, he should not take for granted the statements made in answer to the question, "What is being done about it?" Every statement of action which is not clear should be questioned, "What do you mean by that?" The wisdom of this procedure can best be illustrated by the case of the parent who relates that the child has temper tantrums. To, "What do you do about his temper tantrums?" the mother replies, "I ignore them." This is a psychologically sound method of handling temper tantrums. But a child whose temper tantrums are ignored will not continue to have tantrums because they are futile if there is no audience. Therefore, the counselor was required to follow up with, "What do you mean, you ignore them?" To this the mother replied, "I make him get up from the floor and go to his room." This cannot be labeled as ignoring. The mother's action explains a great deal; the counselor would have been misled had he accepted without question her first explanation.

Certain cases will require additional insights and, consequently, a departure from the structure outlined above. The parents' spontaneous reports will provide the counselor with the necessary leads. An example from the writer's experience will illustrate the point. A mother, during an initial interview, complained of the behavior of the three children and their disobedience. As she related the incidents, she cast sideward glances at her husband in which the counselor thought he saw resentment. Adroit probing by the counselor established the fact that the mother was resentful of her husband because he did not help with the discipline. The father, it transpired, resented his wife's domination of the family and gave tacit approval of the children's disobedience. He relished especially in their son a defiance he did not dare exhibit. The counselor would not have gained this fundamental insight into the reason for the family problem had he not been alert to the non-verbal communication of the mother.

An interview pattern is useful in establishing rapport with parents and for understanding the purpose of the child's behavior. On the strength of the information gained in the interview, the counselor has insight and deeper understanding of the conflict and a basis for an interview with the child. The skilled counselor uses the outline as a guide, deviating from it when the spontaneous verbal and non-verbal communication of the parents warrants it.

REFERENCES

Adler, Alexandra. 1948. *Guiding human misfits: a practical application of individual psychology.* New York: Philosophical Library.

Dreikurs, R., R. Corsini, R. Lowe, and M. Sonstegard. 1959. *Adlerian family counseling.* A manual for counseling centers. Eugene, Ore.: University of Oregon Press.

Garret, Annette. 1942. *Interviewing, its principles and methods.* New York: Family Service Association of America.

Farwell, Gail F., and H. J. Peters. 1960. *Guidance readings for counselors.* Skokie, Ill.: Rand McNally.

Sonstegard, M. December 1954. A center for guidance of parents and children in a small community. *Amer. J. indiv. Psychol., 11,* 81–89.

Chapter 11

PROGRAM APPRAISAL
AND GUIDANCE RESEARCH

The myriad of questions that school personnel must continually ask themselves regarding the appraisal of the elementary school guidance program requires a far more intensive evaluative system than exists today in almost any school. Most school counselors lack the time and the skill to determine the successes and failures of their own programs in guidance and counseling. How, then, can the best methods of guidance be used in any particular situation or with any particular child or at any particular grade level? Determination of this basic problem will solve many of the complexities existing in the elementary school guidance services.

Techniques of guidance research will be discussed in this chapter as a means of furthering the educator's and counselor's understanding of the evaluation problem. Still existing today are those obstacles which have kept the field of guidance from formulating its components into a science; for example, unclear nomenclature, trivial generalities of objectives, uncontrolled complex variables, inability to establish control groups, inadequate samplings. Guidance research has been unable to categorize and classify its components; it has barely begun to identify them.

THE NEED FOR RESEARCH

The articles by Stiller and Cottingham appearing in this chapter point to the need for testing the philosophy, assumptions, and concepts of guidance. They

367

stress the need for both longitudinal experimental studies and small-scale descriptive research.

The first duty of guidance research is to investigate educators' expectations for the guidance process in order to establish existing criteria for guidance evaluation. It is the author's contention that since the objectives of guidance relate so closely to student development, guidance research should be concerned primarily with the adequacy of counselor assistance to the child in the following areas:

1. To assist the child to learn academic content effectively.

2. To assist the child to make decisions regarding his educational and vocational development by considering his abilities, self-concept, and opportunities.

3. To aid the child in acquiring self-understanding and self-acceptance.

4. To help the child develop so that his self-image and aspirations are compatible with his aptitudes.

5. To enable the child to choose between appropriate alternatives to a problem.

6. To improve the child's peer relationships and help him in his social adjustment.

While the above objectives are comparatively general and serve as a starting point of evaluation, additional, detailed research might open for investigation some of the following more specific guidance objectives:

1. The increased understanding of academic content.

2. Improved selection by the child of areas of study appropriate to his abilities and interests.

3. The child's greater knowledge about himself and his perceptions.

4. Increased accuracy in the child's perception of himself in relation to his peers and his environment.

STEPS IN CONDUCTING GUIDANCE RESEARCH

Guidance research necessitates utilization of the following steps:

1. Definition of the problem. The counselor would select a question of importance in regard to a pertinent educational problem. Research might begin by an investigation of how effectively the objectives of elementary school guidance are being achieved in the school. Selection of an issue that the counselor and staff genuinely want to study is important.

2. Establishing the hypothesis. Objectives should be stated in terms of observable and measurable student characteristics and behaviors.

3. Construction of the research design. The researcher identifies his assumptions, limitations, and sources of evidence that will be used to test the hypothesis. The research design requires an evaluation of the instruments to be used and the development of statistical methods.

4. Analyzing data. The researcher should use appropriate statistical pro-

cedures to evaluate the results of the study. Whenever possible, it is important to validate immediate goals against long-term goals of the program.

5. Interpretation of data. In the final step, the researcher states the conclusions, interpreting the results in light of the objectives of the study and the limitations of his research design.

The elementary school practitioner—counselor, teacher, or administrator—interested in studying local guidance problems or basic assumptions related to guidance is referred to an excellent brochure entitled "Operational Studies in Guidance" (1962).

Meaningful research requires continued acquaintance with pertinent literature such as the professional journals of the American Personnel and Guidance Association. Another invaluable resource is the *Review of Educational Research*, a publication of the American Educational Research Association. In three-year cycles, the *Review* summarizes past research and makes suggestions for new studies.

PROBLEMS IN ACCOMPLISHING RESEARCH

Guidance is usually conceived of as service-oriented. Interested and competent researchers are often hindered by a lack of understanding on the part of local administration and staff. The demands for guidance services are great, but recognition of the necessity for local research is still limited. A major hindrance to research is lack of skill and training of researchers. Also, teachers and parents are concerned about which students in the district will be used as either experimental or control elements of the study. Aside from personal and psychological reasons, students might be deprived of certain educational gains because of their selection.

Elementary school guidance is often hampered by the lack of clear, concise, theoretical formulations. Counselors themselves are not even clear about the types of guidance functions that should be carried on by teachers and by counselors. There is certainly a need for a study of those guidance competencies expected of teachers and counselors.

In his article, Stefflre clearly indicates that the results of guidance are not the same for all individuals, and that counselors may be seeking different outcomes with different students. The problem of individual goals in guidance has seldom been attacked except in certain behavioral studies. As Ohlsen (1964) has indicated: "Nonsignificant results often can be accounted for by the investigator's failure to define appropriate criteria for individual clients."

One approach to studying individual goals is to establish for each child some desired modification of behavior. The specific treatment for the individual can then be decided upon. The device for measuring behavior is specified at the time of diagnosis, and results are compared for each individual. This type of research enables the counselor to identify the variables effective in producing change and to answer questions specific to individuals rather than groups. The results of such studies can be reported in terms of percentage of change.

Elementary school guidance research must take into consideration developmental factors. The study must always consider the individual both in terms of his uniqueness and his maturity (Mussen and Jones, 1957). The counselor conducting research with children should first become familiar with some of the basic principles in the area of child development which affect growth and change (Dinkmeyer, 1965; Olson, 1959).

Local research should involve teachers, since teachers can apply research more adequately because of their total involvement in it from the start. This enables them to investigate questions and collect data that is personally meaningful to them. Under these conditions, teachers are able to make inferences and generalizations for practice.

The research needs in elementary school guidance are considerable. Some questions which require study include:

1. What outcomes can be expected of elementary school guidance?

2. Which guidance functions are best assumed by the classroom teacher, counselor, or parent?

3. What are the contributions of the behavioral sciences to guidance practices?

4. What developmental needs go unmet when guidance personnel are not part of the school system?

5. Which techniques and procedures best accomplish certain specific goals?

6. What are the effects of various techniques and how can they be related to specific situations?

Specific studies might also be made which compare techniques such as counseling and information giving; group counseling and group guidance; test interpretation to pupils and test interpretation to teachers, and so on.

Effective decision making depends upon the amount of information available that is valid to the situation. The Bureau of Research Training and Dissemination of the Office of Education has now established ERIC (Educational Research Information Center) to assist in the dissemination of educational research (Walz, 1967).

Stiller points out that a theoretical framework for school guidance is basic to research. He indicates that pre- and post-test measures should be established and techniques and functions evaluated in terms of educational objectives.

Peters and Hansen discuss the rationale and need for research by the school counselor. They present seven competencies necessary for research by the school counselor. They describe various methods of research and procedures for initiating them. A set of research problems, with one criterion for each problem, serve to stimulate the student's thinking about problems in his school and necessary criteria.

Stefflre portrays the present state of guidance research and poses some of the problems which cause the paucity of results, among them: need for clarification of terms, local and descriptive research, and involved statistical manipulation of data hampering progress. He mentions some promising research which offers a brighter horizon for the future.

Cottingham presents an extensive review of the guidance research pertinent to theoretical formulations, guidance functions, and the unmet needs of elementary school pupils. He provides an intensive acquaintance with both theory and research statements related to elementary school guidance. Cottingham encourages in-depth review of behavioral science literature in order to develop a unique elementary school guidance theory. He makes specific suggestions regarding the type of questions and studies which might be undertaken.

REFERENCES

Dinkmeyer, D. 1965. *Child development: the emerging self.* Englewood Cliffs, N.J.: Prentice-Hall.

Mussen, P., and M. Jones. June 1957. Self-conception, motivation, and interpersonal attitudes of late and early maturing boys. *Child Develpm., 28.*

Ohlsen, M. 1964. *Guidance services in the modern school.* New York: Harcourt.

Olson, W. 1959. *Child development.* Second ed.; Boston: Heath.

Professional Development and Research Committee of the New York State Association of Deans and Guidance Personnel. 1962. *Operational studies in guidance.* Great Neck, N.Y.: Great Neck Public Schools.

Walz, G. 1967. Who or what is ERIC? *Sch. Couns., 14* (No. 3).

School Guidance Needs Research*

Alfred Stiller

In recent years, education has come under scrutiny and criticism from experts in diverse fields. Many suggestions have been made to improve the efficiency of education, some of them apolar to each other. In many cases, however, a common proposal for the partial solution of educational ills has been to increase and/or improve the guidance services offered. The result has been a rapid increase in the number of schools offering guidance services and the number of counselors employed. For example, in 1948 there were the equivalent of 450 full-time coun-

* *Personnel and Guidance Journal,* May 1963, vol. 41, no. 9. By permission.

selors in New York State; in 1962 there were 1,975. Open to question, however, is the improvement of the effectiveness of the secondary school as a result of these guidance services and counselors.

Cartwright and Zander (1960) have noted that group dynamics proceeded through at least two identifiable stages in progressing to its present state of development. The first of these was the formulation of theoretical models by outstanding thinkers, based upon their subjective speculations concerning the nature of groups. The second stage saw an empirical rebellion, leading to the testing of propositions about groups and the acquisition of data upon which to base new theories. It is likely that the school guidance movement has progressed through three such stages and is commencing upon a fourth.

Guidance in the school commonly is thought to have begun with the establishment of the Vocation Bureau of Boston in 1908. The ensuing years saw a rapid rise in the number of vocational counselors employed by schools. Their primary function lay in vocational planning so that industry could more effectively utilize high school graduates or dropouts. Vocational planning gradually expanded to include educational planning; the guidance worker now provided educational and vocational information for students. The emphasis was first on the information-giving aspect of guidance and later upon the analysis of the individual with a job requiring his skills or characteristics. Procedures employed were drawn from the fields of education, industrial personnel work, and industrial psychology. In this stage, the guidance worker was thought of as the teacher, manipulator, or benevolent despot for his charges, and stress was placed upon the most effective procedures to be employed in fulfilling this function.

Another stage began when guidance became concerned with meeting the needs of youth as perceived from the frame of reference of the youth themselves. Guidance now drew heavily from clinical psychology and personality theory and became concerned with the establishment of a theoretical frame of reference within which the counselor should work. This necessitated the prior establishment of a theory of personality development upon which the counselor's working referents could be based. The procedures employed by the guidance worker followed from his theoretical orientation; this phase, then, may be characterized by the speculations of outstanding thinkers upon the nature of personality and personality change. The primary example would be the controversy between the psychoanalytic and Rogerian self-theory schools of thought.

During the past decade, emphasis has again shifted to the procedures to be employed and most publications have stressed the pragmatics of the guidance function. Wilkins and Perlmutter (1960) have reviewed the literature in guidance in the years 1957–1960 and have stated that almost no books exist today that deal with guidance theory. Similar conclusions are drawn for periodical articles and for doctoral dissertations. Wrenn (1959) concluded that few authors in the guidance field pretend to possess a consistent philosophy of guidance. Ennis (1960) surveyed a number of standard guidance textbooks and found that they contain a plethora of information about methodology, but little material relating to philosophical or theoretical formulation.

During the past few years, it has been possible to detect a concern by authors over this lack of a philosophical orientation (Ennis, 1960; Wilkins and Perlmutter, 1960; Wrenn, 1959). Articles are now appearing on philosophical issues in counseling (Arbuckle, 1958; Moynihan, 1957); values in counseling (Williamson, 1958); theoretical principles (Tyler, 1958); and a rationale for guidance (Hutson, 1958). It is possible that we are now beginning a new era, one of concern for the theoretical bases of guidance.

NEED FOR THE STUDY

Throughout these past phases, however, most of the theoretical and methodological formulations have been drawn from areas other than school guidance. Sociology, clinical and counseling psychology, industrial personnel work, and vocational counseling have provided the source of theories and practices employed. The major authors read by school counselors today are professors of educational psychology, counseling psychologists, or human relations engineers. Most of the studies upon which conclusions have been based have been performed upon college students or emotionally disturbed youngsters. The bulk of counselor training is performed by psychologically oriented educators or by people who identify themselves as counseling psychologists. The terms "guidance" and "counseling" have a wide range of meanings, depending upon the disciplines which employ them. Thus, Rothney and Roens (1949, p. 8) are able to say that "the guidance program must become essentially a counseling program" and Stewart (1959) can ask that the counselor have "the right to enough time to do his real job . . . to engage in counseling *per* se," while Pepinsky and Pepinsky (1954) can state that the current tendency is to group all psychotherapies under the term "counseling," and Hoppock (1960) can ask that guidance counselors leave psychotherapy to the psychotherapists. To confuse the issue further, counseling psychologists tend to view counseling as a unique discipline which may be applied to any field of work (Arbuckle, 1959; Bordin, 1955).

In this babel of dissenting voices, one point emerges clearly. Little attempt has been made to determine if guidance in the school should differ in any significant manner from that employed in college, industry, or mental health services. Little attempt has been made to discover if the essentially normal, adolescent population with which the secondary school professor works differs significantly from the more mature populations of college and industry, from the intellectually and socially more homogeneous population of the college, or the more abnormal population of the clinic—or if the elementary school population differs from the secondary. Two of the three publications purporting to deal empirically with guidance in the high school (Hartley, 1949; Wrenn and Dugan, 1950) are based upon surveys of existing guidance practices and make no attempt to test the data or to establish a rationale for high school guidance. A noteworthy exception is the longitudinal study performed by Rothney (1958) which set up a guidance program similar to those commonly provided in secondary schools and appraised its effectiveness. Even this study, however, restricted itself to methods currently employed by secondary school counselors and discussed results only in terms of general gain (or lack of it) of a counseled group as against a control group. No attempt was made to investigate the differential effects of various techniques in diverse situations or to establish a theoretical framework for guidance in the secondary school. It would seem that the time is now overdue for an appraisal of the value of guidance in the secondary school, its place in the school organization, and the techniques and procedures which seem to be most effective in achieving the goals of education. Results of this appraisal would have implications for current practices in guidance, the functions and duties of the counselor, and the theoretical or philosophical bases upon which the guidance service should rest.

SUGGESTED PROCEDURE

Because of the present dearth of investigation of guidance in the secondary school, it might be wise to attempt a comprehensive, all-embracing study, both longitudinal and horizontal. The take-off point might be the functions of the counselor as stated by the Committee on Professional Training, Licensing, and Certification, of the American Personnel and Guidance Association. Specifically, these are:

1. To increase the accuracy of the individual's self-percepts.
2. To increase the accuracy of the individual's environmental perceptions.
3. To integrate the individual's self-percepts with environmental realities and perceptions.
4. To present relevant information.
5. To improve the individual's ability to make and execute plans.

The first three of these are psychological in nature, the fourth is reality-based, and the fifth is generally agreed upon as the ultimate aim of all personnel work. Several questions may be raised concerning these functions.

1. *Do these functions contribute to the attainment of educational objectives significantly more than would the absence of these functions?*

Another manner of phrasing the same question would be "Is guidance in the high school worth the additional expense entailed?" It is possible that we are erecting our guidance structures upon quicksand premises. Unless guidance can be shown to contribute materially to the effectiveness of the school, why have guidance?

This question might best be answered by a longitudinal study similar to that of Rothney (1958) in Wisconsin. The major treatment would be an intensive summer training program for selected high school counselors. All students in this summer training program would have had minimal training as psychological counselors, be currently in practice, and possess certification in their field. The training program would attempt to develop in these counselors relatively homogeneous attitudes toward the functions listed above and comparable skills in performing these functions. The counselors would serve as the field force for the implementation of the APGA functions. It would likely be necessary to establish pre- and post-test measures for the following criteria:

a. Improved self-concept.
b. Decrease in dropout rate.
c. Improved school achievement.
d. Decrease in school problem behavior.
e. More realistic educational planning.
f. More realistic post-high school educational or vocational choice.
g. Greater satisfaction with post-high school progress five years after graduation.
h. Decreased incidence of problem behavior (job mobility, anti-social actions) five years after graduation.

2. *Do certain of these functions contribute to the attainment of educational objectives to a significantly greater degree than do others?*

Three of the five counselor functions listed by APGA refer to the personal-social-emotional sphere of counseling. Most counseling psychologists would agree upon these as the most important functions of the high school counselor. However, Ginzberg (1960) argues that it is more important to ensure that information is made available to those who need it than it is to work on psychodynamics. Hoppock (1960) asks counselors to "leave psychotherapy to the psychotherapists." Assuming that personal-social-emotional counseling is being equated with psychodynamics and psychotherapy, Ginzberg and Hoppock are denying that these are the counselor's major functions.

Involved here is the manner in which guidance is to be performed; to this writer this issue is derived from the basic issue of "Should the high school guidance counselor operate as a guidance worker or as a psychological counselor?" It would be wise to test, then, if psychological counseling is more effective than information-giving in improving the individual's ability to make and execute plans as tested by criteria *b* through *h* above.

Also at issue is the question of group work. Individual counseling has traditionally been considered as the *sine qua non* of personnel work; however, Hoppock argues that more can be accomplished through group guidance. Counseling psychologists will counter with group counseling. It is likely that this question can be answered only in terms of the protagonists. However, it seems wise to attempt to measure the effectiveness of various techniques and functions in terms of their furtherance of educational objectives.

The most effective way to study the entire question might be to train counselors in the Ginzberg-Hoppock procedures and to compare the results obtained by these counselors against the results obtained by those counselors mentioned in the preceding section. Care would be required to ensure that degree of training, schools, and population groups were comparable.

An interesting corollary to this study would be to administer diagnostic personality instruments to all counselors to determine if certain techniques are more effective with certain syndromes of counselor personality characteristics. Evidence already exists in the literature to support this view.

3. *Are the functions of the guidance counselor as seen by other sources more realistic for secondary schools in terms of their specific problems?*

The secondary school is beset by many problems which may affect the adequacy of guidance. Most pupil-counselor ratios are in the neighborhood of 400 or more to one, and the counselor is expected to work to some degree with each of his charges (Boy, 1960). In addition, the counselor carries a plethora of other duties, some of which may be identifiable as guidance functions, some of which are purely administrative or clerical, all of which are considered to be important in some way to the functioning of the school, and none of which may be considered as counseling. An important factor here might be the administrator's concept of the role to be played by the counselor; the literature suggests that in many cases administrators are more secure if their counselors deal more with information-giving and with sub-administrative details rather than with personal-social-emotional adjustment. This concept of the administrator is likely to be a limiting factor to the role which the counselor may play in actuality, regardless of the attitudes of his teachers. A complementary problem is the lack of communication between administrators and counselor-trainers.

The concept of role would of necessity include the concepts which students, parents, and teachers might carry of the counselor's role. These might also act as limits to the degree to which the counselor might act as he perceives his role.

The basic issue here is the degree to which lack of time, money, personnel, and training may affect the functions of the guidance worker. Evidence obtained from this and the preceding two sections should be made available to administrators and counselor-trainers alike; hopefully, this might result either in a modification of the expectations of administrators or of the training of counselors or both.

4. *What are the variables which might influence the effectiveness of counseling in the secondary school?*

Hoppock (1960) argues that the limitations of time prevent the high school counselor from carrying on the type of individual counseling which is reported in the literature. Training (or the lack of it) might likely be another limitation. Ginzberg (1960) has pointed out that adolescents are "labile" in their thinking and planning, while Labrant (1955) refers to differential growth patterns between boys and girls and to the need for students to make vocational choices before they are sufficiently mature. Kvaraceus, *et al.* (1959) have stated that the lower social class has a culture all its own, with its own beliefs and customs, which might indicate a social class differential in perceptions of school and of guidance. College-bound students might have perceptions of the guidance function different from those of noncollege-bound students. The high school guidance counselor is acting as an agent of society; as such, he may be more limited in his work than is the college or vocational counselor. Peters and Farwell (1958) have pointed out several aspects of high school guidance which differ significantly from personnel work in other areas.

Any of the variables mentioned above, and likely some not yet mentioned, may serve to differentiate the manner in which high school guidance must be practiced from personnel work in other fields. The literature must be surveyed to determine empirically those variables which might affect the practice of guidance in the high school. Researches would then be designed to test the effects of these variables. While it is impossible at this moment to outline these designs, it is expected that they would fit into the framework of the longitudinal studies mentioned earlier; that is, these would be shorter, simpler studies, horizontal in nature, but performed in the same schools as are participating in the longitudinal study.

The American Personnel and Guidance Association has recently issued a policy statement on counselor education. The formulation of training standards presupposes a knowledge of the counselor's duties and functions, yet there is ample evidence that various groups differ in their perceptions of the counselor's role. A research program such as that discussed above should assist immeasurably in clarifying concepts of the counselor's role and functions.

REFERENCES

Arbuckle, D. S. 1959. A review of Carolyn A. Secrest's article entitled, New dimensions in counseling students. *Personnel guid. J.*, 37, 519.

―――. 1958. Five philosophical issues in counseling. *J. counsel. Psychol.*, 5, 211–215.

Bordin, E. S. 1955. *Psychological counseling.* New York: Appleton.

Boy, A. V. 1960. The captive client. *Sch. Couns.*, 8, 28–31.

Cartwright, D., and A. Zander. 1960. *Group dynamics.* New York: Harper & Row.

Ennis, Mae. 1960. The need for a philosophy of guidance still haunts us. *Voc. guid. Quart.*, 9, 138–140.

Ginzberg, E. 1960. Guidance-limited or unlimited. *Personnel guid. J.*, 38, 707–712.

Hartley, D. 1949. *Guidance practices in the schools of New York State.* Albany, N.Y.: State Education Department. Mimeographed.

Hoppock, R. March 1960. *An irreverent look at a sacred cow.* Address delivered to the New York State Counselors Association.

Hutson, P. W. 1958. The rationale of guidance. *Bull. NASSP*, 42, 121–128.

Kvaraceus, W. *et al.* 1959. *Delinquent behavior.* Washington, D.C.: National Education Association.

Labrant, L. 1955. Mental health practices in the high school grades. *Mental health in modern education.* 54th Yearbook, National Society for the Study of Education. Chicago: University of Chicago Press.

Moynihan, J. F. 1957. The philosophical aspects of guidance. *Rev. educ. Res.,* 27, 186–191.

Pepinsky, H., and Pauline Pepinsky. 1954. *Counseling: theory and practice.* New York: Ronald.

Peters, H. J., and Gail F. Farwell. 1958. What is different about high school counseling? *Sch. Couns.,* 5, 67–70.

Rothney, J. W. M. 1958. *Guidance practices and results.* New York: Harper & Row.

————, and B. A. Roens. 1949. *Counseling the individual student.* New York: Holt, Rinehart and Winston.

Stewart, C. C. 1959. A bill of rights for school counselors. *Personnel guid. J.,* 37, 500–503.

Tyler, Leona E. 1958. Theoretic principles underlying the counseling process. *J. counsel. Psychol.,* 5, 3–8.

Wilkins, W. D., and Barbara J. Perlmutter. 1960. The philosophical foundations of guidance and personnel work. *Rev. educ. Res.,* 30, 97–104.

Williamson, E. G. 1958. Value orientations in counseling. *Personnel guid. J.,* 36, 520–528.

Wrenn, C. G. 1959. Philosophical and psychological bases of personnel services in education. *Personnel services in education.* 58th Yearbook, Part II, National Society for the Study of Education. Chicago: University of Chicago Press.

————, and W. E. Dugan. 1950. *Guidance procedures in high school.* Minneapolis: University of Minnesota Press.

The School Counselor

as a Researcher*

Herman J. Peters / James C. Hansen

Every professional school counselor spends a part of his time in research activities. Such scientific study is essential not only to the development and continuation of an effective guidance program, but also to the success of the entire school effort.

No school person is in a more strategic position to study pupils in their de-

* *The School Counselor,* March 1964, vol. 11. By permission.

velopmental progress than the school counselor. His contacts with students are uniquely advantageous, different from those of other staff members. Thus, he is in an excellent position to collect and organize useful information for research.

The counselor also has a fluid time schedule, which permits him to give attention to the research function in a variety of school activities under variable conditions.

A truly effective counselor must play a dual role, that of school counselor and observer. As a disciplined observer, he is a scientist who engages in continuous research to develop a more accurate and meaningful understanding of the pupil as well as the guidance process. In this way he is able to increase his professional competence.

NEED FOR RESEARCH

Is there a real need to do research in the elementary and secondary school guidance programs?

The applicability of university and clinical research to elementary and secondary school settings has been too easily accepted. Perhaps some findings are translatable. However, the significant differences in cultural dimensions and in pupil development, educational program and purposes at the two school levels necessitate research within each respective framework.

College and university counselor education programs for the preparation of school counselors must focus on the school guidance function in the appropriate locale. The school guidance research studies and conceptualizations available are minimal.

Thus, the assumption of any similarities between college or clinical counseling and the school guidance function should be verified by research rather than adopted on a basis of faith.

Guidance practices cannot consistently grow in effectiveness unless they are evaluated by counselors using a variety of kinds of research. Research is necessary for the continued improvement of the guidance program. Without it, it is difficult to tell whether the guidance program is truly effective, actually meeting the needs of the students and implementing its unique function in the total school program.

The contribution of guidance functions to the instructional program, extra school activities and administration needs to be enhanced through research. It is more economical to tie together the implications of guidance follow-up studies or community surveys for instructional revisions than for the instructional committee to conduct similar and overlapping studies. A follow-up study gives an opportunity to reflect on the activities of the school, the guidance program itself, and to identify the particular emphases for improvement as seen by former students. Community surveys provide a means of assuring that the staff knows and understands the community it serves and that the school is attuned to the community's educational needs.

One of the most promising frontiers of research is that which deals with the process of pupil development in the educational setting. Such research requires an understanding of the nature of the individual in successive stages of his educational development and his ability to cope with his total life space.

Further, research data can help the student to look at his promise for becoming his optimal self in future settings.

A framework for research on student development demands understanding of the student's relationships with others in the setting in which he is being educated. It necessitates understanding the on-going culture in which the individual student and counselor find themselves.

COMPETENCIES NEEDED

School counselors must have a continuing curiosity about their work. This curiosity must be enflamed by disciplined research rather than consumed by the enervating rituals and routines of the guidance program. The spirit of inquiry, the essence of learning, is an essential ingredient of counselor education. Initiated in the counselor's preparation, the spirit of inquiry can propel itself into his career in school guidance, with particular emphasis in research.

The competencies of the school counselor for research center in the following areas:

1. Experience in developing, identifying, and resolving questions about the guidance function.

2. Knowledge of different types of research and the inherent demands of each for rigorous, reputable accomplishment.

3. Understanding of implications for one's school guidance program from research reports in appropriate journals.

4. Ability to assess student educational development in the local school against a backdrop of national information.

5. Ability to determine discrepancy between student potential and performance and its possible significance.

6. Ability to analyze guidance test data and record data.

7. Skills to conduct research relevant to achievement, study skills, career thinking, personal development, and follow-through studies.

These competencies require a school counselor's continuing study of the conceptualization of the guidance function, processes, and instruments. These seem to bring to life the developmental psychology of pupil growth and the changing cultural scene. Out of these competencies arise the specifics of the nature of research in the school guidance function.

NATURE OF RESEARCH

Research extends our knowledge. It gives us additional bases for making decisions, but it does not give us the decision. At its best, research creates new problems for further study, always protecting its invigorating characteristic.

There are different research roads for various purposes. The historiographic, the survey-descriptive, the longitudinal or developmental, the case study and the experimental—these are the approaches available to the school counselor.

Historiographic research is one way for the school counselor to identify tendencies, themes and patterns, either of pupils or of the school, which have impact on the current guidance function.

Research to verify observed grading patterns may show the counselor that in his school a "C" grade is achieved by many high ability pupils because there are so many of them. Thus, to be "average" in this particular school is quite unlike the normal distribution about which he has heard so much. The study of this pattern and its persistence over a period of years will yield a history of great moment and impact on the guidance program.

The disciplined research method of historiography may seem to merely confirm what is "easily observable." Research often does just this, but it does far more. It orders the information into patterns for deeper interpretation by the thoughtful counselor. It verifies or nullifies the authenticity and credibility of that which just seemed to be.

The *survey-descriptive* research approach provides a method to secure evidence about conditions in the guidance program as they now exist.

The survey of study skills and attitudes of pupils, for example, gives a picture for action today. In future years, similar surveys may yield different results. The survey of pupil college choice will alert the school counselor to check the usefulness of his educational information resources.

The careful use of the survey method necessitates skill in its instrumentation and discerning judgment in interpreting the results, as is true for any research method.

Longitudinal or *developmental* studies are of special interest to school counselors. Because the proper guidance function is developmental, this research approach provides a sound basis for studying boys and girls.

The central purpose of developmental research is to discover directions, predispositions, precipitators, trends, rates and changes in the life-space progress, particularly educational progress, of pupils.

The developmental approach provides a basis for examining incipiency of selected behavioral patterns. The onset of underachievement is a guidance concern that can be studied in this way. Further, this approach assists the counselor in distinguishing between transitory incidents in a pupil's developing behavior and negative and positive patterns emerging with their life-long implications.

A basic research approach for emphasis of the guidance function is the *case study* method. The case study uses all relevant data about an individual to assist the counselor in understanding the pupil in the study of himself rather than as a passive object of study by the counselor.

This method depends on completeness of data, synthesis of data in picturing the life stream of the individual and consequent promise of behavior of the individual based on the material at hand. The case study is an excellent research approach in which to involve other school staff.

A research approach of great emphasis is the *experimental* method. The experimental research method is distinguished by the degree of control over the variables studied and the carefully delimited dimensions of the study.

The chief difficulty lies in a design to be sure that the variables controlled are, in fact, isolable from other potentially influencing factors. The chief advantages of the experimental approach is that it gives vividness to a determinant affecting the conditions under study. It must be kept in mind that even though one variable is isolated, the human situation results from a complex interactive process of many variables. However, the one-by-one study of them makes sharper analyses of the problem.

This method is particularly useful in researching guidance functions involving process, e.g., counseling. Various facets of the counseling process can be changed and studied for their implications.

USEFULNESS OF DATA

The data resulting from the research methodology are useful only if the study has been designed with care and sound judgment has been used in making inferences and drawing generalizations. The cause and effect conclusion is too often the Achilles heel of research.

Another variable outside the focus of the research may have been the factor making for a difference or causing it not to occur. Multiple variable control is needed, and with it comes the need for more research, understanding, and skill.

But it should be remembered that the school counselor can initiate less complicated research as a basis for deepening his professional school counselor role, with more involved research functions in the future.

INITIATING RESEARCH

Before he can do any research, a counselor must choose a research project that will answer or help to answer a problem of some importance. Then he must organize a plan, carefully setting up his objectives, his criteria, and the populations to be included.

Materials must then be collected and arrangements made for optimum observations or measurements. Then the research procedures start.

After the data have been collected, they must be analyzed. In reporting the findings of the research, counselors should strive for the same precision and simplicity as in the research itself.

Research questions may focus on the following key points:

1. What is the problem?
2. For what questions are answers being sought?
3. What is said in the literature about the problem?
4. What are the *precise* procedures to be used to solve the problem?
5. How do I plan to report the findings?
6. What recommendations for action in my school will be made?

7. What further research is prompted by this study?

8. How may I report this to the personnel and guidance profession?

DIFFICULTIES

One wonders why more guidance research has not been done in the elementary and secondary schools. Loughary (1961) found, when he questioned many school counselors, that most of the responses were covered by the following generalizations:

1. I don't have time to carry on research. What with my other responsibilities, I never seem to complete my counseling and other assigned guidance duties, let alone doing a study.

2. Administrative policy makes it difficult for me to conduct research. My administrators don't want students used as guinea pigs. They say school board members would ask, "If you don't know that counseling works, why are we paying for it?"

3. I don't feel that I have the necessary research skills to do serious experimental work.

Lack of time is an answer given to many questions that involve work. Although the time schedule is not rigidly set, most counselors find that they are kept busy with their counseling interviews, recordings and scheduling, in addition to meetings and other educational tasks. Many school systems cannot afford adequate staff for their counseling service; therefore, many counselors are carrying a heavy load of counselees.

Guidance workers who are sincerely concerned with experimental research often find themselves lacking the skills that are necessary for effective research programs. These counselors did not have sufficient exposure and training in college to feel adequately prepared in research activities. They did not know how to keep thorough and accurate records. They did not know how to compile information they collected and organize it into a brief but enlightening report.

Probably some counselors who had been exposed to the techniques of carrying on research lacked the individual enthusiasm to do the extra work and planning that is necessary for research.

SUGGESTIONS

Many problems present themselves that would have guidance implications in any secondary school setting. A list of some of these may spur school counselors to initiate research or to extend it to new areas. Consultive help may be secured from colleagues, university staff, or state department.

... Table 1 suggests one criterion for judging the outcome of research on each problem. If the guidance function is applied to the problem, there ought to be a difference in the criterion. This difference should be more than what one might reasonably expect if the guidance function had not been applied to the problem.

Of course, other factors may change the criterion. However, if other conditions in the school are observed as having no appreciable change during the research, it is at least a matter for thought that the guidance function did have impact on the criterion.

TABLE 1/ CRITERIA FOR JUDGING THE OUTCOME
OF RESEARCH ON GUIDANCE PROBLEMS

Pupil-Problem Centered Research

Problem	*Criterion*
1. Counseling potential drop-outs	Number remaining in school
2. Course selection	Selection in terms of ability
3. Knowledge of self	Congruence with test-inventory-observation results
4. Level of aspiration of high ability pupils	Selection of courses prerequisite to higher goals
5. Use of encouragement	Greater observed productivity of pupils after encouragement

Guidance Process Centered Research

Problem	*Criterion*
1. Junior high pupils have concerns of high school rather than college	Content of counseling tapes—recorded topics
2. Counselor initiated counseling	Number of continued contacts
3. Questioning versus pupils leads	Number of continued pupil flow remarks with pupil leads
4. Counselor talk	Word count versus pupil
5. Case staffing	Increase of participants

Guidance Profession Centered Research

Problem	*Criterion*
1. Role commitment	Diary choices of guidance functions over others
2. Analysis of cumulative records	Use versus omissions and positive versus negative statements
3. Prognosis of algebra	Study which test best predictor
4. Follow-up	Former student recognition of guidance services

SUMMARY

Today's school counselor must spend a part of his time in research. Without research, the guidance function will be a superstructure of activities based on a pinhead of substantiation. Without research, the school counselor will be tempted to yield to research data from other closely related disciplines whose focus is on adults or the mentally ill.

The research competencies needed by the school counselor center on the very heart of the spirit of effective inquiry. The school counselor has a number of research approaches for his many varied concerns. Care must be given to thoughtful inference and generalization from research studies.

The chief deterrent to research lies in school counselor reluctance. Research can be started on a number of the school counselor's immediate daily challenges.

Active research by the school counselor is needed as a basis for doing a more effective guidance job. Guidance research is essential if the school counselor is to gain the fullness of professional stature that he is seeking.

REFERENCE

Loughary, J. W. 1961. *Counseling in secondary schools.* New York: Harper & Row.

Research in Guidance:
Horizons for the Future*

Buford Stefflre

The present relationship between research and practice in guidance is much like the relationship between research and practice in other areas of education. If we did, in the name of guidance, only those things that research has proven to be worth doing, we would have a good deal of free time on our hands. We act largely in the name of the three great educational motivators—instinct, inertia, and imitation! And yet, on the horizon we see the promise of better things.

Present knowledge in guidance can be divided into three categories. There is a very small category of knowledge that we know to be true as a result of sound research evidence. There is an extremely large category of "knowledge" that we "know" from common sense or scholastic revelation; such knowledge may be said to be part of the "conventional wisdom." Finally, there is a category of knowledge that is growing rapidly that indicates what we do not know! Well-designed research in guidance typically results in transferring "knowledge" from the second category to the third one. The most common conclusion reached as a consequence of carefully designed research in guidance is the verdict—"not proven."

* *Theory Into Practice*, 1963, vol. 2, no. 1. By permission.

PRESENT STATE OF GUIDANCE RESEARCH

To be more specific with regard to our present situation, let us take a look at the research that deals with the value of counseling. In reviewing this research, the most defensible conclusion is that there is no solid evidence that counseling helps its recipients. An optimistic reaction to this same evidence is contained in the article "Counseling Theory" in the *Encyclopedia of Educational Research,* in which Leary and Harvey (1960) are quoted as follows: "The steady growth in prestige of . . . [psychotherapy] in the teeth of these two obstacles—its unscientific status and its inherent threats to the conscious ego—is a remarkable testimony to its basic effectiveness or to the capacity of otherwise intelligent professional workers to deceive themselves" (p. 347). Regardless of our interpretation of the lack of proof regarding the value of counseling, the fact remains that such proof is not now existent. The difficulty of gathering evidence in this field is tremendous, inasmuch as the goals that we might evaluate are not the same for all classifications of individuals. In short, we are not always certain of what we are trying to accomplish in school counseling, but it seems clear that we are trying to achieve different ends with different students. In some cases we are trying to make a child more free in the expression of his impulses; in others we are trying to make him more controlled and more subject to the dictates of society. In some cases we are trying to get him to raise his level of aspiration; in others we are trying to get him to be more "realistic." Thus, counseling programs are now found in schools, not because of sound research evidence as to their value, but rather because it is the considered opinion of specialists, teachers, students, administrators, and community members that counseling is a worthwhile educational activity.

Essentially the same conclusion is inevitable when we consider the value of systematic high school guidance programs. The best research in this area is reported by Rothney and Roens (1950) in *Guidance of American Youth: An Experimental Study* and Rothney (1958) in *Guidance Practices and Results.* These studies both come to the conclusion that some value (though much less than was anticipated) probably accrues to the high school student who receives counseling. While these are the most definitive attempts to illustrate and prove the value of high school guidance programs, their findings cannot be interpreted in any clear-cut fashion. The first study separated students into experimental and control groups on the basis of matching rather than randomization. The second study does not spell out exactly what the treatment effect was that the experimental group received; that is, the reader does not know what "counseling" meant in this context. The most defensible conclusion to be drawn from these two studies is that doing *something* is generally better than doing nothing. The results of both research studies, while not at all clear-cut in favoring the counseled group, can best be explained by the so-called "Hawthorne effect," which was discovered long ago in industry and is instinctively understood by the physician who supplies his patient with a placebo in the expectation that attention will succeed where more verifiable science falters.

To illustrate further the present state of guidance research, we can point to the fact that our nomenclature is so ambiguous that we are not even certain how many counselors we have working in the United States, how many schools have guidance programs, exactly what a counselor does, or how many counselors we still need. (One study of visiting teachers found that fifty different titles were used to designate this specialist!)

There is no clear and agreed-upon job description for school counselors; they are, in fact, engaged in a variety of tasks. Some function almost as psychologists, some as quasi-administrators, some as disciplinarians, some as liaison men trafficking in college admissions, some even as heavy-handed advice-givers and soothsayers—and this list is not exhaustive. Because of this lack of agreement with regard to the counselor's role, his education neither fits his present function nor reflects precisely what the universities training him think he should do. Research has not helped us to describe the function we are talking about, the specialist who is performing the function, or the purpose for which he was hired.

Furthermore, there is a large hiatus between guidance practice and the research that has been done. Practice seems to move by instinct and inertia, while researchers talk only to each other, and sparingly at that. An example of the lag between research and practice is the present expansion of elementary-school guidance programs. All over the country, administrators are seeking and hiring elementary school counselors. There is as yet, however, no research evidence indicating that the people will be helpful. Certainly there are those who believe fervently that if guidance is good it is good at all levels. There are also those who think that if it is difficult to cure "maladjustment" it is better to prevent it, and the way to prevent it is to work with students at the youngest possible age. Such reasoning may or may not be logical, but it is certainly not based on research. Again, then, we find the field moving on the basis of faith, hope, "expert judgment," but not on the basis of research evidence.

SOME OBSERVATIONS ON RESEARCH NEEDS

In view of the present state of affairs, how can research be used to aid guidance practice and, in turn, the total educational activity of the schools? First, we need, as a profession, to come to some agreement in regard to what we mean by such terms as *counselor, pupil-personnel services, guidance,* and *discipline.* Until we have done this job of thinking through and defining, it seems unlikely that we will make any significant progress in research in this field. What guidance most needs at this time is a Linnaeus!

Second, we need much research that is local and descriptive. That is, we need much study of the process of guidance rather than of its ultimate product.

Such studies are best done by local school counselors and do not involve any ultimate "proof" of the value of their work, but rather describe for us what they are doing. Such local research obviously should not be done without a careful consideration of its effects on the local setting, because it may intrude on the personal values of the professional staff or the community, it may offend certain groups or alter relationships within the school, it may use time which we can ill afford for such purposes. Before beginning such research, counselors should carefully consider who should be consulted and whether the results will be worth the effort. Once such consequences are considered, however, there still might be much room for research studies that tell us how a counselor spends his day, what the perception of the community is with regard to the guidance program, what teachers see as their responsibilities for guidance, and other practical "bread and butter" questions.

Third, we need to recognize that knowledge of human behavior is not confined to the quantitative sciences. Certainly there is much more to be learned about the nature of adolescence from reading Salinger's *The Catcher in the Rye* than from reading the most recent issue of the *Journal of Consulting Psychology*. Guidance persons, like many workers in education, have blinded themselves to the humanities as a way of understanding behavior. We have leaned too long and too heavily on numbers. Do we learn about old age only by reading journal articles on gerontology, or can we not also learn by studying the self-portraits of Rembrandt? Before guidance can make significant contributions to education, it must turn again to the sources that traditionally have both satisfied and aroused our curiosity about the human condition. These sources are the literary and visual arts, and while they do not replace the need for more systematic statements, they certainly should supplement our exercises in the quantitative and the minute.

Fourth, we must recognize that along with a human need to "know" we have an equally human need "not to know." Some of our very supersophisticated research designs grow out of the latter need. The insistence on complete randomization when we know that it is impossible to achieve, the use of very involved statistical manipulations for data that do not merit such careful treatment, the obsession with assumptions underlying statistics when their violation sometimes does not really alter the conclusions—all are evidences of our need not to know. Such a need, perhaps stemming from the guilt of some unresolved academic voyeurism, needs to be brought out into the open and clarified if we are going to make progress in research in guidance. Absolute, ultimate answers— free from the pedant's attack—will not soon be found in guidance research.

Fifth, we must be more concerned about illuminating ends and less concerned about examining means. Certainly the kind of clarification offered by Barry and Wolf (1957) in *Modern Issues in Guidance Personnel Work*, which helps us sort out the purposes of guidance programs, is much needed. We cannot expect any dramatic breakthrough in guidance, or for that matter in education, until we have clearly thought through what it is we are trying to do. We could make a plea, then, for less correlation and more conceptualization.

Sixth, in some cases we ought to delay research and substitute demonstration projects. In elementary school guidance, for example, it seems that there is no general agreement as to what the program should involve. Since we know very little about the field, perhaps our "research" should deal with the evolving of theory rather than its testing. Demonstration or pilot projects would permit us to try out various approaches to this new field. One school, for example, might hire an elementary school counselor who behaves and is trained much like a secondary school counselor. Another could have a psychologist who might serve as a resource person on child growth and development. A third might hire a social worker to carry on therapy with children. There are many other possibilities within this field. Trying out several methods in schools is one way to begin to decide what is the best use of the elementary school counselor and to determine what problems evolve from various approaches. Such research, which would be essentially theory-building, is much needed in guidance.

HORIZONS FOR THE FUTURE

Now let us look at some promising research which offers a brighter horizon for the future. Major longitudinal studies, such as Flanagan's Project Talent and Super's Career Pattern Study give us much hope. These studies promise no immediate answers to our questions, but they they will provide us with a base of data which will permit sounder research and study. They may well do for our understanding of guidance what the Terman studies did for our understanding of the gifted student.

A second kind of study that has much promise is exemplified by Coleman's (1961) *The Adolescent Society*, which examines the values and attitudes of schools and their impact on the learning and behavior of youth. Coleman has pointed to the importance of considering not only the individual but also the context within which the individual learns. Such studies may constitute a major breakthrough in understanding the behavior of adolescents and the levers instrumental to changing it.

A third kind of research is exemplified by Jahoda's (1958) *Current Concepts of Positive Mental Health,* in which she does a splendid job of classifying the definitions of mental health and helping us see that before we can work for mental health we need to agree on what it is. This kind of taxonomic conceptualization is badly needed in the whole field of guidance.

Still another kind of research which leads to optimism is that done by Bandura and Walters (1959) in which they investigate the backgrounds of aggressive adolescents—*Adolescent Aggression: A Study of the Influence of Child-Training Practices and Family Interrelationships.* Few studies have explored so many stereotypes so completely. This is an excellent example of research that transfers knowledge from our original second category—things that we know we know simply because they are part of the conventional wisdom—to our third category—things that we know we do not know. This kind of iconoclastic, stereotype-breaking research is badly needed.

Finally, the studies of H. H. Anderson of Michigan State University, in which he compares the values of children in such countries as Russia, Germany, Mexico, and the United States, provide a valuable perspective to workers in guidance as well as to others in education. Anderson's research is the kind that will pull us out of our provincialism and permit us to see that the world is larger than one school system or one country.

CONCLUSION

These five kinds of research seem to me to be the sort that will lead guidance out of its present state into a more promising future. They have in common a strong belief that counting is not a substitute for thinking! Too much guidance research has been concerned with the manipulation of figures; too little of it, with the manipulation of ideas. The horizons for the future depend on the clarification of concepts more than they depend on the calculation of figures.

In summary, then, the present state of guidance research is not reassuring. We are not able to demonstrate the value of what we are doing, nor are we even able to agree on who is doing it nor on what should be done. As a result, we make radical moves, for example, in increasing the number of elementary school counselors before we have any clear understanding of why we are doing what we are doing. We need clarification of concepts, we need a return to the importance of the humanities, we need local descriptive studies, we need to understand *why* we act, as well as *how* we act, and most of all, we need to know when we do not know. We must unmask easy answers and reveal that they are often but fraudulent substitutes for hard questions.

REFERENCES

Bandura, A., and R. H. Walters. 1959. *Adolescent aggression: a study of child-training practices and family interrelationships.* New York: Ronald.

Barry, Ruth, and Beverly Wolf. 1957. *Modern issues in guidance-personnel work.* New York: Bureau of Publications, Teachers College, Columbia University.

Coleman, J. S. 1961. *The adolescent society: the social life of the teenager and its impact on education.* New York: Free Press.

Jahoda, Maria. 1958. *Current concepts of positive mental health.* New York: Basic Books.

Leary, T. F., and J. S. Harvey. 1960. Counseling theory. In *Encyclopedia of educational research.* Third ed., New York: Macmillan.

Rothney, J. W. M. 1958. *Guidance practices and results.* New York: Harper & Row.

————, and B. A. Roens. 1950. *Guidance of American youth: an experimental study.* Cambridge, Mass.: Harvard University Press.

Research Voids in Elementary
School Guidance*

Harold F. Cottingham

Within the total guidance movement, the emphasis upon the development of guidance concepts and practices applicable to the elementary school is not only of recent origin but is of such intensity and tempo that many unresolved issues are arising. An examination of the research and discussion literature reveals at least three significant areas in which deficiencies appear to exist: (a) theoretical formulations of the nature of elementary guidance, (b) the guidance function within instruction (the teacher's guidance responsibilities) and beyond (the counselor's role), and (c) unmet needs of elementary pupils. It is the purpose of this article to examine briefly some of the guidance literature for evidence of research on these three important aspects of guidance in the elementary school.

ASSUMPTION AS TO THE NATURE
OF ELEMENTARY GUIDANCE

Basic to a review of selected literature sources is a brief description of the salient characteristics of elementary school guidance as revealed by prominent writers in the field. Guidance and counseling in the elementary school can be viewed in a contextual relationship with several larger elements: the goals of education, the guidance function in education, the guidance function in the elementary school, implementation of the guidance function through the guidance process, and guidance and counseling outcomes. The goals of education from such sources as the White House Conference, described by Tyler (1960) or Chandler (1961), must subsume goals that can be attained through guidance activities. The goals of education, whether they be societal in origin as enunciated by Hutson (1958) or psychosocial in origin, as set forth by Mathewson (1957), are implemented by administrative, instructional, and guidance activities, respectively, according to Tiedeman and Field (1962). Within the broad goals of education, the guidance function, as distinct from instruction, emphasizes decisions, goals, plans and value judgments while instruction stresses the acquisition of knowledge, skills, concepts, and facts (Cottingham, 1962). The "guidance learnings" described by Hill (1966), which comprise the guidance function in education, are identified by Tiedeman and Field (1962) with the

* *Elementary School Guidance and Counseling,* 1967, vol. 1, no. 3.
  By permission.

construct of discontinuity but have not been entirely agreed upon by other guidance theorists. In addition to Tiedeman's (1964) definition of guidance being "the science of purposeful action," such authors as Mathewson (1962), Shoben (1962), Katz (1963), and Weitz (1964) have also attempted to define the construct of guidance; Katz refers to "the guidance intervention" and Shoben to "social reconstruction."

Farwell and Peters (1957) listed several differential factors characterizing elementary school guidance. While not defining the precise nature of the guidance function in the elementary school, Hill (1963), Meeks (1962), ASCA (1964), Patouillet (1964), and Cottingham (1966) have outlined the nature and the purposes of guidance work in elementary schools. With few exceptions, the developmental character of educational experiences as described by Mussen (1963) is strongly supported by those concerned with the definition of the elementary school guidance function.

In implementing the guidance function at the elementary school level, many authorities agree that it is carried out both within and beyond instruction. This point is stressed by the ASCD Yearbook (1955), Cottingham (1962), Watson (1964), and Peters and others (1965). The guidance function is administratively placed among several pupil personnel services as reported by the Council of Chief State School Officers (1960), Johnson and others (1961), and Kehas (1966). As a function, guidance can be sub-divided into such areas as behavior assessment, counseling, consulting, and coordination, with a liaison role in the school and community being a pervasive element, according to Miller (1961) and Wrenn (1962).

Assessing the outcomes of the guidance process calls for an examination of human behavior changes in terms of (1) the acquisition of skills, knowledge, and facts (societal expectations) as well as (2) maturity as related to reality, others, self, and values and meaning (self needs). Such sources as the ASCD Yearbook (1955) and Weitz (1964) have identified societal expectations while Raebeck (1959), Mathewson (1963), Kelley (1962), and Tiedeman (1964) have described personal meanings and behavior related to self needs.

RESEARCH ON CONCEPTUAL FOUNDATIONS, OR ELEMENTARY GUIDANCE THEORY

In spite of the many recent publications in the field of elementary guidance and counseling, few, if any, have devoted much discussion to the theoretical bases for either the guidance function or the counseling process in the elementary school. This situation is due to a number of factors, not the least of which is the lack until recently of solid, creative or empirical research leading to the nature of guidance theory, regardless of educational level. Only since 1957 has the *Review of Educational Research* included chapters dealing with the theoretical foundations of guidance, personnel work, and counseling (Kehas, 1966). During this same period, a limited number of writers were struggling with this same problem: Wrenn (1959), Miller (1961), Tiedeman and Field (1962), Mathewson (1962), Shoben (1962), Beck (1963), Weitz (1964), and Tiedeman (1964). The current concern for developing acceptable theoretical formulations of purposes, functions, and practices characterizing the guidance process or function in education is predicated on the need for independent theories of guidance (Kehas, 1966) not immediately derived from other disciplines.

Current periodical literature appears to emphasize the descriptive features of elementary guidance rather than the conceptual elements undergirding such activities. Smith (1963) and Wilson (1964) stressed the need for guidance activities as preventive measures. The general features of guidance programs for elementary schools were outlined by Cottingham (1959), Meeks (1962), and Hill (1963). Support for the concept of developmental and preventive guidance is evidenced in articles by Bosdell (1960), Farwell (1961a), Peters (1963), and Royster (1964). Harris (1959) has identified several principles from developmental psychology which presumably are applicable to the elementary school.

As a sub-aspect of guidance, the core process of counseling has been currently described theoretically by both Stefflre (1965) and Blocher (1966), although no specific reference was made to elementary school counseling by either author. Except for efforts by Dinkmeyer (1965) and Krumboltz and Hosford (1967) who have issued position papers on "developmental counseling" and "behavior counseling," respectively, little has been written on counseling theories uniquely applicable to the elementary school. Dinkmeyer indicated his Adlerian position is modeled after Hummel's (1962) ego counseling. Peters (1959) examined differential factors between elementary and secondary school counseling but offered no theoretical bases. Some writers such as Freer (1962) see the teacher as a counselor, while the majority view counseling as the responsibility of a separate, professionally trained person. The latter group includes Newman (1956), Harrison (1961), Cassel (1963), Meeker (1963), and Helpern (1964).

Presently, further research on various aspects of guidance in the elementary school appears to be seriously hampered by language and function identification problems. If some agreement can be reached on the nature and characteristics, including the conceptual foundations, of the guidance function in the elementary school, subsequent research efforts will be greatly enhanced. Not only will this permit a greater ease of communication, but more importantly, research can focus on comparable phases of functions, responsibilities, and behavior changes so that controlled and related studies can be conducted. This relatively common frame of reference, if generally accepted, could also pave the way for subsequent research aimed at re-examining specific assessment or helping functions, teacher and counselor activities, and ultimately, programming approaches suitable for various categories of pupil needs under different educational conditions.

RESEARCH ON GUIDANCE
RESPONSIBILITIES OF TEACHERS
AND COUNSELORS

A study of research related to personnel and their guidance responsibilities indicates a fourfold approach to this problem: (a) the counselor's actual or perceived ideal role, (b) needed functions (services) and recommended personnel who should provide them, (c) the guidance role of the classroom teacher, and (d) an analysis of broad pupil needs and recommendations for services and personnel to meet their needs. Very little carefully designed research has focused on the specific concerns teachers have as they work with children in meeting their guidance (and instructional) needs.

The roles and functions of elementary school guidance personnel have been the subject of much discussion and considerable research. McDougall and Reitan (1963) and Shertzer and Lundy (1964) examined the image of the counselors as perceived by the school administrator. Foster (1965) made a regional study of the counselor educators,' state supervisors', elementary principals', and elementary counselors' perceptions of the role and function of the future elementary counselor. Bosdell (1960) explored role perceptions of teachers, counselors, principals, and school psychologists toward each other while Gatchel (1958) obtained teachers' reactions to specific guidance services in a 1958 study. Muro (1965) studied perceptions of the elementary guidance specialist by teachers and principals. McCreary and Miller (1966) analyzed the qualifications and functions of elementary counselors in California. Two counselor roles, consultant and psychotherapeutic, were compared through experimental and control groups by Oldridge (1964), while Jones (1966) evolved a competency pattern for elementary school counselors from criteria reviewed by a jury of both state and national counselor educators.

Research on counseling activities or total guidance program features has increased. Hart (1961) surveyed the need for a guidance counselor among St. Louis elementary teachers. Reactions to available or potential services were studied by Parmer (1960) and Riccio and Wehmeyer (1961) who examined guidance services recommended by public and parochial teachers and the demand for psychological services in 28 elementary schools of Columbus, Ohio. Wieland (1966) conducted a national survey of some 220 school counselors, 84 school psychologists, and 49 school social workers in common communities to determine duplication and uniqueness of duties. Illustrative of the recent research made possible by Title V-A of NDEA is a project report by Miller (1964) who described a series of studies dealing with dropouts, underachievers, articulation problems, and experimental counseling in California. In the narrower vein of evaluative research, outcomes of selected activities by counselors and teachers were analyzed by Martin (1959) and Bancroft (1962). Also part of a national pattern are the IRCOPPS researches reported by Shaw (1965) and Byrne

(1966). The former described a regional study at UCLA based on the hypothesis that the guidance specialist's prime responsibility is assisting in the provision of an optimum climate for learning. Byrne's project, at another of the four IRCOPPS centers (Maryland), hypothesized that a new type of in-school pupil service worker could replace the more traditional counselor, psychologist, social worker, nurse, and similar personnel. Some of the theoretical as well as the practical difficulties in the evaluation process have been described by Peters (1964) and Peters and others (1965). Eddleman (no date), in a broader perspective, examined the research role of the elementary counselor.

Much has been written on the question of responsibility for counseling in the elementary school; most writers concur in the fact that the elementary counselor carries the primary responsibility, although others may assist. Such researchers as Hart (1961), McKellar (1963) Raines (1964) and Nitzschke and Hill (1964) have examined the functions that are or should be provided by elementary counseling personnel. In addition, many discussion articles have expressed opinions on the role and function of the elementary counselor. Among those expressing themselves seriously on this subject are SRA (1960), Farwell (1961b), Harrison (1963), Meeks (1963), Brison (1964), Kaczkowski (1964), Smallenburg (1964), Peters and Hansen (1964), Mahan (1965), Ohlsen (1965), Reaves and Reaves (1965), and Zaccaria (1965). Purkey (1962) offered a narrative report of an elementary counselor's work day. Wrenn (1962) surveyed a national sample of elementary counselors and obtained their opinion regarding future functions. An outline of services which an elementary counselor might appropriately perform was suggested by Nelson (1962).

Most of the above writers agree on a threefold function of the elementary counselor: counseling (individual and group), consulting (with parents, teachers, and other pupil personnel specialists, administrators), and coordination (liaison) with school staff and with community and school resources. These roles include making comprehensive studies of pupils, counseling, providing pupils with information (personal and environmental), and supplying pupil information to school and community personnel. The stress upon the elementary counselor being a pupil personnel services team member is generally evident, although some writers use the term guidance worker in preference to counselor. As to the actual job function of the counselor, McCreary and Miller (1966) found that in California counselors spent 50% of the time working with pupils, 17% with teachers, 10% with administration, 12% with parents, and 11% with probation, welfare and other agency officials. Somewhat unique roles for the counselor were described by Farwell (1961 *b*) and Mahan (1965), Farwell emphasized the counselor's responsibility for developmental counseling (as opposed to complete client centeredness or mechanistic guidance services) while Mahan charges the counselor with changing "perceptual sets" of people toward things, themselves, and others. He should also assist in improving the quality of teacher-pupil interaction.

RESEARCH ON PUPIL NEEDS

Apparently only limited research to identify specific unmet needs of elementary school pupils has been conducted. Contrariwise, many extensive studies and committee work on general concerns of youth have been reported in the literature. Few of these endeavors, however, have sought to elicit from youth themselves or their teachers the explicit areas or types of problems not being resolved by available personnel or resource units.

The place of research findings as a basis for individual systems of child study is reflected in such broadly designed studies as the Kowitz and others study (1965) which examined the guidance needs of 1760 children in the primary grades of a Texas community. These researchers concluded that teachers could categorize pupil problems at the second-grade level as enrichment, personal-social, learning (educational) or average-normal (present conditions adequate). Another experimental program which sought to assess ways of pupil diagnosis and help was reported by Lafferty and others (1964). For some years, the child guidance conference and the child study program concept as developed by Prescott at the University of Maryland, described by Richardson (1958), have been used by elementary schools. Traditional sources and types of data for understanding pupils such as cumulative records, interviews, observations, test results, anecdotal records, and sociometric information are recommended by Willey (1960), DeHaan (1961), Hatch and Costar (1961), Ahmann and Glock (1963), Peters and others (1963), and Peters and others (1965). Basic principles for studying children's behavior are reiterated by Moustakas (1957), Ausubel (1959), Dinkmeyer (1961), Slobin (1964), and Marshall (1964). Current trends in approaches to behavior assessment according to Carnes and Doughtie (1966) reflect greater concern for multiple causation, impinging cultural factors, and such non-cognitive elements as creativity, anxiety, and stress.

Personality variables were studied by Feldhusen and Thurston (1964) who examined anxiety level and integration of self concept and found that low anxiety level children had higher mean scores than high anxiety level children on integration of self concept as rated by psychologists. Watson (1964) also reported on Operation Self Concept, a longitudinal study designed to help children with self-understanding and self-concept development. Lighthall (1963) studied children's responses to personality questionnaires. Peer studies are reported by Cassel and Gilbert (1964) and Spaulding (1964). The former compared peer status ratings of pupils with their guidance data and learning efficiency indices, while the latter reviewed empirical research of peer and school influence on personality development. Child behavior problems were examined by Peterson and others (1961), Mangan and Shafer (1962), and Rice (1963), who studied pupil problems as related to parental attitudes, children's attitudes toward behavior, and referral behavior problems. Chance (1961) reported that with first-graders, the time of independence training by mothers was significant.

In the area of pupil identification, two studies examined high learning ability in relation to seventeen physical, social, and intellectual variables and types of problems reported by primary teachers. The authors of these studies were Klausmeier (1959) and Kowitz and others (1965). The latter study reported that 63.4% of the boys had learning-educational problems as compared to 43.7% of the girls. Radin (1963) categorized the behavioral concerns of elementary pupils as follows: academic, social, conflict with authority figures, and overt behavioral manifestations. The Higher Horizons Project of New York City, reported by Hillson and Nyers (1963), illustrates a demonstration project that focused on helping culturally deprived youth reach new goals.

CONCLUSIONS AND RECOMMENDATIONS

A review of selected literature sources revealed only limited research dealing with the three aspects of elementary guidance under investigation. In light of these findings, it is suggested that future research efforts to improve guidance in the elementary school be directed toward three types of problems. Of primary concern is the need to develop an acceptable conceptual foundation for elementary school guidance, compatible with guidance theory in general and with the objectives of elementary education. Another deficiency is the lack of significant research which attempts to examine the guidance functions that can be normally assumed by the classroom teacher, those guidance responsibilities with which she can use some assistance, and those problem areas where referred resources or counselors are needed. Finally, research in depth is needed to reveal the specific types of unmet needs, both personal and educational, which characterize various groups of children such as underachievers, dropouts, pre-delinquents, and the socially maladjusted.

Looking to the future, several recommendations as to possible research activities in each of the three deficiency areas will be proposed. The problem of evolving an acceptable series of conceptual formulations characterizing elementary guidance theory demands a thorough literature search, as well as subsequent acceptance of a tentative position statement by representatives of several disciplines and associatives identified with elementary education. More specifically, an adequate rationale for elementary school guidance requires an initial review of behavioral science literature, both the research and theoretical formulations, to produce evidence of the unique elements of elementary guidance theory. Since the conceptualization of elementary school guidance as an independent area, distinct from other disciplines, is just emerging, the primary source of theoretical formulations must be existing literature, including educational philosophy, psychology, anthropology, and sociology. The involvement of elementary teachers, supervisors, and administrators, as well as counselor educators, counseling supervisors, and elementary counselors, in the evolution of a conceptual statement is necessary to determine its practicality. An accompanying bit of supportive research might include an analysis of child development research literature to identify both societal and psychological needs of pupils, on which a sound theory of elementary guidance should be predicated.

Research efforts to identify the guidance function of the elementary teacher demand both theoretical and practical endeavors. Initially, it is necessary to determine the teacher's perception of her instructional and guidance responsibilities, once they have been conceptually differentiated. Conceivably, certain responsibilities could have either classification, depending upon certain circumstances, and upon the conceptualization of the guidance function. A second phase of research efforts could involve an assessment by a sample of elementary teachers of the use and value of noninstructional procedures for helping children, either as part of their instructional and/or guidance functions. The construct being studied would focus upon the question of pupil needs which teachers feel they can meet in implementing their guidance function as opposed to their opinion of guidance needs of pupils that other personnel can better provide. An auxiliary phase of the research might seek to obtain responses from teachers as to learning principles or philosophical assumptions to which they adhere in child-teacher relationships, since the guidance functions also presuppose some type of pupil-centered orientation. Another related study might examine the reasons elementary teachers are not able to carry out their guidance function, assuming a philosophical acceptance of the responsibility.

In the area of unmet pupil needs, additional research should focus more precisely on types of unmet needs of specific groups of pupils. Research designed to identify these needs could well involve both teacher and children. Teachers could be asked to classify and describe pupil needs that present personnel and resources are unable to meet. Their opinion on future or anticipated needs, as well as their difficulties in current attempts to resolve pupil concerns, could also be obtained. Furthermore, the different pupil needs of selected groups, such as underachievers, potential dropouts, pre-delinquents, and socially maladjusted pupils as perceived by teachers should be ascertained. Another direction such research could take would be the analysis of pupil records, case conferences, and observation reports to identify evidence of unmet needs of elementary school pupils. Finally, pupils themselves, at selected grade levels, could be given the opportunity through free expression and other unstructured situations to respond to generalized stimuli centering on school and home life. By comparison and careful analysis of these data, utilizing the various sources described, common types of unmet pupil needs could be determined. Further research, utilizing controlled and experimental conditions might then be designed to apply corrective measures with certain types of pupil concerns.

REFERENCES

Ahmann, J., and M. D. Glock. 1963. *Evaluating pupil growth*. Second ed.; Boston: Allyn and Bacon.

American School Counselor Association Committee Report (Anna R. Meeks,

Chairman). October 1964. *Dimensions of elementary school guidance.* (Also in *Elem. Sch. Guid. Counsel.,* 1967, *1,* 163–187.)

Association for Supervision and Curriculum Development. 1955. *Guidance in the curriculum.* Washington, D.C.: National Education Association.

Ausubel, D. P. 1959. Developmental issues in child guidance: plasticity, direction, and conformity. *J. Nat. Ass. Women Deans Couns., 22,* 106–112.

Bancroft, J. F. 1962. *A study of teachers' effectiveness in performing guidance services in the intermediate grades of public elementary schools.* Ames, Iowa: University of Iowa. Doctoral dissertation.

Beck, C. E. 1963. *Philosophical foundations of guidance.* Englewood Cliffs, N.J.: Prentice-Hall.

Blocher, D. H. 1966. *Developmental counseling.* New York: Ronald.

Bosdell, B. J. 1960. Guidance in the elementary school. *Univer. North Dakota Coll. Educ. Rec., 65,* 88–92.

————. 1958. *Perceptions of guidance services as related to personality needs and job tile.* Urbana, Ill.: University of Illinois. Unpublished doctoral dissertation.

Brison, D. 1964. The role of the elementary guidance counselor. *Nat. Elem. Princ., 43* (No. 5), 41–47.

Byrne, R. H. 1966. *The problems and design of a research in elementary school counseling.* American Personnel and Guidance Association Convention, Washington, D.C.

Carnes, E. F., and E. B. Doughtie. 1966. The appraisal function. *Rev. educ. Res., 36,* 288–297.

Cassel, R. N. 1963. Teacher and counselor. *Education, 83,* 259–262.

————, and M. Gilbert. 1964. Comparing peer status ratings of elementary pupils with their guidance data and learning efficiency indices. *J. genet. Psychol., 105,* 139–142.

Chance, J. 1961. Independence training and first graders' achievement. *J. consult. Psychol., 25,* 149–154.

Chandler, B. J. 1962. Implementing two vital teacher functions: guidance and instructions. *Couns. Educ. Supervis., 1,* 166–169.

————. 1961. *Education and the teacher.* New York: Dodd, Mead.

————. 1959. Guidance. *Grade Teacher, 76,* 56.

Cottingham, H. F. 1966. The counselor's role in elementary school guidance. *High Sch. J., 49,* 204–208.

Council of Chief State School Officers. 1960. *Responsibilities of state departments of education for pupil personnel services.* Washington, D.C. National Education Association.

DeHann, R. F. 1961. Using test results in pupil guidance. *Nat. Elem. Princ., 41* (No. 2), 23–26.

Dinkmeyer, D. April 1965. *A theory of child counseling at the elementary school level.* Speech delivered to the American Personnel and Guidance Association Convention, Minneapolis, Minn.

————. 1961. Understanding children's behavior. *Elem. Sch. J., 61,* 314–316.

Eddleman, R. R. (no date). The research role of the elementary school counselor. *Research and the Counselor.* Jefferson City, Mo.: Guidance Services Section, State Department of Education. Mimeographed.

Farwell, G. F. 1961*a*. Continuity in the guidance program. *Educ. Leadership, 18,* 338–342.

——. 1961*b*. The role of the school counselor. *Couns. Educ. Supervis., 1,* 40–43.

——, and H. J. Peters. 1957. Guidance: a longitudinal and differential view. *Elem. Sch. J., 57,* 26–31.

Feldhusen, J. F., and J. R. Thruston. 1964. Personality and adjustment of low and high anxious children. *J. educ. Res., 57,* 265–267.

Foster, C. M. 1965. *Perceptions of the role and function of the elementary school counselor.* Lafayette, Ind.: Purdue University. Doctoral dissertation.

Freer, J. J. 1962. The teacher as counselor. *Education, 82,* 366–368.

Gatchel, M. H. 1958. *The elementary classroom teacher's personal opinion concerning several aspects of an organized guidance program at that level.* Norman, Okla.: College of Education, University of Oklahoma.

Harris, D. B. 1959. What child development has to say to guidance workers. *J. Nat. Ass. Women Deans Couns., 22,* 99–105.

Harrison, E. L. 1963. The elementary school counselor's unique position. *Sch. Couns., 11,* 107–110.

——. 1961. The counselor's role in the early identification of gifted children. *Personnel guid. J., 39,* 735–738.

Hart, R. N. 1961. *An analysis of the position of the elementary school guidance counselor.* Los Angeles: University of Southern California. Doctoral dissertation.

Hatch, R. N., and J. W. Costar. 1961. *Guidance services in the elementary school.* New York: Little, Brown.

Helpern, J. M. 1964. The role of the guidance consultant at the elementary school. *B. U. J. Educ., 146* (No. 3), 16–34.

Hill, G. E. April 1966. *Guidance for children in elementary schools.* Speech delivered to the American Personnel and Guidance Association Convention, Washington, D.C.

——. 1963. Guidance in elementary schools. *Clearing House, 38,* 11–16.

Hillson, H. T., and F. C. Meyers. 1963. *The demonstration guidance project 1957–1962.* New York: New York Board of Education.

Hummel, R. C. 1962. Ego-counseling in guidance: concept and method. *Harvard educ. Rev., 32,* 463–482.

Hutson, P. W. 1958. *The guidance function in education.* New York: Appleton.

Johnson, W. F. *et al.* 1961. *Pupil personnel and guidance services.* New York: McGraw-Hill.

Jones, C. R. 1966. *A competency pattern for elementary school counselors.* Lubbock, Tex.: Texas Technological College. Doctoral dissertation.

Kaczkowski, H. R. 1964. *Role and function of the elementary school counselor.* Urbana, Ill.: University of Illinois. Mimeographed.

Katz, M. 1963. *Decision and values: a rationale for secondary school guidance.* New York: College Entrance Examination Board.

Kehas, C. D. 1966. Theoretical formulations and related research. *Rev. educ. Res., 36,* 207–218.

Kelley, E. C. 1962. *Another look at individualism.* Detroit, Mich.: Wayne State University.

Klausmeier, H. J. 1959. Identifying children through measurements. *Education, 80,* 167–171.

Kowitz, G. T. *et al.* 1965. *Guidance needs in the primary grades.* Houston, Tex.: Bureau of Educational Research and Services, University of Houston.

Krumboltz, J. D., and R. E. Hosford. 1967. Behavioral counseling in the elementary school. *Elem. Sch. Guid. Counsel., 1,* 27–40.

Lafferty, J. C. *et al.* 1964. A creative school mental health program. *Nat. Elem. Princ., 43* (No. 5), 28–35.

Lighthall, F. F. 1963. Defensive and nondefensive change in children's responses to personality questionnaires. *Child Develpm., 34,* 455–470.

McCreary, W. H., and G. Miller. 1966. Elementary school counselors in California. *Personnel guid. J., 44,* 494–498.

McDougall, W. P., and H. M. Reitan. 1963. The elementary counselor as perceived by elementary principals. *Personnel guid. J., 42,* 348–354.

McKellar, R. L. 1963. *A study of concepts, functions and organizational characteristics of guidance in elementary schools.* Tallahassee, Fla.: Florida State University. Doctoral dissertation.

Mahan, T. W., Jr. 1965. Elementary school counselor: disturber of the peace. *Nat. Elem. Princ., 44* (No. 4), 72–74.

Mangan, T., and D. Shafer. 1962. Behavior problems of children as viewed by children in the fifth through eighth grades. *J. educ. Res., 56,* 104–106.

Marshall, H. 1964. Behavior problems of normal children: a comparison between the lay literature and developmental research. *Child Develpm., 35,* 469–478.

Martin, L. W. 1959. *A study of the effect of selected guidance activities upon elementary school children.* Columbia, Mo.: University of Missouri. Doctoral dissertation.

Mathewson, R. H. 1963. *The meaning of maturity.* Lecture in guidance and student personnel services. Athens, Ohio: Ohio University.

——— 1962. *Guidance policy and practice.* Third ed.; New York: Harper & Row.

———. 1957. *A strategy for American education.* New York: Harper & Row.

Meeker, A. M. 1963. *Teachers at work in the elementary school.* Indianapolis, Ind.: Bobbs-Merrill.

Meeks, A. R. 1963. Elementary school counseling. *Sch. Couns., 10,* 108–111.

————. 1962. Guidance in the elementary school. *Nat. educ. Ass. J.*, *51* (No. 3), 30–32.

Miller, C. H. 1961. *Foundations of guidance.* New York: Harper & Row.

Miller, F. W. 1961. *Guidance principles and services.* Columbus, Ohio: Merrill.

Miller, G. 1964. New directions in elementary school guidance. *Calif. Educ.*, *2* (No. 1), 5–6.

Moustakas, C. 1957–1958. Spoiled behavior in the school-age child. *Child Study*, *35*, 16–21.

Muro, J. J. 1965. *The elementary guidance specialist as perceived by elementary school teachers and elementary school principals.* Athens, Ga.: University of Georgia. Report based on a doctoral dissertation.

Mussen, P. H. 1963. *The psychological development of the child.* Englewood Cliffs, N.J.: Prentice-Hall.

Nelson, R. C. 1962. Counselors in elementary schools: promise and proposal. *Guid. J.*, *2*, 47–57.

Newman, W. H. 1956. A full-time counselor in an elementary school. *Elem. Sch. J.*, *56*, 354–357.

Nitzschke, D. F., and G. E. Hill. 1964. *The elementary school counselor: preparation and functions.* Athens, Ohio: Center for Educational Research and Services, College of Education, Ohio University.

Ohlsen, M. M. 1965. The elementary school counselor. *South Carolina Guid. News*, *14* (No. 3).

Oldridge, B. 1964. Two roles for elementary school guidance personnel. *Personnel guid. J.*, *43*, 367–370.

Parmer, O. E. 1960. Psychological services in twenty-eight elementary schools of Columbus, Ohio. *J. exp. Educ.*, *29*, 119–131.

Patouillet, R. 1964. *Elementary guidance process and content.* Report of the Fourth Annual All-Ohio Elementary School Guidance Conference.

Peters, H. J. 1963. Fostering the developmental approach in guidance. *Educ. Forum*, *28*, 87–93.

————. 1959. Differential factors between elementary and secondary school counseling. *Sch. Couns.*, *7*, 3–11.

————, and J. C. Hansen. 1964. The school counselor as a researcher. *Sch. Couns.*, *11*, 165–170.

———— et al. (Eds.) 1963. *Guidance in the elementary school: selected readings.* New York: Macmillan.

———— et al. 1965. *Guidance in the elementary schools.* Skokie, Ill.: Rand McNally.

Peters, M. 1964. Evaluating the guidance program. *Nat. Elem. Princ.*, *43* (No. 5), 26–27.

Peterson, D. et al. 1961. Child behavior problems and parental attitudes. *Child Develpm.*, *32*, 151–162.

Purkey, E. 1962. Elementary school counseling. *Nat. educ. Ass. J.*, *51* (No. 9), 18–20.

Radin, S. S. 1963. Mental health problems of school children. *J. Sch. Hlth, 33,* 252.

Raebeck, C. April 1959. *Teacher guidance—three dimensional teaching experience.* Speech delivered to the American Personnel and Guidance Association Convention, Cleveland, Ohio.

Raines, B. 1964. *The role of the counselor in the elementary schools of Ohio.* Athens, Ohio: Ohio University. Doctoral dissertation.

Reaves, G. C., and L. E. Reaves, III. 1965. The counselor and preventive psychiatry. *Personnel guid. J., 43,* 661–664.

Riccio, A. C., and D. J. Wehmeyer. 1961. Guidance services recommended by public and parochial elementary school teachers. *Educ. res. Bull., 40,* 12–18.

Rice, J., Jr. 1963. Types of problems referred to a central guidance agency at different grade levels. *Personnel guid. J., 42,* 52–55.

Richardson, S. 1958. Techniques of studying children. *Calif. J. elem. Educ., 26,* 227–236.

Royster, W. 1964. Guidance in the elementary school. *Nat. Elem. Princ., 43* (No. 5), 6–10.

Science Research Associates. November 1960. Roles of guidance workers in the elementary schools. *SRA Guild, Newsletter.*

Shaw, M. C. 1965. Testing a model for the provision of guidance services. *Elem. Sch. Guid. Couns., 1* (No. 2), 13–16.

Shertzer, B., and C. T. Lundy. 1964. Administrator's image of an elementary school counselor. *Sch. Couns., 11,* 211–214.

Shoben, E., Jr. 1962. Guidance: remedial function or social reconstruction? *Harvard educ. Rev., 32,* 430–433.

Slobin, D. I. 1964. The fruits of the first season: a discussion of the role of play in childhood. *J. humanis. Psychol., 4* (No. 1), 59–79.

Smallenburg, H. 1964. Studying the elementary guidance program. *Nat. Elem. Princ., 43* (No. 5), 15–18.

Smith, H. 1963. Preventing difficulties through guidance. *Education, 83,* 266–269.

Spaulding, R. L. 1964. Personality and social development: peer and school influences. *Rev. educ. Res., 34,* 588–598.

Stefflre, B. (Ed.). 1965. *Theories of counseling.* New York: McGraw-Hill.

Tiedeman, D. V. 1964. Purposing through education: the further delineation of goal and program for guidance. In E. Landy and P. A. Perry (Eds.), *Guidance in American education: background and prospects.* Vol. I. Cambridge, Mass.: Harvard University Press.

———, and F. L. Field. 1962. Guidance: the science of purposeful action applied through education. *Harvard educ. Rev., 32,* 483–501.

Tyler, R. W. 1960. Educational objectives of American democracy. In E. Ginzberg (Ed.), *The nation's children.* Vol. 2. New York: Columbia University Press.

Watson, D. 1964. A teacher looks at guidance. *Nat. Elem. Princ.*, *43* (No. 5), 37–40.

Weitz, H. 1964. *Behavior change through guidance*. New York: Wiley.

Wieland, R. 1966. *A comparative study of the duties performed regularly by school counselors, school psychologists and school social workers working together in selected school systems*. Tallahassee, Fla.: Florida State University. Doctoral dissertation.

Willey, R. D. 1960. *Guidance in elementary education*. Revised ed.; New York: Harper & Row.

Wilson, L. A. 1964. Needs for guidance in the elementary school. *Peabody J. Educ.*, *41*, 289–295.

Wrenn, C. G. 1962. *The counselor in a changing world*. Washington, D.C.: American Personnel and Guidance Association.

————. 1959. Philosophical and psychological bases of personnel services in education. In N. B. Henry (Ed.), *Personnel services in education*. Part II. Yearbook of the National Society for the Study of Education. Pp. 41–81.

Zaccaria, J. S. 1965. Varied contributions of guidance. *Education*, *86*, 75–77.

Name Index

Subject Index

411